With respect and affection;

Tom Martin

SOVEREIGNTY AND COINAGE IN CLASSICAL GREECE

THOMAS R. MARTIN

Sovereignty and Coinage
in Classical Greece

Princeton University Press
Princeton, New Jersey

Copyright © 1985 by Princeton University Press

Published by Princeton University Press, 41 William Street, Princeton,
New Jersey 08540
In the United Kingdom: Princeton University Press, Guildford, Surrey

All Rights Reserved

Library of Congress Cataloging in Publication Data will be found on the
last printed page of this book

ISBN 0-691-03580-6

Publication of this book has been aided by a grant from the Paul Mellon
Fund of Princeton University Press

This book has been composed in Baskerville by Chiron Inc.

Clothbound editions of Princeton University Press books are printed on
acid-free paper, and binding materials are chosen for strength and
durability. Paperbacks, although satisfactory for personal collections,
are not usually suitable for library rebinding

Printed in the United States of America by Princeton University Press,
Princeton, New Jersey

CONTENTS

ABBREVIATIONS

In general, the abbreviations listed in *l'Année philologique* and *Numismatic Literature* will be used, with the following additions and modifications. Full titles are given in the bibliography and at the first citation of an item in the notes (except for book reviews). The usual practice thereafter will be to employ short titles for books and to shorten or, when appropriate, to omit the titles of articles while giving the journal references. To avoid potential confusion, I follow the style of citation of the American Numismatic Society for numismatic journals which have multiple series, giving only the year of the volume, and not its series number. For convenience, the most frequently used short titles of books are included in this list.

ACGC	Colin Kraay, *Archaic and Classical Greek Coins* (Berkeley, 1976)
ANSMN	*American Numismatic Society Museum Notes*
ArchDelt	*Archaiologikon Deltion*
ArchEph	*Archaiologike Ephemeris*
BMC	*British Museum Catalogue of Greek Coins*
CAH	*The Cambridge Ancient History*
CH	*Coin Hoards* (Royal Numismatic Society, London)
Essays	A. R. Bellinger, *Essays on the Coinage of Alexander the Great* (New York, 1963, Numismatic Studies 11)
FGrH	*Die Fragmente der griechischen Historiker*
FHG	*Fragmenta Historicorum Graecorum*
GFS	J.A.O. Larsen, *Greek Federal States* (Oxford, 1967)
GHI	M. N. Tod, *A Selection of Greek Historical Inscriptions. Vol. II. From 403 to 323 B.C.* (Oxford, 1948)
HM	N.G.L. Hammond and G. T. Griffith, *A History of Macedonia. Volume II. 550-336 B.C.* (Oxford, 1979)
HN	Barclay V. Head, *Historia Numorum* [2] (Oxford, 1911)
IG	*Inscriptiones Graecae*
IGCH	*An Inventory of Greek Coin Hoards*, ed. M. Thompson, O. Mørkholm, and C. M. Kraay (New York, 1973)

LT	Marta Sordi, *La lega tessala fino ad Alessandro Magno* (Rome, 1958)
ML	Russell Meiggs and David Lewis, *A Selection of Greek Historical Inscriptions to the End of the Fifth Century* (Oxford, 1969)
Monnayage	Georges Le Rider, *Le monnnayage d'argent et d'or de Philippe II frappé en Macédoine de 359 à 294* (Paris, 1977)
NotSc	*Notizie degli scavi di antichità*
OGIS	W. Dittenberger, *Orientis Graeci Inscriptiones Selectae* (Leipzig, 1903-1905)
RE	*Real-Encyclopädie der classischen Altertumswissenschaft*
SEG	*Supplementum Epigraphicum Graecum*
*SIG*³	W. Dittenberger, *Sylloge Inscriptionum Graecarum* ³ (Leipzig, 1915-1924)
SVA	*Die Staatsverträge des Altertums*
YCS	*Yale Classical Studies*
ZfN	*Zeitschrift für Numismatik*

PREFACE

Greek coins can exert a powerful attraction on those who are fascinated by the *Realien* of ancient Greece. Perhaps because ancient historians can learn so much from other physical remnants of classical antiquity, especially inscriptions, we are eager to use coins extensively, too, as clues in our reconstructions of Greek history. Ancient Greek coinage, however, is a notoriously treacherous source of historical evidence. With the subject of sovereignty and coinage, particular difficulties arise because the coins usually lack overt indications of chronology and because the topic of the so-called right of coinage, so often mentioned by modern scholars, is very nearly invisible in the ancient literary and documentary sources. Keeping the limitations imposed by the nature of the evidence in mind, I have tried in this work to use coins as guides to a clearer understanding of one aspect of ancient Greek history. My curiosity was originally provoked by the reliance of scholars on a historical model which explains the minting of classical Greek and Macedonian coinages as primarily motivated by a desire on the part of the state to produce symbols of its political sovereignty. For many reasons, this model is unsatisfactory. A historical model seems preferable which posits practical economic concerns as the principal consideration in the minting of coinage in this period. Classical coins should not be understood as the functional equivalents of modern national flags in the symbolic assertion of an abstract notion of political sovereignty.

Practical necessities have limited me to the use of published numismatic material, and even there significant limitations must be acknowledged. Even though this preface is being written in 1984, the most recent issue of the invaluable publication *Coin Hoards* which I have been able to use belongs to 1981. The statistics on hoards used here are therefore inevitably out of date. Fortunately, the validity of the argument does not depend on hard numbers. Since, however, legitimate doubts can arise about the ways in which and the extent to which the evidence of coin hoards should be used in historical arguments, I have tried to make my assumptions plain where hoards are concerned.

Since so many different types of coins are discussed in the course of this study, considerations of expense ruled out any attempt at comprehensive illustration. Photographs of most of the types mentioned are available, however, in the plates of the standard reference works, such as Colin Kraay's *Archaic and Classical Greek Coins* (Berkeley, 1976). I am grateful to the Dewing Greek Numismatic Foundation for permission to publish photographs of examples of a few of the types of coins which are especially important to my argument. All the coins illustrated belong to the Foundation and are on loan to the Fogg Art Museum, Harvard University, Cambridge, Mass.

Many people have helped me in many ways in the writing of this book. Even a detailed recitation of their various kindnesses would fail to do more than to hint at how much I owe them. Under the circumstances, I hope that the listing of their names, poor recompense though it is, will show them that I am conscious of my debt. In the case of this book, it is particularly important to stress the formulaic *caveat* that those who have helped me should not be thought responsible for anything here which is wrong or seems wrongheaded. In addition, the expression of my thanks to those who gave me their opinions should not be taken to imply that I have persuaded them to accept the historical model presented in this book.

For reading parts or all of the text in various stages of reworking (some very early on), I am indebted to Ernst Badian, S. C. Bakhuizen, Thomas N. Bisson, G. W. Bowersock, T. V. Buttrey, W. Robert Connor, Giles Constable, Nancy J. Moore, R. M. Errington, Adalberto Giovannini, Philip Grierson, Christian Habicht, N.G.L. Hammond, Albert Henrichs, R. Ross Holloway, John H. Kroll, Carey McWilliams, William E. Metcalf, M. Jessop Price, P. J. Rhodes, Klaus Rosen, Alan M. Stahl, Joseph R. Strayer, Ronald S. Stroud, Margaret Thompson, and Nancy M. Waggoner. Their comments and advice contributed to a final

version of the book that is much changed from what they origi-
nally saw and is, thanks to their help, greatly improved.
Others have helped in other ways. I received bibliographic
help with the history of the Hapsburgs from Steven Ozment.
Scott Bradner, Gregory Crane, Lorna Holmes, Kenneth Morrell,
and Jeffrey Wills helped with word processing and computer use.
Michael Padgett energetically aided the verification of refer-
ences. Margaret D'Ambrosio, of the Library of the American
Numismatic Society, helped with bibliographic problems.
Joanna Hitchcock, of the Princeton University Press, provided
exemplary guidance throughout the process of publication. Her
secretary, Carol MacKinnon, deserves special thanks, as does
Barbara Stump for copy editing. The services of Gary Bisbee, of
Chiron, Inc., made possible computer typesetting. Pamela
Marshall provided timely and meticulous assistance with
proofreading. Janet Dockendorff facilitated the photographing
of the coins for the plates.

The support of my family was constant throughout the long
process of finishing this project. The help of my wife Ivy was
truly essential at all stages.

It is inevitable that a scholar's professional indebtedness will
remain forever unpaid. I am happy to be able to acknowledge
just how deep in debt I find myself.

Thomas R. Martin
Cambridge, Massachusetts

CHRONOLOGICAL TABLE. Thessaly from the End of the Fifth Century B.C. to the End of the Fourth Century

This selective list of dates is appended only to serve the reader's convenience, not to stand in any sense as an attempt at a definitive chronology for the often obscure history of Thessaly in this period. The dates offered are necessarily almost all tentative or approximate, even when "*ca.*" is not used.

ca. 404	Lycophron of Pherae fights against Larissa in an attempt to become leader of the Thessalian Confederacy and to "unite" Thessaly.
ca. 400	Archelaus, king of Macedonia, intervenes in Larissa
393–391	Amyntas III, king of Macedonia, in exile in Thessaly; restored by the Thessalians in 391
ca. 385	Jason becomes tyrant of Pherae
late 370s	Jason elected leader of the Thessalian Confederacy, thereby formally "uniting" Thessaly
370–369	Jason's brothers, Polydorus and then Polyphron, succeed him as leader of the Thessalian Confederacy
369	Alexander of Pherae, nephew of Jason, becomes leader of the Thessalian Confederacy. The Aleuads of Larissa invite Alexander II of Macedonia to intervene; he garrisons Larissa and Crannon
368–364	Pelopidas intervenes in Thessaly on several occasions, acting against Alexander of Macedonia and Alexander of Pherae
361/0	Athenians make alliance with some Thessalians against Alexander of Pherae
358(?)	Alexander of Pherae assassinated; Aleuads of Larissa invite Philip II of Macedonia to intervene against his "tyrannical" successors in Pherae

354/3	Philip II again intervenes in Thessaly on the side of Larissa against Pherae and the Phocians; eventually victorious, he expels the tyrants of Pherae and Pagasae, and is elected leader of the Thessalian Confederacy
352(?)	As leader of the Thessalian Confederacy, Philip punishes Pharcadon and Tricca
late 350s	Strained relations between Thessalians and Philip over revenues and Philip's actions in Pagasae and Magnesia
349/8(?)	Philip again expels a tyrant from Pherae
346	At the end of the Sacred War, Philip restores Thessalian status in the Delphic Amphictiony
344 – 342	Philip reforms tetrarchic government in Thessaly and garrisons Pherae (and Pagasae as well?)
338/7	Thessalians join Philip's League of Corinth
336/5	Alexander III elected leader of the Thessalian Confederacy (and restores Aleuads to power at Larissa?)
330	Most Thessalian cavalrymen in Alexander's army return home
early/middle 320s	Food shortage in Thessaly, probably caused by extended drought
323	Thessalians desert Antipater after death of Alexander to fight with Greeks in Lamian War
322	Antipater defeats Greeks at Crannon and sacks Thessalian cities
321	Thessalians again revolt, incited by the Aetolians, but they are defeated by Polyperchon
after 319	Cassander wins control of Thessaly
302	Demetrius Poliorcetes invades Thessaly and takes Pherae; Cassander recovers his losses upon Demetrius' departure for Asia

SOVEREIGNTY AND COINAGE IN CLASSICAL GREECE

INTRODUCTION

The contents of Greek coin hoards discovered in modern times allow us to see what a wealthy Greek in Thessaly of the mid-third century B.C. would find when he inspected the contents of his well-stocked cash box. The newest and shiniest pieces in his cache were coins which had been minted recently in neighboring Macedonia by the king Antigonus Gonatas, whose military power allowed him to dominate the political scene in Thessaly and much of the rest of mainland Greece as well. There were other Macedonian royal coins present, too, but they were not so fresh because some of them had been minted as long ago as the reigns of Philip II (359–336 B.C.) and Alexander the Great (336–323 B.C.). In addition to these coins from Macedonia, this prosperous man found in his collection of the money of the day coins from other cities and kingdoms to the east of his homeland which bore the portraits of rulers such as Lysimachus or Seleucus; some of these coins were quite new, and some were not. The Greek coins in the collection also ranged from old to new, with tetradrachms of Athens numerous and themselves ranging in their various ages from very recent to as old as perhaps a century. Not so varied in their ages or their appearances, however, were the familiar local coins of Thessaly which this hypothetical Thessalian had in his possession. As a group, these coins were quite old and all, or almost all, products of the same mint, that of the city of Larissa. They all looked alike, with the facing head of a woman on one side and a grazing horse on the other. The man was not surprised at the age and therefore at the generally bad condition of these local coins in his collection because, as a local resident, he knew full well that the mints of Thessaly no longer produced coins in his time and that all the local pieces he possessed had been minted decades earlier. Their circulation for many years had given them a dull and worn look, but they were still valuable. It was only petty pride that would require a man to pay his debts entirely in shiny, new silver coins.[1]

This picture of the coinage in Thessaly around 250 B.C. contrasts sharply with that of the coinage in the same area a century before. An equally wealthy ancestor of this third-century Thessalian would not find any Macedonian coins in his cash box of 350 B.C. Instead, his collection consisted entirely of Greek coins, again with a good number of Athenian pieces, as well as coins from other Greek states, but the Thessalian coins looked somewhat different from those of his third-century counterpart. Coins of Larissa predominated numerically, but their conditions and their types both varied. This diversity in the appearances of his local coins struck their owner as only natural because the mints of Thessaly in his lifetime, as they had done for a century or more, continued to produce new coins to join in circulation their older products from previous years, which were often different in their designs.

Although the evidence which has survived from the period before 350 B.C. in Thessaly makes it difficult to speak with certainty about this still earlier period, it does seem reasonably certain that the picture from, say, 450 B.C. looked in its overall lines much like that from 350 B.C. The great contrast comes from a comparison of the situation in the third century B.C. with that of previous centuries, and this striking contrast presents the historian and the numismatist with an interesting and significant puzzle. Why were the mints of Thessaly, and in particular the once prolific mint of Larissa, no longer minting coins in the mid-third century as they had done in the previous two centuries? Why were Macedonian coins so common in Thessaly in the third century B.C., when they had been unknown there a hundred years before? What did the presence of these royal coins signify for the political and economic status of the region in that period?

The answers given to these questions have remained the same throughout the course of modern scholarship, even though they require us to accept as historical fact a remarkable scenario for which there is no support in the ancient sources. Since the

---

[1] Theophrastus, *Characters* 21.5.

nineteenth century, scholars have often assumed that local Thessalian coinage ended in the later fourth century B.C. because a Macedonian sovereign, who has been variously identified, forced the mints in Thessaly to close and imposed on the Thessalians the use of Macedonian royal coinage. This ruler took these actions, it must be assumed in this argument, because the nature of his sovereignty demanded no less when he deprived the Thessalians of their traditional autonomy in the interest of Macedonian royal sovereignty. That is, he suppressed local autonomous coinage in Thessaly because a supreme and exclusive monetary prerogative was a royal right, a privilege indissolubly tied to rule.

As we will see, this sort of explanation for the end of local coinages has found a far broader application in ancient Greek history than only in the case of Thessaly. In particular, it has been used to justify the view that the kings of the Hellenistic period regularly suppressed Greek coinages as an expression of their sovereignty as monarchs whose rule was originally based on a Macedonian model of kingship. W. W. Tarn, for example, in reference to mainland Greece during the reign of Antigonus Gonatas in the third century B.C., maintained that "Greek towns as a rule lost the right [of coinage] when incorporated in the [Macedonian] kingdom."[2] More recently, Edith Schönert-Geiss has expressed the opinion that this situation began to prevail as early as the reigns of Philip and Alexander.[3] The present state of the numismatic evidence for the Hellenistic period, to say

[2] *Antigonus Gonatas* (Oxford, 1913), p. 197. Cf. Attilio Mastrocinque, "Storia e monetazione di Mileto all'epoca dei Diadochi," *AIIN* 27–28 (1980–1981), p. 62, for a recent statement of the view that subject cities in the Hellenistic period issued royal coin types (if they minted any coins at all), while independent cities issued autonomous coinages or posthumous Alexanders. He refers to this view as the "*lex Seyrig*," based on the remarks of Henri Seyrig in, for example, "Aradus et sa pérée sous les rois Séleucides," *Syria* 28 (1951), pp. 206–220 = *Antiquités Syriennes* (Paris, 1953), pp. 185–200, an important discussion to which I will return in the Conclusion. For a fuller discussion of the situation in the Hellenistic period, see Claire Préaux, *Le monde hellénistique. La Grèce et l'Orient (323–146 av. J.-C.)*, vol. 1 (Paris, 1978), pp. 280–294 ("la monnaie royale").

[3] See her wide-ranging discussion "Das Geld im Hellenismus," *Klio* 60 (1978), p. 132.

nothing of the often obscure and controversial nature of the historical evidence, makes it difficult to assess the relation between sovereignty and coinage in that era. It is probably a safe bet that no simple answer will do. I contend, however, that if the Hellenistic kings in the third century actually did suppress Greek coinage as a matter of policy concerning a theoretical notion of sovereignty, it was not because they had found a precedent for such a policy in the actions of the Macedonian kings in the fourth century, or indeed elsewhere in the history of the classical Greek world.

The purpose of this study is to investigate the relationship between sovereignty and coinage in the Greek world of the classical period. The emphasis will of necessity be on the fourth century B.C., where most of the relevant evidence is to be found, and the nature of the evidence calls for considerable attention to be paid to the Macedonian kings of this period as they become more actively involved in the affairs of the Greeks. My goal is to clear the field of a misleading preconception about the relationship between sovereignty and coinage and to suggest an evaluation of the importance of coinage as a component of the political sovereignty of the Greek states and the Macedonian kings. The results of the investigation, it may be hoped, will shed some light on the relative importance for coinage of abstract or theoretical political considerations *versus* economic and financial concerns in this period of transition from the world of the fractiously independent Greek states to a world at the mercy of the superpowers we call Hellenistic monarchies. As will become clear later, I believe that those who would emphasize the "political sense" of ancient Greek coinage almost to the exclusion of practical considerations have put the emphasis in the wrong place. The idea that coins functioned primarily as political symbols misrepresents the fundamental significance of Greek coinage.[4]

---

[4] Moses Finley discusses the "political sense" of coinage in *The Ancient Economy* (London, 1973), pp. 166–169. For him, the "Greek passion for coins" was "essentially a political phenomenon." Coins functioned as "the traditional symbol of autonomy." This idea often appears in modern specialized scholarship. For recent examples, see Ed. Will, "Les sources des métaux monnayés dans le monde grec," in *Numismatique antique. Problèmes et méthodes*, ed. J.-M. Dentzer, Ph. Gautier, and T. Hackens (Nancy, 1975), p. 102: "Le monnayage est l'un

Since on a general level this study concerns the notion of sovereignty, it will not be out of place to offer a definition of what will be understood here by the word "sovereignty" in the context of the ancient world. A political state must possess the power to establish and to fulfill some goals in the political, economic, social, and other areas of government if it is to exist and to function properly.[5] The ability to exercise this power can be called sovereignty, the ability which belongs to the sovereign in the state. It is necessary to say "ability" rather than "right" because the sovereign need not conceive of his sovereignty as an abstract notion in order to exercise his power. If anachronism is to be avoided, sovereignty in this context must be examined in concrete terms.

On this definition of sovereignty, the study of sovereignty and its components within the context of political history is the search for answers to questions such as who is the sovereign, what is the nature and the extent of the power exercised by the sovereign, how is this power vested in the sovereign, and so on. The historian interested in a particular place at a particular time can try to answer these questions, and others like them, through analysis of different types of evidence, which might be summarized under three headings: actual constitutional documents such

des signes de l'*autonomie*, sinon de l'*eleutheria*, et ce symbole dût devenir plus cher aux cités à mesure que leur autonomie et leur liberté furent plus fréquemment mises en question"; M. M. Austin and P. Vidal-Naquet, *Economic and Social History of Ancient Greece: An Introduction* (Berkeley, 1977), pp. 56–58, on the invention of coinage: "One must emphasize especially the development of civic consciousness: in the history of the Greek cities coinage was always first and foremost a civic emblem. To strike coins with the badge of the city was to proclaim one's political independence."

[5] For the idea that a state has goals, see, for example, Aristotle, *Politics* 7.1326a13, 1328a35–37. My definition of sovereignty is obviously not meant to be original or comprehensive. Since the emphasis here is on sovereignty as it applied to the relation of the state with other states, I will leave aside other components of the idea relevant to the internal workings of a state, such as the need to have some person or institution in the society with the power of final decision (Aristotle, *Politics* 7.1328b13–15). Modern scholarship on this and all other aspects of sovereignty is of course vast. For one example of a wide-ranging approach to the subject, one can see Bertrand de Jouvenel, *Sovereignty. An Inquiry into the Political Good*, trans. J. F. Huntington (Chicago, 1957).

as the political charters common in modern states; other contemporary sources pertinent to the issue of sovereignty such as discussions and surveys of constitutional history or treatises on political philosophy which reflect on current and past government; and the historical facts as revealed by sources which are not themselves directly concerned with the notion of sovereignty as a historical or theoretical subject. For the subject at hand, an investigation of political sovereignty must rely most heavily on the last category of evidence because the first two categories are largely lacking.[6] In fact, Macedonian monarchy has left us even fewer materials with which to study its nature than have the classical Greek city-states, which eventually fell under Macedonian domination in the fourth century. But the study of sovereignty in this period seems worthwhile despite the difficulties, because these years saw the embryonic development of an institution, Hellenistic monarchy, which was to dominate the Greek world of city-states and confederacies for three centuries. Indeed, from a certain perspective, one can say that the kind of monarchy over mixed populations that arose from the events of the later fourth century B.C. set the scene for the political history of the Mediterranean area for nearly two millenia. For the Greeks, at least, the Roman and the Byzantine emperors were the recognizable successors of the Hellenistic kings.

Finally, it should be explained how a study of coinage will contribute to our understanding of sovereignty in this period. When in the 350s B.C. Philip II began to expand his power southward beyond the natural geographical boundaries of his homeland into neighboring Thessaly, the way was opened to a clash between the sovereignty of this energetic king and the sovereignty of the Greek states with which he came into contact. Since the Greeks lacked the political unity and the military strength which would have been necessary to defeat Philip decisively, on a realistic appraisal this clash could end in only a

---

[6] Victor Ehrenberg, *The Greek State* [2] (London, 1969), provides a convenient survey with extensive bibliography of numerous topics in the study of the classical and Hellenistic states conceived as political forms. A review of his discussions of sovereignty as a general topic (see his index on p. 302) gives an idea of the sort of material available for study.

limited number of ways. The two sides could fight to a stale-
mate, necessitating at least a temporary return to the situation of
the past when they existed as separate and distinct political entities moving in different orbits. Alternatively, Philip could win a
decisive victory. After such a success, Philip was unlikely to
leave matters just as they had been before. His options were to
make the Greeks his subjects and destroy the political independence of their states by incorporating them into the Macedonian
kingdom, or to create a new political structure which would
somehow incorporate the formal sovereignties of both sides in a
viable and realistic way.

Thanks to his diplomatic and military prowess, Philip soon
gained control of Thessaly, and after the battle of Chaeronea in
338 B.C. against an alliance of the Greek states opposing him, he
was clearly the dominant power in mainland Greece. But military realities and Philip's ambition combined to rule out the
option of making the Greeks his subjects. At Chaeronea, Philip
had only defeated the Greek forces in the field. He had not
stormed their walled cities, and his desire to invade Asia to fight
the Great King of Persia meant that the effort which would be
required to subject the Greeks was bound to delay his dream, if
not wreck his plans entirely. Storming cities was no simple
matter, as Philip remembered from his fruitless siege of Perinthus
a few years earlier. It suited Philip better to secure the cooperation of the Greeks, or at least their grudging acquiescence, in his
great design to invade the territory of the Persian Empire. There
was nothing to do, therefore, but to work out something new
between the Macedonian king and the Greek states, and that is
just what was done in the so-called League of Corinth. Under
the guise of a traditionally Greek notion of hegemonial alliance,
the clash between Macedonian and Greek sovereignty was
resolved, which is not to say that basic tensions were cleared
away.

The problems caused by competing claims of sovereignty
which faced Philip and the Greeks were not wholly new. In the
fifth century B.C., the Persian kings had for a time explicitly
extended their sovereignty over parts of Greece and Macedonia,
and the infamous King's Peace of 387/6 B.C. had vividly

demonstrated the superior, if distant, power over the Greeks of the Great King of Persia. But never before had it been necessary to work out some kind of long-term political arrangement between a neighboring but foreign king who wanted to be seen, so far as possible, as a hegemonial leader in traditional Hellenic fashion, and Greek states that had been defeated but not subjected. In the circumstances which characterized Philip's rise to dominance in Greece, and his successors' efforts to continue that dominance, the claims of Macedonian royal sovereignty and of Greek civic sovereignty were bound to conflict. The ways in which these conflicts were settled offer clues about what each side considered important within the sphere of its own sovereignty. Although he built with the elements of traditional Greek political structures, Philip did forge a new political arrangement, and Alexander willingly inherited and continued his father's creation. After Alexander's death, various successors contributed to the shaping of this new arrangement as the institution of Hellenistic monarchy gradually developed. Throughout this formative period, the shape and the extent of royal sovereignty were undergoing change as new ideas and different traditions contributed to its development from a purely Macedonian original model. These changes naturally had implications for Greeks as well as Macedonians.

Perhaps it is true of most cultures in most periods of history, but certainly Macedonian royal sovereignty was defined more by practice than by theory. Recent scholarly work has emphasized that the sovereignty of the Macedonian kings rested to a far greater degree on the individual king's personal qualities and effectiveness as a leader than on any securely rooted and codified constitutional arrangements.[7] Under such circumstances, it is obvious that preconceived notions about the nature of royal sovereignty and its relationship to the sovereignty of other states which are derived from the study of sovereigns at other times and in other places are liable to be misleading if applied

[7] See, for example, Robert Lock, "The Macedonian Army Assembly in the Time of Alexander the Great," *CP* 72 (1977), pp. 91–107, esp. p. 98; R. M. Errington, "The Nature of the Macedonian State under the Monarchy," *Chiron* 8 (1978), pp. 77–133.

uncritically. I believe that just such a notion has dominated scholarly thinking about control of the monetary system as a component of sovereignty in the case of the relations between the Macedonian kings and the Greek states of the mainland. The basic assumption about sovereignty and coinage which lies behind the commonly accepted view that Macedonian kings suppressed Greek coinages in favor of their own royal coinages can ultimately be discovered in the tenets of political philosophy of the Middle Ages concerning the inalienable rights of rulers. From this origin, and not from thorough study of the evidence of the classical period, this assumption passed into the canons of modern scholarship on classical Greek antiquity. The noted economist F. A. Hayek, for example, applies this principle to antiquity and the Middle Ages in his discussion of the origin of the governmental prerogative of making money in what might be called a definitive general statement of the traditional view:

It is evident that, as coinage spread, governments everywhere soon discovered that the exclusive right of coinage was a most important instrument of power as well as an attractive source of gain. From the beginning the prerogative was neither claimed nor conceded on the ground that it was for the general good but simply as an essential element of governmental power. The coins served, indeed, largely as the symbols of might, like the flag, through which the ruler asserted his sovereignty, and told his people who their master was whose image the coins carried to the remotest parts of his realm.[8]

This sort of generalization on essentially theoretical grounds, however, is only an assumption based on modern preconceptions about the relation between sovereignty and coinage in classical antiquity which attributes to coins a primary function akin to that of modern national flags, whether as symbols of might or autonomy or sovereignty or whatever notion one wishes to append. For this reason, a study of the relevant coinage of the period, in conjunction with a new examination of the ancient historical evidence, should contribute to a clearer understanding of

[8] F. A. Hayek, *Denationalisation of Money: The Argument Refined. An Analysis of the Theory and Practice of Concurrent Currencies* 2 (London, 1978), p. 25. For the symbolic function of flags, see the references in n. 24 of the Conclusion.

Macedonian royal sovereignty at a time when this sovereignty was being transformed in unexpected and unprecedented ways and also provide evidence for a sounder evaluation of at least certain aspects of the significance of classical Greek coinage.[9]

In particular, the importance of control of the monetary system as a component of sovereignty is worth investigating because in clashes of sovereignty this control can be a bitterly contested issue. This is clear, for example, from the events of other historical periods, such as the Middle Ages.[10] This study will investigate whether there were precedents for exclusive control of the monetary system as a necessary component of sovereignty when the successors of Alexander the Great finally decided at the end of the fourth century that they, too, were kings.

The first step in this study will be to look at the history of the idea that Macedonian kings suppressed autonomous coinages in fourth-century Greece, because only a thorough investigation of the background of this idea can demonstrate why it has been so strong and so widespread, and why it needs to be discarded. This investigation of scholarly opinion will concentrate on the primary exhibit in the case for suppression as a Macedonian policy, the case of Thessaly in the time of Philip, Alexander, and the early successors. Thessaly must receive detailed attention because the idea that a Macedonian sovereign suppressed Thessalian coinage represents the clearest demonstration of how a mistaken conception of the relationship between sovereignty and

---

[9] It is not my intention to try to cover all the aspects which one might postulate as necessary in a comprehensive evaluation of the significance of Greek coinage. There is, for example, the legal aspect of coinage. The Greek word for coin, νόμισμα, implies by its relationship with the word for "custom" or "law," νόμος, a normative role for coinage in the context of the financial and commercial transactions which had to take place for the state to function. This view is implied by the remarks of A. Giovannini on the fifth-century Athenian Coinage Decree in his *Rome et la circulation monétaire en Grèce au IIe siècle avant Jésus-Christ* (Basel, 1978), pp. 75–76. Professor Giovannini has kindly informed me that he intends to pursue this view further in print.

[10] One scholar of modern monetary theory summarizes the general view of why this should be so: "La monnaie est plus liée à l'exercice du pouvoir souverain qu'à la notion même d'Etat." See Dominique Carreau, *Souveraineté et coopération monétaire internationale* (Paris, 1970), p. 23.

coinage can lead to faulty historical reconstruction. The case of Thessaly clearly reveals that when scholars are confronted with a Greek coinage that ends at a time when the issuing state has been in some way subordinated politically to a more powerful state, the standard opinion on the relationship between sovereignty and coinage in the classical Greek world can serve as support for the assumption that the more powerful state suppressed the coinage of the less powerful state. It is obvious, then, that if the case of Thessaly can be shown to have been misinterpreted, an important justification will be removed for applying this assumption across the board in Greek history.

The next step in this study will therefore be a reassessment of the evidence to show that suppression of Thessalian coinage is not likely to have been a Macedonian policy. Rather, it will become clear that economic failure leading to financial weakness in the cities in Thessaly at the end of the fourth century, at a time when Macedonian royal coinage became both popular and plentiful in Greece, is a more plausible reason for the end of Thessalian civic coinage at this time. Finally, the Macedonian, Persian, and Greek evidence for strict control of the monetary system will be discussed to see what, if any, historical precedents there might have been for regarding such a policy as an integral component of political sovereignty or as necessary for the symbolic assertion of the political existence of the state.

It is, of course, impossible to prove beyond any doubt that the continuation of local coinage by Greek states under Macedonian control meant that the kings did not believe that, under optimum conditions, their sovereignty would require them to establish a purely royal monetary system even in the Greek states. That is, one might formulate an alternate hypothesis to explain a Macedonian failure to suppress Greek coinages which would include the notion that the Macedonian kings, looking back to Greek or Macedonian precedents, felt the theoretical need to impose the use of royal money, and only royal money, on all the peoples under their control. This hypothesis would then explain the continuation of Greek coinages by the assumption that the kings did not, for practical reasons of statecraft, insist on the exclusive monetary prerogative to which they were in theory entitled. This sort of hypothesis, for example, might be used to explain Frederick Barbarossa's failure in the Middle Ages to abolish the right of coinage of the Italian cities despite his claim in the Constitution of Roncaglia (A.D. 1158) to an exclusive monetary prerogative.[11]

The problem with this alternate hypothesis is that it cannot be tested. There is no ancient source like Barbarossa's Constitution which announces the position of Philip II and his successors on the Macedonian throne concerning the question of who should mint coins, nor is there any source which indicates that anyone in the classical period whether Greek or Macedonian held the same opinion as Barbarossa on the relationship between sovereignty and coinage, or indeed held any clear opinion on this issue at all. If this study demonstrates that no good evidence exists for the suppression of Greek coinages by a Macedonian king, and that the evidence for control of coinage by Greek states suggests economic motives for the regulation of the production of coins, it would seem fair to say that the burden of proof should fall on those who wish to maintain that in the classical period a close relationship between an abstract notion of political sovereignty and the minting of coins was perceived on a theoretical level and exercised in practice.

The formulation of a plausible explanation of the facts as we have them concerning sovereignty and coinage in classical Greece calls for a fresh examination of all the relevant evidence. That examination must begin with the history of scholarly opinion on the reason for the end of Thessalian coinage in the fourth century B.C.

[11] The constitution is reproduced in *Monumenta Germaniae Historica, Legum,* vol. 2, ed. G. H. Pertz (Hanover, 1837, repr. 1925), pp. 111–112. On his policy, see H. Koeppler, "Frederick Barbarossa and the Schools of Bologna: Some Remarks on the 'Authentica Habita,'" *English Historical Review* 54 (1939), pp. 577–607. On the controversial nature of the rights claimed in the Constitution, see Georges Blondel, "Etude sur les droits régaliens et la constitution de Roncaglia," in *Mélanges Paul Fabre. Etudes d'histoire du Moyen Age* (Paris, 1902, repr. Geneva, 1972), pp. 236–257; Irene Ott, "Der Regalienbegriff im 12. Jahrhundert," *Zeitschrift der Savigny-Stiftung für Rechtsgeschichte, Kanonistische Abteilung* 35 (1948), pp. 234–304; Peter Munz, *Frederick Barbarossa: A Study in Medieval Politics* (London, 1969), pp. 166–170.

ONE. SCHOLARLY OPINION ON MACEDONIAN KINGS AND THESSALIAN COINAGE

The fate of the coinage of Thessaly in the classical period presented a puzzle to those scholars who first studied these coins in a comprehensive fashion. The cities of Thessaly minted a large number of different coinages in the fifth and fourth centuries, but at some point all these civic coinages came to an end and were eventually replaced in the second century B.C. by a federal coinage. Since the ancient sources did not directly reveal the solution to the puzzle of the precise date and the reason for the cessation of civic coinage in Thessaly, scholars had to produce a solution based only on indirect evidence, the uncertainty of which was often unacknowledged. As it happened, a scholarly consensus on the question of the fate of Thessalian coinage was established on the basis of an unexamined assumption about the relationship between political sovereignty and the right of coinage. An explanation of the origin of that assumption must be our first concern.

1
The Assumption behind the Scholarly Consensus

The history of the idea that fourth-century Macedonian kings abolished at least some Greek coinages in favor of their own coins is linked to the history of ancient numismatics as a scholarly discipline. This idea was developed not from study of the ancient Greek situation but, rather, from theories based on the history of other periods. In fact, the strength and persistence in modern scholarship of the idea that fourth-century Macedonian kings suppressed autonomous Greek coinage in favor of their own royal coinage as a matter of policy, which was determined by the nature of their rule, is only comprehensible when one considers the general background of this idea in the history of European political theory on sovereignty, especially the sovereignty of monarchs.

This subject received a comprehensive treatment in the sixteenth century in the famous work on sovereignty of the French political philosopher Jean Bodin (1530–1596). His *Six livres de la république*, first published in 1576, was an attempt to elaborate an absolutist theory of sovereignty based on Bodin's decided preference for monarchy.[1] To make his case, Bodin produced an extremely detailed list of the characteristics and attributes of sovereignty which this absolute sovereign must possess. The comprehensiveness of his definition of sovereignty set Bodin apart from his predecessors in political philosophy, whose traditional views on sovereignty he inevitably inherited, and the wide scope of his thought and of his research for evidence to support his views allowed him to discuss the issue of the sovereign and his coinage in unprecedented detail.

The power to coin money was seventh in Bodin's extensive list of the necessary attributes of a sovereign.[2] In summary, his position was that the right of coinage is the exclusive prerogative of the sovereign, who must suppress all other coinages in his realm and should never grant permission to anyone else to issue coins. A uniform monetary system naturally results, and Bodin recommended that the sovereign emulate the ancient Roman

[1] For the view that Bodin was the originator of modern study of sovereignty as a theoretical concept, see Robert Derathé, "La place de Jean Bodin dans l'histoire des théories de la souveraineté," in *Jean Bodin. Verhandlungen der internationalen Bodin-Tagung in München* (Munich, 1973), p. 245. For the sake of convenience, Bodin will be cited from the edition by Kenneth Douglas McRae, *Jean Bodin. The Six Bookes of a Commonweale* (Cambridge, Mass., 1962), who has compared the various original editions of Bodin's work. For discussion of Bodin's general theory of sovereignty and further bibliography, see Julian H. Franklin, *Jean Bodin and the Rise of Absolutist Theory* (Cambridge, 1973); George H. Sabine (revised by Thomas Landon Thorson), *A History of Political Theory*[4] (Hinsdale, Ill., 1973), pp. 377–385.

[2] Bodin gave all the attributes of sovereignty in book 1, chapter 10 of the *Six livres*, pp. 153–182 in the McRae edition.

Emperors and Charlemagne by allowing only one central mint, to ensure close control of a single coinage for the protection of all.[3]

Bodin's formulation of a theory of sovereignty was especially influential because it represented a culmination of centuries of European thought on the topic. Already in the thirteenth and fourteenth centuries, for example, the elaboration of the notion of the inalienability of *regalia*, "royal rights," made it easy to reach the conclusion that a king might need to suppress nonroyal coinages. These *regalia* were the rights and functions which a kingdom had to exercise if it was to exist and to flourish. Since from a certain perspective in political philosophy an individual king was in effect only a trustee of the powers and responsibilities conferred on him by his royal office, he lacked the right to alienate these essential components of his office's sovereignty to the detriment of his successors and of the state itself. Such was the kernel of the theory of the inalienability of sovereignty as it emerged in this period.[4] The right of coinage was one of the "royal rights." This meant that the sovereign, from the very fact of his possessing sovereignty, was forbidden to invest anyone else with the authority to mint coins. It was a necessary conclusion, therefore, that all nonroyal coinages would have to be eliminated to achieve and maintain a uniform monetary system.[5]

Significantly, this same conclusion also emerged in the great monograph on the theory of money written by Nicole Oresme in the fourteenth century, a treatise which advanced arguments

[3] Book 6, chapter 3, McRae edition, pp. 687–700.

[4] On the subject of inalienability, see Peter N. Riesenberg, *Inalienability of Sovereignty in Medieval Political Thought* (New York, 1956).

[5] Riesenberg, *Inalienability*, pp. 5–9, points out that no firm list of the *regalia* that could not be alienated was ever drawn up, but the control of coinage was definitely one of the rights at issue (cf. p. 30). See, for example, the law in the thirteenth-century Spanish code *Fuero Viejo* that makes "Moneda" one of the four things a king cannot alienate "por razón del señorío natural," quoted by Salvador Minguijón, *Historia del derecho español*[4] (Barcelona, 1953), p. 97. Not every contemporary thinker, however, believed that a uniform monetary system was absolutely necessary. See Romualdo Trifone, "La variazione del valore della moneta nel pensiero di Bartolo," in *Bartolo di Sassoferrato. Studi e documenti per il VI centenario* (Milan, 1962), vol. 2, p. 698.

against the notion that a ruler could manipulate the monetary system absolutely as he pleased.[6] The main point of the work was to argue that the sovereign's monopoly over coinage arose not from an absolute royal right or from ownership of the coinage, but from practical necessity in the interests of the public, whose property the currency really was.[7] The sovereign is to control the coinage for the benefit of the community, and this benefit must be ensured by the suppression of other domestic coinages besides the royal, whether counterfeit or valid. Foreign coinages that threaten the domestic monetary system must be suppressed, by war if necessary.[8]

It would be hard to imagine a stronger statement than Oresme's in favor of the idea that the sovereign should control the monetary system so as to provide a uniform circulation of coinage, by means of the suppression of competing mints if need be. That this statement came from a theorist who also held that the sovereign did not possess this control over the monetary system as an inalienable right meant that both sides in the theoretical debate over the origin of the sovereign's monetary prerogative could be made to agree on the practical point under discussion. They agreed that a king was required by his status and office to restrict the right of coinage only to royal mints throughout the territory over which he exercised sovereignty. On this point, the streams of opinion converged, culminating in Bodin's great work.[9]

[6] For Oresme's work and career, see Emile Bridrey, *Nicole Oresme. Etude d'histoire des doctrines et des faits économiques: la théorie de la monnaie au XIVᵉ siècle* (Paris, 1906), with the important reviews by A. Dieudonné, *Revue numismatique* 1909, p. 93; and A. Landry, *Le Moyen Age* 22 (1909), pp. 145–178; A. D. Menut, *Maistre Nicole Oresme. Le livre de Politiques d'Aristote* (Philadelphia, 1970).

[7] See Hector Estrup, "Oresme and Monetary Theory," *Scandinavian Economic History Review* 14 (1966), p. 116.

[8] In the French version of his treatise, Oresme expanded the recommendations in this area made in the Latin version. See Bridrey, *Oresme*, pp. 209–211.

[9] Subsequent specialized discussions on the subject of the sovereign and the monetary system essentially echoed the views which had been elaborated in the political philosophy of the thirteenth and fourteenth centuries. The German scholar Gabriel Biel (1430–1495), for example, in his major treatise on money written in the fifteenth century (first published in 1542), repeated the opinion

Bodin marshaled examples from both ancient and modern history to support his views on the subject of the sovereign and the monetary system. From the Roman Republic came proof that the sovereign power in the state had the power to determine the value of coinage. From the Roman Empire, he cited a law ascribed to Constantine which punished counterfeiting as treason. In other words, an offense against the sovereign's coinage constituted *lèse-majesté*.[10] Moving immediately from ancient history to more modern, Bodin remarked that the same punishment applies even to those who issue good coinage without the sovereign's permission. And in any case, such permission ought never to be granted to a subject because to do so would compromise the sovereignty of the sovereign. Francis I of France (1515–1547), Bodin noted, suppressed the traditional coinage of numerous nonroyal mints in France, and the "estates" of Poland at about the same time issued an edict which denied that king Sigismund II Augustus (crowned 1530, sole ruler 1548–1572) had the power to bestow the right of coinage on the duke of Prussia, because that right was inseparable from the crown.[11]

All of Bodin's evidence up to this point pertained either to

---

that in theory only the highest sovereign, in this case the Emperor, enjoyed the right of coinage. In practice, he admitted, others exercised this right from immemorial custom or failure to acknowledge the Emperor's superior suzerainty. See his *Treatise on the Power and Utility of Moneys*, trans. Robert Belle Burke (Philadelphia, 1930), pp. 31–32.

[10] McRae edition, p. 176. The law of Constantine is apparently *Codex Theodosianus* 9.21.1 of A.D. 317, which punished only the counterfeiting of gold as treason rather than as fraud. See Philip Grierson, "The Roman Law of Counterfeiting," in *Essays in Roman Coinage presented to Harold Mattingly*, ed. R. A. G. Carson and C.H.V. Sutherland (Oxford, 1956), p. 248.

[11] McRae edition, p. 176. For the monetary policy of Francis, see A. Blanchet and A. Dieudonné, *Manuel de numismatique française* (Paris, 1912–1936), vol. 2, pp. 131–133. For the grant of the right of coinage to Albrecht of Brandenburg, duke of Prussia, in 1525 under the rule of Sigismund I (1506–1548), see Arthur Engel and Raymond Serrure, *Traité de numismatique moderne et contemporaine* (Paris, 1897–1899), vol. 1, pp. 380–381, 533–535. Sigismund's arrangement with Albrecht itself necessitated the suppression of various mints and the centralization of royal authority over coinage, a reform which was elaborately justified in 1526 by Nicolaus Copernicus in his treatise *Monetae Cudendae Ratio*, written at the request of the king.

ancient Roman or to modern European history. Greek antiquity did not appear in his catalogue of historical evidence for the inalienability of the right of coinage. The situation changed, however, when he continued his discussion on the further topic of the importance of the sovereign's image on his coinage.[12] The citations here ranged from Theseus, the legendary king of Athens, through Darius, the Great King of Persia, to Commodus, Emperor of Rome. As part of this catalogue, Bodin mentioned Philip II of Macedonia (359 – 336 B.C.) as the first to coin money in Greece (*sic*) with his own image on it. These pieces, he added, were called *Philippaei*, in imitation of the Persian kings, who called their gold pieces *Dariques* after the image of king Darius (521 – 486 B.C.) which they bore. For Bodin, the placing of the king's own image on his coinage smacked of vanity more than anything else, but it is noteworthy that Philip made an appearance here as an example of a sovereign who insisted in an innovative fashion on his monetary prerogative. As it happens, Bodin had nothing explicit to say about Philip's effect on Greek coinages, but he did remark later on in his work that Philip subjected to himself almost all of Greece.[13] Given these two assumptions, it would be a simple matter to draw the inevitable conclusion that Philip as sovereign of most of Greece insisted on his prerogative over coinage there as well as in Macedonia.

By the time of Bodin, then, the idea had been established as a commonplace of educated opinion that a ruler should insist on a uniform monetary system for his own benefit and for the benefit of his subjects.[14] A scholarly consensus existed that only the

---

[12] McRae edition, pp. 176 – 177.

[13] Book 6, chapter 2 (McRae edition, p. 659).

[14] Political philosophers after Bodin generally reflected his view on this question. See, for example, Bernardo Davanzati, *Lezione delle monete* (presented orally 1588, publ. 1638), in *Ecrits notables sur la monnaie, XVIe siècle. De Copernic à Davanzati*, ed. J.-V. Le Branchu (Paris, 1934), vol. 2, p. 237; Rienier Budelius, *De monetis et re nummaria libri duo* (Cologne, 1591), pp. 19 – 20, 734 – 745; Geminiano Montanari, *Della moneta* (1687), in *Scrittori classici italiani di economia politica. Parte antica*, vol. 3 (Milan, 1804), pp. 36 – 37. Cf. A. E. Monroe, *Monetary Theory before Adam Smith* (Cambridge, Mass., 1923), pp. 91 – 92. The influence of Bodin is still felt. See, for example, Dominique Carreau, *Souveraineté*, p. 39: "Avec ces divers auteurs et surtout Bodin la monnaie apparaît definitivement comme un attribut de la souveraineté. Elle s'inscrit donc dans la construction

sovereign should coin and that extreme measures were justified to prevent exceptions. When in the century after Bodin's classic doctrine of sovereignty had been established scholarly work began to be focused on Greek coinage, the view so persuasively argued by Bodin (and validated by the lessons of modern history above all) passed as part of the common wisdom of political philosophy. This assumption about sovereignty and coinage stood ready as a convenient and respectable aid for the investigation and interpretation of such an imperfectly understood and poorly documented subject as ancient Greek coinage. Numismatists and historians interested in ancient Greece, who otherwise found themselves very inadequately furnished with interpretative tools for their task, naturally found it comfortable to rely on this aid, even though it had come into being on the basis of evidence from other times.[15] If we now turn to the case of Thessaly, we can see how this old assumption about sovereignty and coinage was used to solve the puzzle of the end of Thessalian coinage, thereby setting the stage for the use of the same assumption in other puzzling cases as well.

2
The Case of Thessaly

Historians of ancient Greece writing in the seventeenth and eighteenth centuries disagreed on what Philip had done when he intervened in Thessaly. Some accepted the favorable interpretation of Philip's actions to be found in Diodorus, who reported that the Macedonian king made the Thessalians his friendly allies. [16] Others, however, preferred the reports of Demosthenes

---

doctrinale de l'Etat et de ses prérogatives." Cf. F. A. Hayek, *Denationalisation,* p. 25.

[15] In the first modern handbook designed for historians interested in numismatic evidence, for instance, Charles Patin argued that the use of precious metals in coinage was denied to subject lands. See his *Introduction à l'histoire par la connaissance des médailles* (Paris, 1665), p. 6.

[16] See, for example, Samuel Pufendorf, "De rebus gestis Philippi Amyntae F.," in *Dissertationes Academicae Selectiores* (Lund, 1675), pp. 175–176; Charles Rollin, *Histoire ancienne* (Paris, 1740), vol. 3, pp. 477, 514; Abbé Gabriel Bom-

and Justin that Philip made himself the absolute master of Thessaly at the expense of Thessalian freedom.[17] In fact, it was even argued that Thessaly so completely lost its political autonomy during Philip's reign that the region was politically incorporated into the Macedonian kingdom. The definitive statement of this extreme view came in the work of the Scottish historian John Gillies. Justifying his interpretation by reference to the *Third Philippic* of Demosthenes, Gillies argued that "Philip finally settled the affairs of that distracted country; having taken on himself the whole management of the revenue, and having divided the territory into four separate governments, in order to weaken the force of opposition, and to render the whole province more patient and submissive under the dominion of Macedon."[18] Gillies summarized his view by saying that Thessaly was "reduced to a Macedonian province."[19] Strictly speaking, the word "province" in the first quotation might be understood only as a loose expression meaning "area" or "land," but the second quotation reveals what Gillies truly meant to say: Thessaly became, in a political sense, part of the Macedonian kingdom. This view represented the ultimate extrapolation from Demosthenes' account, and the words "Macedonian province" were to become almost a slogan in nineteenth-century scholarship on Philip and Thessaly. Although Gillies' policy against citing secondary sources makes it uncertain whether this idea was original with

---

mot Mably, *Observations sur les Grecs* (Geneva, 1749), p. 182; Temple Stanyan, *The Grecian History* (London, 1751), vol. 2, pp. 237–238, cf. pp. 289–290, 333–334; Oliver Goldsmith, *The Grecian History from the earliest State, to the Death of Alexander the Great* [2] (London, 1800), vol. 1, pp. 445–446, vol. 2, p. 10. On such early, and often apologetic, treatments of Philip, see Arnaldo Momigliano, "George Grote and the Study of Greek History," in *Studies in Historiography* (London, 1966), p. 58.

[17] See, for example, Jacques de Tourreil, *Démosthène. Oeuvres* (Paris, 1721), vol. 1, pp. 213–214, 239, 247, vol. 2, pp. 357, 379; Thomas Leland, *The History of the Life and Reign of Philip King of Macedon* [2] (London, 1775), vol. 2, pp. 108–109; Carlo Denina, *Istoria politica e letteraria della Grecia libera* (Venice, 1784), p. 151.

[18] *The History of Ancient Greece, its Colonies and Conquests* (London, 1786), vol. 2, p. 497.

[19] Vol. 2, index, *s. v.* Thessaly (no page number).

him, his espousal of it certainly foreshadowed the common nineteenth-century assumption that Philip II in fact turned Thessaly into a Macedonian province. [20] Eight years after the publication of Gillies' work, the great numismatist Joseph Eckhel stated in his monumental survey *Doctrina Numorum Veterum* (Vienna, 1792–1798) that Thessaly lost its autonomous coinage when it became subject to Philip II, either as a result of the "impotence" of the cities or because its *jura* had been lost through a change in the form of government. Eckhel justified this statement by no explicit citation of either ancient sources or modern ones. [21]

Why, then, did Eckhel conclude that Philip's intervention in Thessaly brought the end of local Thessalian coinage? If by "impotence" he meant only that the cities of Thessaly might have lacked the resources to continue minting coins, this was a reasonable guess about the potentially devastating economic and financial consequences of an invasion by a much stronger military power. Eckhel's alternate explanation for the end of Thessalian coinage, however, depended on the unstated assumption that a change of government brought about by subjection to a

[20] Although Gillies prided himself on his knowledge of the ancient sources in general and of Demosthenes in particular, he disdained reference to contemporary scholarship. See vol. 1, preface, pp. vi-viii, vol. 2, p. 430. For Gillies, Philip was a monarch whose devouring ambition pushed him to the brink of tyranny over the "degenerate republics" of Greece. See his fascinating work *A View of the Reign of Frederick II of Prussia; with a parallel between that Prince and Philip II of Macedon* (Dublin, 1789).

[21] Vol. 2 (1794), p. 132: "Ab eodem Philippo Thessalia Macedonibus servire coacta, ejus urbes sive per impotentiam, sive amissis per mutatam reip. formam juribus cessavere signare monetam eo tempore, quo maxime monetae aeneae usus invaluit." Eckhel referred only to Justin 7.6.7–9, for the view that Philip occupied Thessaly in order to add the Thessalian cavalry to his Macedonian army. Elsewhere Eckhel revealed that he had also read Demosthenes and Diodorus, as well as various modern historians reaching back to the sixteenth century, only some of whom he listed by name. See vol. 2, pp. 82, 88–95. He could well have known Gillies' work. A German version of it was begun in Leipzig in 1787, and an English edition was published in Basel in 1790. In Eckhel's own time, monetary unity between Austria-Hungary and most of the states of Germany had been mandated by international agreement. See Engel and Serrure, *Traité de numismatique moderne et contemporaine*, vol. 1, pp. 129–132.

king led to the end of local coinage.[22] Eckhel, of course, did not decide between his alternate explanations, apparently because he felt unsure about the details of the historical situation which might explain the numismatic facts in the case of Thessalian coinage.[23] Scholars who came after Eckhel, however, lacked his caution. They unequivocally made what had been for Eckhel one possible explanation of the end of Thessalian coinage in the fourth century B.C. the standard view on the subject.

About a century after the appearance of the *Doctrina Numorum Veterum*, Ludwig Müller explained the end of Thessalian civic coinage in line with Eckhel's second suggestion and added what was to become a commonplace in the scholarship to follow: Philip not only suppressed Thessalian coinage, he replaced it with his own royal coins minted at various locations throughout Thessaly.[24] In other words, the king enforced a uniform, royal monetary system. This idea obviously also depended on the same unstated assumption about the relation between sovereignty and coinage as did Eckhel's second suggestion, but in this case the conclusion to be drawn about the historical situation was even more striking. Philip's intervention in Thessaly led to the introduction of an entirely new, foreign monetary system. Given the Greek tradition of minting numerous local coinages and of the circulation of different coinages in the same area, this enforcement of a uniform system of royal coinage would have been a radical innovation. With no apparent qualms about the probability of such a move by Philip, however, Müller

[22] That Philip reduced Thessaly to a state of formal subjection was the lesson taught by histories like that of Gillies, but none of these histories had said anything about the fate of Thessalian coinage under Macedonian rule.

[23] Eckhel accepted the idea that cities which were subject to kings, if they were to mint any coins, could only issue coins of royal type. When they regained their autonomy, these cities would issue their own coins. See his remarks in *Doctrina*, vol. 1 (1792), p. LXXXI. He described the right of coinage as *pars autonomiae*. For his views on the right of coinage as a prerogative of sovereignty, see his discussion entitled *de jure feriundae monetae* in vol. 1, pp. LXX–LXXVIII.

[24] Since Müller does not refer to Eckhel's views on Thessalian coinage, it is impossible to say whether he had been influenced by the work of his predecessor on this point.

constructed an elaborate scheme for the numismatic reorganization of Thessaly. As part of his exhaustive treatment of Macedonian royal coinage during the reigns of Philip II, Alexander, and Philip III, Müller identified the mints in Macedonia and in Greece where he imagined the issues of the Macedonian royal system had been struck. He was very clear about his method of identification. Since the coins bore numerous monograms, symbols, and letters, they must (he argued) have been minted in many different cities. Potential mint cities could be identified by determining which cities were in a relation of dependence to the Macedonian kings such that royal coins could have been struck there. The final step in identification of mints was to establish a correspondence between the results of this historical research and an analysis of the signs and symbols on the coins, which Müller assumed to be indications of the location of the respective mints. This process applied to the reign of Philip II as well as to those of Alexander and of Philip III.

Müller proceeded on the assumption that wherever the Macedonian kings exercised sovereignty, they must have suppressed local autonomous coinage in favor of their own royal coinage. Reasonably enough, Müller recognized that the Macedonian kings had not been able to achieve the same degree of effective sovereignty everywhere in Greece. For the reign of Philip II, for example, Müller postulated three gradations of Greek sovereignty ranging from the complete abolition of civic autonomy, with direct administration by Macedonian officials or supporters, to the retention of local autonomy with only formal recognition of the hegemony of the Macedonian king.[25] Müller believed that Philip was in a position to have his own royal coins struck in any of the cities of Greece except those that retained local autonomy. In the process of identifying these royal mint cities, Müller placed the cities of Thessaly in the least-independent category. In his view, Philip overturned the constitutions of the free cities of Thessaly by dividing the country into tetrarchies, each governed by a separate administrator. Furthermore, Philip es-

---

[25] *Numismatique d'Alexandre le Grand suivie d'un appendice contenant les monnaies de Philippe II et III* (Copenhagen, 1855), pp. 54–62, 362–363.

tablished dynastic governments in the individual cities which
were entirely dependent on him and comparable to the hated
Spartan decarchies. In this way, Thessaly lost its political
independence and became a separate province under the Macedonian king. Therefore (and here the unstated assumption about
sovereignty and coinage came into play), there could be no question but that Philip would have had his coins struck in at least
some Thessalian cities. [26]

It is significant that Müller held the view that Thessaly
became a Macedonian province under Philip II. He clearly took
this idea from modern sources because all his references to
ancient sources on this question concern periods later than the
fourth century. [27] He seems to have relied on the work of
Wilhelm Wachsmuth in particular for the idea that Thessaly
became, for all practical purposes including control of the monetary system, part of the kingdom of Macedonia. [28]

Once he had accepted the modern idea that Thessaly became
politically part of Macedonia, it was a simple matter for Müller
to postulate that the cities of Thessaly were sufficiently dependent on Macedon so as to be forced to cease production of their
own coins and to issue Macedonian coinage instead. He set out,
therefore, to correlate the signs and symbols on certain Mace-

[26] P. 366.

[27] See his n. 22 on p. 366, for a reference to p. 65, n. 9, where he cites the following ancient sources: Polybius 4.76.2; Livy 34.1 (presumably an error for
34.51.3 − 6); and the list of the kings of Thessaly from the Armenian version of
Eusebius, cited as *Chronica* I, 39 (*sic*). This last citation presumably refers to J.
B. Aucher, *Eusebii Pamphili Chronicon Bipartitum, Pars I* (Venice, 1818), p. 339.
This list will be discussed in chapter 6, where the appropriate references to the
list of kings in the editions of the *Chronica* by Schoene and Karst may be found
in n. 39. In his n. 21 on p. 366, Müller does refer to Demosthenes' reports that
Philip had enslaved Thessaly.

[28] *Hellenische Altertumskunde aus dem Gesichtspunkte des Staats* [2] (Halle, 1846),
vol. 1, p. 715. Wachsmuth described Thessaly under Philip II and Alexander
as "so gut als makedonische Provinz." He knew of Gillies' history, which he
listed in his section "über Quellen und Hülfsbucher." It was, however,
Wachsmuth's practice to minimize reference to secondary works in his narrative,
with the result, as he himself stressed, that it would often be difficult for the
reader to tell whether his views were original or not. See the preface to his first
edition (1828), pp. xiv-xvi.

donian royal issues with similar types found on Thessalian autonomous issues. Finding such correlations in five cases, he identified Macedonian mints in Magnesia, Melitea, Lamia, Pharsalus, and Tricca. [29] In some instances Müller was clearly only clutching at straws. For example, the correlating symbol for the issue supposedly struck at Lamia was an amphora. Since Lamian autonomous silver coins had an amphora as the reverse type, Müller assumed that Macedonian coins featuring an amphora as an adjunct symbol would have been minted in Lamia because the amphora was the Lamian type *par excellence*. It apparently made no difference that contemporary Lamian bronze coins could have a completely different reverse type (Philoctetes in various postures), [30] or that the amphora was hardly an unusual coin type, as Müller himself admitted. This identification as a Macedonian mint seemed all the more certain because he believed that the city had been occupied by a Macedonian garrison under Alexander and served as headquarters for the Macedonian commander Antipater in the Lamian War against the Greeks after the death of Alexander. [31]

The other identifications of Macedonian mints in Thessaly were on an equally slippery footing. For Melitea, Pharsalus and Tricca, Müller had nothing to go on but the symbols of a bee, a horse's head, and a coiled serpent respectively, and even these correlations were less than perfect. Coins of Melitea indeed had a bee as reverse type, but they could also have a bull or a lion's head. [32] Pharsalian coins had horsemen on the reverse as well as simple horses' heads, [33] and in any case, the parts of a horse were common types almost everywhere. The Macedonian coins with the adjunct symbol of a coiled serpent were given to Tricca because that city's coins had an Asclepius reverse type, which, however, never consisted of only a coiled serpent and was by no

---

[29] *Numismatique*, pp. 182–189.

[30] See B. V. Head, *Historia Numorum* 2 (Oxford, 1911), p. 296.

[31] This identification as a garrisoned city came from J. G. Droysen, *Geschichte des Hellenismus I: Geschichte der Nachfolger Alexanders* (Hamburg, 1836), p. 65.

[32] Head, *HN*, p. 301.

[33] Head, *HN*, p. 306.

means the only civic type in use.[34] For Magnesia, Müller could
point to the report in Demosthenes of Philip's fortifications there
to support his identification based on the symbol of a prow. But
this identification was only a measure of desperation because
Müller could find no other city in Philip's dominions with a
prow symbol. Furthermore, the coins of Magnesia with the prow
symbol were all considerably later in date than the reigns of Philip and Alexander.[35] Finally, Müller's system meant that the most
important city of Thessaly, Larissa, had no mint at all under
Philip.

Müller's entire method of identification of Macedonian mints
in Greece was unreliable at best, and his Thessalian mints were
certainly not among the most plausible of his numerous identifications of mint cities. The evidence was simply much too vague.
Nevertheless, his method of identification based on the adjunct
symbols of Macedonian royal coins retained its scholarly respec-
tability long enough to influence Percy Gardner in his standard
work, the *British Museum Catalogue of Greek Coins. Thessaly to
Aetolia* (London, 1883). Gardner concluded that "it is almost
certain that the abrupt cessation of the issue of Thessalian money
took place at the time of the termination of Thessalian autonomy
in B.C. 344–2 . . . the probability is that any money issued in
Thessaly during the latter half of the fourth century would be of
the regular Macedonian types."[36] Gardner was plainly rephras-
ing in his own words the conclusions which Müller had used to
establish a chronological peg for the end of fourth-century Thessalian coinage. The assumption of a close connection between
sovereignty and coinage represented the basis of all these scholars' views, whether they acknowledged it or not.

Barclay V. Head, Gardner's close colleague at the British
Museum for sixteen years,[37] incorporated his friend's work on

[34] Head, *HN*, pp. 310–311.
[35] Head, *HN*, p. 300. Cf. *IGCH* nos. 239, 306, 313, as corroboration of
Head's date (no earlier than the second century B.C.).
[36] Pp. xxvi-xxvii. He specifically refers to Müller here.
[37] See P. Gardner, *A History of Ancient Coinage 700–300 B.C.* (Oxford, 1918),
p. xii.

Thessalian coinage into his own great work, *Historia Numorum*. [38]
Head reported that the loss of autonomy was the reason for the
end of local autonomous coinage and the imposition of Macedonian royal coinage, but he evidently considered this point to
be so devoid of controversy that further explanation or reference
was unnecessary. Müller's identifications of so many mint cities
made Head uneasy, but he went no further than to urge great
caution. [39] For present purposes, it is both ironic and telling that
Gardner himself eventually went much further. By 1918 he had
completely abandoned Müller's results: "The subject of his
[Alexander's] mints from which coins were issued has not yet
been systematically attacked since L. Müller wrote, half a century ago. Müller's classification is quite out of date, and would
not now be accepted by anyone." [40] In effect, Gardner had
discredited Müller's system, although he could not quite bring
himself to abandon it completely, even in the face of his own
arguments which demanded such a course. With admirable good
sense he reasoned that "Philip's coins are Macedonian only."
Suppression of local coinage he could accept, but there was no
evidence he could see for Macedonian mints in Greece in Philip's time. [41]

Nevertheless, Gardner left open the possibility that
Alexander's coins might have been struck in civic mints by his
permission. [42] But he did not say whether complete suppression of
local coinage had to precede the granting of permission to mint
royal coins. The situation had become extremely muddled, but
at least Müller's work seemed to be dismissed. So, what of Thessaly? History came to the rescue. Since Thessaly had become
part of Macedonia and ceased to be a Greek state, Gardner

[38] 1st ed. (Oxford, 1887), p. 246; 2nd ed. (Oxford, 1911), p. 290.

[39] 2nd ed., p. 244.

[40] *History*, p. 428. See A. R. Bellinger, *Essays on the Coinage of Alexander the
Great* (New York, 1963), pp. 24–26, for further discussion of the history of the
rejection by scholars of Müller's system.

[41] P. 427. Gardner believed that Philip's policy in Thessaly reflected an
awareness of the policy on the right of coinage of the Athenians in the fifth century B.C., as revealed by the famous Athenian Coinage Decree. The implications
of this document will be discussed later in chapter 9.

[42] P. 429.

found it still reasonable to continue to argue that Philip had suppressed Thessalian coinage.[43] Even though Müller's results had been spurned, his influence persisted. The perceived connection between sovereignty and coinage was so strong that it could survive even the demolition of a large part of the evidence Gardner himself had claimed in its support in 1883. The idea that Thessaly had become a Macedonian province overshadowed all other considerations, even at the risk of an inconsistent historical interpretation.

Heirs to Gardner's position continued to appear among the scholars of the twentieth century. Fritz Herrmann used Thessaly's alleged status as a Macedonian province in the usual way as a chronological peg to answer the very difficult question of when the fourth-century silver coinage of the important mint of Larissa ended.[44] No reference was necessary. In the same casual way, the distinguished numismatist Ernest Babelon repeated Müller's view on Thessalian coinage without acknowledgment.[45] The same view appears much later in the second edition of Charles Seltman's well-known book on Greek coinage.[46] Not surprisingly, ancient historians in the twentieth century often adopted the same position as had their numismatic colleagues. The clearest application of Müller's original bequest to Thessalian history came in H. D. Westlake's *Thessaly in the Fourth Century B.C.* (London, 1935). Although Westlake did not regard Thessaly as formally part of Macedonia under Philip II and was careful to say that Thessaly became "virtually a Macedonian province" which "retained the semblance of freedom without its substance," he nevertheless added the following statement to his description of Philip's actions: "Another indication of more stringent Macedonian control lies in the cessation of city-coinage, which was not revived until the end of the century. Nor did Philip introduce a tetrarchy-coinage, but in pursuance of

---

[43] Pp. 354, 427.

[44] "Die Silbermünzen von Larissa in Thessalien," *ZfN* 35 (1924–1925), p. 49.

[45] *Traité des monnaies grecques et romaines*, vol. 4 (Paris, 1926–1932), p. 213. This volume was edited posthumously in five fascicles by his son, Jean Babelon, but the views were those of his father. See the preface.

[46] *Greek Coins*[2] (London, 1955), p. 161.

a general change in his monetary policy, he forced the Thessalians to use Macedonian coins. This humiliating measure may have caused some resentment, coinage being regarded as a symbol of autonomy, but it was endured with resignation."[47] That Westlake gave no reference for this view reveals his debt to the consensus of earlier scholarship. The argument had come full circle. The chronological *terminus* of Thessalian autonomous coinage, which had been established by reference to history, could now be used to establish the historical "fact" of the humiliation of the Thessalians by Philip.

Westlake's picture of the fate of Thessaly and its coinage held the field until, in 1961, A. R. Bellinger called the attention of the International Numismatic Congress to the implications to be drawn from the composition of the hoard which is now *IGCH* 168.[48] He suggested that the contents of this hoard of coins indicated that the autonomous coinage of at least one Thessalian city, Larissa, continued to be minted until approximately 325 B.C., although Philip had forbidden the other cities in Thessaly to mint their own coins. In other words, Bellinger recognized that the numismatic evidence could not support the assumption that Philip put an end to the coinage of Larissa, but he still found it reasonable to assume that the king would have wanted to suppress the coinages of other cities which were not, in Bellinger's opinion, as closely allied with Philip as was Larissa. The old assumption about sovereignty and coinage was still implicitly at work, and it remained potent in the authoritative standard work on Greek coinage of this period by Colin Kraay. He essentially accepted Bellinger's position by saying that Larissa was probably the only Thessalian mint still issuing silver coins in the period after 344 B.C. when Philip imposed "direct Macedonian rule."[49] Kraay's reliance on the assumption that the

[47] P. 204.

[48] "The Thessaly Hoard of 1938," in *Congresso internazionale di numismatica Roma 1961: II Atti* (Rome, 1965), pp. 57–60. In his *Essays*, p. 42, Bellinger suggested that it was no longer safe to assume that Philip's coins had been minted anywhere except in Macedonia.

[49] *Archaic and Classical Greek Coins* (Berkeley, 1976), pp. 117–119. Cf. his *Greek Coins and History* (London, 1969), pp. 14–17.

Macedonian king naturally suppressed Greek coinage where he could was further shown by his flat assertions that the installation of Philip's garrisons brought an end to the autonomous coinages of Ambracia and of Thebes.[50]

The pervasive nature of the consensus which had been established regarding the close connection between sovereignty and coinage is illustrated even more clearly by the recent work of the ancient historians who reflect the views both of older and of contemporary numismatists. For example, N.G.L. Hammond, in the second edition of his *A History of Greece to 322 B.C.* (Oxford, 1967), maintained the older view by stating that the cities of Thessaly ceased to issue their own coinages under Philip and used the coinage of Macedonia.[51] In another historical survey from 1975, Claude Mossé repeated this view that Philip imposed the use of Macedonian coins on the Thessalians.[52] Other historians have taken over the more recent numismatic opinion expressed by Bellinger and ceased to ascribe the responsibility for the end of all Thessalian coinage to Philip. J. R. Ellis, whose position represents the most comprehensive treatment of the subject by a recent historian, has argued that Larissa continued to mint silver during Philip's reign and that the Thessalian confederacy began to mint bronze at the same time. These coinages were suppressed, he has suggested, by Alexander *ca.* 328/7 B.C.[53] Marta Sordi and G. T. Griffith, however, have made Antipater responsible for the suppression of Thessalian coinage after the Lamian War of 323 – 322 B.C.[54] Finally, Edith Schönert-Geiss has now reiterated the view that under Philip and Alexander the occupied Greek states were required to cease minting their own

[50] Pp. 126 and 112–114, respectively.

[51] P. 567.

[52] Ed. Will, Claude Mossé, and Paul Goukowsky, *Le monde grec et l'orient. Tome II. Le IVe siècle et l'époque hellénistique* (Paris, 1975), p. 56.

[53] *Philip II and Macedonian Imperialism* (London, 1976), p. 238.

[54] Sordi, "La dracma di Aleuas e l'origine di un tipo monetario di Alessandro Magno," *AIIN* 3 (1956), p. 19, and *La lega tessala fino ad Alessandro Magno* (Rome, 1958), pp. 275–293; Griffith, in N.G.L. Hammond and G. T. Griffith, *A History of Macedonia. Volume II. 550– 336 B.C.* (Oxford, 1979), pp. 535–536.

coins and, in some cases, to produce Macedonian coinage instead.[55]

By now it should be clear that all modern scholarship on this topic has been written under the unacknowledged influence of a very old, very strong, and quite unexamined preconception about sovereignty and coinage. Since the numismatic evidence now shows that Philip II was not the sovereign responsible for the end of civic coinage at Larissa, most scholars confine his role to the suppression of other Thessalian coinages. The responsibility for the end of the coinage of the major mint of Larisssa is then to be shifted to a different Macedonian sovereign. In this process of historical interpretation, the idea that the Macedonian sovereign insisted on an exclusive monetary prerogative has remained strong in the scholarly consensus on the fate of Thessalian coinage. For this reason, the possibility has been overlooked that the situation in classical Greece might have been very different from that postulated as an ideal by Bodin. It is time to investigate that possibility, beginning with an examination of Thessalian coinage.

[55] "Das Geld im Hellenismus," *Klio* 60 (1978), p. 132.

TWO. THESSALIAN COINAGE

1
The Background of Thessalian Coinage

For reasons which remain unclear, the cities of Thessaly issued no coinage until the fifth century B.C, considerably later than the earliest Greek states to coin, and a decade or more later than most of their neighbors.[1] Unfortunately, the chronology of the coinages of Thessaly is obscure in the extreme. As is the case with most classical Greek coins, Thessalian coins lack overt indications of chronology, such as the years of an ancient era or the names of eponymous magistrates. Moreover, the archaeological evidence which could help establish chronology is sadly lacking for Thessaly. So far as one can tell, the situation seems to have been somewhat as follows.

Sometime after 500 B.C., the city of Larissa began to mint coins with local types, but on a weight standard which conformed to that in use in the Persian Empire.[2] Why should Larissa begin to mint coins at just this time and on a standard which conformed to that of Persian money? The reason probably had nothing to do with considerations of commercial convenience in trading with the neighboring areas to the north which were using a Persian-type standard. It is more likely that Larissa began to issue coins on this occasion because there was a need to make official payments in an appropriate form. Thrace and Macedonia under Persian control had to pay tribute to the Great King like

[1] See Kraay, *ACGC*, p. 115. The large hoard from Asyut of the late archaic or early classical period, which includes coins from numerous Greek mints, has no Thessalian coins. See M. J. Price and N. M. Waggoner, *Archaic Greek Coinage. The Asyut Hoard* (London, 1975). For its date, see also the reviews by C. Kraay, *NC* 1977, pp. 189–198, and H. Cahn, *SNR* 1977, pp. 279–287.

[2] Kraay, *ACGC*, p. 115. The date is established from criteria of style (e.g., the incuse reverse) and from the implications of the weight standard.

the other areas of his empire.[3] In the 480s B.C., the Aleuads of
Larissa voluntarily placed their city under Persian control and
promised eager support to Xerxes.[4] From Xerxes' point of view
as Persian King, Larissa was now another one of his subjects and
therefore owed him tribute like any other similar city.[5] Perhaps
the Aleuads shrewdly anticipated this requirement and offered
the king their new silver money, minted on a standard chosen for
Persian convenience, as a "voluntary contribution" to Xerxes'
expenses as a gesture of goodwill, or perhaps it was that Xerxes
informed his new subject city of the expected tribute and the
desirability of paying in cash rather than in kind or in bullion.
Payment in coin was customary for the tribute-paying Greek
cities of the Persian Empire in western Asia Minor, and the
coinage initiated at Larissa would have been particularly
appropriate for the purpose.[6]

This explanation for the origin of coinage at Larissa would
account for Larissa's status as the only Thessalian city to coin
before the Persian Wars. Larissa was the only Thessalian city to
submit to Xerxes before he actually appeared in Europe, and
thus it was the only city in the region to require coinage for state
payments of this sort.[7] Whatever the truth of the matter may be,
there is no indication that the beginning of coinage in Thessaly
had anything to do with notions of coinage as a symbol of state
identity or of political independence or of any such concept of
sovereignty. The minting of coinage in Thessaly began too long
after minting had become common in other Greek states for this
sort of reason to have been its impetus. The Thessalian confederacy, which was already in existence as an independent

---

[3] Herodotus 7.108.1. Mardonius procured the subjection of Thrace and Macedonia to the Persian king on his expedition in 492 B.C. See H. Castritius, "Die
Okkupation Thrakiens durch die Perser und der Sturz des athenischen Tyrannen
Hippias," *Chiron* 2 (1972), pp. 1–15; R. M. Errington, "Alexander the Philhellene and Persia," in *Ancient Macedonian Studies in Honor of Charles F. Edson* (Thessaloniki, 1981), pp. 139–143.

[4] Herodotus 7.6.2.

[5] Herodotus 7.130.3.

[6] Polycritus, in Strabo 15.3.21 (C735) = *FGrH* 128 F 3a (Polykleitos).

[7] Herodotus 7.172.1.

political entity well before this time, was issuing no coins of its own.[8]

After the Persian Wars, probably sometime still in the first half of the fifth century, coinage began to be produced at more than one Thessalian mint. Now production was on a Greek weight standard, the so-called Aeginetan standard, which was in use in the neighboring areas to the south. Two different groups of related silver coinages on this new standard have been identified, each produced at multiple mints.[9] One group has as its obverse type a man wrestling a bull, and as its reverse type a horse surrounded by letters to indicate the identity of the particular issuing mint. The known mints for this group are Larissa, Crannon, the Perrhaebians, Pharcadon, Tricca, Pherae, and Scotussa. The first five of these mints are all in northern Thessaly, while the last two are not far from each other at the southern end of the region. It has been usual to refer to this coinage as "federal," or as the output of a "monetary union," but this terminology is misleading if it implies a close connection with the Thessalian confederacy. Nothing on the coins indicates that this coinage was meant to represent an official product of the confederacy or to serve as a symbol of its independent existence.

This is not to say, however, that the coinage might not have been produced by the various city mints as a convenient and commonly agreed upon medium of payment for expenses that would be incurred by the cities acting in concert. A uniform coinage, for example, would have been an advantage for the payment of troops in an army composed of contingents from different cities because coins of a very similar appearance would have made it easier to reassure Thessalian soldiers who were unfamiliar with this strange new phenomenon of coined money that everyone was in fact getting the same compensation for his services. If a drachm minted at Larissa closely resembled a drachm minted at, say, Crannon, then the troops from neither city would have cause to worry that their silver was less valuable than their

[8] On the confederacy, see J.A.O. Larsen, *Greek Federal States* (Oxford, 1968), pp. 12–26, 281–294, and the following chapter of this study.

[9] Kraay, *ACGC*, pp. 115–116.

fellows'. Similarity of type, in addition to consistency in weight standard, was desirable to forestall, so far as possible, disputes over pay which could only harm morale and military efficiency. When the value of money depended on the intrinsic value of the material used to make it, as was the case with ancient Greek silver coinage, this sort of consideration about the form of money was far from minor, especially in regions new to the use of coins. In this sense, then, this coinage might be considered a joint effort, but it would probably be going too far to think that the coinage in some important way served as proof of the political identity of the confederacy as a whole, or even of the minting cities as some sort of separate political unit.

The second group of coins also has uniform types, the forepart of a horse on the obverse, and an ear of grain on the reverse accompanied by a legend giving the abbreviated name of the mint. The names are Scotussa, Methylion (location unknown), and "of the Thessalians." Unfortunately, there is no certain way to tell whether this group is earlier or later than the first group, or contemporary with it, or whether all three mints of this group produced simultaneously. The standard view is that these issues began later than those of the first group, with Pherae as the mint issuing coins inscribed not with the city's name but rather with the legend "of the Thessalians." The issues of the first group are assumed to continue, with Tricca replacing Crannon, but Pherae dropping out. Pharsalus at the same time begins to issue coins with types of her own which seem not to be related to those of either of the two groups. Only tentative suggestions are possible for the chronologies of these various coinages, and this situation makes historical interpretation virtually impossible. Peter Franke, the first to identify the "Thessalian" issue, places it between *ca.* 470 and 460-450 B.C., at a time when the confederacy is said to have been in turmoil and without a leader in office on the currently accepted view of fifth-century Thessalian history.[10] The "Thessalian" issue would be a true federal coinage at least in the claim expressed by its legend, but as Franke says, the

[10] "Phethaloi – Phetaloi – Petthaloi – Thesssaloi. Zur Geschichte Thessaliens im 5. Jahrhundert v. Chr.," *AA* 85 (1970), pp. 91–93.

sources for Thessalian history in this period are so poor that
questions about the significance of this particular coinage can
only be asked, not answered. We might speculate, for example,
that this ostensibly federal issue was actually minted by a single
city such as Pherae in the context of a struggle with a rival such
as Larissa over which city would control the functions of the confederacy (such as issuing a coinage in extraordinary circumstances). Alternatively, we might postulate that the coinage
was produced from the monetary contributions of various cities
to serve as a uniform means of payment for a national army or
for allied support or even for hired mercenaries. We cannot even
tell whether this coinage was meant to replace civic coinages, or
only to supplement them. All we can say with confidence is that
this "Thessalian" issue lasted for only a short period and therefore seems to have been associated with some sort of extraordinary circumstances. In ordinary times, there was no federal
Thessalian coinage.[11]

Toward the end of the fifth century, silver coinage in Thessaly
begins to take on a new look. In reference to the most important
mint in Thessaly, Colin Kraay in his standard handbook says
that "at the end of the fifth century the federal type is at last
abandoned even at Larissa."[12] The "federal type" (youth wrestling bull/horse or horse's head) is replaced by a female head in
profile (assumed to be the eponymous nymph Larissa) on the
obverse and a horse on the reverse (Plate 1, no. 1). Fritz Herrmann in his pioneering study of the silver coinage of Larissa postulates a strong artistic influence on the die-cutters of Larissa
from Peloponnesian coin types of this period.[13] It seems clear
that this change in types resulted from the desire of the Larissa
mint to be up-to-date in the style of its dies, as we can see from
the next change of type to take place. The profile head at

---

[11] The fifth-century Peloponnesian coinage inscribed "of the Arcadians"
presents problems of interpretation which are analogous to those of this Thessalian coinage. On this coinage attributed to the Arcadian League, see Kraay,
ACGC, pp. 97–98.

[12] *ACGC*, p. 116.

[13] "Die Silbermünzen von Larissa in Thessalien," *ZfN* 35 (1924–1925), p. 37.
He places the change *ca.* 420 B.C.

Larissa is soon replaced by a facing head in direct imitation of
the famous head of the nymph Arethusa engraved on the coins of
Syracuse by Cimon at the end of the fifth century.[14] The stun-
ningly beautiful nymph of Syracuse became the model for
facing-head imitations on coins throughout the Greek world in
the fourth century, and the motive for these changes was clearly
the wish to copy the latest fashion in numismatic art.[15] In other
words, the mint of Larissa made its major changes in type for
aesthetic and not for political reasons. The change from the so-
called federal type described by Kraay to the more strictly local
type of the nymph's head cannot be invoked as an indication of
factional strife in the Thessalian confederacy which led Larissa to
adopt a new coin type, or of any other phenomenon of this sort.
The Larissaeans wanted the look of their coinage to be à la mode,
and other Thessalians apparently felt the same way. As always,
exact chronology is unobtainable, but at some point in the fourth
century the mints of Metropolis, Gomphi/Philippopolis, Pharsalus, and Pherae adopted a facing head for their silver coinage,
and Meliboea and Pharsalus for their bronze.[16]

As one sees from the list in the *British Museum Catalogue* for
the Greek coins of Thessaly, quite a few more civic mints
operated in the region in the fourth century than had in the fifth.
Although bronze coinage for small denominations was the most
common innovation, new silver coinages also appeared in every
part of the country except southern Pelasgiotis. One of the new
bronze coinages bore the legend "of the Thessalians," the same
as had its counterpart minted in silver in the preceding cen-

[14] Herrmann, p. 50, who dates the change to *ca.* 395 B.C.

[15] See K. P. Erhart, *The Development of the Facing Head Motif on Greek Coins
and Its Relation to Classical Art* (New York, 1979), pp. 181–187, 241–243. For
a similar explanation of a conspicuous feature in the appearance of a very different coinage, see John H. Oakley, "The Autonomous Wreathed Tetradrachms
of Kyme, Aeolis," *ANSMN* 27 (1982), pp. 16–20. He adds support to the view
that the design of the enigmatic wreathed tetradrachms of Asia Minor, which
began to be minted in the second century B.C., was only the latest fad in coin
design.

[16] See the catalogue in Percy Gardner, *BMC Thessaly to Aetolia* (London,
1883).

tury. [17] Once again, some mint in Thessaly had issued coins which carried the claim to be in some sense the products of a united state of Thessaly. We are regrettably no better informed about this fourth-century "Thessalian" issue than we are about the earlier one. The coins can only be dated on stylistic grounds, which means that they could belong almost anywhere in the century. [18] Recent suggestions for their chronology place these coins *ca.* 361/0 or *ca.* 336 B.C.[19] But these are only speculative dates established by supposed connections to historical events, and they have no special claim to authority. No reliable historical interpretations can be based on the alleged chronology of these bronze coins, and all we can be certain of is that the issue was neither plentiful nor of long duration. [20] Just as in the case of the fifth century "Thessalian" issue in silver, this "federal" coinage seems to have been a short-lived phenomenon which presumably occurred under unusual circumstances. The particular circumstances in which this one issue was produced are simply not recoverable, but we can draw a conclusion about ordinary conditions. The confederacy of the Thessalians in the fourth century, just as in the fifth, did not issue any coinage under normal circumstances. As we can tell from the numerous issues of civic coinages in Thessaly in the fourth century, the coining of money was traditionally the province of the cities, not of the confederacy. This point must be kept in mind for the discussion in the following chapter.

The great majority of these various civic coinages are known

[17] Franke, *AA* 85 (1970), pp. 90–91 (illus. p. 87, no. 20). On the spread of bronze coinages as regular, small denominations in the mints of mainland Greece in the first half of the fourth century, see M. J. Price, "Early Greek Bronze Coinage," in *Essays in Greek Coinage presented to Stanley Robinson*, ed. C. M. Kraay and G. K. Jenkins (Oxford, 1967), pp. 90–104.

[18] The profile head could be as early as *ca.* 400, as at Larissa and Pharsalus. These coins are so small that judgments based on the style of the head are difficult to make.

[19] Franke, *AA* 85 (1970), p. 90; M. Sordi, "La dracma di Aleuas e l'origine di un tipo monetario di Alessandro Magno," *AIIN* 3 (1956), p. 20. J. R. Ellis, *Philip II and Macedonian Imperialism* (London, 1976), p. 238, misinterprets the comments of these scholars in suggesting the coinage began in 344.

[20] Franke, *AA* 85 (1970), p. 90.

only from specimens preserved in modern collections, and these are usually coins whose circumstances of discovery are unrecorded. Therefore, with no information on where the coins were found, in what archaeological context, and in company with what other coins, it is impossible to reconstruct patterns of monetary circulation or even secure chronological *termini* for the coinage in question. In the absence of detailed die studies of the various Thessalian coinages, such specimens from modern collections can tell us only that the coinages they represent were produced at some point during the classical period, and that much only because the style of the coins marks them as products of that general chronological period. Coins found in hoards can fortunately be more helpful.[21]

2
The Evidence of Hoards

Even though the minting of coins began in Thessaly early in the fifth century, no Thessalian coins are included in the two hoards from the fifth century which are on record as having been discovered in Thessaly. These hoards contain only staters of Aegina (with the possible exception of one odd Chian piece).[22] Since the largest denomination struck in Thesssaly in this period was the drachm on the Aeginetan standard, these staters of Aegina represented a denomination twice as large as the largest

[21] If they were available, detailed reports of coins found in archaeological excavations in Thessaly could also do much to improve our knowledge of monetary circulation in the region.

[22] *IGCH* 21 (near Triccala, *ca.* 450–440: 35 staters of Aegina and one archaic stater of Chios, perhaps intrusive). The hoard is a mix of fresh and worn pieces, to judge from the illustrations in Mando Caramessini-Oeconomides, "Deux trésors de statères éginètes du Cabinet des Médailles d'Athènes," *SM* 30 (1980), pp. 81–90; *CH* 1.25/5.11 (Karditsa/Myrina, *ca.* 440: 149 staters of Aegina). This hoard also consists of worn and fresh pieces, to judge from the illustrations in Caramessini-Oeconomides, "The 1970 Myrina Hoard of Aeginetan Staters," in *Greek Numismatics and Archaeology. Essays in Honor of Margaret Thompson*, ed. Otto Mørkholm and Nancy M. Waggoner (Wetteren, 1979), pp. 231–239, pls. 27–28. The Aeginetan staters in these hoards are thought to have been produced *ca.* 500–480 B.C. (p. 238).

available local unit of currency. Such larger pieces would have been more convenient for savings purposes because a greater value could be stored with a smaller number of pieces, and these hoards are probably savings hoards which are not wholly representative of monetary circulation in Thessaly in the fifth century.[23] That is, the absence of Thessalian local coinage from these hoards does not mean that the Thessalians were not using their own coins. The composition of these hoards does show, however, that from the earliest stages in the history of the Thessalian monetary system, foreign coins were in use in Thessaly and could even be preferred to local coinage for some purposes.

The first hoard from Thessaly to contain local coins includes thirty triobols of Pharsalus, five triobols of neighboring Phocis to the south, and twelve staters of Aegina.[24] This could be either a savings or a circulation hoard. Perhaps similar was another hoard, described as a "small find," whose only recorded piece is a drachm of Pharsalus.[25] Neither the places of discovery nor the

---

[23] For bibliography on hoards and coin finds in general, see Philip Grierson, *Bibliographie numismatique* (Brussels, 1966), pp. 30–32. On the classification of hoards into different types such as savings hoards, see, for example, Grierson, *Numismatics* (Oxford, 1975), pp. 130–136; Michael Crawford, *Sources for Ancient History* (Cambridge, 1983), pp. 190–202 (who rightly points out that rigid classification of hoards into types can be misleading). Hoards intended to preserve "savings," as Grierson puts it (p. 135), "tend to be selective, containing high-value coins in preference to low-value ones and better specimens of such coins, unworn ones if possible, rather than inferior ones." It will be obvious that strict classification of hoards is not always possible, especially in the case of small hoards. A poor man who wished to hoard some savings, for example, might not be able to be especially selective in choosing coins in a fine state of preservation, and he might only be able to afford to put away small-denomination coins. In this case, his savings hoard, assembled over a period of time, might resemble in its contents a hoard assembled on the spot from the coinage in circulation at a particular place at a particular time (a so-called circulation hoard). It is also possible that a hoard could be unrepresentative of contemporary circulation even if it was deposited not long after the date of its latest coin. See, for example, M. Thiron, *Les Trésors monétaires gaulois et romains trouvés en Belgiques* (Brussels, 1967), pp. 24–26. Cf. Crawford, "Money and Exchange in the Roman World," *JRS* 60 (1970), p. 40.

[24] *IGCH* 45 (Thessaly, late 5th-early 4th cent.; state of wear not recorded).

[25] *IGCH* 49 (Thessaly?, 400–350; this coin, *NC* 1932, pp. 202–203, no. 5, shows almost no signs of wear).

dates of these hoards are very certain, but a reasonable guess would be that they were hidden in the vicinity of Pharsalus in southern Thessaly in the first half of the fourth century B.C. It is also only a guess thanks to the small and imperfectly known sample, but the absence of other Thessalian coinages from these hoards suggests that, in this period anyway, Thessalian civic coinages tended to stay in their own local areas and were supplemented especially in large denominations by "foreign" Greek coinages on the same weight standard, the Aeginetan (in use in neighboring Phocis as well).

The hoards of silver coins found in Thessaly which seem to date from approximately the mid-fourth century are more numerous.[26] It is fruitless to try to give precise dates to these hoards because they do not come from securely dated archaeological contexts and consist exclusively of Greek coinages whose chronologies are themselves poorly established. That they belong to the middle two quarters of the century is fairly certain, to judge from the general style of the coins in them and from the absence of the Macedonian royal coins which begin to show up in Thessalian hoards in the last quarter of the century.

After the two hoards already mentioned which contain coins of Pharsalus as their only Thessalian coins, there are a dozen hoards of the mid-fourth century currently on record as coming from Thessaly and its perioikic territory.[27] Coins of Larissa appear in eight of these twelve hoards, and they are the only Thessalian coins present. One of the four remaining hoards contains two small coins of Cierium, a town in the area Thessaliotis in the southwestern part of Thessaly. Another of the four includes coins of the city of Heraclea Trachinia and of the tribal

[26] There are too few hoards with bronze coins to allow even speculation about the chronology of Thessalian bronze coinage. Edgar Rogers, *The Copper Coinage of Thessaly* (London, 1932), accepts the idea that Thessalian silver coinage and most bronze coinage came to an end in 344, when "Philip made Thessaly a province of the new Macedonian empire" and "Macedonian money with symbols indicating various cities of Thessaly and Magnesia" took the place of Thessalian coinages. He does suggest, however, that some bronze issues may have gone on longer (pp. 10–11).

[27] *IGCH* 52, 55, 56, 61, 62, 71, 96, 97; *CH* 1.27, 1.33. *CH* VI (1981) is the most recent volume I have been able to use.

states of the Aenianes and of the Oetaei. All three are located at
the very southern edge of Thessaly in perioikic territory, that is,
outside the boundaries of Thessaly proper. The other two
hoards have neither Thessalian nor perioikic coinage in their
contents. The majority, if not all, of these twelve hoards appear
to be circulation hoards. The extent to which coins of Larissa
predominate as the Thessalian coinage most commonly found in
these hoards is even more remarkable when one considers that
the coins of the city of Pherae, Larissa's powerful rival for the
leadership of Thessaly in this period, are completely absent from
the hoards.

Their absence is difficult to interpret, to say the least. One
explanation could be that the frequent occurrence of coins of
Larissa in these Thessalian hoards reflects a level of mint production in that city which greatly outstripped that of any other
Thessalian city, in particular Pherae. The statistics may have
been distorted, however, by modern factors affecting the rate of
recovery of ancient coin hoards. On the same site now as in antiquity, Larissa is the largest town by far in modern Thessaly. It
may well be the case that more hoards with coins of Larissa are
known than any other kind because more excavation (archaeological and especially nonarchaeological) has gone on in the
vicinity of Larissa than anywhere else in Thessaly. One can
suspect that many of the hoards which have become known with
provenances listed only as "Thessaly" were discovered in and
around Larissa in the course of modern agricultural and architec-
tural development. Ancient Pherae, by contrast, is on the site of
the modern village of Velestino, a far smaller and less developed
place than modern Larissa.[28] Coin hoards with coins of Pherae
may be missing because much less deep digging has been done in
the area of that ancient city.[29] If it was usual in this period for

[28] See Friedrich Stählin, *Das hellenische Thessalien* (Stuttgart, 1924), p. 105.
For the distribution of the modern population of Thessaly, see Michel Sivignon,
La Thessalie. Analyse géographique d'une province grecque (Lyon, 1975), pp.
189–196.

[29] One gains an idea of what have been the principal areas of interest in the
archaeology of Thessaly from C. J. Gallis, "A Short Chronicle of Greek
Archaeological Investigations in Thessaly from 1881 until the Present Day," in
La Thessalie, Actes de la Table-Ronde 21–24 Juillet 1975 Lyon, ed. B. Helly

local Thessalian coinage to stay very much in its local area, then it would be possible to think that the pattern of modern excavation helps to explain, at least in part, the peculiar predominance of the coins of Larissa in the hoards in question. Nevertheless, it seems clear from the volume of surviving specimens that Larissa produced a more significant and prolific coinage than did Pherae.

If a tendency toward circulation limited to the local area was generally true of civic coinage in Thessaly, it is least noticeable in the case of the coinage of Larissa. Although a northern Thessalian city, her coins turn up in two hoards from the far southern part of the region.[30] And in addition, coins of Larissa are the only Thessalian silver coinage to occur in hoards found outside Thessaly and its border areas which can be dated to the second and third quarters of the fourth century. There are nine such hoards. Three were found at different locations in the Peloponnese and contained only one drachm of Larissa each. Small numbers of coins of Larissa also turn up in one hoard from Delphi and in four hoards from Macedonia. One other hoard from Macedonia, however, contains sixty-two drachms of Larissa.[31] Most of these hoards, to judge from their contents, are

---

(Lyon, 1979), pp. 1–30. *IGCH* 141 from Volos, some fifteen to twenty kilometers from Velestino, is, of the hoards recorded in *IGCH*, the one found closest to the site of ancient Pherae. E. Kirsten, *RE*, suppl. 7, col. 1017, *s. v.* "Pherai," reports a hoard which he apparently assumed came from the vicinity of Pherae in 1937. He reports only that it contained "thirteen coins of Athens, two of Alexander and one of Lysimachus" and was in the Numismatic Museum in Athens. I suspect that these coins actually formed part of *IGCH* 168, which gradually came to light in just this period. On the circumstances of its discovery and its contents, see T. R. Martin, "A Third-Century B.C. Hoard from Thessaly at the ANS (*IGCH* 168)," *ANSMN* 26 (1981), pp. 51–77 (which does not consider the coins mentioned by Kirsten).

[30] *IGCH* 56 (Domokos), 71 (Lamia).

[31] *IGCH* 70 (Kirrha, near Delphi, 350–325), 74 (Mageira, Elis, *ca.* 330–325), 76 (Kyparissia, Messenia, *ca.* 327), 103 (Malandreni, Argolis, 4th cent.), 371 (Chalcidice?, *ca.* 348), 384 (Palatitsa, Macedonia, mid-4th cent.), 385 (Kalamaria, near Thessalonike, *ca.* 340–335: the hoard with 62 drachms of Larissa), 386 (Vergina, *ca.* 340–330). The dates of these hoards are reasonably secure because (except for 103) they all contain coins of the Chalcidian League, or of Macedonian kings.

circulation hoards, but this evidence is certainly too limited to indicate that the coinage of Larissa normally enjoyed a large circulation outside its local area. Nevertheless, these finds from outside Thessaly do help to make clear the status of Larissa as the most important mint in Thessaly. Only its coins found their way over the Thessalian border in any significant numbers (on present evidence). Clearly, we must look above all at the coinage of Larissa in order to understand the fate of autonomous civic coinage in Thessaly.

Before we do this, however, one other very striking feature of the twelve Thessalian hoards already mentioned deserves notice. Foreign Greek coinages occur in all of them. There are coins from Boeotian mints, especially that of Thebes, in eleven of the twelve hoards, and coins from Opuntian Locris in eight. Boeotia and Locris border on Thessaly in the south and southeast, but the town of Sicyon is far distant in the Peloponnese. Nevertheless, its coins turn up in six of the hoards. Coins of Aegina occur in three of the hoards, with coins of Argos, Phlius, and Athens in one each. The overwhelmingly most common denomination in which these foreign coinages occur is the stater, a large denomination which, of the mints of Thessaly, only Larissa, Pherae, and Gomphi/Philippopolis ever produced even under extraordinary circumstances.[32] The largest denomination minted anywhere in Thessaly in the fourth century was usually the drachm, and the local need for larger denominations was apparently satisfied under normal conditions by the use of nonlocal coins on (for the most part) the Aeginetan standard. The only non-Aeginetan coin in these hoards is "at least" one Athenian tetradrachm in *IGCH* 52 (there may have been more, according to the information on which the description of its contents in *IGCH* is based). This appearance in a Thessalian hoard of a coin on the Attic standard may be in this case an isolated phenomenon, but it does look forward to the characteristic make-up of Thessalian hoards in the last quarter of the fourth century, when Attic-standard coinages are common. Since the Attic-standard tetradrachm was almost three times as large a denomination as the Aeginetan-

[32] *ACGC*, p. 115.

standard drachm, it could find a useful place as a very large denomination in a monetary system which lacked a comparable unit.[33] Such large denominations would have been convenient for savings and for large payments. At the very least, one lost less time counting out large sums in tetradrachms rather than in drachms or triobols. The presence of non-Thessalian coinages with Thessalian coinages in Thessalian hoards and the willingness on the part of Thessalians to make use of these coins which their presence implies are important points to notice.[34] The tradition in Thessaly of relying on foreign coinages as well as on local ones was well established before the first appearance in Thessalian hoards of truly foreign currency, the royal coins of the Macedonian kings.

On the evidence currently available to me, there are eight hoards (or perhaps only seven) which have been found in Thessaly and can be dated approximately to the last quarter of the fourth century B.C. on the basis of the Macedonian royal coins which they contain.[35] Again, the majority are certainly circulation hoards, but two of them may be savings hoards.[36] The coins of Larissa, found in five of the eight, continue to be the most frequently occurring Thessalian coinage. Coins of Pharsalus occur in two of the hoards, and one of perioikic Lamia turns up in one of them. No other Thessalian civic coinages appear. Coins of

[33] These calculations are based on the standard weights given in *ACGC*, p. 329.

[34] The presence of foreign Greek coinage in even small Thessalian hoards suggests that the presence of non-Thessalian coinage in Thessaly was not unusual.

[35] *IGCH* 80 (12 tetr. of Ph.; 10 tetr. of Alex.), 82 (6 tetr. of Ph.; 30 tetr. of Alex.), 93 (28 tetr. of Ph.; 31 tetr. and 3 dr. of Alex.), 111 (4 tetr. of Ph.; 29 tetr. of Alex.), 117 (1 tetr. and 1 dr. of Alex.); *CH* 1.40 (13+ tetr. of Ph.; 19 tetr. of Alex.; 1 tetr. of Ph. III), 2.51 (2 tetr. of Ph.; 2 dr. of Alex.), 2.52/6.20 (1 tetr. of Ph.; 2 tetr. of Alex.). *IGCH* 117 may belong much later than 300 B.C., if the Thessalian League coins reported in it are not intrusions. If the hoard which Kirsten reported (*RE*, suppl. 7, col. 1017) is not part of *IGCH* 168, it probably belongs later than 302 B.C., where he puts it. The coins of Lysimachus seem not to appear in hoards in Greece until somewhat later, to judge from the hoards in *IGCH*.

[36] *IGCH* 80, 82.

Locris occur in six of the hoards, while coins of Thebes appear in four.

These statistics come as no surprise in the light of the composition of the Thessalian hoards already presented. Rather, the striking feature of these hoards is the presence of coins of the kings of Macedonia. Tetradrachms (and no other denomination) of Philip II occur in seven of the eight hoards.[37] Coins of Alexander III appear in all eight hoards: tetradrachms in seven, drachms in four. A tetradrachm of Philip III turns up in one hoard. The occurrence of Macedonian royal coinage in Thessalian hoards, often in large numbers, is usual from this point on and throughout the third century B.C, but it is extremely important to notice when these coins first begin to appear in Thessaly. Coins of Philip II never appear in the hoards of the fourth century without coins of Alexander III, which means that no coins of Philip occur in hoards which date to his reign. Moreover, the first Thessalian hoards to contain coins of Philip and of Alexander date to the end of the latter's reign in the late 320s B.C. One of these hoards, *IGCH* 80, contains only tetradrachms of Philip II and of Alexander III, and may, therefore, be a savings hoard because it lacks small denominations entirely. The date of the hoard (*ca.* 320 B.C.) comes from the date of the latest Alexander coins in it, but strictly speaking, one cannot be certain that the tetradrachms of Philip (if they are lifetime issues) had not been circulating in Thessaly much earlier, when they were first made part of a savings cache which was hidden for the last time *ca.* 320. But there are two other hoards, *CH* 2.51 (323–320 B.C.) and *CH* 2.52/6.20 (*ca.* 320 B.C.), whose composition and small size mark them as circulation hoards and which similarly contain tetradrachms of Philip and drachms of Alexander (no tetradrachms of Alexander in *CH* 2.51). One gains the impression that the royal coins of Philip and of Alexander did not begin to show up in Thessalian circulation in sufficient quantity to make their way into local hoards before the 320s.

Tetradrachms of Athens occur in five of the eight Thessalian hoards known from the last quarter of the fourth century. In two

---

[37] Only *IGCH* 117, whose composition is problematic, lacks coins of Philip.

of these hoards, both of good size, there are more Athenian coins than any other single type of coinage (if one regards the coinages of Philip and of Alexander as separate types).[38] This, too, is something new in Thessalian hoards. The appearance in Thessaly of silver coins both of Athens and of Alexander, which were minted on the Attic weight standard, means that use of coins not on the Aeginetan standard was becoming commonplace in Thessaly. For the moment, it is sufficient to point out that the shift away from a monetary system in Thessaly consisting almost entirely of Aeginetan-standard coinages did not occur during the reign of Philip, whose silver coinage was minted on a standard different from both the Aeginetan and the Attic.[39] If it had, we would have found at least some Thessalian hoards with Philip's coins as their only Macedonian coins.

We can see from the statistics on the contents of third-century Thessalian hoards that local Thessalian coinage becomes rarer in Thessalian monetary circulation in this period. The coins of Larissa, present in thirteen of twenty Thessalian hoards dating to the latter half of the fourth century, occur in just five of twelve in the third century. Coins of Lamia turn up in three of the twelve, coins of Pharsalus in one.[40] Thessalian coins are present in large numbers in only one of these third-century hoards, *IGCH* 168 with 156 drachms of Larissa in a total of 591 coins. Furthermore, the coins of Larissa in this hoard are all of the same type and generally quite worn. This fact, when viewed in conjunction with the statistical contrast between the frequency of occurrence of the coins of Larissa in hoards of the fourth and third centuries, indicates that the end of civic coinage at Larissa should lie

---

[38] *IGCH* 93: 34 out of 112; *CH* 1.40: 43 out of 90+.

[39] On the question of the standard of Philip's coinage, see *ACGC*, p. 146; Georges Le Rider, *Le Monnayage d'argent et d'or de Philippe II frappé en Macédoine de 359 à 294* (Paris, 1977), pp. 343–363.

[40] *IGCH* 133, 141, 144, 146, 150/*CH* 6.23, *IGCH* 159, 162, 168; *CH* 1.52, 2.72/3.43, 6.24; Mando Caramessini-Oeconomides, "Contribution à l'étude du monnayage d'Alexandre le Grand. À propos d'un trésor inédit du Musée numismatique d'Athènes," in *Studia Paulo Naster Oblata I. Numismatica Antiqua*, ed. Simone Scheers (Leuven, 1982), pp. 89–98. If the hoard reported by Kirsten is a separate one (*RE*, suppl. 7, col. 1017), it is another third-century hoard without Thessalian coins.

somewhere in the latter part of the fourth century or the early part of the third. Since coins can appear in hoards long after the coinage to which they belong had ceased to be produced, statistics on the occurrence of coins in hoards are far too imprecise an indication of numismatic chronology to provide help in establishing with any accuracy when the mint of Larissa closed.

The only method which can at present assist us in establishing a date for the end of local coinage in Thessaly on the basis of the numismatic evidence alone is the analysis of comparative states of wear. In this case, we can compare the condition in hoards of Thessalian coins, whose dates are unknown, with the condition of Macedonian royal coins, whose dates are much better known. As part of a separate study, I have tried to establish a chronology in this way for the silver coinage of Larissa, using the limited evidence available.[41] In summary, the situation seems to be as follows. By the second half of the fourth century, the civic mint of Larissa was producing only one type of silver drachm (the denomination most commonly found in hoards). The obverse bore the head of a woman facing three-quarters left, the reverse a lone horse grazing. Eventually the mint restricted its production, so that only very minor variations of the reverse type differentiate the coins. The horse, for example, can stand with legs straight or legs bent, but it always faces right (Plate 1, no. 4). On earlier issues of this type it had sometimes faced left, or had been accompanied by a standing man or a foal (Plate 1, nos. 2–3). The type with facing head l./horse r. is the last issue of silver drachms to be minted at Larissa, as the hoards show. While earlier hoards with coins of Larissa have a variety of the city's types in their contents, hoards of the late fourth and early third centuries have only the facing head l./horse r. type.

This striking uniformity is best illustrated by the third-century hoard *IGCH* 168 from near Larissa.[42] Its 156 drachms of Larissa represent one of the largest single groups of such coins ever found together, but it has only this one type of facing head

---

[41] "The Chronology of the Fourth-Century B.C. Facing-Head Silver Coinage of Larissa," *ANSMN* 28 (1983), pp. 1–34.

[42] See Martin, *ANSMN* 26 (1981), pp. 51–77.

l./horse r. If other types had been in production at the same time, they should have appeared in this large find. But if the uniformity of type of the drachms of Larissa in this hoard shows that this type was the mint's last, the general condition of the coins is equally revealing. The majority are quite worn, and some are worn very severely. This implies that these coins had been in circulation for a long time, and the very small number of minimally worn coins further indicates that there was no current production. Otherwise, we should expect to find a much larger number of fresh-looking coins which had not circulated for long at the time when the hoard was assembled for hiding. The date of the hoard is not entirely certain, but in any case, it cannot be earlier than *ca.* 250 B.C., to judge from the dates of the various third-century royal coinages included in the hoard. This means that the end of this issue of silver drachms at Larissa should fall somewhere well before the middle of the third century. Since there is no evidence that the mint continued to produce any kind of coinage in any metal or denomination after the end of this particular issue, the date for the termination of the facing head l./horse r. type will also be the date of the end of civic coinage at the most important mint of Thessaly.[43]

Since these coins of Larissa typically offer no independent indications of their absolute chronology, other methods have to be found to date them. In 1925, Fritz Herrmann used the criteria of style in conjunction with allegedly historical facts to date the facing head l./horse r. type (which he split into two groups) to the period *ca.* 395 – 363 B.C.[44] Since he had no hoard evidence to use as a check on his conclusions, however, he did not place this type last in his arrangement of the various facing head types of silver coinage from the mint of Larissa. Nor were his historical facts more than a set of assumptions, which were grounded in the view that Philip II suppressed autonomous coinage in Thessaly in 344/3 B.C. It is now possible to see from the hoard evidence that Herrmann's date for this type is impossible and that

---

[43] There are no specimens known of any later issue from Larissa after the type found in *IGCH* 168.

[44] *ZfN* 35 (1924 – 1925), pp. 1 – 69.

the end of coinage at Larissa came later than 344/3 B.C. On the
basis of the comparative states of wear in hoards of coins of
Larissa and of Macedonian royal coins of Philip II and of Alexander III, it appears that the final issue of silver coinage at
Larissa came to an end *ca.* 320 B.C. This judgment is based
above all on the condition of the drachms of Larissa as compared
to the condition of the drachms of Alexander III. Since these
drachms of Alexander were not minted on the same standard as
those of Larissa, they are not the same in weight or value, but
they are the closest match available when one looks for coins that
perhaps experienced conditions in circulation similar to those
experienced by the drachms of Larissa (Plate 1, nos. 4–5). It is
significant, therefore, that when comparison is possible from evidence presently available, the facing head l./horse r. silver
drachms of Larissa exhibit signs of wear comparable to those
exhibited by Alexander drachms which were minted late in the
king's reign, or in the early years after his death in 323 B.C. One
can reasonably conclude from this evidence that the final silver
issue of the Larissa mint came to an end in the later 320s or early
in the next decade. It must be made unmistakably clear that the
evidence on which this judgment is based is much scantier than
is desirable. At this date, only five hoards have been published
in sufficient detail to allow any comparison between the state of
wear of Larissa drachms and Macedonian royal coins (drachms
and tetradrachms). Furthermore, the numbers of coins involved
are very small with the exception of the hoard *IGCH* 168.[45]

It will be obvious that any conclusion about the date of the
end of silver coinage at Larissa can be only tentative. And about
bronze coinage there is almost no useful evidence.[46] Nevertheless, the numismatic evidence presented here is important
because it does not support the long-held view that Philip II

[45] See the discussion in Martin, *ANSMN* 28 (1983), pp. 1–34.

[46] From the good condition of a specimen in a mid-third century hoard, how-
ever, it has been suggested that this coinage may have continued down into the
third century B.C. See J. H. Kroll, "A Chronology of Early Athenian Bronze
Coinage, *ca.* 350–250 B.C," in *Greek Numismatics and Archaeology. Essays in
Honor of Margaret Thompson,* ed. Otto Mørkholm and Nancy M. Waggoner
(Wetteren, 1979), p. 152.

suppressed all autonomous Thessalian coinages in 344/3 B.C. If
he had, we should not find in the hoards (as we do) Larissa
drachms which are usually as well or better preserved than tetradrachms of the 340s and resemble in their condition drachms of
the period *ca.* 325–320. The evidence is scanty, but it does have
a cumulative force.

Unfortunately, the available evidence pertains only to Larissa
in even any potentially substantive fashion. [47] In other words, the
hoards cannot help us to assess the validity of Bellinger's assumption, already mentioned in the preceding chapter, that only
Larissa continued to mint coins in Thessaly after Philip II reorganized Thessalian government in the later 340s B.C. [48] There are
simply too few coins by far in the hoards from cities other than
Larissa to allow even speculation about the chronologies of these
coinages based on hoard evidence. Of the numerous Thessalian
mints operating at some point in the fourth century (excluding
perioikic mints), only those of Cierium (once) and of Pharsalus
(twice) are represented in the hoards of the middle and late
fourth century. It is therefore obvious that the absence in the
hoards of the coins of cities other than Larissa is not evidence
that Philip suppressed the coinages of these cities. These
coinages are exceedingly rare in the hoards at all times. For
example, as mentioned earlier, coins of Pherae never appear in
fourth-century hoards (or in third-century hoards, for that
matter), even though the city was certainly minting coins in the
fourth century. On the other hand, coins of Pharsalus turn up in
two hoards before 350 B.C. and then are absent from the hoards
of the mid-century, until they recur in a hoard of the late 320s

[47] In the nineteen Thessalian hoards on record as dated between *ca.* 325 and
200 B.C. (twenty hoards if Kirsten's hoard, *RE*, suppl. 7, col. 1017, is counted as
a separate entity), the most frequently occurring Thessalian coins other than
those of Larissa are from Pharsalus: *IGCH* 111 has four, *CH* 2.51 has two, and
CH 6.24 has forty. Coins of perioikic Lamia occur in four hoards: *IGCH* 133
has one, *IGCH* 159 has one, *CH* 2.52/6.20 has one, and *CH* 6.24 has thirty-
seven.

[48] "The Thessaly Hoard of 1938," in *Congresso internazionale di numismatica.
Roma 1961: II. Atti* (Rome, 1965), pp. 57–60.

B.C. and one of the "late fourth century."[49] The number of coins in the latter two hoards is too small to yield significant results, even if the conditions of the coins were known. But at the very least, this scanty record does not support the idea that Philip put an end to the minting of coins at Pharsalus in the 340s. If anything, it means that Pharsalus did mint some coins in the later fourth century, a suggestion which finds support in the appearance in a hoard of *ca.* 270 B.C. of the largest single group of the coins of Pharsalus yet to be found in one hoard (forty in all).[50]

In sum, then, the numismatic evidence can disprove some views on the fate of Thessalian coinage, but leaves the question open on others. It is safe to say that the hoard evidence cannot be cited in support of the idea that Philip II suppressed the autonomous coinage of Larissa in 344/3 B.C. Furthermore, the evidence from Thessalian hoards runs strongly counter to the assumption that Philip meant his own royal coins to replace local coinage in Thessaly starting in the late 340s B.C. First, there are no hoards from Thessaly consisting only of Philip's coins, nor even any hoard containing Philip's coins with a mixture of the local and southern Greek coinages so common in fourth-century Thessalian hoards. We should certainly expect to find such hoards if Philip had suppressed Thessalian local coinage and enforced the use of his own coins. It is obviously a misconception to think that Philip flooded Thessaly with his coinage. Second, the only denomination of Philip's silver coinage found in fourth-century Thessalian hoards is the tetradrachm. None of Philip's smaller silver coins, and only one bronze coin, has been found in fourth-century Thessalian hoards.[51] Philip's denominations in silver smaller than the tetradrachm do occur in two fourth-century hoards found elsewhere in Greece, one from Boeotia (1 stater in a total of 29) and one from Megara (1 stater and 17 tetrobols in a total of 789), and more than half of a sizable Ambracian hoard buried *ca.* 280 B.C. consists of Philip's silver

[49] *IGCH* 45 (late 5th-early 4th cent.: thirty triobols); *IGCH* 49 (400–350: small find of drachms); *CH* 2.51 (323–320: two triobols); *IGCH* 111 (late 4th cent.: four drachms or fractions).

[50] *CH* 6.24 (six drachms, thirty-four diobols).

[51] *IGCH* 116 (Thessaly?, *ca.* 300).

tetrobols (*ca.* 33 of 60+).[52] In the light of this evidence, it would be theoretically possible to assume that Philip imposed only the use of tetradrachms on the Thessalians as a major and ceremonial coinage indicative of his superiority, but any such assumption seems highly unlikely. Since it seems inconceivable that Thessalian coinage could have been replaced by Philip's tetradrachms alone without any small change in silver, if any such replacement actually took place, we should find some trace of Philip's smaller denominations in a Thessalian hoard like *IGCH* 111, whose mixture of denominations indicates that the hoard probably represents a sample of the coinage in circulation in the late fourth century. But this hoard has only tetradrachms from Macedonia.

Although bronze coinage may have been of lesser significance than silver, the nearly complete absence of Philip's bronze coins from Thessalian hoards stands in sharp contrast to the situation in Macedonia (where Philip's coins naturally represented the principal coinage in circulation during his reign), whose circulatory pattern Thessaly should mirror if it became a "Macedonian province." Only one bronze coin of Philip appears in a very late fourth-century hoard which is perhaps from Thessaly, but his bronzes are found in eighteen hoards from Macedonia and the north.[53] These bronzes should be numerous in Thessalian hoards if Philip imposed the use of his own coinage on the Thessalians in order to create a new monetary system there.

Of course, these arguments cannot disprove Bellinger's theory that Philip allowed Larissa to continue minting coins but denied that right to other Thessalian cities. That theory can only be evaluated in the context of the historical evidence to be presented next. Nevertheless, there is one further piece of numismatic evidence which deserves mention here. At some point in Philip's reign, the name of the Thessalian town of Gomphi

---

[52] *IGCH* 65, 94, 147.

[53] *IGCH* 116 (Thessaly?); from Macedonia, *IGCH* 383, 387, 388, 389, 390, 394, 397, 404, 406, 407, 413; *CH* 3.23, 4.27, 5.29, 6.16, 6.17, 6.18, 6.22.

was changed to Philippopolis.[54] The reason for the change and
its precise date are obscure, but it may have come as a result of
Philip's aid in the fortification of the town against potential
incursions by the Athamani to the west.[55] The important point is
that the town issued silver coins under its new name, "the *polis* of
Philip."[56] These coins have as their obverse type the facing
female head which became so popular in Thessaly in the fourth
century, and their attribution to Gomphi/Philippopolis is assured
by the appearance of a similar type on bronze coins which bear
the original name of the town, Gomphi.[57] The chronology of the
coins of Gomphi/Philippopolis is impossible to determine with
any accuracy, and so the possibility cannot absolutely be ruled
out that its coinage was suppressed by Philip at the same time as
the coinages of all other Thessalian cities except for Larissa. But
surely the fact that a silver coinage was initiated in Gom-
phi/Philippopolis during Philip's reign is circumstantial evidence
against the idea of a general suppression by Philip of local Thessalian coinage outside Larissa.[58]

   The question of a possible suppression of Thessalian coinage
by Alexander is harder to answer on the basis of the purely numismatic evidence. As mentioned earlier, the specimens of the
final issue of drachms of Larissa which appear in hoards with
drachms of Alexander appear to be approximately contemporary
with the Alexander issues of *ca.* 320 B.C. Since the chronology
cannot be pinned down precisely, one could assume that the
mint of Larissa closed either during the later years of the reign of
Alexander or within several years of his death in 323 B.C. The
hoard evidence, therefore, cannot be used in good conscience to
disprove Ellis' theory that Alexander in 328/7 B.C. ordered the

[54] Stephanus Byz., *s. v.* "Philippoi."

[55] Stählin, *Das hellenische Thessalien*, p. 126.

[56] *ACGC*, p. 119.

[57] *HN*, p. 295.

[58] Since no silver coins under the name of Gomphi are known, the coins bearing the legend "of the Philippopolitans" must represent the initiation of a silver
coinage for the town. Head in *HN* makes the bronze coins later than the silver.
The occurrence of a bronze coin of Gomphi in a Macedonian hoard of *ca.* 275
B.C. (*IGCH* 451) is circumstantially in favor of this relative chronology.

suppression of the coinage of Larissa (the only Thessalian coinage still being issued at this date, on his view). To do so would be to place too much confidence in the accuracy of the chronological information to be derived from criteria of comparative wear and in the representativeness of the sample of coins known from hoards which has been used in this analysis. It can only be pointed out that the evidence, as it stands at present, does not support the hypothesis that Alexander aimed to replace Thessalian coinage with his own. (Ellis does not in fact say that this was Alexander's aim, but his argument surely implies that it was.)

Such a hypothesis could conceivably be argued from the relative paucity of Thessalian hoards containing Thessalian coins whose dates of hiding can be securely placed in the early or middle years of Alexander's reign, as compared with the number of hoards of this type which are dated "*ca.* 350 B.C.," i.e., under Philip's reign.[59] But if this hypothesis were true, one would have to ask, where are the hoards with Alexander's issues from his lifetime which would have replaced the local Thessalian coinages? Only two fourth-century Thessalian hoards containing Macedonian royal coins but no Thessalian coins are so far known, and neither of them could have been hidden before Alexander's death because they contain either very late lifetime issues from the East or early posthumous issues of Alexander.[60] These are the first Macedonian coins to be found in Thessalian hoards.

It is important to point out, then, that it is not the case that Thessalian coins are missing from the hoards of Alexander's reign, but rather that (on the traditional hoard chronology) the hoards themselves are missing. They are missing because it appears to have been customary to date fourth-century Thessalian hoards which lack Macedonian royal coinage as "*ca.* 350 B.C.," presumably on the assumption that if the hoards were later in date, they would have contained coins of Philip II. Since, however, neither Philip's nor Alexander's coins appear in

[59] Only *IGCH* 71 is given a date which could potentially fall in Alexander's reign (*ca.* 350–325), and it is from perioikic Lamia. *IGCH* 52, 55, 56, 57, 61; *CH* 4.20, 4.21, 5.20 are all dated roughly to the period around 350 B.C.

[60] *IGCH* 80 (near Larissa, *ca.* 320), 82 (near Karditsa, *ca.* 315).

Thessalian hoards before the end of Alexander's reign, this assumption is invalid. It is quite possible that some of the hoards currently dated to the middle of the century actually belong later in the third quarter of the century and represent the "missing" hoards. To be sure, no absolutely definitive proof can be adduced from the numismatic evidence against the theory that Alexander suppressed Thessalian coinage in order to replace it with his own royal issues, but the absence of Alexander's coins from hoards before the end of the 320s B.C. would then be difficult to explain. The view expressed by Sordi and Griffith that Antipater suppressed Thessalian coinage after the Lamian War of 323–322 B.C. is compatible with the numismatic evidence. Only the historical evidence, therefore, can help us decide if either of these two latter views should be accepted.

As the final bit of background for the picture which will be drawn from the historical evidence in the discussion to follow, it will be appropriate to summarize the monetary situation in Thessaly in the later fourth century. Thessalian local coins continue to occur as significant and generally consistent percentages of the total contents of Thessalian hoards throughout the second half of the fourth century B.C. They do not abruptly disappear from circulation, as they would have if their use had been forbidden in favor of Macedonian royal coins. In general, the traditional pattern of monetary circulation in Thessaly continues. That is, local coinages in denominations no larger than the drachm are supplemented by non-Thessalian coinages in denominations generally larger than the drachm. The non-Thessalian coinages, once almost exclusively on the Aeginetan standard, are now on both the Aeginetan and the Attic standards. Attic-standard coins come to Thessaly both from Macedonia to the north and from Athens to the south. As illustration, one can look to *IGCH* 111, a hoard found near Larissa or Crannon (a town about twenty kilometers to the southwest of Larissa) and dated to the "late 4th century B.C." In a total of *ca.* sixty-nine silver coins, the hoard contained eight drachms and two smaller fractions of Larissa, four drachms or fractions of Pharsalus, one stater of the Opuntian Locrians, ten staters of Thebes, and three staters of Sicyon. In addition to these familiar Aeginetan-standard coinages, the hoard also contained four tetradrachms of Philip II, twenty-nine tetradrachms of Alexander III, and eight tetradrachms of Athens. Since the hoard includes small local denominations and its coins were worn (according to its original description by W. Schwabacher), it is very likely to have been a circulation hoard. In fact, this hoard is probably typical of late fourth-century circulation in Thessaly. Macedonian coins, especially tetradrachms as a convenient large denomination, were beginning to circulate along with Athenian tetradrachms, but the traditional mix of local Thessalian coins and southern Greek coinages on the Aeginetan standard persisted. Macedonian drachms gradually made their way into Thessaly as well, as we can tell from their occurrence in small numbers (many fewer than the tetradrachms) in late fourth-century Thessalian hoards.[61] Any historical reconstruction of the events which might have affected Thessalian coinage in this period should be compatible with this reconstruction of monetary circulation.

[61] *ICGH* 93 (three drachms), 117 (one); *CH* 2.51 (two), 2.52/6.20 (one).

THREE. THESSALY BEFORE PHILIP II

Thessaly was not the sort of place Socrates cared to visit, even when the alternative was death, but the area and its proverbial wealth did have attractions for other famous contemporaries who liked their luxuries, such as Gorgias the sophist.[1] The luxuries which Thessaly had to offer were those of a region fertile enough to produce more agricultural products than its population consumed, an especially fortunate status in rocky and mountainous mainland Greece, where other areas could find themselves dependent on imported foodstuffs.[2] Thessaly lacked the mineral resources to compare with the silver deposits of Attica or the veins of gold in Thrace, and she had neither the harbors nor the geographical location to become a prosperous commercial crossroads like Corinth or Megara.[3] But the broad plain of Thessaly made up for these deficiencies with its abundant production of grain and ample pasture for raising horses.[4] The revenue supplied by such products made possible the purchase of commodities which Thessaly lacked by nature, such as the silver necessary for the raw material of the coinage which various Thessalian cities began to mint in the fifth century B.C. and continued to produce in the fourth century.

[1] Plato, *Meno* 70a-b; Isocrates, *Antidosis* 155–156. On the luxury of the Thessalians, see Critias, frag. 31 (Diels-Kranz, *VS* 6).

[2] Xenophon, *Hellenica* 6.1.11. Cf. Isocrates, *On the Peace* 117.

[3] Justin's reference (8.3.12) to gold mines in Thessaly is a mistake. For Thessaly's resources, see R. J. Forbes, *Studies in Ancient Technology*, vol. 8 (Leiden, 1964), pp. 224–225. Cf. M. Cary, "The sources of silver for the Greek world," in *Mélanges Gustave Glotz*, vol. 1 (Paris, 1932), pp. 133–142; Ed. Will, "Les sources des métaux monnayés dans le monde grec," in *Numismatique antique. Problèmes et méthodes* ed. J.-M. Dentzer, Ph. Gautier, and T. Hackens (Nancy, 1975), pp. 97–102.

[4] For the geography of Thessaly, see Michel Sivignon, *La Thessalie. Analyse géographique d'une province grecque* (Lyon, 1975), pp. 13–16, 23–33.

The geography of Thessaly set it apart from the rest of Greece, and in a fundamental way the social organization of the land reflected that separateness. If any region of Greece was appropriate to become a Macedonian province, Thessaly was it. Hemmed in by mountains on all sides with only a narrow access to the sea and the easier routes of communication and commerce with other regions of Greece which the sea offered, while bordered on the north by the Macedonians, who were only semi-Hellenized in Greek eyes, and on the west by the rough and ready Epirotes, the Thessalians maintained their traditional social organization on into the classical period, despite its contrast to that of almost all their Hellenic neighbors to the south. As we will see, the social organization of Thessaly resembled that of Macedonia in important ways.

In Thessaly, an aristocracy of powerful families dominated the social and political scenes. These aristocrats controlled large numbers of people who were in a state of subordination to them, the *penestai.* [5] One such aristocratic master in the early fifth century B.C. was Meno of Pharsalus, an ancestor of the eponymous interlocutor in Plato's dialogue *Meno.* The earlier Meno had the private resources to help the Athenians financially in a military campaign in the north of Greece to the truly enormous total of twelve talents (enough money to pay the crews of twelve fully manned warships for a month), and militarily with two hundred private cavalrymen (perhaps three hundred; the sources disagree). By comparison, the city of Athens herself at the start of the Peloponnesian War in 431 B.C. mustered only twelve hundred

[5] Archemachus frag. 1, *FHG* 4, p. 314; Demosthenes 23.199. See Detlef Lotze, Μεταξὺ ἐλευθέρων καὶ δούλων. *Studien zur Rechtsstellung unfreier Landbevölkerungen in Griechenland bis zum 4. Jahrhundert v. Chr.* (Berlin, 1959), pp. 48–53; I. A. Shishova, "The status of the *penestai*," *VDI* 3 (133) 1975, pp. 39–57 (in Russian with English summary); M. I. Finley, "Was Greek Civilisation Based On Slave Labour?", in *Economy and Society in Ancient Greece* (London, 1981), pp. 98, 114, 140; G.E.M. de Ste. Croix, *The Class Struggle in the Ancient Greek World* (London, 1981), pp. 150, 153–154; Yvon Garlan, *Les Esclaves en Grèce ancienne* (Paris, 1982), pp. 115–116. Against the argument that the *penestai* can be understood as serfs (as by de Ste. Croix), see M. I. Finley, *Ancient Slavery and Modern Ideology* (London, 1980), p. 70.

cavalry.[6] Whether Meno's astounding private resources in men and money were typical of many Thessalian aristocrats is impossible to say, but tradition in the fourth century had it that in very early times one "share," the minimum holding of an aristocrat, was supposed to furnish forty cavalry and eighty heavy infantry.[7] Meno is the proof that this tradition of men of enormous personal power as the rule in Thessaly must be taken seriously, and the conservatism of the social organization of Thessaly reflected this reality of a necessarily limited number of extremely powerful aristocratic families as the holders of real political influence in Thessaly.

When city-states of the familiar Greek type developed in Thessaly, the aristocrats wasted no time in establishing themselves as the sources of power and influence in them.[8] Throughout the classical period, as all the sources make clear, the famous aristocratic families were closely linked to and even identified with the cities they dominated, as for example the family of the Aleuads with the city of Larissa. At the very beginning of the fifth century B.C., the poet Pindar saw fit to stress the intimate relationship between the aristocrats and the cities they controlled in an ode which referred in its second line to "blessed Thessaly." For this poet from neighboring Boeotia, it was both flattering and true to tell his audience that "ancestral and trusty governance of cities belongs to the aristocrats."[9]

Aristocratic domination produced unrest among the *penestai* and the nonaristocratic but free population of Thessaly.[10] But the

[6] Demosthenes 13.23, 23.199; Thucydides 2.13.8. Cf. R. S. Bluck, *Plato's Meno* (Cambridge, 1961), pp. 120–126.

[7] Aristotle frag. 497 (Rose). On this fragment, see H. T. Wade-Gery, "Jason of Pherae and Aleuas the Red," *JHS* 44 (1924), pp. 55–64.

[8] On the development of city-states in Thessaly, see Ulrich Kahrstedt, "Grundherrschaft, Freistadt und Staat in Thessalien," in *Nachrichten von der Gesellschaft der Wissenschaften zu Göttingen aus dem Jahre 1924. Philologisch-Historische Klasse* (Berlin, 1925), pp. 128–155; M. M. Austin and P. Vidal-Naquet, *Economic and Social History of Ancient Greece: An Introduction* (Berkeley, 1977), pp. 79–81.

[9] *Pythian* 10, lines 71–72.

[10] Xenophon, *Hellenica* 2.3.36; Aristotle, *Politics* 2.1269a36–b12, 5.1305b28–30.

real trouble came from the top, and the most serious Thessalian
political problem was the chronic inability of the aristocrats to
get along with one another. Factional strife was a way of life in
Thessalian cities, as the power of one group of aristocrats in a
city was from time to time violently supplanted or superseded by
that of another group. In even the most important cities, *stasis*
could become so severe that the feuding aristocrats found themselves reduced to the unhappy expedient of choosing a mediator
at the head of a peace-keeping military force. If things went
well, the mediator used this private army to reconcile the hostile
factions and to restore the *status quo ante*, but it was also possible
for the mediator to use his force to tyrannize those whose stability and security he was supposed to restore.[11] This same sort of
violent strife existed on the regional level between the rival aristocratic oligarchies in different cities as they attempted to win
dominance over each other.[12]

Perhaps as a response to the dangers posed by so much strife
and lack of cooperation, in the archaic period the Thessalian
aristocrats put together a confederacy to provide both an organizational framework for concerted military action when necessary
and an institutional channel for diverting their competitive energies *vis-à-vis* one another into what they could hope would be a
constructive form of leadership by consent. The confederacy
consisted basically of an assembly of members who voted on
matters of common concern (national security and foreign policy) and of an elected leader whose principal duty was to lead
the military forces of the confederacy when common action had
been decided on. Since, so far as we can tell, the truly nonmili-
tary duties of the leader were few if any, the rhythm of the confederacy's military expeditions determined the activity level of
the leader in his official capacity. In times of peace he had essentially nothing to do.[13] But this institution had its uses. An

[11] Xenophon, *Hellenica* 6.1.2–3; Aristotle, *Politics* 5.1306a26–30.

[12] Thucydides 1.111.1, 4.78. For a brief discussion of *stasis* in Thessaly until
the time of Philip II, see Andrew Lintott, *Violence, Civil Strife and Revolution in
the Classical City 750–330 B.C.* (London, 1982), pp. 269–271.

[13] Sordi, *LT*, pp. 334–340; Larsen, *GFS*, pp. 12–16; L. H. Jeffery, *Archaic
Greece: The City-States, c. 700–500 B.C.* (London, 1976), pp. 71–72.

elective office for the leadership of the considerable military forces of a united Thessaly and the supervision of the minimal national administrative machinery required to make the system work provided a suitable goal for aristocratic ambition. It was after all easier, safer, and cheaper to win glory and status in competition with one's fellow aristocrats by securing election to the leadership than by trying to defeat them in the field or wear them down by siege. And a national army, even if in existence only when summoned to fight, represented the best defense of a fertile land not on good terms with its neighbors.[14] If the aristocrats were lucky, their confederacy would protect them from their own tendencies toward civil war, as well as from outside enemies more prone to attack a divided country than a unified (when necessary) whole. The Thessalian confederacy was the weapon to defend the traditional and cherished Thessalian way of life, so comfortable for those at the top, against internal and external threats. The function of the confederacy was, in the end, social as well as military.[15]

Before we proceed any further, two points of correspondence between the social and political organization of Thessaly and of Macedonia should be made. First, Macedonian society at the level which mattered was, like Thessalian, constituted of important aristocratic families jealous of their status and power. The term "baronial" has been used to describe both societies, and with justification. The lords of Macedonia and of Thessaly were the mainsprings of power and of potential discontent in the respective lands. Second, both Macedonia and Thessaly had governments organized on monarchical lines. Macedonia had a true king in the normal sense of the word, but his tenure of the throne depended on his ability to marshall and to maintain a consensus among his fellow aristocrats, rather than on constitu-

[14] Neighboring Phocis was an ancestral enemy: Herodotus 8.27. See G. A. Lehmann, "Thessaliens Hegemonie über Mittelgriechenland im 6. Jh. v. Chr.," *Boreas* 6 (1983), pp. 35–43.

[15] The propaganda associated with the confederacy and its leadership makes this point clear. See section 4 below on "the *nomos* of the Thessalians."

tional arrangements.[16] In Thessaly, the government was the confederacy, but its elected leader closely resembled a king in his
power and prerogatives, as other Greeks recognized (as we will
see). The Thessalian "king" held his office expressly at the will
of his fellow aristocrats, from whose ranks he had been chosen.
Neighbors together to the north of the contemptuously proper
Greeks of the mainland, the Macedonian and the Thessalian aristocrats shared certain fundamental assumptions about the way a
society should be arranged which would have made the union of
the two lands at least theoretically plausible. The question to be
answered is whether there was an intersection between possible
theory and actual practice.

The Thessalian confederacy endured into the classical period,
and its main features are the points which require discussion in
order to compare the political organization of Thessaly before
the intrusion of the Macedonian kings in the mid-fourth century
B.C. with that afterward. If the political organization of Thessaly
looked significantly different in the later fourth or early third
centuries from the way it did earlier, we can then try to reconstruct Macedonian policy from the changes. There is, however,
one important methodological problem in making an accurate
comparison. Since some of the evidence on the earlier political
organization of Thessaly comes from sources which themselves
date to the period of Philip II and later, it is possible that the
picture of earlier times presented by these sources incorporates
distortions of, or even falsehoods about, earlier history created
under the influence of later developments. That is, even an
unbiased later source could misrepresent little-known earlier
institutions by incorrectly extrapolating from a later and better-
known situation, while a tendentious later source could consciously distort or completely falsify the past in order to provide a
precedent for contemporary action. In other words, thanks to
the state of the evidence, the question remains open as to how
much of the early history of the Thessalian confederacy (or to

[16] On the nature of the Macedonian monarchy, see, most recently, R. M.
Errington, "The Nature of the Macedonian State under the Monarchy," *Chiron*
8 (1978), pp. 77–133; Hammond, *HM*, pp. 3–31.

put it in Greek terms, the history of Thessaly's "ancestral constitution") was accurately known in the mid-fourth century B.C,
and how much, if any, of this history was made up at that time
(or later) for tendentious reasons to justify innovations in the
structure and organization of the confederacy in the interests of
the Macedonian kings. The best propaganda for a new policy
was an old precedent, even if ancient history had to be created to
find one.[17]

For present purposes, therefore, an analysis of the evidence
requires an approach different from that of the comprehensive
modern works which describe the confederacy in detail.[18] Strict
attention will be paid here (so far as is possible) to the dates of
the sources. Since any innovations in the confederacy made by a
Macedonian king belong to the years of Philip's reign or later,
the first step in each relevant category of evidence will be to
examine the sources which are earlier than Philip's reign, to see
what picture of the confederacy emerges from them, before trying to integrate this earlier evidence with that from sources of
Philip's reign and later. Naturally, this procedure will not produce a full and integrated picture of the federal organization of
Thessaly in the classical period. That sort of treatment is already
available in the works of Sordi and Larsen cited in the previous
note. What is needed is to look at the evidence in such a way
that the chances for misunderstanding the meaning of the actions
of the Macedonian kings in Thessaly are reduced as much as possible. To serve that goal, the evidence has been organized into

[17] For the hypothesis that the First Sacred War was just such an invention to
serve the purposes of Philip in Thessaly and Phocis, see N. Robertson, "The
Myth of the First Sacred War," *CQ* 28 (1978), pp. 38–73. For a different view,
however, see Lehmann, "Der 'Erste Heilige Kreig'—eine Fiktion?" *Historia* 29
(1980), pp. 242–246, and *Boreas* 6 (1983), p. 37, n. 12, with reference to others
who reject Robertson's argument.

[18] Sordi, *LT*, pp. 313–343; Larsen, *GFS*, pp. 12–26, 281–294. Since the
treatise Περὶ πολιτείας attributed to Herodes Atticus provides no evidence
relevant to this discussion, the question of its date and the reliability of its information on the situation in fifth-century Thessaly can be passed over here. On
these issues, see Umberto Albini, *[Erode Attico] περὶ πολιτείας* (Florence, 1968),
pp. 11–23; G.E.M. de Ste. Croix, *The Origins of the Peloponnesian War* (Ithaca,
1972), p. 35, n. 65.

four categories which will be discussed in turn on the basis of the information available from sources earlier than the reign of Philip. This chapter will then close with two additional points about Thessalian political traditions which facilitate the transition to the period of Philip.

1
Regional Organization: The Tetrads

By the time the sources have anything to tell us about the Thessalian confederacy, we find that Thessaly as a geographical unit was divided into four unequal areas referred to as tetrads.[19] This fourfold division existed before the appearance on the scene of Philip of Macedon in the 350s B.C.[20] The political significance of this division is obscure. One hint, however, can be extracted from two inscriptions found in Athens which date to the mid-fourth century just before Philip became deeply involved in Thessaly. They concern a treaty between the Athenians and the Thessalian confederacy which, in the usual fashion, must be sworn to by both sides. In the general agreement, polemarchs appear in the list of officials of the confederacy who must swear to the treaty, and in the second inscription, which gives the names of those who actually did swear, the polemarchs are four in number and designated by the name of a tetrad.[21] The combined evidence of these two texts shows that the polemarchs had a connection both with the confederacy and with the tetrads, which means that the tetrads in turn had some official connection with the confederacy. Unfortunately, we are at a loss to know how that connection worked, and to what, if any, extent it con-

[19] See the map at the end of Friedrich Stählin, *Das hellenische Thessalien* (Stuttgart, 1924).

[20] *Iliad* 2.711–759; Hecataeus, *FGrH* 1 F 133; Simonides frag. 198 (Bergk); Hellanicus, *FGrH* 4 F 52; Herodotus 1.56–57.

[21] *IG* II² 116 (361/0 B.C.), 175. For discussion of the context, see *SVA* II, no. 293; Jack Cargill, *The Second Athenian League: Empire or Free Alliance?* (Berkeley, 1981), pp. 83–87.

cerned more than military administration and organization.[22]

One final piece of evidence remains to be mentioned at this point. In Euripides' *Alcestis*, which was set in Thessaly, Admetus tells "the city-dwellers and all the tetrarchy" to celebrate the recovery of his wife from the dead (lines 1154–1155). Some of the modern translators of Euripides have thought that he meant Thessaly as a whole to be understood by this term, but the word, taken by itself, should refer to one of four areas of rule rather than to one area which was divided into four parts. It seems better to think that in using this word Euripides was anachronistically looking forward to the situation of his own day when Pelasgiotis (where the action of the drama takes place) was one of four administrative divisions of Thessaly and could plausibly be called a "tetrarchy."[23] Strictly speaking, this passage does not tell us that officials called tetrarchs existed in Thessaly at the time of Euripides. That tetrarchs do not appear in the Athenian inscription of 361/0 B.C. which lists the officials who must swear to the treaty with the confederacy suggests that they were not in existence in the mid-fourth century. This point about the existence of tetrarchs before the time of Philip has to be made because it is often assumed that tetrarchs existed in the early period and were replaced by polemarchs in a major reform in the first half of the fifth century B.C.[24] In fact, all the sure evidence for the existence of tetrarchs in Thessaly comes from sources no earlier than the time of Philip. Discussion of this evidence will therefore be postponed for the moment, in the interest of looking first at the evidence from the period before the time of Philip.

---

[22] On the early history of the tetrads, see F. Gschnitzer, "Namen und Wesen der thessalischen Tetraden," *Hermes* 82 (1954), pp. 451–464; Sordi, *LT*, pp. 313–320.

[23] See the commentary on these lines of A. M. Dale, *Euripides. Alcestis* (Oxford, 1954).

[24] Sordi, *LT*, p. 107; Larsen, *GFS*, p. 23; Griffith, *HM*, p. 530.

2

Neighboring Peoples: The *Perioikoi*

By the classical period, the Thessalians had brought several neighboring groups under their control: the Magnesians on the east and southeast, the Perrhaebians on the north and west, and the Phthiotic Achaeans on the south and southwest. In addition to these major groups, the Thessalians also controlled other, smaller peoples who are difficult to identify precisely. The ordinary contemporary description of all these peoples seems to have been "all the tribes round about," which is as precise as the Thessalians needed or cared to be, but the same thing could be summed up by the word *perioikoi*.[25] These neighbors did not, however, become Thessalians in the political sense by a merger of their territory in a union with Thessaly, as we can tell from the continued presence of the perioikic groups as voting representatives of the Delphic Amphictyony.[26] The Thessalians were also members of the Amphictyony, and they remained separate from their neighbors in this organization throughout this period. The relationship between "all the tribes round about" and the Thessalians was one of control of inferiors by superiors.

For the other Greeks, this control meant that the surrounding peoples were the subjects of the Thessalians. [27] The interesting questions for our purposes are to whom of the Thessalians these peoples were subject, and what exactly their subjection entailed. Thucydides says without qualification that each of the perioikic groups was subject to the "Thessalians," which could mean that he was being imprecise if these peoples were, properly speaking, subject not to the Thessalians as a whole but only to a certain group, for example, each people to a certain city. On the other

[25] On the *perioikoi* and related subjects in the early history of Thessaly, see F. Gschnitzer, *Abhängige Orte im griechischen Altertum* (Munich, 1958, Zetemata, vol. 17), pp. 1–6; M. M. Austin and P. Vidal-Naquet, *Economic and Social History of Ancient Greece: An Introduction* (Berkeley, 1977), pp. 84–86; Anthony Snodgrass, *Archaic Greece* (Berkeley, 1980), pp. 87–90; G.E.M. de Ste. Croix, *The Class Struggle in the Ancient Greek World* (London, 1981), p. 160.

[26] On the composition of the Amphictyony, see Georges Roux, *L'Amphictionie, Delphes et le temple d'Apollon au IVᵉ siècle* (Lyon, 1979), pp. 1–19.

[27] Thucydides 2.101.2, 4.78.6, 8.3.1; Xenophon, *Hellenica* 6.1.7, 6.1.9.

hand, Thucydides' usage would be correct if the perioikic groups were subject not to separate cities but to the Thessalian confederacy, which was referred to as "the Thessalians" in this sort of political context. Herodotus provides the evidence which shows that Thucydides was formally correct. He reports that in or shortly before 510 B.C, the Thessalian "king" and a thousand cavalry were sent to Athens to help the tyrant Hippias against his enemies.[28] This help was dispatched in accordance with a treaty between the Thessalians and the family of Hippias, the Peisistratids, and the Thessalians sent their "king" and their troops "by common decision." This latter expression indicates that the Thessalian confederacy as a group representing all the Thessalians voted to send its leader and some nationally marshalled troops to Athens.

The explicit involvement of the confederacy is important here because Herodotus is much more succinct slightly further on in his work when he describes the offers of help made to this same Hippias after his defeat and forced withdrawal from Athens. The tyrant's friends were genuine, and he received from them generous offers of new locations in which to govern. One of these offers, Herodotus says, came from the Thessalians, who offered Hippias the harbor town of Iolkus.[29] The significant point about this offer is the location of Iolkus. It was a city in the perioikic area of Magnesia.[30] The Thessalians who offered to give away Iolkus can only have been the confederacy, which was allied with Hippias. It appears, therefore, that the Thessalian confederacy, when so moved, could dispose of perioikic territory as it wished. Whether this ability was, strictly speaking, a matter of right or of power, or of both, does not really matter. The point is that the subjection of the perioikic areas was to the confederacy.[31] How this worked in everyday practice, when affairs were not so pressing that a common decision was made to give away territory, is difficult to say. From Xenophon's description

[28] 5.63.3.

[29] 5.94.1.

[30] On the location of Iolkus, see Stählin, *Das hellenische Thessalien*, pp. 75–76.

[31] Sordi, *LT*, pp. 340–343, followed by Griffith, *HM*, p. 291, argues that these areas were subject to individual cities.

of the arrangements made by Jason of Pherae for the perioikic peoples after his election to the leadership of the confederacy in the first half of the fourth century B.C., one receives the impression that the subjection of these groups entailed, in other than extraordinary circumstances, the fulfilling of financial and military obligations. According to Xenophon, one of Jason's arguments in favor of his own election to the post of leader of the confederacy was that the "tribes round about" were subject when Thessaly had a leader and that they then furnished considerable numbers of light-armed troops and paid tribute.[32] This indeed proved to be the case once Jason became the leader of the confederacy. He acquired a huge number of peltasts for his national army and received tribute in the amount set (according to Jason) in the distant past by Scopas, presumably one of his predecessors in the leader's office.

Two points of special interest emerge from this crucial and unique passage in Xenophon. First, Jason won election by winning over (by force and by persuasion) cities in Thessaly, and he assigned the military obligations of the members of the confederacy by city.[33] In other words, the important constituent units of the confederacy in the fourth century were the various cities of Thessaly. Whatever the formal role of the tetrads and their officials like the polemarchs, the cities were the entities that mattered. This situation naturally reflected the reality of the political organization of Thessaly in the fourth century, by which time there were various cities in the region large enough to issue their own coinages. When one thinks of the Thessalian confederacy, it is important to think of the cities of Thessaly as its functional reality and not of some elaborate federal organization with a large-scale and effective bureaucracy.[34] Jason of Pherae issued

---

[32] *Hellenica* 6.1.9, 6.1.12, 6.1.19.

[33] 6.1.5, 6.1.7, 6.1.19, 6.4.29.

[34] Larsen's discussion in *Greek Federal States* perhaps conveys the wrong impression. The cities of the Perrhaebians seem to have constituted the functional units of their *koinon*. See B. Helly, "Une liste des cités de Perrhébie dans la première moitié du IVᵉ siècle avant J.-C.," in *La Thessalie, Actes de la Table-Ronde 21–24 Juillet 1975 Lyon,* ed. B. Helly (Lyon, 1979), pp. 165–200.

his orders to the cities because they were the sources of the confederacy's strength.

The second point is to be found in Jason's remarks about the subjection of the perioikic peoples when Thessaly had a leader. His argument in favor of having a leader reveals what we should have expected in any case in the light of the geographical and social background of the situation. The perioikic peoples were not always in actual subjection to the Thessalians, regardless of whether the Thessalians or anyone else considered them to be their subjects. It is easy to understand why. When the aristocrats of Thessaly in their characteristically faction-ridden fashion could not agree on a leader of their confederacy, they were unable, in the absence of an acknowledged supreme military commander, to marshall a national army strong enough to compel all the perioikic peoples, safe in their mountain strongholds, to fulfill their obligations. And in any case, those obligations may have been rather hazy in times of peace when no troops were needed and when, in the absence of an expensive federal bureaucracy to maintain in peacetime as well as in war, no obviously justifiable use could be found for tribute otherwise destined for and justified by the demands of a common defense. Financial exploitation of the perioikic peoples by the confederacy was simply not possible without a strong national army and a dynamic leader.

When the confederacy was unable to exploit the neighboring peoples for its corporate benefit, the various most powerful cities situated near the perioikic territories could step in to demand that their neighbors fulfill certain financial obligations to them.[35] One hint from the period before Philip II that this was so is provided by the fifth-century coinage of the Perrhaebians, which exactly resembles that of Larissa, their very powerful immediate

---

[35] Griffith, *HM*, p. 291–293, is right to emphasize the *de facto* nature of this arrangement. Sordi argues, *L T*, p. 343, that the confederacy officially condoned the practice.

neighbor, and the coinages of several other smaller cities near Larissa.[36] One might imagine that this coinage was designed to facilitate commercial transactions in the area, with Larissa serving as some sort of central market. But the subordinate status of the *perioikoi* perhaps suggests another explanation. That the Perrhaebians minted a coinage mimicking that of their powerful neighbors suggests that they had to make payments to the Larissaeans. This suggestion can be confirmed later when we turn to the evidence on the perioikic peoples from the time of Philip and beyond. In any case, it would be a mistake to try to construct an elaborate and precise model of the legal relationship (to use an anachronistic expression) among the confederacy, the cities of Thessaly, and the *perioikoi*. A reasonable reconstruction of actual practice would be that the confederacy, through its leader, administered and exploited the *perioikoi* by means of the cities, which alone were in any practical position to check on the fidelity of the neighboring peoples in fulfilling their obligations to the general community. It is easy to imagine the leader of the confederacy sending instructions to Larissa, the gist of which was "Make certain the Perrhaebians pay their tribute on time and in the proper amount, and then send it along to me as soon as possible." It is also easy to imagine the Larissaeans making certain that the Perrhaebians paid even when no instructions were sent by the leader, or no leader was there to send them. The people of the city of Pherae could do the same for the perioikic Magnesians, who were nearby, and so on. For the receivers of tribute, it is simpler and more profitable to keep a system of tribute-payment in operation continuously rather than to crank up the necessary machinery intermittently. The *perioikoi* were the subjects of the confederacy, but the cities were the confederacy.

---

[36] F. Herrmann, "Die thessalische Münzunion im 5. Jahrhundert," *ZfN* 33 (1922), pp. 33–43, whose conclusions on the "Münzunion" are open to question. The status of the small cities in Larissa's orbit can be compared to those which Jason is made to describe as "dependent on" the Pharsalians (Xenophon, *Hellenica* 6.1.8).

3
The Leader of the Confederacy

Since, as we will see, Philip and after him Alexander served as the leader of the Thessalian confederacy, it was through this post that they would have made any changes in the political organization of Thessaly. We need to know what they inherited as the traditional prerogatives and limits of their office in order to be able to judge the significance of what they did while holding it.

The most significant evidence for this discussion is the consistent reference by fifth-century authors to the leader of the confederacy as a "king." In an ode of 498 B.C. which refers to "blessed Thessaly," Pindar describes the race of men descended from Heracles as ruling over Thessaly as kings. [37] Pindar meant the Aleuads of Larissa. [38] Herodotus also describes the Aleuads of the time of the Persian Wars in the early fifth century B.C. as "kings" of Thessaly. This was not, however, a term exclusively for the well-known Aleuads as leaders of the confederacy because Herodotus also calls the obscure Cineas who was sent by the confederacy to help Hippias a "king." [39] Thucydides uses the same term to describe Echecratidas, father of the exiled Thessalian whom the Athenians tried unsuccessfully to restore in the mid-fifth century B.C.[40] It is instructive that non-Thessalian writers in the fifth century, who had to convey the nature of things to their audiences in a comprehensible way, perceived the nature of the office as monarchical and royal. Whether or not the Thessalians themselves used the title "king" before the fourth century to

[37] *Pythian* 10, line 3. Anacreon earlier used the colorless word ἄρχος in an apparent reference to the leader of the Thessalian confederacy: 107 (Diehl), D. Page, *Epigrammata Graeca* (Oxford, 1975), Anacreon XIII, p. 7. Cf. Dionysius of Halicarnassus 5.73.3, 5.74.3 (1022, 1025–1026 Reiske), perhaps relying on Theophrastus.

[38] *Pythian* 10, lines 64–72.

[39] 5.63.3, 7.6.2. Cineas' city is unknown. See N. Robertson, "The Thessalian Expedition of 480 B.C.," *JHS* 96 (1976), p. 105. N.G.L. Hammond, "The Narrative of Herodotus VII and the Decree of Themistocles at Troezen," *JHS* 102 (1982), p. 78, n. 18, believes we should translate 7.6.2 with "rulers of Thessaly," not "kings of Thessaly."

[40] 1.111.1.

refer to the leader of their confederacy we cannot tell because no evidence from Thessaly itself is extant. But the evidence for at least the perception of the leader as a king by other Greeks must be kept in mind as part of the background for discussion of the election of Philip to the leadership of the confederacy.[41]

From Xenophon, we learn the term which was usually employed in a technical sense to indicate the leader of the confederacy in the fourth century. Xenophon reports that Jason of Pherae needed to explain to another prominent Thessalian his desire to become ταγός of all the Thessalians. To secure this post, Jason required the agreement of the cities of Thessaly, the constituent units (practically speaking) of the confederacy. Xenophon applies the same term to the successors of Jason.[42] There is no other literary source which allows us to confirm Xenophon's usage, nor does any epigraphical source provide indisputable proof of the use of ταγός for the leader of the confederacy. But inscriptions do show that the word was used in Thessaly in an official sense, and its rarity in the prose of Xenophon's time means that Xenophon was not simply using a common word to describe an uncommon institution.[43] Although the dangers are obvious in relying on the etymology of a word as indicative of the function which the word described at any one time, especially when the function in question could have changed over time, it is nevertheless worth noticing the basic meaning of the word ταγός. This noun is related to the verb τάσσειν ("to draw up into battle order") and should refer in the first place to a military leader or commander, to the head of an army. For the basic

---

[41] A king at the head of a confederacy is attested for the Paeonians in the third century B.C. See Luigi Moretti, *Iscrizioni storiche ellenistiche*, vol. 2 (Florence, 1975), p. 25, on *SIG*³ no. 394, with references to other such arrangements in the north of Greece. He refers to "il problema della coesistenza di due forme politiche teoricamente antitetiche: regno (βασιλεία) e federazione (κοινόν)." The case of Thessaly shows that this coexistence was feasible for a long period of time and suggests that theory mattered little in such arrangements.

[42] *Hellenica* 6.1.8–9, 6.1.12, 6.1.18, 6.4.28, 6.4.33–37.

[43] *IG* IX.2, 257 and 517. Cf. Pollux 1.128.

meaning of the term, any notion of civil rule would probably be secondary to that of military command.[44]

The leader of the Thessalian confederacy in the fourth century was, it seems, principally, and perhaps exclusively, a military leader whose duties and responsibilities were the same as those carried by leaders like Cineas, who led the Thessalian cavalry to Attica at the end of the sixth century, and like Jason, who organized a national army and its finances.[45] The leader's political role was to carry out the will of the members of the confederacy on matters of national security and foreign policy once they had reached a common decision, as they did, for example, in the case of Cineas' mission, and might have done if they had had the time in the case of Brasidas' transit of their land with a military force in 424 B.C.[46] A strong leader would naturally have a considerable influence on the decisions reached by the confederacy, as the case of Jason makes clear. Jason had his own force of mercenaries to make his efforts at friendly persuasion quite compelling, and the grandiose plans for the conquest of Greece, Macedonia, and Persia which Xenophon has him outline as the program of the Thessalian national army were his own initiatives, which the confederacy would rubber-stamp.[47]

The leader of the Thessalians had the opportunity to make of the office what he could, based on his personal ability to compel,

[44] See H. Frisk, *Griechisches etymologisches Wörterbuch*, vol. 2 (Heidelberg, 1970), s. v. ταγός; τάσσω. This contrasts with, for example, the primary association of *rex* with civic responsibilities. On *rex*, see Emile Benveniste, *Le vocabulaire des institutions indo-européennes* vol. 2 (Paris, 1969), pp. 9–15. Without reference to Thessaly, Robert Drews, *Basileus. The Evidence for Kingship in Geometric Greece* (New Haven, 1983), ch. 4: "The Hereditary *Basileis* of the Archaic and Classical Period," pp. 116–128, argues that military responsibilities were often the primary concern of Greek "kings."

[45] The reference to the leader of the confederacy as the ἄρχων in *IG* II² 116, lines 23, 33, 34, of 361/0 B.C., is explicable on historical grounds. Since Alexander of Pherae had prior claim to the title of ταγός, his opponents who made this treaty with the Athenians had to use another title for the moment to refer to the leader of their rival version of the confederacy.

[46] Thucydides 4.78.3–5. Brasidas crossed the region with the help of various Thessalian friends, despite the opposition of other Thessalians who said that he should not cross without the consent of the Thessalians as a whole.

[47] Xenophon, *Hellenica* 6.1.8–12.

to persuade, and to unite. He needed to use that ability to become an acknowledged leader of a powerful national army, and in addition he had to be able to make certain that the requisite tribute was collected from the *perioikoi* and deposited in the federal coffers rather than exclusively in those of the various large cities which dominated the respective perioikic regions. There was, to be sure, a good deal of room for sharp accounting practices and outright cheating in the collection and forwarding of funds because the confederacy lacked an elaborate federal bureaucracy to oversee federal finances on a long-term basis. The financial arrangements of the confederacy were necessarily *ad hoc* because they were limited and determined by the willingness of the cities to contribute to the federal treasury. But the willingness of the cities to pay depended, in the final analysis, on the ability of the leader of the confederacy to ensure their cooperation. To be effective, the leader had to be able to finance his army as well as to lead it in battle. He had to dominate the cities of the confederacy and the peoples of the perioikic territories.

If a leader could perform his duties successfully, how long was he expected to continue in office? The fifth-century references to the leader as a king imply that he served for life. Local confirmation of a term of office that was at least longer than annual comes from a fifth-century inscription at Delphi which refers to polemarchs to indicate chronology.[48] The highest federal official, the leader of the confederacy, would have been the natural choice as an indicator of chronology if his office had been annual, as the choice of the general as the eponymous magistrate of the reconstituted Thessalian confederacy in the Hellenistic period demonstrates.[49] Since the polemarchs are the eponymous officials in this fifth-century inscription, we must conclude that the term of the leader's office made him inappropriate

---

[48] *SEG* 17 (1960), no. 243. See Sordi, *LT*, pp. 344–347; G. Daux, "Dédicace thessalienne d'un cheval à Delphes," *BCH* 82 (1958), pp. 329–334.

[49] On this office, see Herwig Kramolisch, *Demetrias II. Die Strategen des thessalischen Bundes vom Jahr 196 v. Chr. bis zum Ausgang der römischen Republik* (Bonn, 1978, Beiträge zur ur- und frühgeschichtlichen Archäologie des Mittelmeer-Kulturraumes, vol. 18), p. 3.

for indicating chronology (on the assumption that there was a leader of the confederacy at the time).[50] The same seems to have been true in the fourth century as well.[51] This fact alone, however, does not prove that the leader served for life. Any term longer than a single year would have been useless for chronological purposes in the Greek system, which reckoned on the large scale in units of one year.[52]

Confirmation that the ταγός usually did serve for life, at least by the first half of the fourth century, comes from Xenophon's account of the careers of Jason of Pherae and his successors.[53] When Jason was made leader of the confederacy by consent, there was no leader already in office because the violent efforts of Lycophron of Pherae to become leader of Thessaly at the end of the fifth century B.C. had split the confederacy.[54] This sort of internal strife among the Thessalian aristocrats was probably far from rare when it came time to elect a new leader, and one can imagine that long periods could pass while no leader was in office. Jason based his arguments in favor of his own election to the post on the military benefits to be expected under his leadership in preparation for war on Macedonia, Greece, and Persia. There is no indication that Jason expected his term of office to

[50] Sordi, *LT*, pp. 107–108, believes that the leader's office was in abeyance after the battle of Tanagra, when the inscription was set up.

[51] Werner Peek, "Griechische Inschriften," *Athenische Mitteilungen* 59 (1934), p. 57, no. 15: the Thessalians make a proxeny award which appears to be dated by the names of two groups, who are designated as the προστατεύοντες, not by the name of the individual leader of the confederacy. See Sordi, *LT*, p. 333. It is conceivable, however, that the reference to the groups in this text served to indicate not the year but only a certain period within the year, as is the case, for example, with the references to prytanizing tribes in Athenian decrees.

[52] The reference in *IG* IX.2, 257 (Thetonium, fifth cent. B.C), to ταγά and ἀταγία has been taken to refer to the office of the leader of the confederacy, in which case an indefinite tenure of the office would be implied. The words may refer, however, only to "wartime and peacetime," and not to the leader's office. For discussion of these words, see C. D. Buck, *The Greek Dialects* (Chicago, 1955), p. 226; J. Chadwick, "ταγά and ἀταγία," in *Studi linguistici in onore di Vittore Pisani* (Brescia, 1969), vol. 1, pp. 231–234; J. T. Hooker, "Thessalian ΤΑΓΑ," *ZPE* 40 (1980), p. 272.

[53] *Hellenica* 6.1.2–19, 6.4.20–37.

[54] *Hellenica* 2.3.4.

be anything less than lifelong, and his successors certainly tried to hold the office for life. Their opponents elsewhere in Thessaly were no doubt unhappy about this fact, but that dissatisfaction made no difference unless backed by superior military force, which the opponents on their own could not marshall.

The perception of the leader of the confederacy as a king and his lifetime tenure of office raise an additional issue concerning the office. What happened when one leader died and a new one had to be selected? What were the criteria of selection? Obviously the most important ones should have been the ability of the candidate to gain the support of the majority of the Thessalian aristocrats and to perform the military duties demanded of his office, but the evidence from the period before Philip suggests that another criterion figured in the selection process which again helps to explain why non-Thessalians thought of the leader of the confederacy as a kind of king. That criterion was kinship. If the family tree sketched by J. S. Morrison for the Aleuads is right, that family practically monopolized the leadership of Thessaly in the late sixth and early fifth centuries, passing the highest federal office from father to son, or perhaps to a close male relative.[55] This situation obtained without any doubt by the fourth century, as we see from the careers of Jason and his relatives at Pherae as the leadership of the confederacy passed from one male member of the family to the next.[56] Once a strong family had one of its members elected as the leader of the confederacy, it evidently tried hard to keep the office in its male line.[57] Of

[55] "Meno of Pharsalus, Polycrates and Ismenias," *CQ* 36 (1942), pp. 59–61.

[56] Sordi, *LT*, p. 336, states that by this period the office was "elective" rather than "dynastic," a legalistic conception which underestimates the strength of the tendency for a family to keep a firm grip on its prerogatives. Alexander of Pherae claimed the office as his by inheritance (Diodorus 17.4.1). Cf. Arnaldo Momigliano, "Tagia e tetrarchia in Tessalgia," *Athenaeum* 10 (1932), pp. 52–53. One might profitably compare the history of the Hapsburgs, who struggled to establish a hereditary right to be elected monarchs. See, for brief discussion, Fritz Hartung, *Deutsche Verfassungsgeschichte vom 15. Jahrhundert bis zur Gegenwart*[7] (Stuttgart, 1950), pp. 34–36; R. A. Kann, *A History of the Hapsburg Empire 1526–1918* (Berkeley, 1974), pp. 54–62, 125–129. .

[57] The story of Thargelia the Milesian as "queen of Thessaly" for thirty years after the death of her husband the "king" is a romantic fiction. For the story, see H. Dittmar, *Aischines von Sphettos* (Berlin, 1912), p. 277, frag. 21 = *Anonymi*

course, it is very unlikely that the office became an automatically inherited one *de jure* in the way that a proper kingship was because the selection of the leader had to be accomplished by the members of the confederacy. But the tendency for the office to be inherited *de facto* nevertheless was present, as a result of the realities of family politics and also of the natural inclination to give the office to a man who could be expected to provide the same qualities of leadership as had his father or his uncle or his brother. From time to time, the office moved from one family to another as conditions in Thessaly changed, in much the same way that royal lines change in countries ruled by proper kings.

The nature of the leader's office as revealed by evidence earlier than the reign of Philip II is easy to summarize. It was overwhelmingly military with concomitant financial responsibilities. A very important component of these military and financial responsibilities was the enforcement of the "subjection" of the people of the perioikic areas in the interest of the confederacy. The leader was not ordinarily concerned with other areas of government such as the administration of justice on the civic level. There was, however, no set of hard and fast rules on the federal level to define precisely the scope of the leader's power, nor the extent of the cooperation required of the members of the confederacy. The situation remained fluid. A strong leader could go further than others of lesser strength or charisma in exercising his prerogatives for the "common interest."

In this type of constitutional situation, the possibilities for disagreement and even violent strife were many. Given the tradition of factional strife among the Thessalian aristocrats, one has no difficulty understanding how disputes arose over whether the leader of the confederacy was doing his duty in the proper way. In the absence of explicit constitutional guidelines in codified form, arguments were inevitable over what the proper way was. That the Thessalians in fact had a strong tradition that there was a proper way for their leader to behave can be seen from the

---

tractatus de mulieribus II, in A. Westermann, *Paradoxographoi* (Brunswick, 1839), p. 217.

fourth and final category of evidence on the political organization of Thessaly before the time of Philip II of Macedon.

4
The *Nomos* of the Thessalians

The Greek word νόμος presents notorious difficulties to the
English translator because it simultaneously embodies notions of
what the modern interpreter must call "custom" and "law."
Although the word can mean "statute law," it would be misleading to think of this sense for νόμος and its associated adjectives
and adverbs in the context of Thessalian tradition. In the history of Thessalian social and political life, the expression "the
nomos of the Thessalians" refers to the notion that there was a
way in which things should be done, and that was the way in
which they had traditionally been done to the satisfaction of the
aristocratic community in Thessaly. If this notion seems short
on specifics, that is only proper. Customs change or evolve into
new forms, and therefore ideas of what is proper can change.
But the idea that *something* is proper endures. As a result, there is
always the possibility of arguing that the customs of the day have
gotten away from the "genuine" old style of behavior. In a
society with minimal record keeping at best (with no permanent
federal headquarters for the confederacy, archives are inconceivable), the "ancestral constitution" was going to be a matter of
dispute among those who wanted to remember its provisions to
their own political advantage. But there were certain very
important points about the *nomos* of the Thessalians which could
not be disputed. These are the points one must consider as the
background for understanding the significance of what happened
once the *nomos* of the Thessalians had to find room for a direct
Macedonian influence.

Once again the discussion begins with Pindar's ode in honor
of a young Thessalian athlete. At the conclusion of the poem,
Pindar praises the family of his patron, Thorax the Aleuad,
because "bearing on high the *nomos* of the Thessalians they
increase it. Ancestral and trusty governance of cities belongs to

the aristocrats."[58] Pindar did not mean his audience to think of any particular event when they heard these flattering words. Rather, he was emphasizing the idea that the Aleuads deserved praise because they were behaving in the traditionally accepted and proper fashion for the aristocratic rulers of Thessaly. In the case of the Aleuads, the rule in question covered both their ancestral city, Larissa, and the confederacy. Since Pindar speaks here of governance of cities in the plural, his reference is to the confederacy, which was made up of cities by the fifth century B.C., and all indications are that Thorax was indeed the leader of the confederacy by the date of the poem.[59]

Xenophon's account of Jason's rise to leadership of the confederacy reveals the specifics which Pindar's poetry conceals. Xenophon, Jason's contemporary and therefore in a position to know his reputation, says that Jason was great in Thessaly because, to be sure, he had a large army of well-trained mercenary soldiers and many allies, but also because he became leader of the Thessalians "in accordance with their *nomos*."[60] The speech which Xenophon wrote for Jason to explain his motives for wanting to become the leader shows what this *nomos* was. The leader had to receive the recognition of the cities of Thessaly; that is, he had to be elected by the members of the confederacy. Although Jason had the power to compel the cities to recognize him by defeating them in battle, he wanted to be elected by the power of persuasion rather than by force.[61] Jason got his wish and was made leader "by common agreement."[62] The text of the Thessalian-Athenian treaty made less than a decade after Jason's death proves that Xenophon is presenting an accurate picture of the *nomos* of the Thessalians. There one reads that the leader of the confederacy whom the Athenians agree to

[58] *Pythian* 10, lines 69–72 (Snell): ἀδελφεοῖσί τ᾽ ἐπαινήσομεν ἐσλοῖς, ὅτι / ὑψοῦ φέροντι νόμον Θεσσαλῶν / αὔξοντες. ἐν δ᾽ ἀγαθοῖσι κεῖται / πατρώϊαι κεδναὶ πολίων κυβερνάσιες.
[59] Sordi, *LT*, pp. 65–66.
[60] *Hellenica* 6.4.28: διὰ τὸ τῷ νόμῳ Θετταλῶν ταγὸς καθεστάναι.
[61] 6.1.5–13, esp. 7–8.
[62] 6.1.18: ὁμολογουμένως ταγὸς τῶν Θετταλῶν καθειστήκει.

defend is the one "whom the Thessalians chose."[63]

The same treaty is also revealing in its stated intent to defend the confederacy and its leader against tyranny.[64] The threat of tyranny at the time the treaty was made came from Alexander of Pherae. He had apparently gained the leadership of the confederacy in what could be construed as the traditional fashion, but now he had betrayed the tradition of his office (so his opponents claimed) by ruling by force, contrary to "*nomos.*"[65] So, it seems, not only did the leader of the confederacy have to secure his election by common consent; he also had to retain the common recognition of his status by the cities of Thessaly as time passed. He would become a tyrant if he lacked the "common agreement" of the Thessalians. It was probably Isocrates' aim to persuade the successors of Alexander of Pherae to secure this common agreement when he wrote to them advising against trying to become tyrants in Thessaly, as their local advisers were pressing them to do. Those advisers, said Isocrates, were the sort of men who undertake deeds "most contrary to *nomos.*"[66] As usual, Isocrates' advice went unheeded, but his letter does provide further contemporary evidence for the acknowledged importance of the tradition of appointing a leader of the Thessalian confederacy by consent rather than by force.

There is one other important constituent of the *nomos* of the Thessalians as it applied to the leader of the confederacy. Jason of Pherae was murdered by a band of young conspirators before he could launch any of the great campaigns of conquest which Xenophon claims as his intention. No motive for the killing is reported, although Xenophon says that the Greeks were relieved at the news of Jason's death because they feared he was turning into a tyrant.[67] Jason was succeeded as leader of the confederacy

[63] *IG* II² 116, line 18 (*SVA* II, no. 293).

[64] Lines 19, 31.

[65] Diodorus 15.61.2–3; Plutarch, *Pelopidas* 26, 31–32.

[66] *Letters* 6.12. For the date and the authenticity of the letter, see Georges Mathieu, *Isocrate. Tome IV*, ed. with Emile Brémond (Paris, 1962), pp. 168–170.

[67] *Hellenica* 6.4.31–32. Cf. Joshua Mandel, "Jason: The Tyrant of Pherae, Tagus of Thessaly, as Reflected in Ancient Sources and Modern Literature: The Image of the 'New Tyrant,'" *Rivista storica dell'antichità* 10 (1980), pp.

by his brother Polydorus, and then by his brother Polyphron, who murdered Polydorus to take his office. Xenophon comments that Polyphron made his short tenure of the office like a tyranny, and fortunately Xenophon explains how. While leader of the confederacy, Polyphron executed nine prominent citizens of Pharsalus and exiled many from Larissa.[68] Polyphron clearly overstepped the bounds of his office by interfering in the affairs of the cities, in this case by undertaking to administer "justice" on the civic level by the use of force. In other words, noninterference in the affairs of the cities of the confederacy by its leader was part of the *nomos* of the Thessalians. Only when a tyrant threatened the confederacy or its leader could the leader justifiably interfere in a Thessalian city, or at least that is the implication of Xenophon's account and the text of the treaty with the Athenians. Under normal circumstances, civic concerns were not the business of the leader of the confederacy.

Whatever else it might have meant, then, the *nomos* of the Thessalians by the fourth century demanded that the leader of the confederacy win and keep the consent of the cities to his holding office, and that he eschew interference in the affairs of the cities unless a tyrannical conspiracy was in the making. If he respected the *nomos* of his land, the leader of the Thessalian confederacy had the chance to function as the commander of a formidable military force which was drawn from the manpower of the cities of Thessaly and its neighboring areas and was financed by the resources of both. If he proved to be popular with his fellow aristocrats, the leader could usually pass his office on to his heir with the consent of the confederacy. In sum, the *nomos* of the Thessalians stood for the mutual expectations of the Thessalian aristocrats that they would govern themselves by persuasion and not by force. One can see from the best documented example of the selection of a leader of the confederacy that such expectations were more utopian than realistic. Jason of Pherae was able to persuade the other cities of Thessaly and the aristocrats who controlled them to support his election because he

---

47–77.

[68] *Hellenica* 6.4.33–34.

possessed the personal mercenary army to compel obedience to his wishes, if it came to that.   But it should not be overlooked that Jason did achieve a real measure of popularity in Thessaly by his insistence on his respect for custom and his reluctance to use force. His propaganda worked. The lesson was there for anyone who cared to learn it.

This brief analysis of the political organization of Thessaly before the time of Philip II based on the sources of the period is not meant to present a full picture, but only to present the evidence in such a way that our idea of what Thessaly was like before the entry of Philip remains uncontaminated by inference drawn from potentially tendentious sources of Philip's own time and later. Before we proceed to the history of Thessaly in the latter half of the fourth century B.C., however, two further points must be made in preparation for the discussion to follow. These points concern not Thessalian political institutions properly speaking but, rather, Thessalian political traditions.

At the beginning of this chapter, reference was made to the factional strife which characterized Thessalian political life and the remedy adopted in desperate times of putting affairs completely in the hands of a mediator backed by troops. We know for certain that in the fourth century a "mediating magistrate" with full powers was appointed in Pharsalus and in Larissa, two of the three most important cities in Thessaly.[69] The third of these cities, Pherae, could have used one as a remedy for the string of political murders it experienced in the same period. These incidents reveal a traditional tendency to look to a strong individual at the head of an army to bring back social and political harmony when ordinary institutions had failed to preserve it. In a sense, the need for a confederate leader to head the national army in times of danger or of opportunity was analogous to the need for a mediating archon to fight political fires and to resolve social crises. But crisis-management by committee, such as the Athenians tried in 413 B.C., was not for the Thessalians.[70] Only a truly dominant individual could harness the energies of the

[69] *Hellenica* 6.1.2–3; Aristotle, *Politics* 5.1306a26–30.
[70] Thucydides 8.1.

powerful and fractious aristocrats of Thessaly.

This tendency to look for help in times of strife from a strong third party also lies behind the second point to be made here. The aristocrats of Thessaly, like the participants in civil wars elsewhere in Greece, made it a habit to call for military aid from nonlocal sources in their violent disputes with one another or with their neighbors. One party or the other often turned for assistance to powerful Greek states like Sparta, Athens, or Thebes.[71] But the Aleuads of Larissa made it a habit to look for help from sources beyond Greece as well. In the early fifth century, they called on the king of Persia to invade their homeland in hopes of furthering their own advantage, and again at the end of the same century the king was asked to supply troops to help Larissa combat her domestic enemies. In the fourth century, the Aleuads called on the Macedonian king for the same reason.[72] These collaborations with foreign kings presented the same difficulties as did placing the city in the hands of a mediating magistrate. The mediator could turn out to have designs on despotic control that were inimical to the interests of those he was supposed to help. In the early 360s B.C., in fact, King Alexander of Macedonia treacherously occupied Larissa when called in by the Aleuads.[73] But when faced in the 350s with the threat of tyranny from Pherae, their southern neighbor in the rich plain of Pelasgiotis, the aristocrats of Larissa apparently had no choice but to continue to seek their salvation by submitting to the leadership of a non-Thessalian commander who could get the job done. Moreover, the happy experience the Aleuads had with Pelopidas of Thebes shortly before the appearance on the scene

[71] Diodrus 14.82.5–6 (Medius of Larissa asks for troops from the anti-Spartan *synedrion* formed at Corinth and then takes Pharsalus, which had a Spartan garrison); Xenophon, *Hellenica* 6.1.2–16 (Pharsalus asks Sparta for aid against Jason of Pherae); *IG* II² 116 (*SVA* II, no. 293: the confederacy asks Athens for aid against Jason); Diodorus 15.80.1; Plutarch, *Pelopidas* 31–35 (the "Thessalians" ask Thebes for help against Alexander of Pherae).

[72] Herodotus 7.6.2; Damastes, *FGrH* 5 F 4; Xenophon, *Anabasis* 1.1.10; Diodorus 15.61.3.

[73] Diodorus 15.61.4–5. See the general comment of Isocrates, *On the Peace* 118, on the occupation of Thessalian citadels by foreigners as a consequence of the Thessalian propensity for civil war.

of Philip of Macedon shows what they could hope to get from leadership supplied by the right person. Since the example of Pelopidas provides important background for understanding the election of Philip as the leader of the Thessalian confederacy, this episode provides an appropriate transition to the discussion in the following chapter.

When Alexander of Pherae as leader of the confederacy began to behave in tyrannical fashion, the Aleuads of Larissa, from fear of his παρανομία, conspired to overthrow him with Macedonian help. After Alexander of Macedon proved a treacherous ally, the Aleuads turned to Thebes for help. The Theban commander Pelopidas came with an army to Thessaly and succeeded in freeing Larissa from the Macedonian Alexander and in warning Alexander of Pherae to govern according to *nomos*. Harmony was restored.[74] When it failed to endure, Pelopidas returned. At first, Alexander of Pherae had the upper hand, even holding Pelopidas prisoner for a while, but eventually Pelopidas led a predominantly Thessalian army against the forces of Alexander. According to Plutarch, Pelopidas persevered because he hoped to win the glory which came to a man who opposed tyrants ruling "contrary to *nomos* and by force." Unfortunately Pelopidas died in the trying.[75]

The Thessalians who had called upon Pelopidas mourned his death as if he were a Thessalian national hero. The confederacy (as constituted in opposition to Alexander) passed decrees in his honor and set up a statue with a verse inscription at Delphi. The cities sent honorific delegations to the funeral, which was carried out by the Thessalians at their special request. They mourned the loss of their commander and, they declared, their freedom as well. The historical accuracy of Plutarch's life of Pelopidas is certainly open to question because its hero consistently comes off so well, but there is no reason to quarrel with Plutarch's assessment of Pelopidas' standing with the Thessalians after his death.

[74] Diodorus 15.67.3–4; Plutarch, *Pelopidas* 26.

[75] Plutarch, *Pelopidas* 26–32; Polybius 8.35.6–8; Diodorus 15.67.3–4, 15.80. See John Buckler, *The Theban Hegemony 371–362 B.C.* (Cambridge, Mass., 1980), pp. 110–129. On the modern view that Pelopidas reorganized the confederacy, see Sordi, *LT*, p. 207.

The extravagant honors paid the dead man by foreigners marked him as supreme in the fortune of his reputation.[76] The historian of Philip's career in Thessaly does well to remember how the Thessalians felt about a non-Thessalian military man who could lead Thessalian troops effectively in defense of their *nomos* against a tyrant from Pherae. By now, the background should be clear against which the actions of Philip in Thessaly must be seen.

[76] *Pelopidas* 33–34. For the honors paid him, cf. Nepos, *Pelopidas* 5.5. For the statue erected by the "Thessalians," see Adolf Wilhelm, "Zu Ehren des Pelopidas," *Oesterr. Jahreshefte* 33 (1941), pp. 35–45.

FOUR. THESSALY AND PHILIP II

The Thessalians were no strangers to the kings of their northern neighbors in Macedonia. The aristocrats of Larissa in particular had reason to know both the good and the bad points of these powerful and meddlesome monarchs. Thucydides reports that at the time of the Peloponnesian War king Perdiccas of Macedonia was on close terms with "the first men of Thessaly," and he names Nikonidas of Larissa as one of them.[1] At the end of the fifth century, king Archelaus apparently interfered in the internal affairs of Larissa to such an extent that a Thessalian partisan could refer to his aim as enslavement.[2] And as previously mentioned, Alexander II responded to an Aleuad call for help against the tyrannical Alexander of Pherae in the 360s B.C. by occupying Larissa with his Macedonians, whence it took Pelopidas to dislodge him. This treachery was poor recompense for the favor the Aleuads had done his father, Amyntas III, by restoring him to his throne in the late 390s B.C.[3]

By the time Philip II came to power, the Aleuads knew well the potential benefits and risks of calling in a Macedonian king at the head of an army. Recent experience taught that the risks to be run in return for Macedonian aid were very high indeed. Nevertheless, not long after Philip's accession, the Aleuads invited him to bring an army to Thessaly to fight with them against the tyrannical house which ruled Pherae and claimed to represent the legitimate leadership of the Thessalian confederacy. The Aleuads and their allies disputed this claim and called on Philip to help defend the true confederacy. This young

[1] 4.78.2, 4.132.2.

[2] Thrasymachus frag. 2 (Diels-Kranz VS [6]). For the evidence of pseudo-Herodes, see Sordi, LT, pp. 146–151, and the references given in n. 18 of chapter 3.

[3] Diodorus 14.92.3. See Hammond, HM, p. 172.

Macedonian king lived up to their expectations. Pherae was defeated, and Philip returned home without committing any outrages of the sort his grandfather, Alexander II, had perpetrated on his mission into Thessaly. When the threat from Pherae revived in even more dangerous fashion later in the 350s, the Aleuads of Larissa again turned to Philip.[4] This time the confederacy was under attack not only by the tyrants of Pherae but also by the forces of their allies, the Phocians led by the commander Onomarchus. Since Onomarchus was a powerful man who, according to Diodorus, was scheming to gain control of Thessalian affairs, traditional government in Thessaly was in grave danger. That the danger came from the Phocians, the detested enemies of the Thessalians from long ago and their immediate neighbors to the south, made the situation desperate.[5]

Philip persevered. Despite a major defeat which threatened the cohesiveness of his Macedonian army, he managed to unite the other Thessalians under his leadership in the name of the god Apollo of Delphi and to subdue the tyrants and their formidable allies.[6] With his glorious victory, Philip put an end to nearly twenty years of tyranny in Pherae and, therefore, to the claim of the successors of Jason to head the confederacy. He saved traditional government in Thessaly. And by their association with the new conqueror, the Aleuads regained the primacy in Thessalian politics that they had last enjoyed in the fifth century B.C. This was the kind of help for which the enemies of Pherae and of Phocis had hoped, the kind of resolute and unifying military leadership they could not find in their own ranks. Philip the Macedonian had actually accomplished what just a few years earlier the Athenians had sworn by treaty to do but never did: he had protected the Thessalian confederacy against the threat of tyranny.

[4] On these early interventions, see Griffith, *HM*, pp. 218–230, 267–295; T. R. Martin, "Diodorus on Philip II and Thessaly in the 350s B.C.," *CP* 76 (1981), pp. 188–201, and "A Phantom Fragment of Theopompus and Philip II's First Campaign in Thessaly," *HSCP* 86 (1982), pp. 55–78.

[5] Diodorus 16.35.1–2.

[6] For Philip's conspicuous allegiance to Apollo's cause, see Diodorus 16.38.2; Justin 8.2.3.

The king's reward was remarkable. By an unprecedented decision, the Thessalians selected Philip as the leader of their confederacy. G. T. Griffith in his standard work on this period rightly emphasizes the special nature of the Thessalians' decision.[7] A foreign king at the head of a Greek league was truly something new. But in the best Hellenic fashion, the justification for novelty could be found in an alleged evocation or even resurrection of the past. Philip's election, for example, could be excused on the personal level by appeal to his descent from Heracles, the common ancestor of the Aleuads of his day and of the mythological Thessalus, the eponymous hero of the country. As Pindar had remarked, Thessaly was blessed when the race of Heracles ruled.[8]

Another positive item in Philip's background was more recent than his kinship with Heracles. As a teenager, Philip had spent three years in Thebes after Pelopidas took him as a hostage from Macedonia.[9] Although Philip had lived in the house of another Theban, his connection with Pelopidas, whom the Thessalians had so admired, could only serve to recommend Philip. Moreover, Philip had the style that the high-living aristocrats of Thessaly understood and appreciated. He was congenial, hearty to the point of rowdiness, and comfortable in the company of aristocrats who, of necessity, had to tolerate the leadership of one of

[7] *HM*, pp. 221, 278, 285, 294. In the light of the tendency of Greek authors to refer to the leader of the confederacy as a king, Diodorus' statement (16.38.2, for 352/1) that as a result of his actions in Thessaly Philip "increased his kingdom" could refer to Philip's election to that post.

[8] Pindar, *Pythian* 10, line 3; Isocrates 5.32–34 *et passim* (Philip's Heraclid ancestry); W. H. Roscher, *Ausführliches Lexikon der griechischen und römischen Mythologie*, vol. 5 (Leipzig, 1916–1924), *s. v.* "Thessalos," cols. 775–776. For the view that the apologist Antipater of Magnesia proclaimed Philip's legal title to places like Pallene, Torone, Amphipolis, and Ambracia by reference to Philip's Heraclid ancestry and Heracles' exploits in these places, see E. Bickermann and J. Sykutris, *Speusipps Brief an König Philipp* (Leipzig, 1928, Berichte über die Verhandlungen der Sächsischen Akademie der Wissenschaften zu Leipzig, Philologisch-historische Klasse 80,3), pp. 27–29. As P. A. Brunt remarks, there is no reason to think that such genealogies were not believed in the fourth century. See his *Arrian*, vol. 1 (Cambridge, MA, 1976, Loeb Classical Library), p. 464.

[9] See Griffith, *HM*, pp. 204–206.

their own class. [10] As a king of Macedonia, Philip had to deal with the same general social situation as in Thessaly because the Macedonian nobles on whose cooperation his kingship depended had to be treated as social (if not political) equals. [11] But the most important factor in Philip's elevation to the leadership of the confederacy was what he had been able to do. In response to a Thessalian appeal, he had led Thessalian troops to victory in the name of Thessalian political tradition. Since his new post was awarded through the consent of Thessalians, that decision was Thessalian, too. But the legitimacy of Philip's status as leader of the confederacy ironically depended on maintaining a perceived allegiance to tradition. The only way to legitimize a revolution in a conservative society was to link it to the past. [12] In this situation, the pressure to interpret or to recreate the past in the image of the present was going to be strong in certain interested quarters.

We can see that the selection of Philip as leader of the confederacy was acceptable on the level of propaganda because it could be explained as serving the interests of the *nomos* of the Thessalians. Here was a man with aristocratic sympathies whose royal status in Macedonia and demonstrated prowess as a military commander recommended him for the type of duties the leader had to perform. Furthermore, his personal acquaintance with Pelopidas gave hope that he could be the kind of beneficial "mediating magistrate" that his Theban predecessor had been, and which Thessaly needed at the moment (as so often). Above all, Philip's election meant the elimination of tyranny at Pherae as a threat to the confederacy and a return to leadership by consent. There were some in Pherae who would have said that their consent had not been solicited in the making of this decision, but

[10] On the Thessalian manner, see Xenophon, *Hellenica* 6.1.3; Theopompus, *FGrH* 115 F 49.

[11] See Hammond, *HM*, pp. 152–153.

[12] As M. I. Finley points out in *Politics in the Ancient World* (Cambridge, 1983), p. 133, an "appeal to the past was usually a conservative argument against fundamental change, or . . . for a backward change." But Philip was clever enough to use the past as justification for a veiled but radical change in the politics of Thessaly.

they were disqualified anyway by their heretical views on the
way Thessalian government should be run. They had agreed to
bring in the Phocians, of all people. For other Thessalians weary
of factional strife or intent on their own advantage, or both, Philip's election offered the hope of restoring a facsimile "ancestral
constitution" and the national status a more united Thessaly had
commanded in the past. That Philip understood this hope and
capitalized on it is shown by his sworn promise at the time of his
election to restore Thessaly to its traditional position of influence
in the assembly of Greek states which controlled Apollo's temple
at Delphi, the Amphictyony. Since Delphi lay within the bor-
ders of Phocis, the Phocians had been able to deprive the Thessalians of their ancient prerogatives and were not about to recognize Thessalian rights without a fight. Philip swore to win the
war for Thessaly.[13] That solemn promise proved (it could then
be said) the Macedonian king's devotion to the cause of Thessalian tradition. The central fact to remember about the political
climate at the time of Philip's rise to the leadership of the Thessalians in the late 350s B.C. is the way in which radical innovation (a Macedonian in the highest Thessalian office) was introduced under the cover of respect for traditional practices, "in
accordance with *nomos*."

Philip had made a good start in Thessaly. Relations with
members of what was now his confederacy became strained over
the course of the next several years, however, when no progress
was made in keeping the promise to defeat the Phocians in a
sacred war. The strains developed because the new leader was
evidently insisting on the privileges of his office while (in Thessalian eyes) neglecting his duties. For one thing, Philip was
receiving certain substantial revenues in his capacity as leader of
the confederacy. Part of the money came from taxes levied in
markets and harbors, but perhaps the largest sums came from the
tribute paid by the perioikic areas.[14] There was no question that

[13] Demosthenes 19.318.
[14] Griffith, *HM*, pp. 289–291. S. C. Bakhuizen, however, in a forthcoming
article on Magnesia under Macedonian suzerainty which he kindly allowed me
to see, argues that Philip ended the Thessalian perioikic system and incorporated the perioikic areas into Macedonia. I cannot agree, as the arguments in
this chapter show. Cf. below, n. 20, on Strabo 9.5.16.

Philip was entitled to these revenues as leader of the confederacy. The issue was whether the money was being spent in the interest of the membership and not just to further Philip's private activities elsewhere.[15] That sort of dispute is common in any situation in which one official controls community funds more or less independent of a regular accounting procedure which can ensure against fraud.

The sources which imply that Philip received Thessalian revenues illegitimately are either biased or ill-informed. Demosthenes, who clearly falls into the first category, will be dealt with shortly. For the moment, it is enough to mention a passage from the geographer Strabo, writing three centuries after Philip's death. In his survey of Thessaly, Strabo remarks that the people of Larissa in mythological times gained control of the original land of the Perrhaebians in Thessaly and exacted tribute from it until Philip became "lord ($\kappa\acute{\upsilon}\rho\iota o\varsigma$) of these places." This passage cannot be taken to mean that Philip robbed the Larissaeans of revenues to which he was not entitled because Strabo shows understanding neither of the political organization of Thessaly in the fourth century nor of the legitimate claim of the leader of the confederacy to receive tribute from the perioikic peoples in the name of the confederacy. Perhaps Strabo was right if he meant that Philip, like Jason of Pherae, as legitimate leader of the confederacy received the revenues which the Larissaeans were supposed to collect for the confederacy but kept for themselves whenever possible.[16] But Strabo is not by himself a witness for illegitimate (i.e., nontraditional) behavior by Philip in his Thessalian office.[17]

[15] Demosthenes 1.22.

[16] 9.5.19 (C440). Strabo's rather general comment may be based on the evidence of earlier sources such as Polybius 9.33.2 (discussion of the question whether Philip was "lord" in Thessaly) and Isocrates 5.21 (the Perrhaebians were Philip's subjects).

[17] See below, n. 20, on Strabo 9.5.16 (C437). Theopompus, on the other hand, like Demosthenes, is an independent witness whose testimony cannot be trusted. In *FGrH* 115 F 81, he presents a rhetorically slanted reference to Philip's dispatch of a representative "to destroy the Perrhaebians and look after affairs there." It is inconceivable that the leader of the confederacy lacked the right to supervise *perioikoi* by means of a man on the spot to look after "federal" interests.

Of course, Stràbo is not the source which matters in an evaluation of Philip's conduct after his election to the leadership of the confederacy and, therefore, in an evaluation of his actions in Thessaly. That honor goes to Demosthenes. Since Demosthenes launches his attacks on Philip in a series of speeches which begin not long after Philip became the leader of the confederacy, now is the appropriate time to look at the charges brought by the orator against the king. We will proceed through the speeches in chronological order so far as possible. In that way we can keep a check on the consistency of Demosthenes' evidence and on the possibility that Philip abandoned his commitment to the *nomos* of the Thessalians as he served longer in his post and acquired greater and greater power throughout Greece.

The earliest references in Demosthenes to trouble between Philip and the Thessalians come in the first and second orations concerning Olynthus, which are usually dated sometime in the Athenian archon year 349/8 B.C.[18] Since these two speeches are so similar in subject, in structure, and in wording, it is difficult to believe that they were both delivered. Which, if either, was the version spoken by Demosthenes is impossible to know. In both, Demosthenes refers to Thessalian dissatisfaction over Philip's handling of the matters of the fate of the city of Pagasae and of the perioikic area of Magnesia. Pagasae and Magnesia had been under the control of the tyrants of Pherae until Philip's recent victory which led to his election as leader of the confederacy.[19] Demosthenes in *Olynthiac* I.12–13 makes the briefest of references to Philip's intervention in this area during a thumbnail sketch of the king's successes up to the time of his attack on Olynthus. Philip, he says, "first having taken Amphipolis, after this Pydna, then Potidaea, next Methone, thereupon attacked Thessaly. After this, he went to Thrace, having settled matters as he wished in Pherae, Pagasae, Magnesia, and all [that area]. Having thrown out some of those there [i.e., in Thrace] and set

[18] For the dates of Demosthenic speeches, see Raphael Sealey, "Dionysius of Halicarnassus and Some Demosthenic Dates," *REG* 68 (1955), pp. 77–120.

[19] N. D. Papahadjis, "Magnesia polis, 'at the foot of Mount Pelium,'" *Thessalika* 2 (1959), pp. 22–28, argues that the reference to Magnesia is to the harbor town of the Magnetes, not to the perioikic territory as a whole.

up others, he became ill." Demosthenes then mentions the attack on Olynthus, followed by a *paraleipsis* in which he refers to campaigns against the Illyrians, Paeonians, and King Arybbas.[20] In *Olynthiac* I.22, Demosthenes says that "the Thessalians have voted to demand that Philip return Pagasae and have prevented the fortification of Magnesia." In *Olynthiac* II.11, he says that "the Thessalians have voted to demand that Philip return Pagasae and to confer about Magnesia."[21] In *Olynthiac* I.22, Demosthenes adds the information that he has heard a rumor from some people that the Thessalians will no longer hand over to Philip the revenues from their harbors and markets. Since Demosthenes' aim is to convince his audience that Philip is in a precarious position, there is little incentive to believe in the truth of a rumor reported by a man who had heard of Alexander the Great's death in 335 B.C. and produced a witness to back up the story.[22] But even if the rumor about revenues was true, there is no indication elsewhere in Demosthenes or any other source that the Thessalians ever ceased to turn over these revenues to Philip. The granting of these same revenues to Alexander when he succeeded to his father's position as leader of the confederacy supports the assumption that the threat to cut off funds, if it was ever made, was never carried out.[23]

It is easier to believe that the status of Pagasae and of

[20] This passage is probably Strabo's source at 9.5.16 (C437) for the explanation of how Philip made the islands off Magnesia a focus of attention: "Fighting for the leadership, he always used to attack the areas close to him first, and just as he made most parts of the Magnetan land and of Thrace and of the other territory around him Macedonia, so he also took [ἀφῃρεῖτο, an imperfect which could mean "tried to take"?] the islands off Macedonia and made [ἐποίει, "began to make"?] these islands, which had previously been known to none, objects worth fighting for and well known." Bakhuizen in his forthcoming article (see n. 14 above) interprets this passage, in conjunction with other evidence, to mean that Philip incorporated the majority of Magnesia into Macedonia even though the Magnesians retained their identity as an *ethnos*. Strabo, however, is here most likely only offering an interpretation of Demosthenes' comments and is not an independent witness.

[21] It seems likely that these two passages are simply alternate versions of the very same facts.

[22] Justin 11.2.7–8.

[23] Justin 11.3.2.

Magnesia caused problems for Philip and the Thessalians of the confederacy. The location of these places on the gulf of Pagasae controlled the approach to Thessaly from the sea and the route south along the coast to Thermopylae, the gateway to southern Greece. The power of the tyrants of Pherae had been buttressed considerably by their holding Pagasae and Magnesia, and the situation had been made much worse by their allowing the hated Phocians access to these vital spots. That sort of dangerous situation had to be prevented for the future. Therefore, after his victory over Pherae and the Phocians in the late 350s B.C., Philip would have been wise to put garrisons of loyal (and thus predominantly Macedonian) troops into Pagasae and Magnesia until he could be certain that there was no serious threat of losing these strategic locations to hostile forces. It seems almost certain that Philip had introduced garrisons into Pagasae and Magnesia in the late 350s.[24] If Demosthenes is telling the truth about the Thessalian reaction, the confederacy protested as a group.

Even if this is so, it is possible that Demosthenes inflated to the national level complaints which in reality came from the disgruntled leaders of Pherae who had previously controlled Pagasae and Magnesia. They might well have complained because their rivals in Larissa, surely the dominant faction in the confederacy, and their rivals' hand-picked leader, Philip, had connived to get federal approval of garrisons in these sensitive locations. These garrisons meant the Pheraeans had no chance to recover their losses even when Philip was absent. It would be characteristic of Demosthenes to report such complaints from those out of power as if they reflected the national consensus in Thessaly. But this hypothesis cannot be proved, and it is certainly the standard opinion to take Demosthenes' report at face value. In that case, Demosthenes' references to Thessalian demands in the first and second *Olynthiac* orations should mean that the Thessalians of the confederacy had objected, first, to the presence of Philip's forces in Pagasae, a city which was supposed to be an autonomous member of the confederacy without a garrison once the danger of tyranny had passed, and, second, to

[24] Cf. Griffith, *HM*, p. 287.

the plans for a fortified position which Philip had evidently made for Magnesia, an area which he could claim to control as leader of the confederacy. The presence of the leader's troops in Magnesia was perhaps acceptable, but a permanent fort was too much. Since Pagasae in very early times may have belonged to perioikic Magnesia, Philip could have justified his special arrangements for that port city on the grounds that he was returning to the ancestral situation in which Pagasae's military security had been, properly speaking, a concern of the leader of the confederacy.[25] That is just the sort of argument which Philip seems to have used later in the 340s B.C. as camouflage for the changes in tetrarchic government which he introduced, as we will see.

Whether Demosthenes' comments actually refer to a dispute between the members of the confederacy and their leader over garrisons of the sort just described, or to something else entirely, it seems that the matter was straightened out. Nothing is said in *Olynthiac* III about dissatisfaction in Thessaly, although this omission may be of no significance because there is no way to establish beyond doubt that this speech is later than the other two. But there are other hints that the matter had been settled. Diodorus reports that Philip in 349/8 B.C. had to return to Thessaly to expel the tyrant Peitholaus from Pherae again.[26] As Griffith rightly points out, it is hard to believe that Peitholaus had been able to reestablish himself in Pherae while Philip held Pagasae (not to mention Magnesia).[27] His solution to this puzzle is to assume that Diodorus has misreported what was actually a local popular uprising in Pherae against Philip and not a comeback by a once-defeated tyrant.

It is also possible, however, to think that Peitholaus was able to return just because, among other things, Philip was no longer holding Pagasae when the return took place. This possibility becomes more compelling when one considers the implications of Demosthenes' remarks in *Philippic* II.22 (344 B.C.). There he

---

[25] Friedrich Stählin, Ernst Meyer, and Alfred Heidner, *Pagasai und Demetrias. Beschreibung der Reste und Stadtgeschichte* (Berlin, 1934), p. 169.

[26] Diodorus 16.52.9.

[27] *HM*, pp. 319–321.

refers to the time when Philip "was expelling tyrants for them and was giving back Nicaea and Magnesia." Since it is certain that Philip did expel tyrants from Pherae and did give back Nicaea, it makes sense to believe that he "gave back" Magnesia, too.[28] And although Demosthenes does not mention Pagasae here, his failure to raise the question of its status in any of his speeches after *Olynthiacs* I and II suggests that the Thessalians "got Pagasae back" as well as Magnesia, or at least that some satisfactory compromise was reached between the leader of the confederacy and its membership on this point.[29] In other words, Demosthenes' comments on Pagasae and Magnesia can plausibly be explained as referring, at most, to disagreements between the leader of the confederacy on one side and the members of the confederacy on the other over issues of mutual concern. That sort of trouble must have been common throughout the history of the Thessalian confederacy even before Philip's time, if the reports we have about the prevalence of *stasis* in Thessaly are any indication. The controversy over the status of Pagasae and Magnesia was not of such a magnitude that Demosthenes could have expected to find many Thessalians in agreement with his claim in *Olynthiac* II.8 that they now found themselves "the slaves of Philip."

It should be added that "giving back" Pagasae and Magnesia did not mean that Philip abdicated his rights as leader of the confederacy in these places. Pagasae presumably had the same sort of military and financial responsibilities as did the other cities which belonged to the confederacy, and probably with stricter supervision. Magnesia as a perioikic area owed tribute which was collected for the benefit of the confederacy in theory and of the leader in practice. As in the case of the Perrhaebians,

[28] Demosthenes 6.22. Cf. 6.20 for a similar use of the imperfect tense to refer to handing over Potidaea.

[29] Griffith, *HM*, p. 287, says Philip never surrendered Pagasae "so far as we know." But if Philip held on to the city and thereby caused trouble in Thessaly in 344 B.C. (p. 524), why is Demosthenes silent on this point in the *Second Philippic* of the same year? Pagasae appears as an independent city in a list of 325 B.C. from Delphi. See J. Bousquet, "Le compte de l'automne 325 à Delphes," in *Mélanges helléniques offerts à Georges Daux* (Paris, 1974), p. 27, n 1.

Philip continued to maintain his right to this tribute from his "subjects" the Magnesians, as Isocrates calls them.[30]

Potentially more serious objections to the idea of Philip as the public respecter of the *nomos* of the Thessalians are the allegations of Demosthenes that Philip radically altered Thessalian government in the later 340s B.C. on both the civic and the national levels. In 346 B.C., Philip had fulfilled his promise to the Thessalians by finally defeating the Phocians in the Sacred War and by restoring the ancestral privileges of the Thessalians in the Amphictyony to the members of the confederacy. Even Demosthenes has to admit that the king and his Greek allies are on good terms in this period.[31] In speeches written in the years 344–342 B.C., however, Demosthenes tries hard to give the impression that Thessaly is now suffering grievously from the slavery imposed by its erstwhile benefactor, Philip. As always with Demosthenes, it pays to read between the lines. In *Philippic* II.22 (344 B.C.), in the passage which refers to Philip's throwing out tyrants and giving back Nicaea and Magnesia, Demosthenes poses the rhetorical question of whether the Thessalians ever expected to have the *dekadarchia* which they now have.[32] Or, Demosthenes goes on, when Philip was restoring their Amphictyonic privileges, did the Thessalians expect that Philip would appropriate their private resources? Details of these charges are not offered. Demosthenes' answer is obviously no in both cases, but an unbiased reply can be made only after looking at some additional evidence. In the speech *On the False Embassy* 260 (343 B.C.), we read that their desire for Philip's friendship has destroyed the hegemony, reputation, and now the freedom of the Thessalians because Macedonian garrisons are occupying the citadels of some Thessalian cities. Demosthenes does not name these cities or say how many were garrisoned or when. Nor does he comment on any Thessalian reaction to the presence of these garrisons, just as in *Philippic* II he gives no indication of unrest

[30] 5.20.

[31] 5.19–20.

[32] *Dekadarchia* otherwise appears only in Isocrates *Panegyricus* 110 and *Philippus* 95 as a variant for *dekarchia*, the usual term for a Spartan "rule of ten" (e.g., Xenophon, *Hellenica* 3.4.2, 3.4.7, 6.3.8).

or dissatisfaction in Thessaly. Without a doubt, Demosthenes meant his audience to jump to the conclusion that the Thessalians were restive and unhappy with Philip, but it is important to notice that Demosthenes makes no such explicit claim for the period to which the *Embassy* speech refers, as he did for the period after Philip's election to the leadership of the confederacy.[33] The lack of details in Demosthenes' accusations is worth noticing. When he has valid (or even invalid but plausible) charges to press, Demosthenes spells them out.

In the speeches *On Halonnesus* 32 (343 B.C.) and *On the Chersonnese* 59 (342/1 B.C.), one finds the details which reveal why Demosthenes was so vague when accusing Philip of malfeasance in Thessaly in the two earlier speeches *Philippic* II and *On the False Embassy*. It turns out that Philip had campaigned against the city of Pherae and put a garrison into its citadel after a victory over, or a capitulation by, the other side. Since Pherae had previously refused to cooperate with Philip on (it seems) two occasions when he called on it to fulfill its obligations to him as leader of the confederacy, it is obvious that the city had now been forced by Philip, in his capacity as the leader of the confederacy, to fall into line and that an occupying garrison had been introduced to prevent further treason.[34] Once again, Philip had expelled tyrants.[35] In other words, he had done just what had won him favor with the Thessalians some years before. The other members of the confederacy might not relish the prospect of having Macedonian troops in Pherae indefinitely, but recent history showed that lesser measures only ensured the recurrence of very dangerous trouble in that rebellious city. For the good of the confederacy, Pherae had to be subdued and kept under close watch. Philip could therefore excuse the action taken against Pherae by reference to the traditional concern of the confederacy with the threat of tyranny, and he was formally correct to deny

[33] *Olynthiacs* I.22, II.8.

[34] Demosthenes 19.320. See Griffith, *HM*, p. 525, for the second occasion in 344 B.C.

[35] Diodorus 16.69.8.

that he was making war in Thessaly when dealing with Pherae.[36] As the leader of the Thessalian confederacy, he moved against Pherae as the "friend and ally" of the other Thessalians.[37]

This idea of insisting that certain acts of war are merely "police actions" is unfortunately not unfamiliar to historians of the twentieth century, and then, as now, the point of the vocabulary was propaganda. When the orator Hegesippus sneers that of course Philip garrisoned Pherae so that its people could be autonomous, his sarcasm reveals the official Thessalian position on the incident.[38] Pherae was attacked and garrisoned to guarantee the freedom from tyrants of the people of Pherae as well as of the rest of the Thessalians. "Dekadarchy" is, one might guess, a term of abuse to describe the special arrangements made to govern Pherae after this most recent rebellion.[39] The private resources which Demosthenes claims that Philip appropriated for himself can only have been the contributions the leader of the confederacy received from the member cities and perioikic peoples, and Demosthenes' accusation at this point was perhaps inspired by the reimposition on Pherae of the financial obligations which the city had been shirking (to judge from *Embassy* 260). So far, then, the charges raised by Demosthenes seem to have been related to action against Pherae taken in the name of the Thessalian confederacy. But what of the claim in the *Embassy* speech that more than one citadel was garrisoned?

G. T. Griffith has suggested that Larissa suffered the same fate as did Pherae, and this would be a point of crucial importance, if true.[40] Pherae had a history of treason and recalcitrance which could be invoked to justify harsh measures as the requirements of tradition. Larissa, however, had no such record and was in fact the city which had done the most to secure Philip's position in

[36] Demosthenes 8.59.

[37] Demosthenes 9.12.

[38] [Demosthenes] 7.32.

[39] Griffith, *HM*, pp. 527–533. Xenophon's reference (*Hellenica* 6.3.8) to *dekarchia* as a form of tyranny opposed to autonomy, whose members ruled by force rather than according to *nomos*, shows that "rule of ten" was the perfect term of abuse to apply to Philip's avowed policy of respect for Thessalian *nomos*.

[40] *HM*, pp. 525–526.

Thessaly. It would be very difficult to explain the garrisoning of Larissa as an act of federal policy which could be accepted as such by Philip's friends there and by other members of the confederacy. If Larissa was garrisoned, the charade was over, and the leader had plainly revealed himself as a tyrant. The evidence for a garrison in Larissa, however, is illusory.

The case for believing that Philip garrisoned Larissa depends on a reconstruction of the career of a certain Simus of Larissa, an Aleuad who had collaborated with Philip when the latter first entered Thessaly but later fell from the king's favor, according to Demosthenes. Griffith, for example, assumes that Philip expelled Simus from Larissa because Simus had begun to abuse his position in the city. A garrison was then introduced to keep the peace. But the various pieces of evidence from the historical sources which must be put together to form this jigsaw puzzle of a reconstruction do not fit.[41] Similarly, the numismatic evidence which has served to support this reconstruction of Simus' career cannot be relied upon. This evidence consists of a group of silver coins minted in Larissa which bear the name Simus in tiny script.[42] Since the appearance of the name on the coins has been taken as a sign that this Simus was a tyrant in the city, and since the date of the coins has been taken to be the period 353−344/3 B.C., the coins have been used to confirm the view that Philip expelled Simus from Larissa and imposed a garrison. But this interpretation is erroneous. The coins are dated to this period on the basis of the faulty historical evidence just mentioned, rather than on numismatic evidence. An analysis of coins found in hoards shows that in fact the Simus coins belong *ca.* 370−360 B.C., much earlier than previously thought.[43] Therefore, the Simus coins of Larissa provide no help whatsoever in determining what happened to the Simus who, according to Demosthenes, fell from Philip's favor.

[41] For a discussion of this evidence, see appendix 1 on Philip II and the career of Simus.

[42] Kraay, *ACGC*, p. 119. The coins are Group VII, Series R, in Herrmann, *ZfN* 35 (1924−1925), pp. 1−69.

[43] T. R. Martin, "The Chronology of the Fourth-Century B.C. Facing-Head Silver Coinage of Larissa," *ANSMN* 28 (1983), pp. 1−34.

In sum, there is no reason to think that Larissa received a garrison in 344 or 343. Pherae did, and perhaps Pagasae as well, if Demosthenes' plural is to be believed. But this action took place as part of the business of the confederacy, within the context of the *nomos* of the Thessalians. Even when Philip took drastic measures in Thessaly, he found it convenient to ensure their "legitimacy." We might compare the punishment inflicted on Pharcadon and Tricca in (probably) 352 B.C. for treasonous collaboration with Onomarchus. The penalty was carried out by the leader, but it was decided upon by the confederacy. [44] This commitment to "legitimacy" is a point whose significance is not diminished for historical purposes by the acknowledgment that legitimacy and moral right are often far from the same thing. Philip respected the *nomos* of the Thessalians because this policy worked. As Demosthenes had to say, the majority of the Thessalians were satisfied with their Macedonian leader. [45] Philip treated them fairly and to their benefit, and that was freedom enough, for now. [46]

Only one substantive charge remains from Demosthenes' speeches of this period as proof of the "slavery" which Philip imposed on the Thessalians. In *Philippic* III.26 of 342/1 B.C., Demosthenes claims that the king had wronged his allies in Thessaly by "taking away their constitutions and their cities and by establishing tetrarchies so that they may be slaves not only by city [κατὰ πόλεις] but also by tribe [κατ' ἔθνη]." In short, Philip "prescribes for the Thessalians in what way they are to be governed" (*Philippic* III.33). Again, the problem is to disentangle the facts from the rhetoric, especially since some scholars have thought that "tetrarchies" in this passage refers to the same thing as "dekadarchy" in *Philippic* II.22. But Griffith's treatment of this point should kill that impossible idea forever, and we need only concentrate on *Philippic* III by itself. [47] "Slavery by city" sounds like a polemical description of Philip's leadership of the Thessalian confederacy, whose constituent elements were

[44] Sordi, *LT*, pp. 254–256; Griffith, *HM*, pp. 271, 279, 286.
[45] 8.65.
[46] Isocrates, *Letters* 2.20 (343 B.C.).
[47] *HM*, pp. 527–532.

cities, and of the sort of action taken against Pherae, especially if a new "constitution" was installed in that city after the latest rebellion was quelled. The real issue for our purposes, then, is the significance of the tetrarchies which Philip "established" in Thessaly. Can this feature of Thessalian government under Philip's leadership be reconciled with the policy of ostensible respect for the *nomos* of the Thessalians which has emerged from an analysis of the other evidence as Philip's chosen position? The answer to this question is clearly yes. First, the evidence discussed earlier shows that Thessaly had long been divided into four units for certain administrative purposes relevant to the confederacy. On the broad level, tetrarchic government was certainly nothing new in Thessaly. The details of Philip's arrangements are another matter, however, and the most important of these details is the existence of tetrarchs. Contemporary literary and epigraphical sources prove that Thessaly had officials called tetrarchs by the time of Philip.[48] It is usually assumed that these tetrarchs were officials created by Philip to replace the polemarchs known from the earlier evidence, but in fact there is no compelling reason why the tetrarchs could not have simply supplemented the polemarchs as magistrates in the tetrads. A larger number of high local offices would have served Philip's purpose by leaving room for ambitious nobles to serve in traditional posts.[49] But the important issue here is the intended relationship of Philip's tetrarchs to Thessalian tradition. Working

[48] Theopompus, *FGrH* 115 F 208; *SIG*[3] 274 VIII.

[49] Sordi, *LT*, p. 339, and Griffith, *HM*, pp. 533–534, based on the use of the verb καθιστάναι in Theopompus and Demosthenes to describe Philip's actions regarding tetrarchs or tetrarchies, believe that Philip abolished elective polemarchs in favor of tetrarchs whom he appointed to office. The evidence seems far too weak to support this conclusion, and it seems incorrect to say that the "significant thing" (in Griffith's words) in Philip's reform was a change from elected to appointed officials at the head of the tetrads. Philip would have had no trouble having his men elected, if election was the *nomos* of the Thessalians. And why replace the polemarchs if Philip was going to have his men on hand in a position of superior authority in alleged imitation of the "ancestral constitution"? Better to keep the old offices going so that the Thessalian aristocrats could, like the consuls during the Roman Empire, continue to satisfy their ambitions in offices of high (though hollow) status.

strictly from the evidence from sources certainly earlier than Philip, one cannot tell whether Thessaly had officials called tetrarchs before Philip's time. The only hint that they might have existed is the reference to "tetrarchy" in Euripides' *Alcestis* lines 1154–55.

The only other source to testify to the existence of an early tetrarch is an inscription set up at Delphi by a man who himself served as a tetrarch under Philip. The Thessalian Daochus erected a series of statues of prominent members of his family in Apollo's sanctuary and inscribed on the bases the honors each ancestor had earned. Daochus refers to himself as "tetrarch of the Thessalians," which is the same title inscribed below the statue of his fifth-century ancestor Acnonius. [50] It would probably be unwarranted to suspect that this convenient fifth-century precedent for Philip was invented and inserted into the family history of Daochus. Thanks to the testimony of Euripides, we can believe that Acnonius had been a tetrarch of the Thessalians. Philip picked this office to exploit for his own purposes. Precisely what he did with it, we cannot know. The tetrarchs may have continued to exist in the fourth century but without real power until Philip strengthened their position, or he may have restored the office, which could have been abolished at some earlier time or, perhaps, failed to be filled for a long period because factional strife was so intense as to prevent agreement on suitable men to serve as tetrarchs. [51] The significance of Philip's effect on the tetrarchies is not so much in exactly what he did (whatever it was, it was in his own interest), as in how he presented his action. The Daochus inscription shows that Philip linked the present to the past. Philip's tetrarchs were clearly publicized as a return to the provisions of the ancestral constitution. They were to be regarded as part of the *nomos* of the Thessalians. This final point emerges even more strikingly from another inscription among those on the so-called Daochus monument, but discussion of this text must be postponed briefly in order to consider two

[50] *SIG* 3 274 II (Acnonius), VIII (Daochus). See Griffith, *HM*, p. 386, n. 1, p. 539.

[51] For the view that Philip reestablished the tetrarchies, see, for example, George Cawkwell, *Philip of Macedon* (London, 1978), p. 115.

final pieces of evidence on tetrarchies which come from sources no earlier than Philip's time.

From the Aristotelian *Constitution of the Thessalians* comes the information that Thessaly was divided into four parts at the time of the legendary Aleuas the Red, who also assigned the number of cavalry and infantry which each "share" in Thessaly was to provide.[52] It is certainly interesting that in this research on the early constitution of Thessaly, which was most likely compiled during or after Aristotle's stay in Macedonia at Philip's court, it was reported that the fourfold division of the land was the work of Aleuas, like Philip a descendant of Heracles who had been concerned with the Thessalian army.[53] Interest increases when one turns to Plutarch's story of how Aleuas was chosen "king of the Thessalians."[54] He was very unexpectedly picked for the office by the god Apollo in a lottery which was held at Delphi at the request of the Thessalians, who had apparently been unable to make a selection themselves. In other words, the god of Delphi could, if so moved, choose a descendant of Heracles like Aleuas as a suitable though surprising leader for the Thessalians when they could not find someone on their own. The parallel with Philip's case was naturally imperfect (after all, Aleuas was a genuine Thessalian), but suggestive. Since Philip had led the Thessalian army to victory in the Sacred War under Apollo's banner and, it was alleged, in the interests of proper management of his shrine, it was possible to imagine that Apollo had had a hand in the happy coincidence of interests between Philip and the confederacy.[55] In any case, these stories make it clear that Aleuas, the leader of the Thessalians who saw to the tetrads and to the army, represented a convenient model for Philip, who was concerned with the same things. If the tradition about Aleuas

[52] Frags. 497–498 (Rose), on which see H. T. Wade-Gery, "Jason of Pherae and Aleuas the Red," *JHS* 44 (1924), pp. 55–64.

[53] Some of the "constitutions" perhaps belong *ca.* 347–334 B.C. See Ingemar Düring, *Aristoteles. Darstellung und Interpretation seines Denkens* (Heidelberg, 1966), p. 51. The one concerning Athens is later, however. See P. J. Rhodes, *A Commentary on the Aristotelian Athenaion Politeia* (Oxford, 1981), pp. 51–58.

[54] *Moralia* 492A-B (*De fraterno amore* 21).

[55] See Diodorus 16.38.2; Justin 8.2.3; and Griffith, *HM*, p. 274.

represents what the Thessalians even before Philip's time believed about their own distant past (as it probably does), we can again glimpse how Philip operated in Thessaly. As with the tetrarchs, he could use history to justify what he had decided to do in his own interest.

It is easy to believe that Philip relied on his tetrarchs to keep watch on the cities of Thessaly and to make certain that they sent the troops he wanted when he wanted them. One final story from Plutarch hints that the tetrarchs may have also been concerned with collecting the leader's revenues, which we might have expected anyway. According to Plutarch, when a certain Hermon tried to beg off from service as the leader of the Thessalians on the grounds of personal poverty, it was voted that each tetrad would provide him with a ration so that he could take up his office. [56] The moral of the story could be found in the responsibility of the tetrads to supply the leader of the confederacy with the necessary revenues. Who better than a tetrarch loyal to Philip to ensure that the king received the money due him? Tetrarchs who kept a sharp eye out would have been especially valuable in monitoring the flow of revenue from the perioikic peoples to the leader of the confederacy in order to eliminate skimming by the cities. And the same officials could have made certain that the perioikic areas kept their light-armed forces in service to the confederacy up to strength. These duties, which were especially important for a leader who was often not in Thessaly to check on things himself, could easily have been transformed by the rhetoric of Demosthenes into "slavery by tribe" because the perioikic peoples were "the tribes round

---

[56] *Moralia* 822E (*Praecepta gerendae reipublicae* 31). The incident is not dated, but the mention of tetrads could fit just as easily into the classical period as into the period of the refounded confederacy after 196 B.C., where J.A.O. Larsen, "The Thessalian *Tetrades* in Plutarch's *Moralia* 822E," *CP* 58 (1963), p. 240, thinks the incident belongs. The continuing importance of the tetrads in this later period has now been confirmed by the inscription announced by K. Gallis at the Eighth International Congress of Greek and Latin Epigraphy in Athens (October 1982). It must be pointed out, however, that Plutarch in 822E otherwise discusses events from the classical period (concerning Lamachus and Phocion).

about." [57] One might suggest that Philip's tetrarchs were especially concerned with the management of perioikic territory, thus supplementing the preexistent Thessalian administration. [58] The catalogue of Philip's crimes in Thessaly compiled by Demosthenes is now complete. In every case, it seems that Demosthenes is referring to an action which, whatever its sinister character in reality, from the point of view of a pro-Philip propagandist fell under the heading of protection of the interests of the confederacy and of the *nomos* of the Thessalians. With this observation in mind, we can turn in conclusion to the epigram inscribed on the base of the statue of another member of Daochus' family, in this case his ancestor of the same name from the second half of the fifth century B.C. [59] In this autobiographical poem, the elder Daochus is made to say that he "ruled all Thessaly for twenty-seven years not by force but by *nomos*. Thessaly teemed with wealth and the fruits of a great peace."

The elder Daochus' career, as described in this honorific text set up in Philip's time or not long after, could be seen as a precedent for Philip's career in Thessaly (and for that of Alexander, as it turned out). [60] Daochus had "ruled" Thessaly for a long and continuous term of office which covered times of peace. Philip, too, "ruled" Thessaly for a long time, and after 346 B.C. during peacetime. Furthermore, the elder Daochus prided himself in his posthumous poem on his observance of *nomos*, the great concern of Philip as leader of the Thessalians. The choice of what to

---

[57] Theopompus, *FGrH* 115 F 209, echoes Demosthenes' terminology: Thrasydaeus (one of Philip's tetrarchs) was "tyrant over those of his own tribe."

[58] Since the story about Hermon cannot be dated, we lack even a clue as to whether the tetrarchs had special financial responsibilities before the time of Philip. If the story could be shown to belong to the history of Thessaly before Philip, one could surmise that, once again, Philip had exploited Thessalian tradition in making his own arrangements for the Thessalians.

[59] *SIG*[3] 274 VI.

[60] On this monument, see Tobias Dohrn, "Die Marmor-Standbilder des Daochos-Weihgeschenks in Delphi," *Antike Plastik* 8 (1968), pp. 33–53. Steven Lattimore, "The Chlamys of Daochus I," *AJA* 79 (1975), pp. 87–88, has suggested that the date of the monument might be as late as the end of the fourth century, but this seems unlikely. We hear nothing of the family of Daochus after the 330s.

emphasize in this inscription about the career of the fifth-century Daochus cannot be accidental. The Daochus of the fourth century who commissioned this inscribed monument was a partisan of Macedonian rule. It would be incredible if the propaganda about the confederacy which was expressed in the texts on his monument at Delphi, a meeting place for the Amphictyonic council with which Philip had been so concerned, did not coincide with Philip's public position on the nature of his role in Thessaly as the successor of the elder Daochus as "ruler" of the Thessalians. As Polyaenus says, Philip won over the Thessalians "not by arms."[61] The *nomos* of the Thessalians was Philip's weapon.[62] Wielding it deftly, he was able to create a system in professed imitation of an "ancestral constitution" which permitted him to retain effective control of Thessaly through local Thessalian officals even in times of peace, when the Thessalian leader's office had traditionally been weak.[63] As an absentee leader after 346 B.C. (except perhaps for short visits), Philip needed this sort of system to keep watch on the unreliable Thessalians with their history of factional strife.

On the level of moral evaluation, where the form of events matters less than their content, the modern historian may well wish to agree with Demosthenes that the Thessalians were in reality the slaves of the Macedonian king, but the form of that slavery matters if one is to answer other questions. If taken too literally, eloquent appraisals such as Griffith's that the developments of 344–342 B.C. "drew a blanket of darkness and tyranny over Thessaly, effectively and finally stifling freedom" are apt to mislead the unwary.[64] This has certainly been the case with Thessaly, ever since the time of Demosthenes. For this reason, it

[61] *Strat.* 4.2.19.

[62] He probably used this approach in Macedonia whenever possible; the societies were similar, as we have seen. Cf. Arrian 4.11.6, where Callisthenes is made to say that Alexander's forebears had ruled the Macedonians by *nomos*, not by force.

[63] See H. D. Westlake, *Thessaly in the Fourth Century B.C.* (London, 1935), p. 23, on earlier views that Jason of Pherae fabricated a Thessalian "ancestral constitution."

[64] *HM*, p. 535.

was necessary to discuss the evidence in detail and separated along chronological lines.   It must be clear that Philip's policy of public respect for Thessalian *nomos* is the background against which the question of the fate of Thessalian coinage must be seen.   All indications are that Philip's policy remained unchanged in the years after 342 B.C.   The Thessalians retained their treasured primacy in the Delphic Amphictyony, and they were included as independent members of Philip's Hellenic League, formed in the aftermath of the king's victory over the Greeks at Chaeronea in 338 B.C.[65]   That this situation was not entirely a sham is shown by the Athenian embassies which came to Thessaly in the period before Chaeronea to urge resistance to Philip.[66]   If Thessaly had been a province politically incorporated into the Macedonian kingdom, there would have been neither opportunity nor reason for such missions.   After Chaeronea, the "freedom and autonomy" of the members of the Hellenic League were guaranteed.[67]   For our purposes, this is an important point no matter how insincere the guarantee.   In Thessaly, *nomos* remained king of all.   With the election of Philip as their leader, the Thessalians had found a solution to their current problems which could be reconciled with tradition of long standing.   In a time of severe factional strife, they had settled on a third party to serve in a sense as "mediating magistrate" at the head of an army strong enough to quell any rebellion or tyranny.   They had looked to a foreign king for help, an effective if risky business, as they knew from experience.   But this was a foreigner in the mold of Pelopidas, with the added advantage of some dim claim to Thessalian kinship in his mythological ancestry and in his marriages (if that is the right word) to two Thessalian women.[68] He obtained his rule by the consent of the strongest (or at least the most successful) of

[65] *SVA* III, no. 403, b, line 2. (I accept the common view that this text refers to the members of the Hellenic League, the so-called League of Corinth.)

[66] Griffith, *HM*, p. 537.

[67] [Demosthenes] 17.8.

[68] Satyrus F 5, *FHG* 3.161 (Athenaeus 13.557). On the question of his marriages, see A. M. Prestianni Giallombardo, " 'Diritto' matrimoniale, ereditario e dinastico nella Macedonia di Filippo II," *RSA* 6–7 (1976–1977), pp. 81–110.

those who mattered, the aristocrats with ambitions. His changes in tetradic and perioikic administration were, it was said, attempts to get back to the way things were in the good old days of the "ancestral constitution." He kept his hands off civic affairs unless it was a question of danger to the confederacy from tyranny or the like.

These are the arguments, or, rather, rationalizations, the Thessalians could make to themselves in order to stifle feelings of uneasiness and dread about their prospects for the long run as followers of a dynamic, ruthless, and militarily powerful Macedonian king. Such arguments, which reflected the propaganda of Philip, could never obscure the plain truth. Philip controlled Thessaly. What must be emphasized is how he controlled it. Philip's consistent policy was to govern Thessaly "in accordance with *nomos.*" His changes and innovations were such that they could be explained as reversions to ancient precedent. Philip did not make Thessaly into a province of his Macedonian kingdom. This fact bears directly on the hypothesis that Philip imposed the use of Macedonian coins on the Thessalians. Since he exercised power in Thessaly in the guise of a traditional leader of the confederacy, he had an incentive to leave to the cities matters of purely civic concern such as coinage. That was the Thessalian tradition. They had never had a federal coinage which won universal acceptance or lasted for more than a brief period. The traditional Thessalian leader paid no attention to autonomous coinage in Thessaly, and there is absolutely no reason to think that Philip behaved differently.[69] In fact, he had a vested interest in the financial *status quo*. As leader of the confederacy, he received revenue from Thessaly. To have suppressed the local production of coinage could only have interfered with the flow of this money. Fees and taxes would have to be collected in foreign coinage, charges for exchanges between different coinages would have to be paid constantly, and so on. The effect could only have been to produce confusion and even

---

[69] There were no external models, for example, which would have influenced Philip to suppress Greek coinages. See chapter 5 and appendix 2 for discussion of two such models, those of Persia and of Boeotia.

chaos. A shrewd judge of the power of money and of its utility to himself, Philip had every reason to maximize his revenues from all quarters. Closing the mints of Thessaly was not going to help him do that.

The historical evidence confirms the conclusions already drawn from the numismatic evidence. Philip II cannot have suppressed the autonomous coinage of Thessaly as a matter of policy, and there is no reason to think that his political or financial plans could have had that effect even indirectly. In fact, Philip had good reasons to keep matters just as he found them in Thessaly so far as coinage was concerned. We must keep the precedent of Philip's policy clearly in mind as the necessary background to an investigation of the question of what effect Alexander and his successors might have had on Thessalian coinage.

FIVE. THESSALY AND ALEXANDER THE GREAT

When Philip II was murdered in 336 B.C. before he could embark on his campaign against Persia, his son Alexander III moved quickly to assume his father's power and the offices through which it was exercised. Most important, of course, Alexander was acknowledged as king in Macedonia, but he also took care to establish relations with the Greeks which exactly perpetuated those of Philip. This was not a simple matter because many of the Greeks decided to try to deny to the son the leadership they had conceded to the father. But the Thessalians were not among this group. They elected Alexander as the leader of their confederacy in the tradition of passing on the office in the same family when circumstances demanded it, and they voted Alexander the same revenues Philip had received.[1] The new leader of the confederacy had been careful to point out his kinship with the Thessalians through their common ancestor Heracles, an indication that the same concern for Thessalian *nomos* which Philip had affected carried over as Alexander's "Thessalian policy."[2] Since Alexander had been chosen by consent, from the constitutional point of view nothing had changed in Thessaly except the name of the leader of the confederacy. Just as in Philip's time, the *nomos* of the Thessalians was the guiding principle which governed relations between the Thessalians and the Macedonian king.

[1] Justin 11.3.1–2.

[2] Diodorus 17.4.1. On Alexander and Heracles, see P. A. Brunt, *Arrian*, vol. 1, pp. 464–466. For a possible connection between Alexander and the Thessalians based on their relationships to Aeacus, see Marta Sordi, "Aspetti della propaganda tessala a Delfi," in *La Thessalie, Actes de la Table-Ronde 21–24 Juillet 1975 Lyon*, ed. B. Helly (Lyon, 1979), pp. 162–163.

As proof of their loyalty, the Thessalians even voted to march with their leader against Athens to force that city to recognize Alexander as *hegemon* of the Hellenic League which Philip had established after the battle of Chaeronea in 338.[3] As it turned out, Athens and the other recalcitrant Greek states caved in without a struggle before Alexander's persuasive words and powerful army. Alexander was duly recognized by the *synedrion* of the Hellenic League at Corinth as Philip's successor in the post of *hegemon*, and he was given command against Persia.[4] Since the Thessalians were members of this Hellenic League, they enjoyed its guarantee that they could keep whatever constitution they had when they joined the organization.[5] For what it was worth (not much, of course, if Alexander changed his mind), this guarantee confirmed that government in Thessaly would continue along the lines worked out under Philip. In fact, there is no indication that any changes were made in the structure of government in Thessaly during Alexander's reign (336–323 B.C.).[6] Marta Sordi, who believes that Philip II expelled the Aleuads from Larissa in the Simus episode already described, suggests that Alexander restored them to power at Larissa. By doing the Aleuads this favor, Sordi would argue, Alexander gained their willing collaboration in the promotion of his own

[3] Aeschines 3.161. The Thessalians also appear to have taken part in Alexander's attack on Thebes in 335. See Quintilian 5.10.111, with the comments of Brigitte Gullath, *Untersuchungen zur Geschichte Boiotiens in der Zeit Alexanders und der Diadochen* (Frankfurt, 1982), p. 63.

[4] For a recent discussion, see A. B. Bosworth, *A Historical Commentary on Arrian's History of Alexander. Volume I* (Oxford, 1980), pp. 46–51. On *IG* II² 329, see A. J. Heisserer, *Alexander the Great and the Greeks. The Epigraphic Evidence* (Norman, Okla., 1980), pp. 3–26.

[5] See *SVA* III, no. 403, b, line 2; [Demosthenes] 17.8. In an unhistoric piece of rhetoric from the Roman imperial period, Philostratus, *Heroicus* 326 = *Opera*, vol. II, ed. Kayser (Leipzig, 1871), p. 209, line 29 to p. 210, line 7, says that Alexander "enslaved" all of Thessaly except for Phthiotic Achaea, which he freed in honor of Achilles.

[6] None of the interference in Greek governments by Alexander reported in [Demosthenes] 17 pertains to Thessaly, nor do the other sources record any.

interests in Thessaly.[7] Whether or not the Aleuads, or their city
for that matter, had actually lost the favor of Philip, if Sordi is
right that Alexander established good relations with the Aleuads,
this is a clear hint that the young king, like his father, saw the
utility in a connection with his "relatives" (through their common ancestor Heracles). It made good sense to exploit his pre-
tended relationship to those Larissaeans whose maneuvers had
originally made it possible for a Macedonian king to seek his
own advantage under the useful cover of Thessalian *nomos*.

In 334 B.C. Alexander left Europe for Asia, never to return.
At first, the Thessalians seem to have taken the continued
absence of their leader with loyal good cheer, especially since a
large number of Thessalian cavalry were serving with distinction
and earning rich rewards in Alexander's army as it swept the
Persians before it year after year.[8] Despite the urgings of Demosthenes, the Thessalians refused to join the revolt against
Alexander's authority led by the Spartans in 331 B.C.[9] When
Alexander sent home his Greek troops in 330 B.C., the Thessalians brought home on top of their pay a bonus of two thousand
talents as a reward for their meritorious service. (Some stayed on
in Alexander's army as "mercenaries.")[10] These honored
veterans, safely home with their purses full, can have had no
complaints against their leader, and their compatriots at home
apparently felt the same, or at least realized that they should pre-
tend to do so. From this point on in the reign of Alexander, the
sources are silent about relations between the Thessalians and
their nominal leader far away in Asia. Perhaps the Thessalians
thought of him, but Alexander's thoughts were directed elsewhere. Nevertheless, there is no indication that, formally speaking, things had changed. Alexander was still the formal leader of
the confederacy, but the need for his presence in Thessaly was
essentially nil because Thessaly was at peace. Traditionally, the

[7] *LT*, pp. 303–304.

[8] For the Thessalians at the Granicus, see Arrian 1.14.3; Thessalian reinforce-
ments, 1.29.4; Thessalians at Issus, 2.8.9, 2.9.1, 2.11.2–3. They obtained the
largest share of the great plunder seized at Damascus (Plutarch, *Alexander* 24.1).

[9] Aeschines 3.167.

[10] Arrian 3.19.5–7, 3.25.4, 3.29.5; Curtius 6.6.35.

leader of the confederacy had little if anything to do in such periods, and the Thessalians could get along without Alexander. At times Alexander probably felt that same way about all the Greeks, but he had not forgotten about them upon his return to Mesopotamia from India in 324 B.C. When he sent back to Macedonia those soldiers who were unfit for further service, according to Arrian, the king sent with them his general Craterus with instructions "to assume charge of Macedonia, Thrace, the Thessalians and the freedom of the Greeks."[11] It is difficult to tell what these rather vague instructions meant on a constitutional level (on the assumption that Alexander himself conceived of the situation in those terms, which is far from required), but the passage does not imply that any new arrangement for Thessaly was envisioned. Alexander was simply telling Craterus to look out for the king's interests as monarch in the north, as leader of the Thessalian confederacy and, finally, as *hegemon* of the Hellenic League.[12] If nothing had changed for the Greeks, as the expression "the freedom of the Greeks" showed it had not, then nothing had changed for the confederacy. Thessaly was not being transformed into a Macedonian province.

J. R. Ellis nevertheless argues that about 328/7 B.C. Alexander "instructed Antipatros to terminate all coinages under Macedonian control that were not the king's own."[13] These coinages were, on Ellis' view, the gold and silver issues of Philippi in Thrace, the posthumous Philip issues from Macedonian mints, and the silver of Larissa. The last was "to be replaced shortly in Thessaly by regal silver." Especially important here are Ellis'

---

[11] Arrian 7.12.4.

[12] In his speech at Arrian 7.9.4, Alexander is made to say that Philip made the Macedonians "archons" of the Thessalians. This only means that the Macedonians were "rulers" of the Thessalians because their king served as the leader of the Thessalian confederacy. Hermann Bengtson, *Die Strategie in der hellenistischen Zeit*, vol. 1 (Munich, 1937, Münchener Beiträge zur Papyrusforschung und antiken Rechtsgeschichte 26), pp. 27, 38–45, is overly legalistic. The presence of Medius of Larissa in Alexander's entourage afforded the king at least nominal contact with his Thessalian constituency. On Medius, see H. Berve, *Das Alexanderreich auf prosopographischer Grundlage* (Munich, 1926), no. 521.

[13] *Philip II and Macedonian Imperialism* (London, 1976), p. 238, in his appendix "Coinage under Philip and Alexander: Some Observations," pp. 235–239.

speculations about Alexander's reasons for ordering such a dramatic change in the traditional monetary system of Thessaly. He believes that by this date Alexander had established a secure enough power-base of his own that he could "quite openly cut most of the ties inherited from Philip." Moreover, his victories in the East allowed Alexander to establish himself "in his own right as King of Persia." The first of these points is debatable; the second is certainly true. But their relevance to the cessation of autonomous coinage in Thessaly is illusory.

First, whatever one thinks of the idea that by 328 B.C. Alexander "could cut his ties inherited from Philip," there is absolutely no evidence that Alexander cut the tie inherited from Philip of the leadership of the Thessalian confederacy. Why should he have cut it? The arrangement had worked well and presumably helped to finance Antipater's guardianship of Alexander's interests in Greece by the payment of the revenues which the Thessalians had been turning over to their Macedonian leader ever since the late 350s. Antipater could use the money, as Alexander's shipments of cash to him prove. [14] With the greater part of the very effective Thessalian cavalry now home after their release from service in Asia in 330 B.C., there was nothing to be gained and, perhaps, serious trouble to be expected from any change in the long-standing arrangement between the Thessalian confederacy and the Macedonian crown. Does it really make sense to think that Alexander, while busily engaged at the end of the earth in organizing Sogdiana in the winter of 328/7 B.C., gave any thought to the coinage of Larissa or of Philippi or of any other state in Greece so far away?

Alexander's position as King of Persia certainly had nothing to do with the coinage of Thessaly. He did not rule the Thessalians in his capacity as the successor of Darius. But perhaps, on Ellis' view, the acquisition of the Persian throne should be regarded as a stimulus to the kind of absolutist thinking that would require the elimination of all coinages except royal in all areas under Macedonian control. Again, the facts of the matter point to a different conclusion. The Great King of Persia had

---

[14] For example, Arrian 1.24.2, 2.20.5, 3.16.10; Curtius 3.1.1.

never sought to institute a uniform system of currency in the parts of his empire which customarily used coins in financial transactions (i.e., primarily the Hellenized areas of Asia Minor). His western satraps coined in silver, as did numerous Greek cities under his control.[15] The Persian King did reserve for himself the privilege of coining in gold, but that restriction reflected the royal view that the best of everything (in this case, the best of the precious metals) belonged to the King. In fact, the Greek city of Lampsacus in western Asia Minor even issued gold staters with its own types at least intermittently over a period of about sixty years in the fourth century while under Persian control.[16] Evidently it suited the King's purposes to have a non-Persian type of gold coinage available for diplomatic bribery in Greece, and for that reason he was content to have a nonroyal mint coin in gold.[17] The King did not insist on an exclusive right of coinage as an expression of sovereignty.

This situation helps us to understand a famous incident from the reign of Darius (521–486 B.C.) which Herodotus relates.[18] The story is that a certain Aryandes while satrap of Egypt heard that Darius had issued a coinage of the purest gold because, the story goes, Darius wanted to perpetuate his memory by doing something which no other King had done. Wishing to imitate his superior, Aryandes minted a coinage of equally pure silver. When Darius heard this news, he had Aryandes executed on "another charge" that he was a rebel. This accusation of treason had nothing to do with silver coinage because satraps demonstrably were allowed to issue such coins. The King had no cause to dismiss a satrap for minting silver coins. If Darius actually wanted to get rid of a satrap because he resented the satrap's

---

[15] Kraay, *ACGC*, pp. 31–34, 248, 251, 268–311. Cf. S. Hornblower, *Mausolus* (Oxford, 1982), pp. 154–155. For further discussion of coinage in the Persian empire, see M. A. Dandamayev, "Politische und wirtschaftliche Geschichte," in *Beiträge zur Achämenidengeschichte*, ed. Gerold Walser (Wiesbaden, 1972, Historia Einzelschriften 18), pp. 45–48 ("Das Geldwesen"); Richard N. Frye, *The History of Ancient Iran* (Munich, 1984), pp. 116–117.

[16] Kraay, *ACGC*, pp. 248, 251, 259–260. For gold mines near Lampsacus which were active in the period of Alexander, see Pliny 37.193.

[17] See Kraay, *ACGC*, p. 251, with reference to *GHI* 160.

[18] 4.166.

presumption in trying to emulate the prestige of the Great King by, for example, issuing a coinage of legendary purity, the issue was rivalry with the King, not the right of coinage. Herodotus' own comments make the moral clear. [19] The story of Aryandes in no way establishes a connection between Persian royal sovereignty and the right of coinage.

Any assumption that the King of Persia felt such a connection to exist would have to be based on a misconception of what money represented in Persia. From the Persepolis Treasury Tablets of the first half of the fifth century B.C. we gain a clear impression of the role of money in the King's world. These records refer to payments made to workmen in silver in lieu of foodstuffs. The value of the money is clearly indicated. For example, one finds on the tablets phrases such as "sheep and wine serve as the equivalent (of the money): 1 sheep for 3 shekels, 1 jar (of wine) for 1 shekel."[20] On the tablets, this phrase is followed by a compound word that has been taken to mean "fixed by edict," which the editor explains as "(at the rate) fixed

[19] He introduces the story (4.166.1) with the comment that Aryandes was killed because he tried to equal Darius. He concludes (4.166.2) that Aryandes "got what he deserved for his imitation of the King."

[20] George G. Cameron, *Persepolis Treasury Tablets* (Chicago, 1948), pp. 2, 83. (The translation "serve as" appears on the latter page; "serve for" appears on p. 2.) R. T. Hallock, "A New Look at the Persepolis Treasury Tablets," *JNES* 19 (1960), p. 91, suggests "counterpart" as a translation instead of "equivalent." It is not clear from the tablets whether the silver being paid out was in coin or in shekel weights of uncoined silver. One reason to favor the latter alternative is that Persian *sigloi* are normally found in the Aegean area, not in the Persian heartland, and may have been intended primarily for use in that area. It is striking, however, that no reference to silver as payment occurs in the Persepolis Fortification Tablets, which record payments from the period of the late fifth and early fourth centuries B.C. immediately before the period covered by the Treasury Tablets. These payments are exclusively in kind. Payment in silver was apparently an unfamiliar innovation at the time of the Treasury Tablets. Since payment by weights of uncoined silver was not at all a new phenomenon in the East by the time of the Treasury Tablets, the innovative nature of the use of silver recorded in these tablets would be easier to understand if the silver being used was coined. That form of silver was something new and unfamiliar in Persia, whose use would have needed the kind of careful reference found in the Treasury Tablets. For a discussion of both kinds of tablets, see J. M. Cook, *The Persian Empire* (New York, 1983), pp. 85–90.

by edict."[21] In the grain tablets, the amount of the silver being paid varies, most likely as a reflection of the fluctuating price of grain in a period of scarcity.[22] From this evidence, it would be fair to conclude that, at least in the period when the tablets were inscribed, the value of Persian money was officially established in relation to commodities. The mention of an edict to fix the rate of exchange between money and commodities shows that the authority behind this decision was that of the King, especially since the tablets concern royal projects in Persis, the Achaemenid homeland.[23]

In other words, the Persian King (no doubt through a functionary) established the value of his money in terms of commodities so that he could use it to pay people who were accustomed to receiving their wages in kind. Money, whether in the form of coins or of weighed pieces of metal, was a royal convenience to be produced when necessary. The King only had as many coins minted as he needed to pay expenses, preferring to keep his vast wealth in the form of bullion.[24] One might argue that this situation was restricted to the earlier fifth century, when coinage was still being introduced as something new in the Persian Empire, and that by the later fourth century currency was so familiar that there was no need to tariff money in this way. But Daniel Schlumberger's analysis of monetary circulation in the Persian Empire shows that even at this date silver coinage was not the normal means of exchange in the vast majority of the territory of the King.[25] Under such circumstances, it makes sense to think that even as late as the 330s the Achaemenid King still had to decide the value of his money *vis-à-vis* commodities. They remained the most common standard of payment in the Persian

[21] Cameron, *Persepolis Treasury Tablets*, pp. 105–108 (tablet 13).

[22] Hallock, *JNES* 19 (1960), p. 94.

[23] Cameron, *Persepolis Treasury Tablets*, pp. 11–17.

[24] Polycritus in Strabo 15.3.21 (C735), emended to Polycleitus (*FGrH* 128 F 3a). Cf. Herodotus 3.96.

[25] *L'argent grec dans l'empire achéménide* (Paris, 1953), a separate publication of pp. 1–64 of Raoul Curiel and Daniel Schlumberger, *Trésors monétaires d'Afghanistan* (Paris, 1953, Mémoires de la délégation archéologique française en Afghanistan 14).

Empire. [26] I have not found any evidence to prove that Alexander set the tariff for his coinage in the East in terms of commodities, but there is no inherent reason why he should not have done so as the successor of the Persian King. He administered his Eastern kingdom on the Achaemenid model, and his subjects there still needed to know official prices so they could render their tribute in kind and compute their wages. [27]

With these points in mind, we will find it easy to accept that the Great King made no attempt to impose any kind of uniform monetary circulation on the part of his empire which was accustomed to use coinage on a regular basis. Royal Persian coinage, if that is the right term for satrapal silver, circulated together with the civic coinages of the Greek cities of Asia Minor. The impression one forms from the evidence for the minting and circulation of coins in the Persian Empire is that the Persian King cared not a whit about the nature of the monetary system in use among his Greek subjects. He wanted his tribute to be paid, and he did not want any rivals to his preeminent status, but he was not concerned with the details of how his subjects conducted their financial transactions. If they preferred a diverse circulation of different coinages supplied by the products of their own and of Persian mints, that was fine with him. Just let them pay on time and in full. This was the tradition Alexander took over when he ascended the Persian throne. There was nothing in his role as Darius' successor to induce Alexander to terminate any coinages in Greece.

The idea that Alexander's new status as the King of Persia led him by 328/7 B.C. to order the suppression of autonomous coinages even in the Greek homeland has roots that are hard to uncover. In Ellis' case, the idea is simply asserted without discussion. One can suspect that the implicit justification for this idea is analogy with the idea that Alexander, insisting on his rights as a king, demanded the partial or total abandonment of

[26] On payment in kind (usually foodstuffs), see Cook, *Persian Empire*, pp. 70, 86, 140. See appendix 3 on the possible relevance of this evidence for the interpretation of the remarks on coinage in the Aristotelian *Oeconomica*.

[27] On Alexander's administration, see E. Badian, "The Administration of the Empire," *Greece and Rome* 12 (1965), pp. 166–182.

local coin types by the Greek cities in Asia.[28] To my knowledge, this idea and its implications for the history of Alexander's reign have been discussed in detail recently only by A. R. Bellinger in his comprehensive treatment of Alexander's general monetary policy.[29] Since subsequent opinions depend implicitly or explicitly on Bellinger's discussion, it is worth summarizing his views on this important issue. First, when in 334 and 333 B.C. Alexander's conquests in Asia Minor gave him the opportunity to force a uniform currency on the cities of the region, he did not do so. Just as in Greece, imperial coinage did not replace local coinage in Asia Minor. To quote Bellinger:

Alexander came into no vacuum of currency when he brought his money to Asia. Schlumberger's statement of his purpose is very good. "What Alexander intended to do is clear. He intended to give to an empire that did not have it a silver coinage universally acceptable as money, and in so doing, to extend the use of silver money as such (and not as bullion) to the entire territory of that empire." The intention was never entirely carried out, partly, of course, because of the shortness of his life, but, aside from that, it is not likely that the plan itself was ever so complete as to contemplate the retirement of the great variety of silver that was already in use. Whatever the theory, the fact was that there was a supplementary coinage from the cities. [30]

Since Bellinger introduces Schlumberger's view as authoritative, we must consider it fully here. Schlumberger goes on to argue that in the territory of the old Persian Empire Alexander

[28] For this idea in recent scholarship, see, for example, Paul Goukowsky, ed. with Ed. Will, *Le Monde grec et l'orient. Tome 2. Le IV e siècle et l'époque hellénistique* (Paris, 1975), p. 317; W. E. Higgins, "Aspects of Alexander's Imperial Administration: Some Modern Methods and Views Reviewed," *Athenaeum* 58 (1980), p. 138.

[29] *Essays*, "The King's Finances," pp. 35–80. For references to other views, see Schlumberger, *L'Argent grec*, pp. 27–28; Jakob Seibert, *Alexander der Grosse* (Darmstadt, 1972), pp. 42–51. A survey of work on the coinage of Alexander is presented by Georges Le Rider, "Numismatique grecque," in *Annuaire 1968–1969. Ecole pratique des Hautes Etudes. IV e section. Sciences historiques et philologiques* (Paris, 1969), pp. 173–187; *Annuaire 1969–1970* (Paris, 1970), pp. 255–269; *Annuaire 1970–1971* (Paris, 1971), pp. 241–262.

[30] *Essays*, pp. 40–41. The reference is to Schlumberger, *L'Argent grec*, pp. 27–28.

planned to retire the coinage in circulation in favor of his new, imperial coinage on the Attic standard, but he acknowledged that the hoards show almost no signs of any such policy ("les effets du retrait ne se discernent guère"). In the light of this evidence, it seems wholly unnecessary to assume that Alexander had any policy to impose a uniform monetary circulation even in the East outside Asia Minor (which Schlumberger excludes from the "empire" at this point to make his argument). It would be hard enough to assume that Alexander's purpose was only to introduce money as a regular form of payment and exchange into the vast regions of the Persian Empire which did not use coinage but, rather, relied on barter. It might be possible to regard this as a "civilizing" measure intended to bring a more enlightened form of commercial exchange and financial transactions to backward regions, but even this sort of scheme seems wildly impractical. Would Alexander really expect peasants in remote reaches of his empire to start using his silver coins? [31] It is much more likely that Alexander had his own convenience and that of his men in mind when he made arrangements for the production and distribution of his coinage. He had to pay his troops in coin, and their supplies could be much more easily acquired (from the Macedonian point of view) when they could be purchased with currency rather than bartered for (when supplies were to be paid for and not just appropriated). [32] Furthermore, the settlers in Alexander's new colonies in the East were accustomed to using coins, and in their new "Hellenic" foundations they could be expected to stick to their old, familiar habits. [33] The limited

[31] For a general discussion of the restricted effect of a monetary economy on the way of life of peasants, see T. F. Carney, *The Economies of Antiquity: Controls, Gifts and Trade* (Lawrence, Kans., 1973), pp. 100 – 103.

[32] D. W. Engels, *Alexander the Great and the Logistics of the Macedonian Army* (Berkeley, 1978), p. 41, n. 82, categorizes the ways in which Alexander obtained supplies: through purchases, requisitions, and gifts.

[33] Diodorus, 18.7.1, comments on the longing Alexander's settlers in the East had for the Hellenic way of life. On the discovery of a Greek settlement in Afghanistan, see D. Schlumberger and P. Bernard, "Aï Khanoum," *BCH* 89 (1965), pp. 590 – 657. On the coins found there, see Georges Le Rider, "Les monnaies," in *Fouilles d'Aï Khanoum I. Campagnes de 1965, 1966, 1967, 1968,* ed. Paul Bernard (Paris, 1973, Mémoires de la délégation archéologique française en Afghanistan 21), pp. 203 – 205. On hoards found there, see R. Audoin

spread of Alexander's coinage throughout the territory of the Persian Empire was an inevitable, but indirect, consequence of his military and political actions.

Nevertheless, Bellinger (presumably under Schlumberger's influence) states that Alexander's establishment of royal mints in the East in the years 333 to 330 B.C. "had as its purpose the wholesale replacement of the Persian royal coinage by the Macedonian imperial." [34] Since Alexander claimed to be "King of Asia" (i.e., Darius' replacement as Persian King) after the battle of Issus in November 333, [35] it is certainly reasonable to believe that he might have planned to take over the traditional coinage of the Persian King for his own use, especially in areas where it was the only familiar coinage. But there is no evidence that Alexander planned to institute a new policy of monetary uniformity in departure from Persian royal practice. [36]

Bellinger himself points to another explanation. He realizes that Alexander required a large amount of money for his grandiose campaign to the far reaches of the world in the East, and according to Bellinger, the royal mints of Cilicia and Syria were intended to produce that money. [37] Alexander had conquered these foreign, non-Greek cities, and if their local issues of coinage had to be put aside to produce for Alexander, that was an

---

and P. Bernard, "Trésor de monnaies indiennes et indo-grecques d'Aï Khanoum (Afghanistan)," *RN* 1973, pp. 238–289; *RN* 1974, pp. 7–41; C. Y. Petitot-Biehler and P. Bernard, "Trésor de monnaies grecques et gréco-bactriennes trouvé à Aï Khanoum (Afghanistan)," *RN* 1975, pp. 23–69. On the nature of these settlements, see E. Badian, *Greece and Rome* 12 (1965), pp. 177–178.

[34] *Essays*, p. 50.

[35] Arrian 2.14.8–9. See Bosworth, *Commentary*, pp. 232–233. Alexander confirmed the autonomy of the Greeks at the same time (Plutarch, *Alexander* 34.1–2).

[36] On the continuation of local coinage by some Phoenician kings during Alexander's reign, see Fergus Millar, "The Phoenician Cities: A Case-Study of Hellenisation," *Proceedings of the Cambridge Philological Society* 209 (1983), p. 61. Cf. M. J. Price, "On Attributing Alexanders—Some Cautionary Tales," in *Greek Numismatics and Archaeology. Essays in Honor of Margaret Thompson*, ed. O. Mørkholm and N. M. Waggoner (Wetteren, 1979), pp. 241–250.

[37] *Essays*, pp. 54–55. One severe difficulty with Bellinger's formulation of this idea, however, is that he envisions Alexander as having to convey to India enough coin to pay all his troops all the time. That was impossible.

obligation owed the king from his subjects. Bellinger finishes his analysis of Alexander's policy by observing that after the battle of Gaugamela in 331 Alexander produced new issues in the East which augmented the preexisting monetary confusion by adding yet more issues to those already in circulation. Bellinger's suggestion is that after the elimination of the Achaemenid royal house in 330 Alexander had less need to assert his identity as king in Asia and therefore decided to experiment with another approach to the monetary situation in the territory under his control.[38] He also suggests, however, that Alexander opened mints in Asia Minor for gold and for silver in small denominations after 331 as "a belated provision of uniformity in place of the pre-existing confusion."[39] Bellinger summarizes his own views as follows:

Before Gaugamela the empire had two monetary zones: Greece and Asia Minor where the imperial types joined or dominated but did not extinguish the local currencies; Cilicia and Syria where the local currencies were replaced by the imperial. To this period belongs the fiscal purpose of Alexander, as defined by Schlumberger, of eventually achieving monetary uniformity for the empire as a whole. But after Gaugamela a third zone is added, of Mesopotamia and the East in which the pre-existing confusion is not merely tolerated but augmented by the emissions of the conqueror. There is concession to the Persian tradition, as proved by the double darics; concession to the satrapal tradition as proved by the imitation owls. Whether temporarily or permanently the ideal of uniformity is laid aside.[40]

On Bellinger's own evidence, the situation under Alexander is confused and confusing. It would be easier to make sense of the evidence if one laid aside the apparently *a priori* assumption that Alexander ever aimed at establishing monetary uniformity, least of all in Asia Minor, where local Greek coinages were a strong tradition. His decisions on where and when to coin are better understood as *ad hoc* responses to his changing needs as

---

[38] *Essays*, pp. 78–79.

[39] *Essays*, p. 58.

[40] *Essays*, pp. 77–78. See Badian, *Greece and Rome* 12 (1965), pp. 173–175, against Bellinger's assertion that the satraps in Mesopotamia continued to coin under Alexander's rule.

commander and administrator. For example, even as Alexander went farther and farther away from Macedonia and its royal mints, he still needed coins to pay his troops and his expenses. Since these coins were meant above all for Macedonian eyes and Macedonian purses, it was natural and indeed necessary that they carry Alexander's name and types. It was a logistical requirement to have at least some royal mints in the East. If Alexander's coins carried any message to the local inhabitants, who could not read the Greek legends on his coins, that was incidental to the purpose of the king in minting them.[41] Alexander had nothing to gain by trying to accomplish the impossible goal of providing a standard imperial coinage and requiring its usage to the exclusion of all other coinages. The numismatic evidence continues to accumulate to show that this was not his policy.[42]

Nevertheless, even Colin Kraay in his standard work on Greek coinage assumes that the numismatic evidence conforms to the idea that Alexander suppressed Greek coinages in Asia Minor: "The conquest by Alexander the Great of the western satrapies of the Persian Empire was followed by the introduction of uniform regal issues in silver on the Attic standard at a

---

[41] Bellinger, *Essays*, p. 55, regards Alexander's use of his own name and types on coins produced in the East as "one of the most effective kinds of manifesto known to antiquity." Along similar lines, W. B. Kaiser, "Alexander and Mytilene," *Münzen und Medaillensammler Berichte aus allen Gebieten der Geld-, Münzen- und Medaillenkunde* 55 (Freiburg, 1970), pp. 795–800, proposes that the electrum hektai of Mytilene carried the news to the Aegean world that Alexander was the son of Zeus Ammon. M. H. Crawford, "Roman Imperial Coin Types and the Formation of Public Opinion," in *Studies in Numismatic Method Presented to Philip Grierson*, ed. C.N.L. Brooke, B.H.I.H. Stewart, J. G. Pollard, and T. R. Volk (Cambridge, 1983), pp. 47–64, argues that the programmatic aspect of coin types had little effect in the Greco-Roman world, especially below the level of what he calls "the educated classes."

[42] See Otto Mørkholm, "The Hellenistic Period. Greece to India," in *A Survey of Numismatic Research 1972–1977*, ed. R. Carson, P. Berghaus, and N. Lowick (Berne, 1979), p. 66. Cf. the recent assessment of Alexander's fiscal policy by Richard Frye, *The History of Ancient Iran* (Munich, 1984), pp. 147–148: ". . . it is clear that at some time during his rule he decided to issue silver coins on the Attic standard for the empire, while at the same time to allow local coinage to continue."

number of mints in both Ionia and the Hellespontine area; between 330 and 325 most local issues in Asia Minor and the adjoining islands come to an end, except, it seems, at Rhodes, which was not occupied by Alexander or his lieutenants." [43] The unreliability of the implied historical interpretation (Alexander suppressed the Greek coinages of Asia Minor, except for that of Rhodes, in favor of his own royal issues) is patent. Rhodes surrendered to Alexander in 332 B.C. after having served as an important Persian collaborator and was occupied by a Macedonian garrison which was expelled only in 323. In addition, the government was changed from the traditional oligarchy to a democracy. [44] If Rhodes with its history of collaboration, its army of occupation, and its imposed constitution could go on coining under Alexander's reign, it makes no sense at all to think of a conscious policy of suppressing of Greek coinage in Asia Minor which had been introduced and enforced by Alexander.

It seems far more likely that the large-scale production of Alexander's coins in the mints of "free" cities of Asia Minor had the indirect effect of making the production of local types largely superfluous. So much money was being produced by Alexander's agents that the cities could close their mints if they wished, saving themselves the trouble of running a municipal operation. For many local mints, this was probably a decision imposed by the nature of the marketplace. People came to prefer the coinage of Alexander. [45] They could conveniently use

[43] *ACGC*, pp. 249–250. He does not cite the evidence for his view.

[44] Arrian 2.20.2; see Bosworth, *Commentary*, pp. 242–243; H. Hauben, "Rhodes, Alexander and the Diadochi from 333/332 to 304 B.C.," *Historia* 26 (1977), pp. 307–339; R. M. Berthold, "Fourth-Century Rhodes," *Historia* 29 (1980), pp. 45–49; *Rhodes in the Hellenistic Age* (Ithaca, 1984), pp. 33–36.

[45] This was the case with the production of electrum coinage in Asia Minor. See Friedrich Bodenstedt, *Phokäisches Elektron-Geld von 600–326 v. Chr. Studien zur Bedeutung und zu den Wandlungen einer antiken Goldwährung* (Mainz, 1976), p. 19. It is impossible to document the operation of a municipal mint in classical Greece. One suspects that a perhaps substantial capital outlay was required initially for the construction of a mint building, the purchase of slaves to mint bullion into coins, and so on. After these start-up expenses, the city probably expected to make a profit from a well-run mint, or at least not to run a deficit. Cf. Dittenberger, *OGIS*, no. 339 (Sestus, 2nd B.C., on bronze coinage). The closing of the local mint would not have been a financial boon to the city, but at

the Alexander types which were being put into circulation by the
garrison troops Alexander had left behind in the cities and by
others in the king's employ.[46] Alexander needed a steady production of coinage in the strategically crucial area of Asia Minor
to pay those important men who looked after his interests, and
this need can account for the installation of royal mints in the
region. There is no reason to think that they testify to any concern on Alexander's part for a more efficient monetary circulation, or to a megalomaniacal desire to impose a uniform currency
on the entire world. Speculation about possible plans to create a
universally accepted coinage as the sole currency of a uniform
world monetary system is not reason to believe that Alexander
ever told any Greek city it could no longer mint its own coins if
it wanted to and could afford the expense.[47] Alexander's coinage
may have supplanted local coinages in various places because his
royal issues were more desirable for the consumer, but supplantation is a far different historical phenomenon from forced suppression.

There is another point to consider. We cannot be certain
about the status of the cities of Asia Minor, although it is reasonable to think that they were originally members of the League of
Corinth.[48] No other League member is thought to have been

least it did eliminate the necessity for citizens to serve as supervisors of the
operation of the municipal mint, a liturgy which perhaps carried more burdens
than rewards.

[46] That is, garrisons such as the one in Aspendus and men such as Philox-
enus. According to Kraay, *ACGC*, p. 277, the silver coinage of Aspendus continued "through the fourth century." On Alexander's financial and political
arrangements in Asia Minor, see E. Badian, *Greece and Rome* 12 (1965), pp.
166 – 170, and "Alexander the Great and the Greeks of Asia," in *Ancient Societies
and Institutions: Studies Presented to Victor Ehrenberg on His 75th Birthday*
(Blackwell, Oxford, 1966), pp. 37 – 69.

[47] The notion that Alexander must have planned on a uniform world
currency has perhaps flourished because it would fit with the popular picture of
Alexander as an advocate of the "unity of mankind" or even of "Weltherr-
schaft." See Seibert, *Alexander der Grosse*, pp. 207 – 211, on these ideas.

[48] See Badian, *Greece and Rome* 12 (1965), p. 168, and *Ancient Society and Institutions: Studies . . . Ehrenberg*, pp. 37 – 69; A. J. Heisserer, *Alexander the Great
and the Greeks*, pp. 66, 84 – 85, 131 (arguing that some cities were already
enrolled by Philip's generals in 336 B.C.).

ordered by Alexander to stop coining, and the coinage of Corinth where a Macedonian garrison was in place certainly continued under Alexander.[49] Why, then, should Alexander's status *ca.* 328/7 B.C. induce him to suppress the autonomous coinage of one member of the League and not those of others? Larissa was no more under Macedonian control than was occupied Corinth. It is simply illogical to assume that the fate of Thessalian coinage was linked to the status of Alexander in Persia, or to any changes in the nature of the coinage being produced simultaneously in Macedonia. A theory such as Ellis' labors implicitly under the burden of the fallacious assumption that Thessaly became a Macedonian province. This is of course not to say that Alexander as leader of the Thessalian confederacy and of the League of Corinth would have considered it impossible to trespass on the autonomy and privileges of his allies if he saw any advantage to be gained by it. Individual outrages, such as the imposition and support of local tyrants in Greek cities, could be perpetrated without any second thoughts if these separate changes meant a better climate for stability and obedience.[50] But the selective suppression of autonomous Greek coinages could hardly have come under that heading. It might, however, be theoretically possible to argue that suppression in Thessaly was only part of a general and complete suppression of autonomous coinages throughout Greece in favor of royal Macedonian coinage. This sort of comprehensive disregard for the autonomy of the European Greeks would be comparable (though on a grander scale) in its implications for the relationship between Alexander and the Greeks to the edict from the end of the reign which ordered the return of the exiles to those cities from which they had been expelled.[51] But there is no evidence at all for even an attempt at a general suppression of Greek coinage in favor of Macedonian issues during the reign of Alexander.

The final difficulty with Ellis' reconstruction is that it depends

[49] See the discussion to follow in chapter 8.

[50] This is clear from [Demosthenes] 17.

[51] See E. Badian, "Harpalus," *JHS* 81 (1961), pp. 25–31; S. Jaschinski, *Alexander und Griechenland unter dem Eindruck der Flucht des Harpalos* (Bonn, 1981), pp. 62–92.

on the chronology worked out by Georges Le Rider for the coinages of Philip II (lifetime and posthumous) in his monumental study of this extensive body of material.[52] In short, Le Rider postulates that both Philip's gold and silver coinages continued to be minted after his death until *ca.* 328 B.C. For Ellis, then, this date represents the point at which Alexander decided to make significant changes in the coinage of Macedonia by eliminating further production of posthumous coinage in Philip's name so that the only Macedonian coinage would be his own coins, which (on this theory) the Macedonian royal mints had been producing along with posthumous issues of Philip up to now. If Alexander decided to make such changes in Macedonian coinage at this point, the argument goes, then he probably also decided to make significant changes in the Greek coinages under his control. For Thessaly, the change was the suppression of the coinage of Larissa, the last remaining autonomous coinage in the region.

This reconstruction cannot stand, however, because the chronology postulated by Le Rider for the posthumous issues of Philip is untenable.[53] On the contrary, there are strong arguments in favor of the idea that Philip's coinage continued for only a short time after his death in 336 and that the royal mints of Macedonia under Alexander produced Alexander's coins, not Philip's. The numismatic evidence cited by Ellis in support of his theory of a suppression of nonroyal coinages by Alexander in 328/7 B.C. vanishes upon close examination, just as did the historical evidence marshalled to make the same point. We are left with the impression that Alexander, like his father before him, left Thessalian coinage alone.

[52] *Le Monnayage d'argent et d'or de Philippe II frappé en Macédoine de 359 à 294* (Paris, 1977).

[53] An analysis of Le Rider's chronology is presented in appendix 4.

SIX. THESSALY AND THE SUCCESSORS
OF ALEXANDER

By 323, the good feelings produced in Thessaly by the return of the veterans from Alexander's army with their money and their exciting stories about their daring commander had dissipated, to judge from the Thessalian reaction after Alexander's death. At this point, it had been over a decade since the Thessalians at home in their own country had seen the elected leader of their confederacy. Following an Athenian lead (just what they had not done after the death of Philip), the Thessalians almost unanimously joined the Greek movement to destroy Macedonian control in Greece. The Athenians were in the lead because they had reason to fear imminent Macedonian action as a result of Alexander's decision to restore Greek exiles.[1] The Athenians were very seriously affected by the decision because they stood to lose their possession of the island of Samos, which they had taken over after capturing it and banishing its inhabitants. The Athenians simply could not take the chance that Alexander's successor might enforce the dead king's order, and their choice to rebel is easy to understand. The choice of the Thessalians is not so obvious. Tricca, Pharcadon, and Heraclea may have had an important group of men in exile for anti-Macedonian actions, and their return might have boded ill for those in the cities who

---

[1] Diodorus 17.109.1–2, 18.8.1–7; *SIG*[3] 312. On this complicated issue, see Jakob Seibert, *Alexander der Grosse* (Darmstadt, 1972), pp. 170–171; E. Badian, "A Comma in the History of Samos," *ZPE* 23 (1976), pp. 289–294; K. Rosen, "Der 'göttliche' Alexander, Athen und Samos," *Historia* 27 (1978), pp. 20–39; Jakob Seibert, *Die politischen Flüchtlinge und Verbannten in der griechischen Geschichte* (Darmstadt, 1979), vol. 1, pp. 158–162; S. Jaschinski, *Alexander und Griechenland unter dem Eindruck der Flucht des Harpalos* (Bonn, 1981), pp. 124–140.

had stepped in to benefit from their absence.[2] But we do not hear of any potential losses of property by the Thessalians to match the loss the Athenians faced, and perhaps the reasons for the Thessalian decision to rebel were not directly connected with the provisions of the edict on exiles but, rather, had to do with the history of political relations between Macedonia and Thessaly in the preceding thirty years.

First, the argument raised against Philip II long ago, that the Macedonian king in his capacity as leader of the Thessalian confederacy was receiving Thessalian revenues without using them on Thessalian affairs, had applied to Alexander with even greater force. As his father's successor at the head of the confederacy, Alexander had been receiving Thessalian funds from the time of his election in Philip's place. Although no source mentions the disposition of these funds once Alexander had left for Asia in 334 B.C., a good guess would be that Antipater continued to insist on their payment in Alexander's name throughout the king's reign despite the peaceful condition of Thessaly. If so, the dissatisfaction of the Thessalians at the time of Alexander's death would be easier to understand. They knew Antipater for the tough and unyielding character he was, and they probably suspected that he would still want their taxes even with Alexander dead. But Antipater himself had no legitimate claim at all to the leadership of the Thessalian confederacy because he was not related to Alexander. This fact is connected to the second reason for Thessalian feelings after the death of Alexander.

Since Alexander had left no legitimate heir behind in Macedonia and Philip III was absent in Asia (as would be Alexander IV), there was no one locally available whom Antipater could try to have installed as leader of the confederacy as a successor in the traditional Thessalian fashion which Alexander had exploited in succeeding Philip in this post. Both Philip and Alexander had come to Thessaly to be elected to the leadership of the

---

[2] Diodorus 18.56.5. We do not know when these men were exiled. It could even have been after 323. Griffith, *HM*, p. 286, assumes Pharcadon and Tricca had been destroyed by Philip II, but Pharcadon is mentioned at Livy 31.41.8. This could mean either that the town was not obliterated by Philip or that it had been rebuilt by the late third century B.C.

confederacy. Since these great men had been careful to respect the proper ritual for the election of a Thessalian leader, the Thessalians would have expected the same observance of Thessalian custom from the less prestigious leaders left after the death of Alexander. Form matters for those, like the Thessalians, to whom only form remains after their inferiority in power has been *de facto* institutionalized and the real ability to settle their own fate has been taken from them. Any action Antipater might take in Thessaly before a new Macedonian king was formally and properly installed as the leader of the Thessalian confederacy could only be construed as an attack on Thessalian *nomos*, and that was all the Thessalians had left to be proud of and to fight for. Antipater showed his intentions in this direction when he demanded the service of the Thessalian cavalry in his army marshalled to put down the rebellion of the Greeks to the south which had been set in motion by the news of Alexander's death.[3] The Thessalians can have had no doubt that this dragooning meant that Antipater intended to exploit them without even a nod to the requirements of Thessalian *nomos* despite the precedents established by Philip II and Alexander. This recognition can only have outraged the Thessalians after thirty years of at least ostensible Macedonian respect for local traditions in government. A generation had grown up in Thessaly under the arrangement which Antipater unilaterally canceled, and the price for this abrupt change was going to be paid by both sides.

The Thessalians deserted Antipater's army to join the Greek cause at the urging of the Athenians, and the result of the conflict was especially disastrous for the deserters. The war was largely fought in Thessalian territory. After his victory over the Greek army at Crannon in Thessaly in 322 B.C. in the battle which effectively finished the Greek revolt ignited by Alexander's death, Antipater refused at first to make a common settlement with all the various Greek states. Instead, he demanded separate negotiations for peace with each city. When

<hr />

[3] Hypereides, *Epitaphios* 13; Diodorus 18.12.3; Plutarch, *Moralia* 846E (*Vitae decem oratorum*).

the Greeks refused, he began to sack cities in Thessaly in a campaign of terror. The tactics worked. Envoys arrived from the separate cities, whereupon Antipater granted all of them peace "on mild terms." This clemency completely undid the rebel alliance, and all the Greeks except the Athenians and the Aetolians soon came to terms with Antipater. [4] This means that the Thessalians should be numbered among those who benefited from Antipater's new policy. Some of their cities had suffered grievous physical damage, and their territory had been exposed to the ravages of invading and occupying armies for two campaigning seasons. They had survived politically, however, thanks to a timely surrender.

It seems reasonable to think that the Thessalian confederacy was not abolished at this point to make way for some new arrangement formally subordinating the land to Macedonia as a kind of province. When the spoils of Alexander's empire had been divided at Babylon in 323 B.C., Antipater had been given Europe. Parts of Thrace, Macedonia, Epirus, and "all the Greeks" were listed as separate entities under his charge. The Thessalians were neither singled out for any special treatment nor differentiated from the other Greeks. [5] It was unnecessary then to do away with the confederacy, and it was unnecessary a year later. Now, after the lessons just taught by Macedonian terror tactics, an attempt could be made to exploit the traditional links of the confederacy to Macedonian control of Thessaly in a new way by the general who could claim to act for the Macedonian kings in Greece, and that was Antipater. If his reorganizations of the democratic constitutions of other Greek states in favor of oligarchies are any indication, Antipater could have gotten what he needed in Thessaly simply by checking and then purging the roll of delegates who represented the various Thes-

[4] Diodorus 18.17.7. His narrative of the war is in 18.9–18. For details, see Ed. Will, *Histoire politique du monde hellénistique. Tome I*[2] (Nancy, 1979), pp. 29–33.

[5] Arrian *FGrH* 156 F 1.7. On the settlement, see R. M. Errington, "From Babylon to Triparadeisos: 323–320 B.C.," *JHS* 90 (1970), pp. 49–77; Will, *Histoire politique I*[2], pp. 40–43.

salian cities in the confederacy in order to ensure a pro-Macedonian selection was in office.[6]

Whatever it was Antipater did in Thessaly, the Thessalians did not approve. After Antipater had conveniently left Europe for Asia, the Aetolians invaded Thessaly in 321 B.C. and convinced most of the Thessalians to rebel once again. But the commander whom Antipater had left behind in Macedonia, Polyperchon, quashed the revolt in a very bloody battle in Thessaly and, according to Diodorus, "recovered Thessaly."[7] What this second revolt and "recovery" meant for the form and substance of Thessalian government we are not told. It is usually said that the outcome of the events of 322 and 321 B.C. meant the end of Thessalian independence.[8] This generalization is perhaps true at the level of historical interpretation in the abstract, but it is hard to see how the situation in practical terms differed radically from that of Thessaly during the leadership of the confederacy by Philip and then Alexander. Macedonians were controlling Thessaly in, presumably, the manner most advantageous to themselves. It is perhaps conceivable that, for Antipater, advantage demanded that he abolish the confederacy. But he would have been in an excellent position to profit from the now longstanding connection between the leadership of the confederacy and the Macedonian throne once he had returned to Europe from Asia with the new kings in tow.[9] At this point, Antipater could have seen to the formal acknowledgment of Philip III as leader of the confederacy in conformity with Thessalian *nomos*. (Alexander IV was only a baby, so the ticklish question of what to do with the second king could easily be sidestepped for now.) Since Antipater could control Philip, using him as a tool to exercise control over the Thessalians would have made sense. The

[6] For Antipater's oligarchies, see Diodorus 18.18.4–8.

[7] 18.38. On the Aetolian incursion, see H. D. Westlake, "The Aftermath of the Lamian War," *CR* 63 (1949), pp. 87–90.

[8] See, for example, H. D. Westlake *Thessaly in the Fourth Century B.C.* (London, 1935), p. 235.

[9] Diodorus 18.39.7. Antipater returned after the settlement at Triparadeisus, on whose date (321 or 320) see J. Seibert, *Das Zeitalter der Diadochen* (Darmstadt, 1983), p. 78.

exploitation of tradition was the best way to manage recalcitrant and sentimental Greeks.

By 319 B.C., Antipater was dead and Polyperchon had been elevated to the post of guardian of the joint kings Philip III and Alexander IV. In that year, Polyperchon in Macedonia publicized a royal edict which guaranteed to the Greeks, including the Thessalians, the forms of government they had enjoyed under the reigns of Philip II and Alexander.[10] In fact, the edict claimed that this very guarantee had been extended shortly after Alexander's death but had been sabotaged by the Greek revolt which "the generals" had quelled with, it had to be said, considerable harshness toward the cities. Now there was to be a return to the *status quo ante*. If Antipater had ever taken the trouble to decree the formal dissolution of the Thessalian confederacy, Polyperchon as royal guardian in 319 sanctioned its resurrection. Thessaly was not a part of the Macedonian kingdom. If the confederacy had been abolished at some point after the Lamian War (an action for which there is no direct evidence) and if civic coinage had also been suppressed at the same time, now they could both make comebacks. The mints of Thessaly could operate as they had under Philip II and Alexander.

For what it is worth, the evidence from outside Thessaly suggests that Antipater was not the man to make the sort of radical change in the Thessalian monetary system which suppression of the coinage of Larissa (and of any other operating Thessalian mint) would have meant. When the Athenians finally surrendered in 322, Antipater imposed an oligarchy, but he allowed everyone to keep his property.[11] That permission is not consistent with the abolition of civic coinage, and the mint of Athens was not closed. In Corinth, Antipater maintained the garrison

[10] Diodorus 18.55–56. The mention of Tricca and Pharcadon shows that Thessaly was included with the rest of Greece. See Will, *Histoire politique I²*, pp. 48–51. I agree with Ch. Habicht, "Literarische und epigraphische Ueberlieferung zur Geschichte Alexanders und seiner ersten Nachfolger," in *Akten des VI. internationalen Kongresses für griechische und lateinische Epigraphik. München 1972* (Munich, 1973), pp. 367–377, that Philip III and Alexander IV ruled jointly.

[11] Diodorus 18.18.4.

originally associated with the League of Corinth, but the civic mint of Corinth continued to produce local coinage as always. In Macedonia, Antipater apparently reinstituted the production of posthumous issues of Philip II to complement the production of posthumous issues of Alexander (and perhaps the lifetime issues of Philip III, the chronology of which is not precisely established). [12] Whatever this extraordinary proliferation of types of royal coinage meant, it certainly recalled the situation in force under the two previous regimes. Coinage in Macedonia under Antipater overtly recalled the past in the time of Philip as well as that of Alexander. When Antipater became the official guardian of Alexander's successors, i.e., when he was in a position to gain from traditional arrangements which bolstered the power of the Macedonian throne, he had reason to see the past as the best guide to a successful future.

Even if these arguments cannot claim to prove that Antipater did not suppress Thessalian coinage, it cannot be denied that Polyperchon's edict of 319 would have sanctioned its revival, at least temporarily, had the Thessalians so wished. For the situation after 319, there is little to go on, but the scattered evidence from the early Hellenistic period nevertheless hints that the confederacy of the Thessalians did not disappear. If it survived, political tradition was alive in Thessaly. A live political tradition representative of the *nomos* of the Thessalians is not the context in which to look for the imposition of a uniform royal monetary system made possible by the suppression of local coinages in a region which was not a province of Macedonia. The evidence requires review.

Within a year or two of the publication of the edict, Polyperchon had apparently lost whatever influence he had in Thessaly because Cassander operated safely there against him on several occasions during the struggles which eventually ended with Polyperchon's acceptance in 309/8 B.C. of a subordinate position as

---

[12] The posthumous issues of Philip II are Le Rider's groups III from Pella and Amphipolis. See *Monnayage*, pp. 398–399, 433. For some issues from Asia Minor, see Margaret Thompson, "Posthumous Philip II Staters of Asia Minor," in *Studia Paulo Naster Oblata I. Numismatica Antiqua*, ed. Simone Scheers (Leuven, 1982), pp. 57–61.

Cassander's ally. To seal the bargain, Cassander gave Polyperchon (among other things) five hundred Thessalian cavalry to use, a sure sign that Cassander controlled Thessaly.[13] Whether any formal changes in Thessalian government followed on Cassander's establishing himself as the dominant force in Thessaly we cannot know because no source tells us. By 312 B.C., Cassander had created a "general for Greece" whose job above all entailed overseeing the security of central Greece where Cassander's interests were strong.[14] The best guess is that this general was not concerned with the forms of local government and that confederacies such as the one in Thessaly were allowed to continue as convenient intermediaries between the Greek population and the Macedonian overlords and garrisons.[15]

In 307 B.C., Demetrius Poliorcetes came to Greece from Asia "to free the Greeks" from Cassander's domination. Thessaly was not one of the areas Demetrius liberated.[16] Several years later, Demetrius, acting for his father, established a Hellenic League based in Corinth.[17] When in 302/1 B.C. Demetrius led the allied forces of the new organization to the north to take on Cassander, the latter anticipated the attack by taking up a position in Thessaly.[18] Cassander obviously felt he could count on support there and a secure line of communication to Macedonia, which means that Thessaly was still in his orbit. Demetrius made his move by capturing the city of Larissa Cremaste and some nearby settlements in Phthiotic Achaea.[19] He then struck further north into the southern region of Thessaly proper. The city of Pherae had a Macedonian garrison, but Demetrius was able to take the city and to restore "freedom" to its population when the

[13] Diodorus 19.35.2, 19.36.1, 19.53.1, 20.28.3.

[14] Diodorus 19.77.6.

[15] H. Bengtson *Die Strategie in der hellenistischen Zeit* vol. 1, pp. 132–134.

[16] See W. W. Tarn, *CAH*, vol. 6 (Cambridge, 1927), p. 501.

[17] See *SVA* III, no. 446.

[18] Diodorus 20.106–107.1.

[19] For a recent discussion of the coinage which Larissa Cremaste is assumed to have begun to strike after receiving its "freedom" from Demetrius, see C. Heyman, "Achille-Alexandre sur les monnaies de Larissa Cremaste en Thessalie," in *Antidorum W. Peremans sexagenario ab alumnis oblatum* (Louvain, 1968, Studia Hellenistica 16) pp. 115–125.

Pheraeans "called him in."[20] It may not be an accident that the city which voluntarily gave itself up to Demetrius was the same city which had rebelled against the Thessalian confederacy led by Philip II and which had been garrisoned for that reason. Perhaps the Pheraeans (or at least those who found themselves outside the power structure of the government tolerated by Cassander, most likely an oligarchy like those favored by his father, Antipater) were hoping by their defection to Demetrius to escape from a confederacy dominated by Cassander in which they had little sway and large obligations. If so, they failed. When events in Asia made it necessary for Demetrius to leave Greece and his war of liberation not long after the restoration of freedom to Pherae, Cassander recovered the cities which Demetrius had "freed."[21] Cassander had reached an agreement with Demetrius before the latter's departure for the East that all Greek cities would be left free, but Cassander evidently interpreted this commitment in the spirit of Alexander's orders to Craterus twenty years earlier: the freedom of the Greeks needed a Macedonian to look after it.

It would be difficult to argue that any of the successors of Alexander had a genuine commitment to the cause of Greek freedom, or at least any commitment that got in the way of their own aggrandizement. But some of them were very vocal about their loyalty to the cause, if only for purposes of public relations. Cassander, however, was not one of those who proclaimed his love for Greek freedom loud and often. In fact, the sham compact with Demetrius is the only evidence of any public stance on the issue by Cassander. Does this mean that he is a likely candidate for identification as a suppressor of local Thessalian coinage? Since he took over Thessaly from Polyperchon probably not long after 319 B.C., the *terminus* of *ca.* 320 B.C. for the coinage of Larissa could be compatible with suppression by Cassander. It is perhaps significant, nevertheless, that Cassander did not suppress local coinage in Athens, even though he clearly had the power to do so. In 317 B.C., Cassander reached an agreement with the

[20] Diodorus 20.110.
[21] Diodorus 20.111.1−2, 20.112.1.

Athenians which legitimized his control of the city. The terms show just how strict Cassander's domination over these "friends and allies" was to be: a Macedonian garrison was to stay in the port until the end of the war with "the kings"; the city government was to be an oligarchy; Cassander would choose an Athenian suitable to himself as "overseer" of the city. [22] To call this freedom would be stretching a point. It is, therefore, instructive to notice the remaining stipulations of the pact: the Athenians could keep their city, their land, their revenues, their ships, and everything else. This certainly implies that the Athenians could continue to mint their own coins, and there is every indication that they did so. [23]

By 316 B.C, Cassander had taken charge of Alexander IV, the sole surviving legitimate successor of Alexander after the murder in 317 of Philip III by Olympias. He let the boy live, as a prisoner, until after the Peace of 311 B.C.[24] Cassander himself seems to have assumed the title of king only after the assumption of the title by Antigonus and Demetrius in 306.[25] Unfortunately, we are particularly ill informed on Cassander's relations with the Thessalians. If he took any action to change traditional Thessalian government or coinage, we do not know about it. One late source, in fact, shows Cassander allowing traditional institutions to function as of old in this part of Greece. According to Quintilian, when the Thebans after the refoundation of their city by Cassander demanded repayment of a large loan from the Thessalians which Alexander had canceled after his capture of Thebes, the Amphictyonic council heard the case. In other words, Cassander did not, in this instance anyway, exercise direct jurisdiction even in a matter concerning the financial

[22] Diodorus 18.74.

[23] There are no indications of an interruption in production (such as a change in types) in Athenian coinage of the late fourth century, and Athenian coins continue to appear in contemporary hoards.

[24] Diodorus 19.52.4, 19.105.1–4.

[25] Olaf Müller, *Antigonos Monophthalmos und "Das Jahr der Könige"* (Bonn, 1973), pp. 101–105.

well-being of a city in which he had a clear interest.[26] It is also noteworthy that Cassander was conservative in his arrangements for Macedonian coinage during his rule. Precious metal issues continued just as before to carry the names and types of Philip and of Alexander. The name of Cassander was stamped only on bronze small change.[27] There is nothing which speaks against the assumption that Cassander, like his predecessors, followed a *laissez-faire* policy on Greek coinage, which is perhaps another way of saying that he had no discernible interest in the subject at all.

The history of the confederacy of the Thessalians in the last decades of the fourth century B.C. has been traced here as a guide to the actions of the Macedonian kings and commanders who controlled the region, in order to see if politics is likely to have had any direct and intentional effect on the right of the Thessalian cities to issue coins. In my opinion, no such effect is discernible. But perhaps the evidence is hidden from us. One final way to investigate the situation is to look for traces of a fourth-century policy of direct Macedonian interference with Thessalian coinage in the history of Thessaly in the third century. We must search for such traces by asking what, if any, reflection of fourth-century practice is to be found in the relationship between the Macedonian king and Thessalian government in the third century. There are a few scattered but important clues.

When in (probably) 294 B.C. Demetrius Poliorcetes left southern Macedonia after a visit with Alexander, the son of Cassander who had just recently come to the throne, the new king escorted

[26] *Institutio oratoria* 5.10.111. This is not to say, of course, that Cassander could not have controlled or influenced the decision of the council.

[27] Head, *HN*, p. 228; C. Ehrhardt, "The Coins of Cassander," *Journal of Numismatic Fine Arts* 2 (1973), pp. 25–32. When his brother Alexarchus founded a new city called Uranopolis in Macedonia, it issued a complete series of silver coins in typically Greek style with punning types of the universe and Aphrodite Urania. See Head, *HN*, p. 206.; Martin Price, *Coins of the Macedonians* (London, 1974), p. 18; M. Thompson, "The Cavalla Hoard (*IGCH* 450)," *ANSMN* 26 (1981), pp. 40–42. Since this was certainly a special case, given Alexarchus' apparently unbalanced condition and his status as the ruler's brother, it would not be legitimate to draw further conclusions from it about Cassander's attitude toward Greek coinages.

Demetrius as far as Larissa in Thessaly. Since Alexander
suspected that Demetrius, a rival for his position as king, was
actively plotting against him, his trip to Thessaly implies that
Alexander felt relatively secure there. Otherwise he could have
stayed in Macedonia. This detail is a hint that some special relationship still existed between the Macedonian king and at least
the part of Thessaly dominated by Larissa.[28] Subsequent events
indicate that this relationship was probably in some sense a continuation of the traditional arrangement. Demetrius proved
Alexander's suspicion correct by murdering him in Larissa,
whereupon Demetrius was recognized as their king first by the
Macedonians of Alexander's army, and then by the Macedonians
at home after Demetrius' triumphant return at the head of a
unified army.[29] After Macedonia (and, it must be emphasized,
therefore not simultaneously), Demetrius "took possession of"
Thessaly.[30] Plutarch, our source, offers no details, but he implies
that Demetrius "took possession of" Thessaly in much the same
way as he became king in Macedonia, without a fight and with
the "agreement" of the population. Whether the Thessalians
were enthusiastic about the situation does not matter for the
point at hand. If Demetrius did not "take possession of" Thessaly immediately upon assuming the kingship in Macedonia, the
implication is that the leadership of Thessaly was not at this time
automatically a part of Macedonian kingship.

There is every reason to think that Demetrius could have gotten all he needed from the Thessalians by perpetuating the relationship which Philip and Alexander had established (on the
assumption that Cassander had not changed it). After all, he had
imitated them with the establishment of his panhellenic league at
Corinth. He could get Thessalian revenues, Thessalian cavalry,
and an easy entry into Thessalian political affairs as leader of the
confederacy.[31] Nothing more was required. By now, it had been

---

[28] Plutarch, *Demetrius* 36.8−9.

[29] Plutarch, *Demetrius* 36.10−37.

[30] Plutarch, *Demetrius* 39.1: Δημήτριος δὲ μετὰ Μακεδονίαν καὶ Θετταλίαν
ἦν παρειληφώς.

[31] The Antigonids later claimed to be related to the Argead line. See Müller,
Antigonos, p. 115, and Bosworth, *Commentary*, p. 174 (on Arrian 1.29.3), on the
idea of C. F. Edson, "The Antigonids, Heracles and Beroea," *HSCP* 45 (1934),

sixty years since anyone other than the Macedonian king had served as leader of the Thessalian confederacy, except perhaps during the Lamian War, and most likely whatever limits of law or of custom there had originally been to the power of the leader had by now been eroded or forgotten. When Demetrius created a new city named after himself in Magnesia not long after he had "taken possession of" Thessaly, he could have argued that as leader of the confederacy he had a special responsibility and a special right to see to such matters in the interest of the confederacy.[32] That Demetrius was able to include a city as important as Pagasae in his synoecism to form Demetrias, however, is a clue that he did not have to make arguments to get his way. All he had to do was to decide what he wanted. He had the power to enforce his wishes. E. T. Newell thought that one of the things Demetrius wanted was to mint some of his own royal issues in his new city, but this is far from certain.[33] In any case, it has nothing to do with the fate of coinage in Larissa or the survival of the confederacy.

One of the things Demetrius had apparently not wanted to do was to put large military forces into Thessaly. This we know because Plutarch's account of the struggles between Demetrius and Pyrrhus, his erstwhile supporter and now ambitious rival, shows that Pyrrhus overran Thessaly without any difficulty because Demetrius had not occupied the area with a large force. Strong garrisons came only after the invasion had been

---

p. 226, that Antigonus Monophthalmus was actually related to the royal house. On the claim to be descended from Heracles, see Edson, "Perseus and Demetrius," *HSCP* 46 (1935), pp. 191–202. This latter claim, if made already in the time of Monophthalmus, could have served to legitimize leadership of the confederacy, as it had done for Philip II and Alexander.

[32] On Demetrias, see E. Meyer, *Pagasai und Demetrias* (Berlin, 1934), pp. 178–195; V. Milojčič and D. Theocharis, *Demetrias I* (Bonn, 1976, Beiträge zur ur- und frühgeschichtlichen Archäologie des Mittelmeer-Kulturraumes 12). Meyer argues (p. 187) that Demetrias lacked the right of coinage "zufolge ihrer Zugehörigkeit zu Makedonien" except for the "few years" of the rule of Demetrius Poliorcetes. Unfortunately, hoard evidence is lacking for the coins of Demetrius dated *ca.* 290 B.C. by Head, *HN*, p. 294, to which Meyer is referring.

[33] *The Coinages of Demetrius Poliorcetes* (London, 1927), pp. 131–136.

repelled.[34] Evidently Demetrius had felt confident enough in his relationship with the Thessalians to do without such strongholds before. Thessaly was apparently a relatively peaceful place unless attacked by outsiders, another hint that the traditional arrangement between the Thessalians and the Macedonian king was still in effect. More trouble might have been expected and more garrisons might have been required if a new arrangement had been made by which the Thessalians were no longer even nominally independent under their own *nomos* but were instead subjects of the king in the same way as the Macedonians.

Sometime in the early 280s B.C., Demetrius was displaced as Macedonian king by Pyrrhus.[35] Again the meager details supplied by Plutarch are all we have. It appears that even though Demetrius had lost Macedonia, he still retained his influence in Thessaly. Only after Demetrius left Europe for Asia did Pyrrhus as king of Macedonia and on the advice of Lysimachus initiate his attempt "to bring about a revolt in Thessaly," presumably by force of arms.[36] This account implies that Demetrius had retained some tie to Thessaly (in addition to the garrison in Demetrias) which Pyrrhus had not automatically taken over when he became king in Macedonia. One could suggest that the tie was the leadership of the confederacy voted by the member cities of Thessaly, the by now customary fief of the Macedonian king but still something which was supposed to be acknowledged and conferred by the Thessalians. In other words, the confederacy still existed as a functional body, even if its function was only to rubber-stamp.

Plutarch does not explicitly say so, but Pyrrhus did take over control of Thessaly from Demetrius' supporters. There was no one in Thessaly powerful enough to stop him.[37] But what was Pyrrhus' status in Thessaly? Modern scholars usually assume that he became "king of the Thessalians," on the evidence of the list of "Kings of the Thessalians" preserved in the Armenian

[34] Plutarch, *Demetrius* 40.1–2.

[35] Plutarch, *Demetrius* 44; *Pyrrhus* 11.

[36] Plutarch, *Pyrrhus* 12.8.

[37] Only Demetrias was saved. See W. W. Tarn, *Antigonos Gonatas* (Oxford, 1913), p. 102.

version of the first part of Eusebius' *Chronicle,* the *Chronographia.*[38] This chronologically arranged list consists of the Macedonian kings from Philip III to Philip V. The list is preceded by a prose summary entitled "Kings of the Thessalians" which begins with the statement that "for a long time the same ones who ruled over the Macedonians ruled over the Thessalians and the Epirotes."[39] A completely separate list entitled "Kings of the Macedonians" comes before the list entitled "Kings of the Thessalians." The names are the same in both lists, but the numbers of regnal years assigned to each name do not agree in every instance. The implication is that these lists in some sense refer to different offices held by the same people.

Taken together, the list of "Kings of the Thessalians" and the accompanying prose summary are not evidence that the political relationship between the Macedonian kings and the Thessalians had changed after the death of Alexander the Great. The *Chronographia* has no independent value as historical evidence for constitutional change in Thessaly (or in Epirus, for that matter). In the first place, as we have seen, it was common for other Greeks to refer to the leader of the Thessalian confederacy as a "king." A list of the "Kings of the Thessalians" could easily be a list of the leaders of the confederacy. If the relationship between the Macedonian king and the Thessalians had truly changed in a fundamental way so that the Thessalians were the subjects of the king in exactly the same way as were the Macedonians, one would expect, at the very least, to find evidence of a unitary kingship, not two separate kingships. If there were only one office, only one list would have been called for: the "Kings of the Macedonians and the Thessalians."

Second, the format of the list preserved in the *Chronographia* prevents us from knowing what Eusebius' source for the "Kings of the Thessalians" thought the relationship had been between the Macedonian kings and the Thessalians during the reigns of Philip II and Alexander the Great. For reasons which are not

---

[38] See P. Lévêque, *Pyrrhos* (Paris, 1957), p. 163.

[39] For translations, see Alfred Schoene, *Eusebi Chronicorum Liber Prior* (Berlin, 1875), pp. 241–247 (Latin translation); Josef Karst, *Die Chronik des Eusebius* (Leipzig, 1911), pp. 114–116 (German translation).

explained in the *Chronographia*, Eusebius changed his source for the chronology of Macedonian history after the death of Alexander. For the kings of Macedonia from Caranus, the founder of the royal line, to Alexander the Great, Eusebius seems to have relied on Diodorus, but he switched to the work of his contemporary Porphyry for the chronology of the Macedonian kings after Alexander (from Philip III to the end of the monarchy in the second century B.C.).[40] The change of sources is at first glance odd because Porphyry probably relied on Diodorus for his information, and one can only assume that Eusebius, for some reason, found it more convenient to use Porphyry for all of Hellenistic Greek history.[41] Perhaps Porphyry's work was more convenient because it was written specifically to deal with the history of the successors of Alexander, a well-known scheme for historical and chronological treatises from the Roman imperial period.[42]

In any case, regardless of whether Porphyry was in fact Eusebius' source for the "kings of the Thessalians," there is a clear hint in the *Chronographia* that this source realized that the relationship between the Macedonian kings and the Thessalians which it was describing did not begin with Philip III. After an introduction, the prose summary entitled "Kings of the Thessalians" begins its record of the names of the various kings with the statement that "there ruled also over these after Alexander, Arrhidaeus" (with the other names following).[43] The "also" in this sentence suggests that Eusebius' source recognized that the political relationship between the Macedonian kings and the Thessalians did not begin with Philip III and that this source did not imply that any constitutional change had taken place in Thessaly at this point.[44] The source simply happened to begin its

[40] See the headings in Karst's edition, pp. 106, 109.

[41] See Alden Mosshammer, *The Chronicle of Eusebius and Greek Chronographic Tradition* (Lewisburg, Pa., 1979), pp. 130–131.

[42] Arrian (*FGrH* 156) and Dexippus (*FGrH* 100) wrote monographs on "Affairs after Alexander."

[43] Schöne, p. 241 (*iterum*); Karst, p. 114 (*wiederum auch*).

[44] There is no indication in the *spatium historicum* of the *Canons* of the *Chronicle* that any constitutional change took place in Thessaly after the death of Alexander the Great.

chronology with the death of Alexander and therefore referred to the political *status quo* of that time. On the assumption that Porphyry was Eusebius' source for the "Kings of the Thessalians" and that Porphyry in turn relied on Diodorus, it is easy to see how the notion that the Macedonians should be referred to as the "kings of the Thessalians" could find its way into the chronographical tradition which Eusebius used. Diodorus had made this development possible by stating that Philip II "extended his rule" as a consequence of his victory in Thessaly.[45] But, as we have seen, Philip II did not rule in Thessaly in his capacity as Macedonian king. He exercised authority in Thessaly in the traditional Thessalian way as leader of the confederacy, a position which the Greeks equated with kingship. Diodorus' account of Philip's actions in Thessaly did not reveal this crucial fact, which would account for the ignorance of it on the part of those who relied on Diodorus' account for their own interpretations of the history of Thessaly in the fourth century and even later. The lists in the *Chronographia* support the idea that Thessaly did not become part of Macedonia, a "Macedonian province," in the fourth or the third century B.C.

The other evidence for the relationship between the Thessalians and the Macedonian kings after Demetrius Poliorcetes supports the idea that the form of Thessalian government which came into being under Philip II and Alexander continued to exist at least formally long after 323 B.C. There is no direct evidence for the nature of the relations between Thessaly and the Macedonian kings Pyrrhus, Lysimachus, or Antigonus Gonatas, but Tarn thought that Pyrrhus' dedication in the temple of Athena Itonia in Phthiotic Achaea (a deity whose favor the Thessalians traditionally cultivated) after a victory over Gonatas in Macedonia probably meant that Pyrrhus was claiming to be the head of the Thessalian confederacy.[46] Since the Meno of Pharsalus who led the Thessalian cavalry in the Lamian War was

---

[45] 16.38.2: ηὐξηκὼς ἑαυτοῦ τὴν βασιλείαν. The use of βασιλεία here, for example, could have helped to implant the idea that Philip became the king of the Thessalians, even though Diodorus was probably only using the word in the general sense of "rule" or "domination."

[46] *Antigonos Gonatas*, p. 265.

Pyrrhus' maternal grandfather, the Epirote Pyrrhus could claim a kinship with the Thessalians which was considerably closer than the kinship with them which Philip and Alexander had traced through a shared divine ancestor. If Pyrrhus controlled Thessaly in the capacity of the leader of the confederacy instead of merely as the Macedonian king, his rivals and successors had reason to emulate his example in their dealings with the Thessalians by paying at least lip service to the tradition of the *nomos* of the Thessalians.[47]

Justin, echoing the language of his source Pompeius Trogus, says that Antigonus Doson "suppressed" the Thessalians when they rejoiced at the news of the death of Demetrius II in 229 B.C.[48] That Doson had to act in Thessaly as the result of the death of a Macedonian king implies that some special relationship still existed between the Thessalians and the king. Justin naturally assumes that Doson then went on to rule the Thessalians as their king, in the same way Demetrius II had. But the evidence of Polybius shows that the Thessalians were the allies of Doson (and so perhaps had been the allies of Demetrius II as well), not his subjects.[49] The same relationship continued between the Thessalians and Doson's successor in 221 B.C, Philip V.[50] It is an important point that the Thessalians were, properly speaking, allies of Philip V, and not his subjects, because we can glimpse from the literary and epigraphical sources just how intrusive the king's influence was in Thessalian affairs. The Thessalians meant more to Philip than did any of his other allies, thanks to their strategic location on his southern flank and to the

[47] Later evidence reveals a tradition that Lysimachus' father was a Thessalian, the kind of connection which could have been exploited. This tradition is, however, generally rejected. See Helmut Berve, *Das Alexanderreich auf prosopographischer Grundlage*, 2 vols. (Munich, 1926), no. 480; I. L. Merker, "Lysimachos—Thessalian or Macedonian?" *Chiron* 9 (1979), pp. 31–36.

[48] Justin 28.3.14 (*conpescuerit*); prologue to book 28 (*subiecit*).

[49] 4.9.4. Cf. 2.54.4–5. Polybius' reference to the Thessalians as allies is consistent with the assumption that the Macedonian king served as the leader of their confederacy. Cf. Demosthenes' reference to Philip II as the "ally" of the Thessalians (9.12). Polybius' terminology may, however, only indicate the status bestowed by inclusion in the Hellenic League which Doson formed.

[50] Polybius 11.5.4.

long tradition of Macedonian hegemony over their confederacy.[51] As in Macedonia, certain local officials in Thessaly
reported to him (or were supposed to do so, in any case).[52]

A well-known inscription from Larissa demonstrates Philip's
concern for and power over important local matters. After hearing the report of the city's ambassadors, Philip instructed the
Larissaeans to pass a decree extending citizenship to qualified
individuals. When the locals later tried to revoke the grants, he
again intervened politely but firmly to have the disenfranchised
citizens reinstated. [53] In his letters to Larissa, Philip calls himself
simply "king." This was his most important title, the one by
which he was of course known in Macedonia, from where he sent
the letters. By this time late in the third century B.C., "king" was
the title which Philip and his royal colleagues elsewhere in the
Hellenistic world used routinely in their letters, regardless of the
status of those with whom they were corresponding.[54] In the case
of Thessaly, the tenure of the Macedonian kings as the leaders of
the national government for well over a century perhaps meant
that after such a long time no one much cared anymore whether
the leader was called "king" or "tagos." There is, in any case, no
evidence that the confederacy had disappeared in favor of some

---

[51] Livy 32.10.7–8. Cf. 32.10.4.

[52] Polybius 5.26.5. See Ch. Habicht, "Eine neue Urkunde zur Geschichte
Thessaliens unter der makedonischen Herrschaft," in *Ancient Macedonian Studies
in Honor of Charles F. Edson* (Thessaloniki, 1981), p. 196, on a Macedonian
strategos mentioned in a Thessalian document of the time of Philip V.

[53] *SIG*[3] 543. On the date (217 or 216 B.C.), see Ch. Habicht, "Epigraphische
Zeugnisse zur Geschichte Thessaliens unter der makedonischen Herrschaft," in
Ancient Macedonia, vol. 1 (Thessaloniki, 1970), pp. 273–278. Cf. D. Mendels,
"Polybius, Philip V and the Socio-Economic Question in Greece," *Ancient Society*
8 (1977), p. 162; J.-M. Hannick, "Remarques sur les lettres de Philippe V de
Macédoine à la cité de Larissa (*IG* IX, 2, 517)," in *Antidorum W. Peremans sexa-
genario ab alumnis oblatum* (Louvain, 1968, Studia Hellenistica 16), pp. 97–104;
E. S. Gruen, "Philip V and the Greek Demos," in *Ancient Macedonian Studies in
Honor of Charles F. Edson* (Thessaloniki, 1981), pp. 170–171.

[54] As one can see, for example, from the collection of royal letters in C. B.
Welles, *Royal Correspondence in the Hellenistic Period: A Study in Greek Epigraphy*
(London, 1934). The Macedonian material is collected by R. M. Errington,
"Macedonian 'Royal Style' and Its Historical Significance," *JHS* 94 (1974), pp.
20–37.

arrangement which made Thessaly just another part of Macedonia and therefore part of the kingdom.[55]

The continuing existence of the confederacy in the third century would be certain if we could be sure that Mario Segre's date in that period is correct for the Hellenistic inscriptions which show the confederacy of Thessalian cities making decisions as a federal body.[56] But even without the testimony of these epigraphical texts, we can infer the persistence of the traditional form of Thessalian national government in this era from the words of Polybius (4.76.2). He describes the status of Thessaly early in the reign of Philip V as follows: "The Thessalians seemed to be governed according to their own laws and to differ greatly from the Macedonians, but there was no difference; in every way they experienced the same things as the Macedonians, and they did everything which the king's men ordered." The reality of life in such a situation for the Thessalians and those who came into the same circumstances could be very harsh, as Polybius goes on to suggest, and there was no doubt that the king controlled Thessaly. But the appearance of normal government continuing as usual, which Polybius presents as the façade masking royal power, is the point on which we must focus our attention. The "*nomos* of the Thessalians" was formally preserved.[57] Tarn put it well: "The Thessalians can hardly have exercised any free choice in the appointment of Macedonian

---

[55] A contrary view is expressed by J.V.A. Fine, "The Problem of Macedonian Holdings in Epirus and Thessaly in 221 B.C.," *TAPA* 63 (1932), p. 140. Tarn, *Antigonos Gonatas*, p. 206, is wrong about regnal dating in Thessaly. See the commentary to *IG* IX.2, 461a.

[56] "Grano di Tessaglia a Coo," *Rivista di filologia* 12 (1934), pp. 169–193. Larsen, *GFS*, p. 281, assumes the confederacy continues in the third century. Cf. the federal decree for judges from Teos (*Bulletin épigraphique* 1973, 240), which should date to the third century because the year is not given by reference to a *strategos*, as it would be after 196 B.C.

[57] For a different interpretation of Polybius' comments, see John Briscoe, "The Antigonids and the Greek States, 276–196 B.C.," in *Imperialism in the Ancient World*, ed. P.D.A. Garnsey and C. R. Whittaker (Cambridge, 1978), p. 315, n. 10.

kings as presidents of their League; but no doubt all forms were observed."[58]

The evidence for the status of Thessaly in the third century B.C. has been reviewed in order to make clear that, just as in the fourth century, there is no identifiable point in the history of the region during the early Hellenistic period at which it makes sense to assume that Thessalian local coinage came to an end for political reasons. If all indications are that the form of traditional Thessalian government endured on the national level under Macedonian domination, then it makes no sense to assume that the Macedonian kings infringed on Thessalian *nomos* in the area of coinage by closing local mints. There simply is no evidence that the answer to the question of what caused the end of Thessalian coinage lies in the realm of political history. Another solution to the puzzle has to be found.

[58] *Antigonos Gonatas*, p. 207.

SEVEN. THE END OF CIVIC COINAGE
IN THESSALY

The production of coinage, like that of any other thing of value, involves expenses for raw materials, manufacture, and distribution. In the case of ancient coinage in precious metal, the greatest expense was the raw material. Silver and gold were very valuable, and even bronze was not entirely negligible in its value. Above all, any city which wished to issue its own coins had to acquire a supply of the requisite metals.[1] Building and staffing a mint required an initial capital outlay for construction and the purchase of the slaves who would do most, if not all, of the work, but production costs thereafter were, one guesses, not onerous. The slaves had to be maintained along with the mint's physical plant, but nothing lavish was required in either case. Distribution of the coins once minted was simple. The state disbursed payment in its coins to those who were entitled to it, and no expensive bureaucracy was required to handle the state payments of the average Greek city (one imagines; these matters are not of much interest to our sources).[2]

Since Thessaly had no silver mines of its own, the raw material for the silver coinages of the various cities in the region

[1] See Ed. Will, "Les sources des métaux monnayés dans le monde grec," in *Numismatique antique. Problèmes et méthodes*, ed. J.-M. Dentzer, Ph. Gautier, and T. Hackens (Nancy, 1975), pp. 97–102.

[2] For example, the Aristotelian *Constitution of the Athenians* does not indicate who was in charge of the mint at Athens or how it was supervised. On Athenian revenue officials, see P. J. Rhodes, *A Commentary on the Aristotelian Athenaion Politeia* (Oxford, 1981), on *Ath. Pol.* 43.1, 47.2–48.3. We might expect that the idea was to run local mints at a profit after normal operating expenses, or at least not at a deficit. But an investment had to be made to start up a mint, and the capital had to be available to purchase silver bullion for coining.

had to come from external sources, who were not in the business of giving away their silver. It had to be paid for. Thessaly had no gold mines either, and it is highly unlikely that her indigenous supply of copper, for whose existence there is some evidence, produced sufficient quantities of this less valuable metal both to satisfy local needs for coinage and other items in bronze and to serve as a commodity for export in return for silver.[3] Thessaly had no ancient reputation as a supplier of metals. Her income sprang from the soil of her plains. When Thessaly was prosperous, it was thanks to agriculture and animal husbandry. Unlike most of the rest of Greece, Thessaly had considerable land that was flat enough and fertile enough to produce copious amounts of grain for human consumption and grasses for grazing animals.[4] The plain in the west was larger than the plain in the eastern part of the country which Larissa controlled, but the western plain tended to flood and perhaps had substantial sections of forest still standing which prevented agriculture. Too much rain in the winter made this plain a swamp difficult to sow; too little in the summer left it baked hardpan. It was not an easy area in which to raise a full harvest every time. The plain of Larissa was drier and cooler, cold enough to damage vines and trees by freezing.[5] But when things went well, this plain could be lush with grain and support herds of horses. In fact, in good years grain and horses both could be produced in such abundance that there was a surplus for sale in foreign markets. Grain would go to Greek cities that could not feed themselves, such as Athens, and Thessalian horses were so famous that they found

[3] On the mines and metals of ancient Thessaly, see n. 3 in chapter 3.

[4] On the natural characteristics of the region, see M. Sivignon, *La Thessalie. Analyse géographique d'une province grecque* (Lyon, 1975), pp. 13–92.

[5] On the climate and water supply of Thessaly, see Sivignon, *La Thessalie*, pp. 35–66, who remarks that "la pluviosité" in Thessaly is "capricieuse." He records variations in rainfall from one year to the next (1961–1962) at Tricala of 517 to 1244 mm., at Larissa of 343 to 807 mm. Over the course of thirty-five years, the flow of one river measured a low of 281 million cubic meters and a high of 1449 million cubic meters.

buyers in many markets.[6] One of these was Macedonia. The Macedonians appreciated strong, swift horses, and they were willing to pay for quality. Alexander's famous horse Bucephalas was bought from a Thessalian for thirteen talents (an exorbitant price).[7] This sort of "foreign trade" helped Thessalian cities earn, directly or indirectly through taxes and contributions, the capital to buy silver from foreign sources, such as Macedonia. But the agricultural situation was precarious in the east of Thessaly just as in the west. In particular, the plain of Larissa was susceptible to crop failure if the spring rains were tardy or absent because the winter tended not to be wet. Like a risky investment, Thessalian agriculture and animal husbandry offered big rewards and equally great risks.[8] Prosperity was uncertain and transient, a situation reflected, for example, in the municipal revenues of Pharsalus in the fourth century. The city was perpetually fluctuating between a surplus and a deficit.[9] Obviously there was no contingency fund, and the other Thessalian cities likewise endured a precarious position. The most striking confirmation of this fact comes from a well-known inscription found in Cyrene.[10] This text lists the grain supplied by Cyrene to various cities and peoples in mainland Greece and on numerous islands during a food shortage (*sitodeia*) whose date is not specified. The size of the shipments to Thessaly shows that the region, often a grain exporter, was especially hard pressed. The town of Atrax near Larissa received 10,000 measures (*medimnoi*), while Meliboea (either the town in Hestiaeotis or perhaps the settlement in Magnesia) got two consignments totaling

[6] For Thessaly's grain, see H. D. Westlake, *Thessaly in the Fourth Century B.C.* (London, 1935), pp. 4–6; for horses, J. K. Anderson, *Ancient Greek Horsemanship* (Berkeley, 1961), p. 20.

[7] Plutarch, *Alexander* 6.1.

[8] See Sivignon, *La Thessalie*, p. 227, on the variability of the cereal harvest in modern Thessaly. This point has recently been well emphasized in an article which appeared as this book was in the press. See Peter Garnsey, Tom Gallant and Dominic Rathbone, "Thessaly and the Grain Supply of Rome during the Second Century B.C.," *JRS* 74 (1984), pp. 30–35, who furnish detailed statistics on precipitation and crop yields.

[9] Xenophon, *Hellenica* 6.1.3.

[10] *GHI* 196.

28,500 measures. The perioikic Oetaei in the south also received two shipments for a total of 21,400 measures. Larissa itself, the most prosperous city in Thessaly, received 50,000 measures, the same as the great cities of Argos and Corinth. This was a large amount of food. The total for the Thessalians alone is 109,900 *medimnoi.* If these are *medimnoi* on the Aeginetan standard of measure, as Tod suggests in his edition of this text, this total represents the equivalent of almost four million daily rations of grain (assuming a generous allowance attested for the classical period.)[11] Other cities in Thessaly were surely in desperate straits if even Larissa had to rely on imported food. They may have gotten relief shipments of which we have no record, or they may simply have starved because they lacked good connections to foreign suppliers.

The likeliest explanation for the famine in Thessaly and so many other places is a drastic alteration in the normal pattern of rainfall leading to a sustained drought. If the problem had been caused by human manipulation such as faulty distribution, or even simply by price inflation (as has been suggested), we would not expect to find the Thessalians short of food.[12] They had their own supply except when the weather betrayed them. When that happened, they had no nonagricultural resources to fall back on to protect their prosperity, as did Athens with her silver mines or Corinth with her trade revenues. The Thessalian economy

[11] 109,900 Aeginetan *medimnoi* = 164,850 Attic *medimnoi* = 7,912,800 *choinices.* Two *choinices* of barley a day was a good ration; a slave could expect only one. See J. K. Anderson, *Military Theory and Practice in the Age of Xenophon* (Berkeley, 1970), pp. 49–50. D. W. Engels, *Alexander the Great and the Logistics of the Macedonian Army* (Berkeley, 1978), p. 125, argues that the grain ration of Alexander's soldiers was three pounds a day (= two *choinices*).

[12] W. L. Westermann, "New Historical Documents in Greek and Roman History," *American Historical Review* 35 (1929–1930), pp. 16–19, argues that the grain shortage was caused by "price inflation, bad distribution and profiteering." W. W. Tarn, *CAH*, vol. 6, p. 448, suggests crop failure as the reason for the shortage. On the connection of drought, famine, and epidemic disease, see John McK. Camp II, "A Drought in the Late Eighth Century B.C.," *Hesperia* 48 (1979), pp. 397–411, who suggests that there was a severe drought at Athens in this period which lasted three quarters of a century, with devastating consequences for agriculture and general prosperity. See also the remarks on drought of S. C. Bakhuizen, *Mnemosyne* 35 (1982), pp. 436–437.

depended on water, and on just the proper amount, neither too much nor too little. If Thessaly had to bring in food from abroad, the rains must have been at fault, and their failure would have struck at the prosperity of the entire land.

Although no source gives us the dates of the famine which motivated the grain shipments to Greece from Cyrene just mentioned, it is generally agreed that the shortage began at the end of the 330s B.C. and extended well into the 320s.[13] This was just the time when conditions might otherwise have been looking better for the Thessalians. In 330 B.C, Alexander had dismissed his Thessalian cavalry along with the other Greeks in his army. Only 130 Thessalians contracted with him for further service. The rest came home laden with a bonus of two thousand talents in addition to their pay, their booty, and the proceeds from the sale of their horses.[14] Some of this money no doubt found its way into the pockets of merchants, entertainers, and thieves as the troops made their happy way back to Thessaly, but a good deal of it presumably came all the way home. With these funds in hand, the returned veterans had a chance to reestablish a productive peacetime life for themselves and even to embellish their home cities with new or refurbished public buildings.[15]

In addition, the influx of capital could have meant a boost for Thessalian finances to make up for the shortfall of the previous two decades. By 330 B.C, the Macedonian king (or his deputy) had been receiving the revenues due the leader of the Thessalian confederacy for over twenty years. This money was, of course, supposed to be spent on "the common affairs of the Thessalians,"

[13] M. Rostovtzeff, *The Social and Economic History of the Hellenistic World* (Oxford, 1953), pp. 95, 1329, n. 29; S. Isager and M. H. Hansen, *Aspects of Athenian Society in the Fourth Century B.C.* (Odense, 1975, Odense Univ. Class. Stud. 5), pp. 200–208. Confirmation that shortages at Athens occurred later in the 320s comes from the comic reference to Harpalus' gift to a wheatless city (Athenaeus 13.596a-b). Cf. *IG* II² 360.

[14] Arrian 3.19.5–6, 3.25.4; Plutarch, *Alexander* 42.5; Curtius 6.6.35.

[15] The veterans who returned to Pherae seem to have contributed to the construction of a new gymnasium, or to work on the old one. See B. Helly, G. J. Te Riele, and J. A. Van Rossum, "La liste des gymnasiarchues de Phères pour les années 330–189 av. J.-C.," in *La Thessalie, Actes de la Table-Ronde 21–24 Juillet 1975 Lyon*, ed. B. Helly (Lyon, 1979), p. 227.

but already in the early years of Philip's leadership, as we saw, some Thessalians had occasion to complain that the confederacy's income was being spent by the Macedonian king on his own affairs. After the Sacred War had been resolved in the Thessalians' favor in 346 B.C., who was going to dispute the leader's right to spend these funds as he pleased? Protest would have been pointless and dangerous. Since we are told that Alexander received these same revenues after he had been elected to his father's post in Thessaly, we can be certain that Philip continued to siphon away this income throughout his career, and we can guess that Alexander and his agent in Europe, Antipater, did the same while Alexander was king. Another good guess would be that the cities also had less opportunity to skim the federal revenues under the new regime once Philip had installed his collaborators as overseers in Thessaly.

In other words, by 323 B.C. Larissa and the other cities in Thessaly had experienced for thirty years what in the United States today might be called "reverse revenue sharing": the constituent members of the federal organization "shared" their revenue with their chief. This situation did not put the cities of Thessaly in a position to cope easily with the financial pressures of a severe famine, which not only meant added expense in feeding their own populations but also destroyed their revenue from foreign trade in agricultural products. The market for horses, at least in Macedonia, may also have shrunk with the bulk of the king's army far away in Asia. Alexander on campaign to India was not going to be buying any cavalry chargers or draft animals from Thessaly.

With these conditions in mind, it is easy to see how the returning cavalrymen's riches would have been depleted in relatively short order. Naturally, it always cost money to procure the basic necessities of life, to say nothing of acquiring private luxuries and making public contributions. But the great famine meant that food prices were now going to be especially high. We do not know what grain prices were like in Thessaly during this period, but evidence from Athens shows that normal prices could more than triple when supplies were short. At this price (the highest attested for the period), the shipments to Thessaly listed in the Cyrene inscription alone would have cost almost 440 talents (if the measures were Aeginetan). [16] Tod thinks that Cyrene may have provided its grain "not necessarily as a free gift, but more probably at or below the normal price." [17] But even at a normal price of 5 drachmas/*medimnus*, this one instance of relief help was worth over 135 talents. At that rate, the money brought back from service with Alexander was not going to last very long.

It seems possible that by the end of Alexander's reign prosperity was only a memory in Thessaly. Federal revenues had been diverted out of the country for thirty years. Drought had crippled agricultural production and hindered the profitable raising of horses, the market for which had shrunk in any case. There was no longer a large contingent of Thessalians on lucrative service in the East who could send or bring money home. Given an interval of peace and some balmy weather, Thessaly could have regained its prosperity in time. But that chance was lost. The first setback may have been social disruption caused by Alexander's disbanding the Greek mercenary armies of his satraps and his proclamation which ordered the restoration of Greek exiles to their native cities. The precise repercussions these measures had in Thessaly are unattested, but they can hardly have improved matters. There may have been a number of Thessalian mercenaries to accommodate, and there were some Thessalian exiles, as we have seen. [18]

Far worse, however, than any damage done by these provisions of Alexander was the loss incurred in Thessaly as a result of the war which followed on his death. The Lamian War was fought in Thessaly in 323 and 322 B.C. by large and desperate armies. Successful agriculture was almost out of the question in this sort of protracted struggle. [19] And after the bloody battle of

[16] A price of sixteen drachmas *per* Attic *medimnos* is attested at [Demosthenes] 34.39. The normal price was five drachmas.

[17] *GHI*, p. 274.

[18] See E. Badian, "Harpalus," *JHS* 81 (1961), pp. 25–31, on the damage done in Greece by Alexander's actions.

[19] See, for example, the references in Xenophon, *Poroi* 4.9, and *SIG* 3 497, lines 8–9, to the effects of war in preventing cultivation.

Crannon in 322, Antipater and Craterus proceeded to take Thessalian cities by storm.[20] Since the battle of Crannon took place near Larissa, it makes sense to think that Larissa was one of the unfortunate cities singled out for siege and capture. Taking a large city like Larissa was just the sort of object lesson Antipater had in mind to teach the other recalcitrant Greeks. Pharsalus, another important city, definitely suffered this fate.[21] Little imagination is needed to surmise the catastrophic effects of a forcible takeover and sack on a city's financial well-being. If one figures in the costs of supporting an army of occupation for even a short time, the loss becomes staggering.[22] And this was not all. As previously mentioned, in 321 the Thessalians joined the Aetolians in another vain attempt at revolt against Macedonian control. Further financial losses were inevitable.

At the very least, the outcome of the wars of 323–321 B.C. must have brought a large and perhaps even crushing financial loss upon the Thessalians despite Antipater's "mild terms."[23] After the financial drain of the last three decades, there was no chance that the Thessalians had any substantial capital in reserve for rebuilding, or for liquidation of debt by public contributions. The economy was faltering, and the national financial plight was overwhelming. Where was the money to be found to buy silver abroad to be turned into coins at local mints? Moreover, silver may by now have become harder to procure, or at least more expensive. The main source of silver for Thessalian mints had presumably always been nearby Macedonia and Thrace.[24] But it

[20] Diodorus 18.17.7.

[21] Plutarch, *Moralia* 846E (*Vitae decem oratorum*).

[22] As Craterus admitted, the Macedonian army was a great burden even on its friends (Plutarch, *Phocion* 26.6).

[23] Diodorus 18.17.7. Public penury was a common result of war for agricultural communities. See, for example, the Thessalian inscription from the second century B.C. and the parallel cases published by Y. Béquignon, "Etudes thessaliennes," *BCH* 59 (1935), pp. 36–51 (= L. Moretti, *Iscrizioni storiche ellenistiche*, vol. 1, no. 99). This situation is explicitly described in *OGIS* 339, lines 54–58 (Sestus, 2nd B.C.).

[24] On mines in the north, see R. J. Forbes, *Studies in Ancient Technology*, vol. 8 (Leiden, 1964), pp. 224–225; Will, "Les sources des métaux," *Numismatique antique*, pp. 97–102.

seems likely that the amount of silver from these sources available for export to consumers such as the mints of Thessaly had diminished in the face of an increased domestic demand for metal to be made into the royal coinages of Macedonia. Furthermore, there is evidence that the value of silver relative to that of gold had risen by the end of the 320s, a development that may not have hurt those who were not buying silver with gold, but could surely have been part of a general inflation of prices just at the time when the Thessalians were least able to pay.[25]

All these indications of economic failure leading to financial weakness in Thessaly in the late 320s B.C. suggest that Larissa, and any other Thessalian cities with mints still in operation (e.g., Pharsalus), would have experienced great difficulty in finding the funds necessary to carry on the production of local coinage. If the chronological arrangement I have proposed for the fourth-century silver coins of Larissa is correct, it is perhaps no accident that an earlier diversity of coin types produced by the mint eventually dwindled to the production of the single type found in the hoard *IGCH* 168.[26] Fewer types meant fewer production expenses. This de-emphasis on variation for artistic reasons would be consistent with a situation of severe financial strain in the city. When conditions went from bad to worse as a result of drought and war, production of even a single type became financially burdensome, if not completely impossible. The city was not going to be budgeting any major expenditures in its present financial condition and therefore had no real need for new issues of local coinage. The coins already in circulation would easily serve the needs of the reduced level of transactions in the ravaged local economy. Regular production of local coinage was not going to be easy until the situation improved so that new taxes could be imposed or contributions solicited to pay for municipal expenses.

The economic and financial difficulties which the Thessalian cities encountered came, as it happened, not long after the

[25] See Le Rider, *Monnayage*, pp. 439–441; J. R. Melville-Jones, "The Value of Gold at Athens in 329/8 B.C.," *AJAH* 3 (1978), pp. 184–187.

[26] *ANSMN* 28 (1983), pp. 1–34.

production of Macedonian royal coinage substantially increased. As Le Rider has demonstrated, the production of coinage in Macedonia accelerated tremendously with the later issues of Philip II, and Alexander's coinage continued to be copious. The hoards show that these coins had begun to show up in Thessaly by the 320s. This influx of coinage provided a new supply of currency to take up any slack in the volume of coinage in circulation caused by a reduction or a halt in local production. Even though they were on a different weight standard, the tetradrachms of Philip and Alexander would have been welcome, if only because the large denominations in circulation in Thessaly had always come from foreign mints. And now the production of drachms in large numbers under Alexander made available a ready supply of a smaller denomination which, like the royal tetradrachms, was familiar to those Thessalians who had been paid by Alexander and brought their coins home with them. As exact fractions of the Macedonian tetradrachms, these drachms fit conveniently into circulation with their large denomination colleagues. At any rate, the inconvenience inherent in transactions conducted with coins of different weight standards was never a bar to circulation in Greece. Once agricultural production had recovered to the point where a surplus was available for barter or sale, Thessalians could acquire Macedonian coins (or any other, for that matter) in return for their grain or horses. Since Thessaly was in ordinary times self-supporting in food, there was little or no need to buy from foreign markets, and the continuing Macedonian domination meant that the cities of Thessaly had no independent foreign policy to be financed by state expenditures. The Thessalians could do without a domestic supply of coins so long as reliable and popular currency made its way into the country from abroad as payment for Thessalian products. From a practical point of view, the increased production of Macedonian royal coinage and its introduction into Thessaly (above all in the form of Macedonian pay to Thessalian soldiers) made regular production of local coinage in Thessaly superfluous, even if the cities could afford to keep open their mints. The coins of Philip and Alexander arrived in Thessaly as a popular and convenient form of exchange just in the period when they were most needed and most welcome. Macedonian royal policy had nothing directly to do with the fate of Thessalian coinage. A combination of practical factors made it easy for Macedonian royal coinage eventually to supplant local coinage to such an extent that further local production would have been superfluous even for purposes of convenience in exchange. But if the Macedonian kings were not concerned to suppress autonomous coinage in Thessaly, neither did they have any interest in restoring it when the mints closed. The evidence of the historical record coincides with the numismatic evidence in suggesting a date *ca.* 320 B.C. after the Lamian War as the likely *terminus* for silver coinage at Larissa. There is no evidence that any other Thessalian civic mint was able to continue minting silver coins after this date. Bronze coinage may have continued longer. In any case, local coins minted earlier continued to circulate in Thessaly alongside Macedonian issues after 320. [27] The attitude of the Macedonian sovereigns toward coinage in Thessaly, if they thought about the subject at all, was *laissez-faire.*

The resumption of the production of local coinage in Thessaly was long delayed, and when it did come in the second century B.C. after the appearance of the Romans in Greece in force, a federal coinage was created in place of the long-gone civic issues. The motives for the creation of a federal coinage in Thessaly in the changed conditions of the second century are beyond the confines of this investigation, but an explanation is in order for the failure of the local mints of Thessaly to resume production in the years after *ca.* 320 B.C. First, the financial plight of the cities in Thessaly may have improved only slowly, if at all. Rostovtzeff argued that the inflation in prices for most goods in the age of Alexander and the successors was a sign of growing prosperity

---

[27] This is clear from the hoards. *IG* IV, 617 from Argos, dated perhaps to the late fourth century, is a peculiar text which appears to record contributions from (among others) various Thessalian cities. The payments are made both in "Aeginetan" coins (i.e., local coinage on that standard) and in "Alexandrian" coins (i.e., Macedonian royal coinage).

and not of economic bad times.[28] For those like the Thessalians who could under favorable conditions produce a surplus to sell, higher prices meant higher incomes. But it is also true that higher prices discourage consumption and tend to shrink the size of the demand, therefore restricting the income of producers. Despite Rostovtzeff's confident evaluation of the prosperity of Greece in this period, there is evidence that conditions were bad for many people. Under 308 B.C., Diodorus reports that many Greeks from various states enlisted for service in Cyrene because the conditions of life in Greece were so terrible as a result of the wars of the successors.[29] These wars certainly continued to be fought or prepared for in Thessaly in the waning years of the fourth and the opening years of the third centuries. Even friendly forces had to be fed, and the Thessalians were in no position to insist on reimbursement. After all, they were the ones being "protected" or "liberated."

There is another point to be made about Thessalian revenues in the years after *ca.* 320. There are reasons, which I outlined earlier, for thinking that the Macedonian kings kept the confederacy in existence after this date. If they kept that tradition alive, they had every reason to preserve the tradition that they, and not the Thessalians, should receive the revenues of the confederacy. Then in 279 the predatory Gauls invaded, and their route through Greece took them into Thessaly. The barbarian leader Brennus also sent a band of marauders across Thessaly to attack Aetolia.[30] The damage which they must have inflicted can only have made matters worse in Thessaly. Aetolian raids later in the century presumably had a similar effect. [31] Since the evidence for Thessalian history in the third century is scattered and sparse, it would be going too far to claim that we know conditions failed to improve in a significant way. Nevertheless, there is a hint from the end of the century that prosperity had not returned to the land. Inscriptions testify that Larissa had experienced a drop in population which required the intervention of

[28] *Social and Economic History*, pp. 164–165.
[29] 20.40.7.
[30] Pausanias 10.19.12, 10.20.8, 10.22.2–3.
[31] Polybius 4.62.1, 5.99.4–5.

the Macedonian king, Philip V.[32] In sum, it seems possible that the cities of Thessaly failed to resume the production of local coinage because they found themselves unable to afford the expense of silver for coins after the devastation they had suffered in the later fourth century,[33] and they could conveniently continue to use Macedonian coinage which had become well known throughout the Greek world. Their decisions on these matters were their own, not the decisions of a sovereign in Macedonia. In the next chapter, we will see whether there is reason to think that the situation might have been any different elsewhere in Greece.

[32] See the references in n. 53 of chapter 6. For similar enfranchisements at Pharsalus and Phalanna, see *IG* IX.2, 234 and 1228 with *addenda*.

[33] See G.E.M. de Ste. Croix, *The Class Struggle in the Ancient Greek World* (Ithaca, 1981), p. 294, on Rostovtzeff's idea that a shrinking market for exports contributed to a general economic decline in Greece in the fourth century.

EIGHT. OTHER GREEK COINAGES

If we are to evaluate the idea that Macedonian kings had a policy of suppressing Greek coinages, we must look as clearly as the sources allow at other cases besides that of Thessaly. None of these cases can be as well documented as that of Thessaly, but the cumulative evidence is important.

1
The Greeks in the South

The standard handbook of Greek coinage in this period is now Colin Kraay's *Archaic and Classical Greek Coins* (1976). Since so little is known about some Greek coinages, Kraay reasonably enough does not devote equal attention to all issues of coinage. His book does represent, however, the most recent comprehensive treatment of the subject, and for that reason it is the best guide in the sort of survey which is needed here. My discussion will follow the arrangement of his presentation of the coinages within the various regions of Greece, beginning with central Greece.

Boeotia is first on the agenda. By the time Philip II began his reign in Macedonia, the coinage in use in Boeotia was probably minted in Thebes, the capital of the Boeotian Confederacy.[1] This coinage should probably be regarded as federal.[2] There are three series of coins that have to be considered, Kraay's series I(b), I(c), and II. All have the Boeotian shield on the obverse. I(b)

---

[1] For the Boeotian confederacy in this period, see Larsen, *GFS*, pp. 175–180; John Buckler, *The Theban Hegemony 371–362 B.C.* (Cambridge, Mass., 1980), pp. 18–33.

[2] On the finances of the confederacy, see Paul Roesch, *Etudes béotiennes* (Paris, 1982), pp. 297–298; Pierre Salmon, *Etude sur la Confédération béotienne (447/6–386)* (Brussels, 1978), pp. 212–214.

has the legend "of the Thebans" and an amphora accompanied by various symbols on the reverse, while I(c) has the amphora and symbols with personal names as legends. II has a similar reverse but with the legend "of the Boeotians." Kraay dates I(b) to the early years of the fourth century; II to 379–371 B.C., apparently on the assumption that the Boeotian Confederacy was in existence in this period but not firmly under Theban leadership (though Thebes was the capital and mint in his view); and I(c) to 371–338 B.C., the period of Theban hegemony bounded, in Kraay's view, by the battles of Leuctra and of Chaeronea.[3]

This historical reconstruction will not stand. The Boeotian Confederacy under Theban leadership had been dissolved by the King's Peace of 386 B.C., when the Thebans were required to let the cities of Boeotia be autonomous.[4] These terms meant only that the Thebans were stripped of their dominant position in Boeotia and did not prohibit the now free cities of Boeotia from arranging themselves in an alliance, or perhaps even in some other sort of cooperative organization. Other such organizations continued to exist in Greece after 386.[5] After the Theban uprising against a Spartan garrison in the early 370s, the Boeotian Confederacy was reestablished as a federal organization under Theban leadership by 375 B.C., albeit with a new constitution.[6] This new form of an old organization endured even after Philip's victory at Chaeronea in 338 because the Boeotian Confederacy as a unit joined Philip's Hellenic League like the other defeated Greeks.[7]

Nevertheless, 338 B.C. has generally been chosen as the date for the end of coinage produced at Thebes (for the Confederacy) for reasons which are never made explicit. Barclay V. Head implied that the mint at Thebes was closed in 338 because after Chaeronea "Thebes was now degraded from her proud position as head of all Boeotia. . . . Galling in the extreme were the

---

[3] *ACGC*, pp. 111–114. See below, n. 12, on the chronology of series I(c).

[4] Xenophon, *Hellenica* 5.1.31–36.

[5] Larsen, *GFS*, pp. 170–172.

[6] Buckler, *Theban Hegemony*, pp. 15–18.

[7] Larsen, *GFS*, p. 178; Griffith, *HM*, p. 625. See Roesch, *Etudes*, for a study of the confederacy from 338 to 172 B.C.

insults and personal injuries which her citizens were compelled to submit to at the hands of the barbarous Macedonian soldiery [of the garrison]."[8] One suspects that Head, and Kraay after him, saw the presence of Philip's garrison in the Cadmea of Thebes as the sign that local coinage ended in 338.[9] But this is not the whole story. Philip did not "degrade Thebes from her proud position," but he did want to keep the Thebans from threatening him militarily in the future, and he took several steps to ensure his protection. The garrison was one, but so were the rebuilding of the "destroyed" cities of Plataea, Orchomenus, and Thespiae, the restoration of exiles (who would presumably become royal partisans), and the installation of an oligarchic council in the city which could control the Boeotian Confederacy in the king's interest.[10] These oligarchs were Philip's "friends." Forbidding them the right of coinage would have been a strange proof of friendship. It is impossible to believe that a pro-Macedonian Boeotian Confederacy led by a secure Thebes and belonging to the Hellenic League was not able to continue minting local coinage. The argument would hold even if Kraay were right that the issues with magistrates' names are civic instead of federal. Thebes was in Philip's camp after Chaeronea.

The situation at the mint remained essentially unchanged after Chaeronea, although Philip's oligarchic supporters were now the ones to oversee the local operation. The end came in 335 when Alexander in the guise of Greek *hegemon* executed the will of his allies against the rebellious Thebans. He razed the town and sold a huge number of its inhabitants into slavery. A garrison was placed in the Cadmea again, but the city was no more.[11] The physical destruction of the mint at Thebes meant the *de facto* end of local coinage. There is no reason to think that series I(c) necessarily had to end in 338 rather than in 335.[12]

[8] *On the Chronological Sequence of the Coins of Boeotia* (London, 1881), p. 73.

[9] Diodorus 16.87.3; Pausanias 9.1.8, 9.6.5.

[10] See Griffith, *HM*, pp. 610–611.

[11] Diodorus 17.12; Arrian 1.9.9.

[12] Kraay reports the number of issues known from series I(c) as "over forty" (*ACGC*, p. 113). J. Taillardat and P. Roesch, "L'inventaire sacré de Thespies. L'alphabet attique en Béotie," *Revue de philologie* 40 (1966), pp. 85–87, have shown that some of these issues are earlier than 395 B.C. They place the start of

Local coinage could have been revived elsewhere in Boeotia after 335 with Alexander's blessing if any of the cities had so desired. They remained "free" members of the Hellenic League and divided up the territory of Thebes among themselves. [13] If their coins had been their symbols, necessary to their sense of political identity, the Boeotians could have rebuilt the federal mint or started individual civic issues. Apparently they chose neither of these options. On present evidence, it appears that the Boeotians minted no new silver coins until some point well into the third century when they produced a new series of Attic-standard tetradrachms with new types inscribed "of the Boeotians." [14]

The decision not to issue local coinage cannot have been the result of a Macedonian royal policy forbidding autonomous Greek coinage. Other Greek coinages in the general area, such as that of Delphi, continued. The Boeotians produced no coinage of their own after 335 because they decided they needed none. Minting coinage required capital in the first place, even if a profit could perhaps be expected from a well-run mint. The Boeotian cities were perhaps financially too weak to find it easy to produce currency, silver coinage, which had to be financed with capital like any other commodity required by the state. A shortage of funds, for example, would help to account for the slow pace of reconstruction of the "destroyed" cities, which remained incomplete in 335. [15] To add to the burden, the famine of the 320s did not spare the Boeotians. Tanagra and Plataea received grain from Cyrene. [16] Moreover, the Boeotians were sufficiently well supplied with coins to satisfy the needs of local

---

the series *ca.* 400 or a little earlier. Cf. Salmon, *Etude,* pp. 43–47. S. N. Koumanoudes, "Prosopographika Thebaikon nomismaton," *Neon Athenaion* 5 (1964–1966), pp. 62–69, appears to place series I(c) in the period 379–335 B.C.

[13] Larsen, *GFS,* pp. 178–180. Diodorus 18.11.4 shows that Boeotians were among the allies who profited from the destruction of Thebes. See Roesch, *Etudes,* pp. 417–439, on Thebes and the confederacy from 335 to 288 B.C.

[14] *HN,* p. 353. One example turns up in the Sophikon hoard, which is dated *ca.* 230–220 B.C. (*IGCH* 179).

[15] Plutarch, *Alexander* 34.2; *Aristides* 11.9.

[16] *GHI* 196, lines 32, 44.

exchange. Their old issues still circulated, for one thing.[17] For another, the large-scale production of coinage in Macedonia made available a convenient, even desirable substitute for local coinage which had an international appeal no Boeotian issue could match. This is supplantation, however, not suppression. The supplantation took place for economic reasons and at the decision of the Boeotians. In short, it should be clear that the apparent break in production of local coinage in Boeotia which began in the later fourth century was not the result of the enforcement of a policy of suppression set in Macedonia.

We may omit Thessaly, already fully discussed, and turn to Phocis and Locris. The traditional coinage of Phocis was federal in character, and Kraay has plausibly linked the peaks and valleys in the history of its production to the changing needs of the Phocian Confederacy for funds to pay for national defense and, perhaps, for reconstruction after the Persian Wars of the fifth century, and to the changing supply of silver. He puts the end of coinage in Phocis after the conclusion of the Sacred War, which "was ended in 346 by the intervention of Philip, and the total elimination of the political and military power of the Phocians. Any remaining resources were to be devoted to repaying the looted Delphic treasure at the rate of sixty talents a year, and it may be safely assumed that the Phocian coinage came to an end at this time."[18] Certain historical details deserve notice. The fine was levied as a total assessed on "the Phocians," not as a set of separate payments to be made by different bodies. The payments are recorded as from "the Phocians," and the appearance of the federal archon of the Phocians in these records proves the

[17] See, for example, the appearance of Boeotian fractions in *IGCH* 78 from Orchomenus (*ca.* 323 B.C.), a circulation hoard, to judge from the preponderance of fractions.

[18] *ACGC*, p. 121. See Griffith, *HM*, pp. 346, 451. Rainer C. S. Felsch, "Apollon und Artemis oder Artemis und Apollon?" *AA* 1980, pp. 83–84, argues that the beginning of Phocian coinage must be linked to the rise of a national political consciousness *ca.* 570 B.C. after the liberation of Phocis from Thessalian domination. It can be pointed out that a newly liberated state with powerful and hostile neighbors would have had good reason to furnish itself with a coinage in order to finance its defense, as well as the major building program which Felsch also assumes for this period.

federal organization continued to exist.[19] The implication is that some sort of organizational structure was left in place to raise and to send on the money. In, it seems, 338, the payment schedule was relaxed to ten talents a year, and the continuing political identity of the Phocians is attested by their appearance in the partially preserved inscription which is generally assumed to list the members of Philip's League of Corinth.[20] In other words, the Macedonian king did not require the complete abolition of Phocis as a political entity; indeed, it was in his interest to keep it going.[21] It is very likely that the Phocians even after 346, and especially after 338, could have had their own coinage if they so desired. Neither Philip nor Alexander would have forbidden them. If it is true, as usually assumed, that the Phocians did not issue any more coins in the fourth century after the 340s or the 330s, it was their own decision. Whatever money they raised, whether from capital levies on themselves, from import/export fees, or from the sale of commodities to outsiders, had to go to repay Apollo. Those payments could just as well go to Delphi in the form in which they were collected, whether local coins, objects of value, or foreign coins. The Phocians had no need to endure the losses involved in melting down precious metal to mint Phocian coins.[22] Like the Boeotians and the Thessalians a few years later, they would have stopped coining because it no longer made financial sense to try to carry on. Operating in the shadow of the Macedonian king, the Phocians had neither an independent foreign policy nor any significant defense force to finance. Their future, such as it was, was guaranteed by their *hegemon*, the Macedonian king. But he never told them to close their mint. Like the Amphictyons at Delphi, who issued a local coinage in the mid-330s, the Phocians could have minted coins in their own name after 346 if they felt the

[19] Diodorus 16.60.2; *GHI* 172.

[20] *SVA* III, no. 403, b, line 8. See Larsen, *GFS*, pp. 300–302, and especially Griffith, *HM*, pp. 592–593, on this complex situation.

[21] Griffith, *HM*, p. 454.

[22] For the losses involved in melting down old coins to mint new ones, see E.J.P. Raven, "The Amphictyonic Coinage of Delphi, 336–334 B.C.," *NC* 1950, pp. 1–22.

need to have a local coinage in addition to the other coinages, especially Macedonian, in circulation in Greece which could serve their needs for currency in a perfectly adequate fashion. [23]

The case of Locris is desperately obscure. For unknown reasons, the Locrians as a federal organization began to issue a very up-to-date-looking silver coinage at some point in the first half of the fourth century, perhaps *ca.* 380. The sequence of issues lasted until at least *ca.* 340. [24] Kraay makes the good suggestion that during the Sacred War these coins were used to finance military expenditures. Perhaps the end of the war meant that there was no longer any pressing need for local coinage in an area that in the past usually had none. The Locrians, too, belonged to the League of Corinth after Chaeronea. [25] If Locrian coinage came to an end in this period, this had nothing to do with any Macedonian policy on coinage.

Next to be considered are the mints of northwestern Greece. The most remarkable feature of the coinage of this area in the later fourth century is the number of mints which begin to issue a uniform, Corinthian-style coinage, the famous silver *pegasi* with a winged horse as the obverse type. Eleven different civic mints can be identified. [26] The great majority of these coins turn up in Sicily. [27] For the next half century or so these *pegasi*, along with

[23] On Delphi, see Raven, *NC* 1950, pp. 1–22; Kraay, *ACGC*, pp. 121–122; Georges Roux, *L'Amphictionie, Delphes et le temple d'Apollon au IVe siècle* (Lyon, 1979), pp. 129–133; Philip Kinns, "The Amphictyonic Coinage Reconsidered," *NC* 1983, pp. 1–22. Roderick T. Williams, *The Silver Coinage of the Phokians* (London, 1972), pp. 49, n. 2, and 60, n. 3, says that some of the issues of his period V series (the final one) could perhaps go as late as *ca.* 339–336 B.C., but he thinks that Phocis was too devastated for at least a generation after 346 to issue coinage. It must be emphasized that we lack the evidence to establish any closing date for the Phocian mint.

[24] Kraay, *ACGC*, pp. 122–123.

[25] *SVA* III, no. 403, b, line 8.

[26] *ACGC*, pp. 126–127.

[27] For the idea that Corinthian colonies and allies in the northwest minted these coins to help finance the military expedition to Sicily led by the Corinthian Timoleon in 344 B.C., see G. K. Jenkins, "A Note on Corinthian Coins in the West," in *Centennial Publication of the American Numismatic Society*, ed. Harald Ingholt (New York, 1958), pp. 367–379; R.J.A. Talbert, *Timoleon and the Revival of Greek Sicily 344–317 B.C.* (Cambridge, 1974), pp. 161–178; C. M. Kraay, "Timoleon and Corinthian Coinage in Sicily," in *Actes du 8ème Congrès*

those of Corinth, became the main money in circulation in Sicily, probably because they were available in quantity and had a reputation for reliability which made them desirable for trade purposes. There is no suggestion that any of these coinages were affected by the Macedonian king, with one notable exception. According to Kraay, "The Ambraciot series was destined to be cut short, for in 338 the town was captured by Philip and received a Macedonian garrison, so bringing its activity as a Corinthian mint to an end."[28] This statement is presumably based on the same assertion made by Oscar Ravel in his work on the sequence of the *pegasi* issues of Ambracia.[29] Ravel's evidence was Diodorus 17.3.3, where one reads that after Philip's death in 336 B.C. the Ambracians expelled the garrison which Philip had installed and then set up a democracy. It is assumed that this garrison (and an oligarchic government as well?) had been installed by Philip after his victory at Chaeronea in 338.[30] As in the case of Thebes, which also received a garrison after Chaeronea, it is assumed that the presence of garrison troops meant closing the local mint.

This latter assumption simply makes no sense, especially when a city's government is organized to favor the supporters of the Macedonian king (as at both Ambracia and Thebes). It would have been strange politics to install one's collaborators in power and simultaneously deny them the right to mint coins to pay the troops who protected them and the king's interests. Moreover, the Ambracians were members of Philip's League.[31] They might be the hosts of a force "assigned to the common defense," the Macedonian euphemism for a garrison in a Greek city, but the Ambracians were autonomous after Chaeronea. In 336,

---

international de numismatique New York-Washington 1973 (Paris, 1976), pp. 99–105. See, however, R. R. Holloway, "Il problema dei 'pegasi' in Sicilia," *Quaderni ticinesi. Numismatica e antichità classiche* 11 (1982), pp. 129–136, for the evidence that *pegasi* were important in Sicilian circulation before the arrival of Timoleon.

[28] *ACGC*, p. 126.

[29] *The "Colts" of Ambracia* (New York, 1928), pp. 4, 20, with n. 17 on p. 165.

[30] Griffith, *HM*, pp. 612–613.

[31] *SVA* III, no. 403, b, line 6.

Alexander confirmed their autonomy even after they had expelled the garrison and changed their government.[32] The next certain information we have about the status of Ambracia is the report that Pyrrhus took possession of the city and installed his own troops there *ca.* 294 B.C. Cassander's son, Alexander, had been in control of Ambracia before this, and he perhaps had a garrison there, too.[33] It has been suggested that the city had been garrisoned again as early as the end of the 320s at the conclusion of the Lamian War.[34] In any case, the presence of a Macedonian garrison in a Greek city tells us nothing about the fate of that city's coinage, as we see from the case of Athens. No one doubts that the traditional coinage of that city continued throughout the fourth century and on into the third despite the presence of a Macedonian garrison from 322 B.C. on.[35]

The numismatic evidence for the coinage of Ambracia is not copious, but from it one does not get the impression that the city's mint closed down in 338 B.C. Coins of Ambracia turn up in eight hoards dated to the reigns of Philip and Alexander and in eighteen hoards dated to the last quarter of the fourth and the first quarter of the third centuries. Thereafter Ambracian silver disappears from the hoards. The frequency of occurrence of these coins remains fairly consistent throughout the hoards (they are never as common as the coins of Corinth). These limited statistics are not necessarily reliable, and one would like to have detailed information on comparative wear, for one thing. As usual this is impossible, but the scanty data available do not contradict the idea that Ambracia probably issued coins after 338

---

[32] Diodorus 17.4.3.

[33] Plutarch, *Pyrrhus* 6.4–5. For the date, see D. Kienast, *RE* 47, *s. v.* "Pyrrhos" (13), col. 121.

[34] Hermann Bengtson, *Die Strategie in der hellenistischen Zeit*, vol. 1, p. 140, n. 3.

[35] Kraay, *ACGC*, pp. 74–77. Antipater first installed the garrison (Diodorus 18.18.5). For the continuous presence of the garrison, see Ch. Habicht, *Untersuchungen zur politischen Geschichte Athens im 3. Jahrhundert v. Chr.* (Munich, 1979, Vestigia 30), pp. 95–112; against the idea that Antigonus Gonatas deprived Athens of the right of coinage, Habicht, *Studien zur Geschichte Athens in hellenistischer Zeit* (Göttingen, 1982, Hypomnemata 73), pp. 100–107.

B.C.[36] The one salient and incontrovertible fact about the hoards containing *pegasi* of Ambracia is their location. Twenty of the twenty-four hoards come from Sicily, and two others from southern Italy. This particular statistic shows very clearly that the Ambracians were helping to satisfy the demand in Magna Graecia for Corinthian-style coinage which began in the second half of the fourth century. Eventually this demand faded away. It seems very likely that autonomous coinage at Ambracia, which by this time was apparently largely destined for export, ended when the foreign demand for it ended.[37]

There is much less to be said about most other mints in mainland Greece. Athens has already been mentioned. The prolific fifth-century mint of Aegina found no parallel in the fourth. Sporadic issues were produced for local use, but there is no hint of Macedonian interference.[38] As for the numerous mints of the Peloponnese, their often isolated and irregular issues of coinage sputtered on, so far as we know, independent of the Macedonian kings. Only local concerns, and probably the availability and cost of silver, dictated the rhythm of production.[39]

Only one detail deserves mention. Kraay states that the rather more important mint at Sicyon ceased production about 330 B.C.[40] No reason is given for this view. One must suspect that it reflects the now discredited idea of E. Babelon that certain gold and silver coins of Alexander type ("Peloponnesian Alexanders") were minted at Sicyon. A. R. Bellinger, accepting this identification, favored this date for the end of local coinage at

[36] See the appendix on Ambracian coins in hoards.

[37] It is worth pointing out that Kraay argued elsewhere that the earlier production of coinage at Ambracia was sporadic, the result of changing historical circumstances which had nothing to do with considerations of sovereignty and everything to do with the financial condition of the city and the demands of its great ally, Corinth. See his articles "The Earliest Issue of Ambracia" and "The Coinage of Ambracia and the Preliminaries of the Peloponnesian War" in *Quaderni ticinesi. Numismatica e antichità classiche* 6 (1977), pp. 35–52, and 8 (1979), pp. 37–66.

[38] Kraay, *ACGC*, pp. 48–49.

[39] Kraay, *ACGC*, pp. 100–103, 105–107. It is especially regrettable that we know so little about the coinage even of the important city of Argos.

[40] *ACGC*, p. 100.

Sicyon because he postulated the opening of a royal Macedonian mint in the city which operated from 330 to 323 B.C.[41] For Bellinger, this development was the result of Alexander's implementation of a more efficient and, for the Greek cities whose mints were affected, a more oppressive monetary system for the European sector of the Macedonian empire. Bellinger and Kraay presumably would have felt that the presence of a pro-Macedonian garrison in Sicyon in this period, which we hear about because it was expelled in the Lamian War, was further evidence for the closure of the local mint.[42] The city was again garrisoned after the failure of the revolt and remained so under various masters, until Demetrius freed it at the end of the century.[43]

A study of the so-called Peloponnesian Alexanders of Sicyon has shown, however, that there is no reason to believe that any royal issues were produced at Sicyon.[44] With the phantom Macedonian mint of Sicyon dispelled, it is possible to speculate about the fate of local coinage there from the numismatic evidence available. Sicyonian silver coins occur regularly in hoards dated to the later fourth and third centuries. Since these issues have not been systematically classified, it is impossible to decide with confidence when (or perhaps even if) the mint of Sicyon stopped production, either intermittently or permanently. But the information available on the frequency of occurrence of these coins in hoards and on their comparative states of wear suggests that it would be wrong to assume that local coinage necessarily came to

---

[41] *Essays*, pp. 58–60.

[42] *IG* II² 448, lines 46–47. This garrison was probably connected with the tyrant installed with Alexander's blessing. See [Demosthenes] 17.16. On the history of Sicyon in this period, see Audrey Griffin, *Sikyon* (Oxford, 1982), pp. 76–79.

[43] Diodorus 19.67.1–2, 19.74.2, 20.37.1–2, 20.102.2–103.1; Plutarch, *Demetrius*, 25.1.

[44] Hyla Troxell, "The Peloponnesian Alexanders," *ANSMN* 17 (1971), pp. 41–94, esp. 44–50 on these particular issues. This study is not mentioned by Kraay in his discussion of Sicyon. Nancy J. Moore, "The Lifetime and Early Posthumous Coinage of Alexander the Great from Pella" (Diss., Princeton University, 1984), assigns these coins to the Pella mint in the period *ca.* 328–323 B.C.

a halt at Sicyon early in the reign of Alexander.[45] If it did cease at some point in the late fourth century, the situation was probably the same as I have suggested for Thessaly. Sicyon received a large shipment of grain from Cyrene during the great famine.[46] One can suspect that numerous Greek city-states gave up the production of their own coinage *ca.* 320 B.C. for the same reasons: economic crisis leading to financial weakness and the tendency for Macedonian coinage to supplant local coinages in even local circulation.

The remaining important mints are those of Euboea and of Corinth. The coinages of Chalcis and the Euboean Confederacy in the fourth century and later have recently received close attention in a major study by Olivier Picard.[47] Based on a full analysis of the hoards and the sequence of issues of the civic mint at Chalcis, Picard concludes that federal issues (produced at Chalcis) and civic issues alternated. When (on his view) the Confederacy developed in the first half of the fourth century under Boeotian patronage, federal coinage was issued on the Aeginetan standard in use in Boeotia. Later, in the early 350s, the Confederacy shifted its allegiance to the confederacy headed by Athens, and the weight standard of its coinage was also shifted to the Attic in order to facilitate, Picard plausibly suggests, Euboea's contributions to the expenses of military defense against common enemies (especially the Boeotians dominated by Thebes).[48] After Chaeronea, Picard believes, Philip II dissolved the Euboean Confederacy, whose coinage naturally stopped as an indirect consequence of this political decision. At this point, however, the cities of Chalcis (which received a Macedonian garrison), Histiaea, and Carystus began to issue local coinage (Eretria had no coinage of its own until the second century B.C.).[49] So far as one can tell, the interference of various Macedonian sovereigns

[45] See the appendix on Sicyonian coins in hoards.

[46] *GHI* 196, line 12.

[47] *Chalcis et la confédération eubéenne: étude de numismatique et d'histoire (IVᵉ–Iᵉʳ siècle)* (Athens, 1979).

[48] *Chalcis*, pp. 174–175, 344.

[49] *Chalcis*, pp. 252–253. Griffith, *HM*, p. 612, n. 3, suggests Chalcis was not garrisoned until 335 B.C. after the revolt of Thebes.

on the island had no direct effect on civic coinage until Demetrius Poliorcetes revived the Euboean Confederacy in the period
ca. 304–290. The Macedonian garrison in Chalcis stayed in
place under a succession of sovereigns until Antigonus' agent
expelled it in 313, only to reimpose it in 310/9. This garrison
was later thrown out, but Demetrius installed troops when he
became an ally of the city in 304.[50] None of this can be connected directly to any effect on local coinage. When Demetrius
revived the Confederacy, the cities closed their mints so that
they could cooperate in the production of a federal coinage, just
as they had during the earlier history of the Confederacy in the
absence of any Macedonian influence or control. The cities had
no coinage of their own when joined together in a Confederacy
because they were supporting the joint effort financially with
individual contributions. [51] As an ally of the city, not as its ruler,
Demetrius temporarily opened a mint of his own at Chalcis. [52]

Picard assumes that Chalcis had no civic issues from 308 to
304 B.C. as a result of the city's supposed entry into the Boeotian
Confederacy and consequent loss of independence. Furthermore,
membership in the Boeotian Confederacy imposed "the renunciation of all independent coinage." [53] Picard does not indicate whether he means that Chalcis had to give up her coinage
because the Boeotians suppressed it as part of the loss of
independence or because, as usual in federal organizations, all
members were contributing toward the production of a joint
coinage. Since the Boeotians seem not to have been issuing any
coinage in this period, he presumably inclines to the former opinion. But all of this is just an assumption because, as Picard's discussion illustrates, it is quite possible that Chalcis never was a
member of the Boeotian Confederacy but, rather, simply an ally.
At the dissolution of the Euboean Confederacy for unknown reasons *ca.* 290, Chalcis, along with Histiaea and Carystus, resumed
the production of local silver coinage. After a short-lived revolt
from the dominance of Antigonus Gonatas *ca.* 273, Chalcis lost

---

[50] *Chalcis*, pp. 256–267.
[51] Aeschines 3.94.
[52] Picard, *Chalcis*, p. 261.
[53] *Chalcis*, pp. 175, 260–261.

the right of coinage (on Picard's view). Local coinage resumed *ca.* 245 after the death of Alexander, son of Craterus, and an interval of revived activity by the Confederacy.[54]

Two observations should be made. First, Picard's careful study shows that the Macedonian kings in the fourth century and even into the third (before *ca.* 273 on his chronology) did nothing directly to change the traditional arrangements for local coinage on Euboea. Their actions concerning the Euboean Confederacy had an indirect effect on the local monetary system because it was customary on the island for the Confederacy to issue a federal coinage when it was in existence. But it would be a complete misreading of the political situation in this period to say that anything the Macedonian kings did was done as a result of a policy on the right of coinage. Second, even though Picard's work justifies this first point, he appears to subscribe to the notion that the loss of a city's independence required the suppression of its coinage. If Chalcis ever was a member of the Boeotian Confederacy, however, normal federal arrangements of the kind familiar to the Chalcidians would explain the renunciation of local coinage without any assumption of forced suppression. As for the suppression of local coinage said by Picard to be dictated by Antigonus in the late 270s, this is an assumption made under the influence of the tradition on sovereignty and coinage which this study has traced. As Picard himself points out, we know almost nothing about the factors which influenced Greek cities in their choice whether to mint coins or not. We are at a complete loss, for example, to try to explain why Eretria, the neighbor of Chalcis, produced no coinage during all this time. Chalcis itself produced silver coinage only on an irregular pattern in the third century during a period of great prosperity.[55]

Corinth is the final southern Greek city to be treated here. Until the work of Oscar Ravel on the coinage of Corinth, scholars assumed that the city's mint continued to operate as late as the first half of the third century B.C. despite the apparently

---

[54] *Chalcis*, pp. 271–276.
[55] *Chalcis*, pp. 173, 346–347.

continuous presence of a Macedonian garrison on Acrocorinth for almost a century after Chaeronea in 338 B.C.[56] In his work on the *pegasi* of Ambracia, Ravel associated the introduction of the garrison in 338 with the end of local coinage in that city.[57] He had nothing to say, however, about the Macedonian garrison installed at Corinth simultaneously. The end of civic coinage at Corinth came, in his view, *ca.* 300 B.C. when Cassander took the city from Demetrius Poliorcetes and Macedonian coins replaced the "colts" of Corinth.[58] Before we can evaluate the merits of this historical reconstruction, we must examine the numismatic evidence.

The two final groups of Corinthian coinage in Ravel's arrangement are his groups V and VI. He placed the *terminus* of V in 307 B.C. based on a hoard of 196 silver coins found buried in a pot in the modern village of Chiliomodi near Corinth (*IGCH* 85).[59] Included in the hoard were fourteen drachms of Corinth and twelve of Ptolemy, all marked with the same letters (ΔO) on the reverse, and all in FDC condition. Since the hoard also contained twenty-one tetradrachms of Ptolemy in slightly worn condition, Ravel concluded that the Ptolemaic drachms could not have come from Egypt and must have been minted in Corinth to pay the Ptolemaic troops in the garrison which occupied Corinth from, according to Ravel, 308 to 306 B.C.[60] Ravel believed that the same mint officials had been responsible for both the Corinthian and the Ptolemaic drachms, hence the same letters on both series. Since the ΔO coins were the last of group V, Ravel split the difference and made 307 B.C. the *terminus* of the group. Since then, scholars have usually taken 308 – 306 as the period in

---

[56] See, for example, E. T. Newell, *The Coinages of Demetrius Poliorcetes* (London, 1927), pp. 145 – 146. The garrison was originally part of the "common defense force" of Philip's League of Corinth. See [Demosthenes] 17.15 for this force. The garrison stayed in place until Aratus "freed" the city in 243/2. For the date, see R. M. Errington, *Philopoemen* (Oxford, 1969), p. 268.

[57] *The "Colts" of Ambracia*, pp. 4, 20.

[58] *Les "Poulains" de Corinthe*, vol. 2 (London, 1948), pp. 28 – 29.

[59] "Corinthian Hoard from Chiliomodi," in *Transactions of the International Numismatic Congress*, ed. J. Allan, H. Mattingly, and E.S.G. Robinson (London, 1938), pp. 99 – 108.

[60] For Ptolemy's garrison, see Diodorus 20.37.1 – 2; Plutarch *Demetrius* 15.1.

which local coinage came to an end at Corinth. [61] This does not coincide with Ravel's scheme. He imagined that the ΔO Ptolemaic drachms went to pay the garrison troops and that Corinthian issues continued to be produced and to circulate as usual to serve local needs. The end of local Corinthian coinage on his scheme came only with the termination of group VI at the supposed return of Cassander to Corinth *ca.* 300, whose troops Ravel imagined to have replaced the troops of Demetrius Poliorcetes in the city, whose own garrison had in 303 B.C. replaced an earlier garrison installed by Cassander as a replacement for the garrison originally installed by Ptolemy in 308. In short, Ravel argued that beginning with the occupation by Demetrius Poliorcetes, which ended in 300 B.C. on his view, "the regular money (of Corinth) was probably of Macedonian type . . . and under Cassander it completely replaced the colts."[62]

This view is untenable on historical grounds alone, as we will see shortly. But the numismatic situation is also not as simple as is often assumed. The Corinthian coins of Ravel's group VI, put together as a group because they have monograms (the sequence of issues cannot be determined), could have continued beyond *ca.* 300 B.C. In the hoard *IGCH* 147 (dated 280 B.C.), for example, the fourteen specimens of group VI found in it range in condition from "very fine" to "exceedingly fine." The posthumous tetrobols of Philip in the hoard, which appear to belong to the early third century, range only from "fine" to "very fine."[63] This could mean that the group VI coins are later than 300 B.C. More important are three issues of drachms marked by letters

[61] For a recent view, see Andrew Burnett, "The Coinages of Rome and Magna Graecia in the Late Fourth and Third Centuries B.C.," *SNR* 56 (1977), pp. 97–98, 111.

[62] Ravel, *Poulains*, p. 29: "Pendant cette période, la monnaie régulière était sans doute de type macédonien, et, sous Cassandre, elle remplaça complètement les poulains." The sources for the occupation of Corinth by Cassander and Demetrius are given below.

[63] Ravel, *Corinthian Hoards* (New York, 1932), pp. 12–27. The presence of monogram issues in this hoard and their absence from *IGCH* 171, the enormous hoard (3786 silver coins) from Mycenae dated 250–240 B.C., show that these coins cannot be as late as 243–233 B.C., as proposed by C. Oman, "Some Problems of the Later Coinage of Corinth," *NC* 1926, p. 33.

unknown in Ravel's group V. These drachms turn up in *IGCH* 171, a huge hoard dated *ca.* 250−240 B.C. on the basis of the tetradrachms of Ptolemy II which it contains. Coins from group V are present in the hoard, but the specimens with the new letters are uniformly the best preserved of the Corinthian coins. The examples of the rare ΔO type (the final series of group V dated *ca.* 308−306) are perceptibly more worn than are the coins with letters unknown to Ravel. [64] On this evidence, the ΔO coins of group V should not be the final autonomous issues of Corinth whatever one thinks the chronology to be of the issues of group VI. Finally, there are the so-called Peloponnesian Alexanders, Attic-standard tetradrachms which have been assigned to Corinth *ca.* 290−288 B.C. as issues of Demetrius Poliorcetes. [65] As Picard points out, there are good reasons for thinking that these are civic rather than royal issues. [66]

Corinthian coinage apparently did come to an end at some point in the first half of the third century. [67] But there is no evidence at all that this cessation of coinage was caused by the direct action of a Macedonian commander or king. As Ravel concluded, Ptolemy apparently let the mint of Corinth go on with its production of local coinage, so long as it also took care of his need for coined money. After the installation of Ptolemy's garrison in 308 B.C., we next hear of Corinth in 303 B.C. when, as just mentioned, Demetrius Poliorcetes expelled a garrison belonging to Cassander. We do not know when Ptolemy's troops

[64] The new letters, which do not appear in Ravel's "Répertoire des lettres et inscriptions," *Poulains*, vol. 2, pp. 287−288 (no. 1126 with lambda on the reverse is a barbarian imitation), are NO, Y, and Λ. See *Arch. Eph.* 1896, pls. 7.5, 21−22, and 8.20. Notice that the lower feathers of Pegasus' wings are worn away on the ΔO specimens in pl. 7.15−16. The ΔO coins are in better condition than the other letter-marked issues of Ravel's group V, confirming the position of ΔO at the end of the group.

[65] Troxell, *ANSMN* 17 (1971), pp. 44−50.

[66] *Chalcis*, p. 180.

[67] To judge from the hoards listed in *IGCH* and *CH*, Corinthian coins become relatively scarce in hoards dated after *ca.* 270 B.C. Cf. Tony Hackens, "A propos de la circulation monétaire dans le Péloponnèse au III ᵉ s. av. J.-C.," in *Antidorum W. Peremans sexagenario ab alumnis oblatum* (Louvain, 1968, Studia Hellenistica 16), p. 93.

had given way to Cassander's.[68] Demetrius came to Corinth to found a Hellenic League of "free" Greeks, and his garrison was installed, so he maintained, at the request of the Corinthians as protection against Cassander. [69] Ravel, furthermore, was wrong to think that Cassander took Corinth back from Demetrius *ca.* 300. All indications agree that Demetrius' garrison continued to hold the city throughout his lifetime and remained in place under Antigonus Gonatas. [70] The most plausible explanation for the end of local coinage at Corinth is the contraction of the Sicilian market for imported silver coins. [71] When this foreign demand had dropped off and the influx into Corinth of the popular coinage of Macedonia had greatly reduced the need for local production of coinage, the municipal government could respond by closing the mint without inflicting any hardship on the citizenry. If any coins were to be issued, for example to make a "contribution" to Corinth's Macedonian protectors, the coins of choice would be issues on the Attic standard matching those minted in Macedonia.

Despite the uncertainty on details, the cumulative force of the evidence merits emphasis. Nowhere in mainland Greece south of Macedonia does one find a single place whose coinage can reasonably be thought to have come to an end in the fourth century as a result of suppression by a Macedonian king or would-be king. In most cases, the dates of cessation of local coinages are extremely uncertain and have tended to be fixed on *a priori* grounds which reflect the common opinion on sovereignty and coinage. It is certainly true, moreover, that autonomous coinage could continue without hindrance even in cities which were occupied by a garrison. Where we can check, the likeliest

[68] Diodorus 20.103.1–2. Since Ptolemy's forces still held Sicyon in 303 B.C. (20.102.2), they need not have left Corinth as early as 306. O. Mørkholm, "Cyrene and Ptolemy I. Some Numismatic Comments," *Chiron* 10 (1980), p. 156, observing that the date at which Ptolemy gave up Corinth is uncertain, dates the Chiliomodi hoard to 304 B.C.

[69] For the garrison, see Diodorus 20.103.3; for his League, see *SVA* III, no. 446.

[70] Plutarch, *Demetrius* 43.4, 51.1, 53.4.

[71] See Talbert, *Timoleon*, p. 167. Cf. A. R. Bellinger, "Greek Coins from the Yale Numismatic Collection II," *YCS* 12 (1951), p. 255.

explanation for the end of local coinage in this period is lack of financial resources to continue local minting, or at least a clear financial disincentive to continue, coupled with the influx of widely accepted, popular, and convenient issues from the royal Macedonian mints which supplant local issues because local inhabitants preferred the foreign coins to their own. The best assumption is that the Macedonian kings and commanders who exercised control over various cities of mainland Greece did nothing to or about Greek coinage. What we want to know is whether this was the result of an intentional policy to keep hands off Greek coinage in deference to Greek notions of the requirements of local autonomy despite a strong Macedonian tradition of suppressing nonroyal coinages, or simply the reflection of a general lack of interest on the part of the Macedonian kings in the entire subject of Greek coinage. As part of this necessarily speculative inquiry, a few observations are in order on the Macedonian, barbarian, and Greek coinages of the north in the period before the reign of Philip II.

2

Coinages of the North

Despite considerable scholarly interest in the coinages and associated political developments of Macedonia, Thrace, and the surrounding Balkan regions in the sixth and fifth centuries, no consensus has been reached as a result of the bewildering complexity of the numismatic material and the paucity of historical sources.[72] Given the state of the evidence, no one interpretation is likely to be agreed upon in the future. Since the most recent comprehensive treatment of this difficult subject is by N.G.L. Hammond, his arguments offer a logical starting point for this

---

[72] See Doris Raymond, *Macedonian Regal Coinage to 413 B.C.* (New York, 1953), with the review by J.M.F. May in *NC* 1953, pp. 165–170; P. R. Franke, "Geschichte, Politik und Münzprägung im frühen Makedonien," *JNG* 3–4 (1952–1953), pp. 99–111; M. J. Price, *Coins of the Macedonians* (London, 1974), pp. 2–30.

discussion.[73] He argues that coinage began in the Thraco-Macedonian area in the sixth century because there was a foreign demand for the precious metals which the region had in abundance. When the Persians made their way into Europe, demand increased from the silver-hungry Persian Empire. Gold always, and silver sometimes, were exported as raw bullion in response to this demand, but silver was usually sent abroad in the form of coinage. That this coinage was manufactured to serve as a reliable form of bullion is shown by the common practice of minting very large silver pieces, some more than twice the weight of the largest standard Greek silver coin, the tetradrachm.[74]

Since Greek coins were already well known even in Asia, exporting silver as coins minted on the lines of Greek prototypes made good financial sense. In addition, since some of the Greek settlements on the coast acted as middlemen for the silver trade, the barbarian owners of the mines inscribed some of their issues with their names in Greek letters for the convenience of their Greek intermediaries. Some of these Greek cities themselves minted coins if they had direct access to mines. In other words, those tribes and cities in the Thraco-Macedonian region which controlled deposits of precious metal, or had a sure supply of it, minted coins. Since the non-Greek tribes of the region can hardly have had an economy whose internal workings depended on coined money issued to a significant extent in huge denominations and often inscribed in Greek, their coinage seems to have been nothing more than a convenient device to ensure profit from a commodity which they were fortunate enough to have and which others wanted. Their motive for minting coins was financial, not political. This is the clear implication of the explicit connection between the control of mineral resources and the issuance of coinage in this region by kings and tribes at this

[73] *HM*, chapter II, 2: "The coinages of the tribes, cities and kings *c.* 550–480," pp. 69–91; chapter III, 2: "The coinage of Alexander and other Balkan kings," pp. 104–115.

[74] See Hammond's discussion in *HM*, pp. 74–79. Cf. the brief discussion in Price, *Coins*, pp. 3–4.

time. [75] One can suspect that the same motive lay behind the contemporary Greek coinages of the region.

The sporadic production of coinage in the region in the late sixth and early fifth centuries seems closely related to changes in ownership of the various mines in the area brought about by war. For example, the Paeonians issued coins from *ca.* 540 until *ca.* 511 B.C., when a defeat by the Persians allowed their neighbors to move in on most of their sources of silver. The Macedones, the early Macedonians, in about 509 took over the Paeonian chief city Ichnae, the location of a prolific mint. But the city had no mines nearby to go with it, and the Paeonians in the inland areas naturally cut off its supply of silver when it fell into enemy hands. Thus the mint closed. Other tribes, such as the Bisaltae around 500 B.C., started to coin when they managed to take over mines previously exploited by someone else. The first Macedonian royal coinage properly speaking was that of Alexander I, who became king *ca.* 495 B.C.[76] We do not know precisely at what date he began to mint coins.[77] The crucial point is that Alexander began to mint coins when he had captured the gold and silver mines formerly controlled by the Bisaltae. These barbarians had previously issued their own coins for export, and Alexander's first issues mimicked the types and the heavy weights of their Bisaltic predecessors (Plate 2, no. 1). Only the inscriptions were changed to record Alexander's name as the issuing agent. Eventually, and perhaps even very soon, Alexander had new types produced, but his first issues were revealing. If his coinage had been intended as a ringing statement of Macedonian sovereignty and political existence, the assumption by a king with Hellenic pretensions of the types of a barbarian tribe would be inexplicable.[78] Alexander was only doing what his until-then richer neighbors had done: mint coins as a way to profit from mines in one's possession. If Alexander's

---

[75] For this connection, see Hammond, *HM*, pp. 73, 79–80.

[76] Hammond, *HM*, pp. 82–84 (the tribes), 84–86, and 104–110 (Alexander).

[77] Hammond, *HM*, pp. 84–86, 104, puts Alexander's first coins exactly in 479/8, but the evidence is too scanty to support such an exact chronology. Price, *Coins*, pp. 9–10, gives a date of *ca.* 475.

[78] Alexander competed in the Olympic games (Herodotus 5.22).

coinage made any statement, it proclaimed the king's ownership of valuable mineral resources which he wrested from others by force of arms. To make money, he too minted heavy pieces presumably intended for export. The eastern market for silver from the Balkans perhaps shrank after the expulsion of the Persians from Europe in the aftermath of the Persian Wars with the Greeks. Alexander may then have created coins of different weights to serve other markets. How successful he was we cannot really judge, but Macedonia did not develop in the fifth century in any way comparable to the material achievements of some of her Greek neighbors to the south. The important point to remember is that the introduction of Macedonian royal coinage is directly connected with the acquisition of silver mines. When the king did begin to issue coins, his motive was, so far as we can tell, overwhelmingly financial, not a desire to produce a symbol of political sovereignty or of autonomy.

In discussing the identification of some of the unattributed coinages of the region, Hammond rejects an earlier, tentative attribution of a certain issue *ca.* 500 to Therme, a settlement on the site later chosen for Thessalonike in 316 B.C.: "As the Macedonian king held this part of Mygdonia from *c.* 510 onwards, the attribution can be confidently discarded; for there is no doubt that he had a monopoly of coining within his realm."[79] As a statement of fact this may be true, but any implication that the royal monopoly had anything other than a practical justification would be unwarranted. On Hammond's own view, the king owned all the supplies of precious metal in his territory and exploited them for the profit of himself and, no doubt, the nobles on whose support he depended. [80] The types of these coins alone are sufficient to show that they do not belong to Therme. Places like Therme had no tradition of independent coinage because they had no independent supply of silver.

Macedonian royal coinage continued in the fifth and the fourth centuries, though not on a vast scale. The Macedonian

[79] *HM*, p. 113.

[80] *HM*, p. 157. This is clearly true of the mines near Philippi taken over by Philip II.

kings Alexander II and Perdiccas III (370/69 – 360/59) had far less gold and silver at their disposal than did their Illyrian rival, King Bardylis.[81] Coins were not a common component of everyday Macedonian financial life, perhaps because the country was no showplace of urban development. The largest native city, Pella, was no match for the great cities of Greece in the days before Philip II.[82] In the area northwest of Macedonia the export of silver to the north had led by the fourth century to the creation of more silver coinages to exploit the metal resources of places like Damastium.[83] Various Greek cities in the Thraco-Macedonian region were also issuing coinages in gold, silver, and bronze by the same period.[84] But so far there had been no clashes between Macedonian royal authority and Greek settlements which led to any direct consequences for local coinage.[85] When a Greek city in the region stopped minting coins, such as Acanthus *ca.* 380 or a little later, the Macedonian king had nothing to do with it. The Acanthians lost their mines to fellow Greeks.[86] Nor is it necessary to assume that the short-lived bronze coinages issued by cities like Pydna while free of Macedonian interference had any political significance as badges of freedom.[87] The coinages were utilitarian. On their own, and facing likely Macedonian reprisals for collaboration with hostile powers like the Athenians, these cities would have been cut off from Macedonian silver and Macedonian coinage. To pay the

---

[81] Price, *Coins*, p. 19; Hammond, *HM*, p. 192.

[82] Hammond, *HM*, pp. 196 – 197.

[83] See J.M.F. May, *The Coinage of Damastion and the Lesser Coinages of the Illyro-Paeonian Region* (Oxford, 1939).

[84] Kraay, *ACGC*, pp. 135 – 141; cf. Hammond, *HM*, pp. 192 – 193.

[85] Neither Kraay nor Hammond has suggested that any of the Macedonian kings in the fourth century before Philip II suppressed any Greek coinages, nor does the numismatic evidence suggest this.

[86] Kraay, *ACGC*, p. 136; Hammond, *HM*, p. 193.

[87] For this assumption, see A. R. Bellinger, "Notes on Coins from Olynthus," in *Studies Presented to David Moore Robinson*, ed. G. E. Mylonas and Doris Raymond, vol. 2 (St. Louis, 1953), p. 182. Cf. Hammond, *HM*, pp. 192 – 193. Pydna was not issuing a coinage when it fell to Archelaus in 410 B.C. (Diodorus 13.49.1 – 2).

troops whose job was to defend the walls, these cities had to issue coinage in the least precious and therefore least expensive metal. The situation changed soon enough after the accession of Philip. He pursued an aggressive policy toward independent Greek cities in and around Macedonia. It is thus particularly important to have Macedonian tradition in mind when we try to evaluate Philip's policy on coinage in this region. His predecessors on the Macedonian throne had certainly not expected any other Macedonians to issue coins, if only because the king controlled the raw material of coinage and the distribution of the kingdom's finances, but none of them had ever been in a position even to pose for himself the question of what he as king should do about non-Macedonian coinages produced in Macedonia. Before we turn to the status of formerly independent Greek cities in Macedonia under Philip, it will be instructive to review the status of some non-Greeks who also found themselves under Philip's thumb.

In 358 B.C., Philip won a victory over the Paeonians which allowed him to require their obedience to the Macedonians. An abortive revolt in 356 led to the confirmation of their inferior status.[88] Yet the king of the Paeonians continued to mint coins with his own types throughout the reign of Philip. Other barbarians whose destiny Philip controlled did the same.[89] Also in 358, Philip took over the territory in which at least one of the silver mines of the "Illyro-Paeonian" settlement, Damastium, was located.[90] Hammond even speculates that Philip had one of his agents oversee the operation of the local mint. But it did not close. Indeed, it seems to have stayed open until *ca.* 325–320 B.C., when its production came to a halt for what have been called "economic reasons": competition from the abundant coinages of Philip and Alexander made its operation no longer profitable, especially since the local mines were probably no longer so rich. Damastium's neighbor Pelagia continued to coin

[88] Demosthenes 1.23; Diodorus 16.4.2, 16.22.3. See Griffith, *HM*, pp. 212, 251.

[89] Hammond, *HM*, pp. 652, 666, 669.

[90] Hammond, *HM*, p. 668.

until *ca.* 280 B.C., when the Gallic invasions caused great havoc.[91]

There were many Greek cities in the Thraco-Macedonian region which managed as independent states to coexist with the neighboring Macedonian monarchy. Occasionally a place like Pydna might fall under the sway of a Macedonian king for a time, but at the start of his reign Philip was confronted with an array of independent cities to the south and east which could cause him trouble, especially if they acted in concert with his enemies. And some of them had resources he could use. During the course of his reign Philip captured some of these cities, failed in attempts on some, and made alliances with some. For our purposes it is important to know what happened to the coinages of the cities which happened to have them at this period and came under Philip's control. The standard practice has been to assume that local coinage stopped once a city was "incorporated into the kingdom," or "fell under the dominion of Philip," or however one wishes to phrase it. In Kraay's survey, this explanation (explicitly or implicitly) accounts for the end of the coinages of Aenus, Abdera, Amphipolis, the Chalcidian League with its mint at Olynthus, Neapolis, and Thasos.[92] This unaccountably contrasts with the situation at Philippi (the renamed Crenides) which "was permitted by both Philip and Alexander to mint gold and silver in its own name." [93]

The explanation offered for the end of local coinage at these places implies that Philip ordered the suppression of these coinages in favor of his own as an expression of his sovereignty. Some explanation is in order because various Greek coinages in the north do appear to come to an end in the later fourth century. But it is only the traditional assumption on sovereignty and coinage that makes Philip directly responsible through a policy of the suppression of local coinage and that is exploited to supply precise terminal dates for autonomous coinages.

Although the coinages of some of these places have been

[91] May, *The Coinage of Damastion*, pp. vii-viii, 160–163.

[92] *ACGC*, pp. 160 (Aenus), 156 (Abdera), 151–152 (Amphipolis), 138 (Chalcidian League), 150 (Neapolis), 150 (Thasos).

[93] *ACGC*, p. 145.

studied in detail, the numismatic evidence itself, as usual, cannot supply a precise chronology. In the case of Aenus, J.M.F. May in his standard work supplies a *terminus* of 342/1 B.C. because at that date the city "left what remained of the Athenian Confederacy and went over to the Macedonian. Her independence was lost and with it her autonomous coinage came to an end."[94] It is illogical, however, to postulate that a city which voluntarily joined Philip would as a consequence lose its independence and coinage. Far more logical is Griffith's idea that Aenus defected from Athens *ca.* 340–338 and became a member of the League of Corinth as one of Philip's "nominally free allies." [95] If Aenus did join the League of Corinth, the suppression of the city's local coinage cannot have been part of the price of membership, as we have already seen from other cases. Nevertheless, Griffith is unwilling to exclude the possibility that this sort of free alliance meant that Philip ordered the end of local coinage, as we see from his discussion of the status of Abdera:

> Moreover, the silver coinage of Abdera . . . comes to an end now, most probably in the 340s or only a year or two later. This presumably means something, politically, and usually it is taken to mean that Abdera has succumbed now, and is under Philip's control. Though the example of Corinth warns us not to assume that a Macedonian garrison in the citadel is sure to mean the cessation of an independent coinage, and not to make the same connection in reverse without due reserve, here in Abdera this connection in some shape or form does seem required. To infer that the coinage ended by Philip's orders, and from this to infer that Abdera became not his free ally but a subject, would be speculative certainly, and by no means sure to be right.[96]

But again, the accepted date of the end of the coinage of Abdera is based only on guesswork buttressed by the traditional assumption about sovereignty and coinage. May assumed Philip was strong enough by 346 to suppress Abderan coinage and thus put

[94] *Ainos. Its History and Coinage 474–341 B.C.* (Oxford, 1950), pp. 202–203.
[95] *HM*, p. 380.
[96] *HM*, p. 379.

his *terminus* for Abderan coinage at this date.[97] Griffith opts for a different rhythm of issues and suggests 338.[98] Gerhard Kleiner puts the end of Abderan coinage in the reign of Alexander.[99] If Griffith is right that Abdera broke with Athens and joined Philip *ca.* 340–338 as an ally and eventually a member of the League of Corinth, there is absolutely no reason to believe that Philip suppressed the city's coinage. As one plainly sees, the argument that he must have done so is wholly circular.

We know more about Amphipolis. Philip took it by force in 357, exiled his opponents, brought Macedonians into the city's territory, and, it is usually assumed, established one of his royal mints there.[100] After all, this city was hardly a pure Greek city-state. But Crenides, now Philippi, with its Macedonian settlers sent in by Philip, was the same sort of place, and it did have a local coinage under Philip which continued with the same types (but a new inscription) as those on the coinage in production at the time of Philip's takeover. What made Amphipolis so different that its mint had to be closed?[101] The chronology of the fourth-century silver coinage of Amphipolis cannot be independently established, but the assumption that Philip suppressed its coinage contradicts what little evidence we have from the appearance of coins of Amphipolis in hoards. Three fourth-century tetradrachms of the city turn up in two well-published hoards found in the area of Olynthus, one in one hoard and two in another.[102] None of the three belong to what is thought to be

---

[97] *The Coinage of Abdera (540–345 B.C.)* (Oxford, 1966), p. 290.

[98] *HM*, p. 379, n. 4.

[99] "Zur Chronologie der Münzen von Abdera," *JNG* 2 (1950–1951), p. 18.

[100] For the details, see Griffith, *HM*, pp. 351–356. On the royal mint, see Le Rider, *Monnayage*, pp. 323–342, with the critical review by M. J. Price, "The Coinage of Philip II," *NC* 1979, pp. 230–241.

[101] It is true that the hostility of the native population forced Philip to storm Amphipolis; he was called in by the people of Crenides for help against the Thracians. On Crenides, see Griffith, *HM*, pp. 246–248; E. Badian, "Philip II and Thrace," *Pulpudeva* 4 (1983), pp. 55–57.

[102] David M. Robinson and Paul A. Clement, *Excavations at Olynthus Part IX. The Chalcidic Mint and the Excavation Coins Found in 1928–1934* (Baltimore, 1938), pp. 183–190 (hoards IX and X).

the final group of tetradrachms from the mint of Amphipolis.[103] They do show signs of wear, and there is always the possibility that these particular coins were put away years before the hoards were buried *ca.* 348, or that it is an accident that no examples of the final group occur with them. [104] But on this evidence anyway, the question must be left open whether the civic mint of Amphipolis stopped minting tetradrachms as early as 357 B.C. There is no intrinsic reason why a royal mint and a civic mint could not have operated simultaneously for a while. One can compare the situation at Corinth after 308 B.C.

The coinage of the Chalcidian League certainly came to an abrupt end in 348 when Philip destroyed its capital and mint city, Olynthus. [105] Since we never hear of the League again, it presumably passed out of existence. Not so with the other cities of the League besides Olynthus (and Stagira). There is contemporary evidence that they became allies of Philip, with all the freedoms and obligations that ill-defined status carried. [106] Like the Boeotians after the destruction of Thebes, they should have been in a position to mint coins if they had wanted to. But the terrible loss involved in the destruction of the Chalcidice's main city and the capital of the League could not have made that a very easy path to follow financially.

Finally, nothing can be said about the political situation in the cases of Neapolis and Thasos. Neapolis may have stayed out of Philip's grasp until the circumstances of 338 put all the mainland Greeks except the Spartans into his camp. [107] The Thasians show up in the inscription which apparently lists the members of

[103] As classified by K. Regling, "Phygela, Klazomenai, Amphipolis," *ZfN* 33 (1922), pp. 55–63.

[104] A date of *ca.* 348 B.C. for these hoards seems reasonable, but we cannot automatically rule out a later date because some settlement seems to have remained on the site. See W. S. Ferguson, *AJA* 39 (1935), pp. 154–155, and A. R. Bellinger, *Studies . . . Robinson*, p. 185.

[105] Robinson and Clement, *Excavations at Olynthus*, pp. 133–134, 162–163.

[106] Griffith, *HM*, pp. 365–379.

[107] Griffith, *HM*, pp. 364–365.

the League of Corinth.[108] The most plausible explanation for the end of Thasian coinage is the loss of their rich mines on the mainland to Philip and his supporters at Philippi.[109]

When one boils all this down, only Amphipolis is left as the possible recipient of an order from Philip to stop the production of local coinage. But it is far from required that we assume any such order was ever given. That is, the situation could certainly have been that the king simply commandeered the local mint facilities for the convenient production of his own coins at some point after he had acquired the nearby mines of Mt. Pangaeum in 356 and gave no thought to the status of the local coinage. As for the Amphipolitans, with no independent foreign policy to finance and confronted with an influx of Macedonians who would prefer Macedonian money, what need had they for their own issues? Who was going to ask this busy and ambitious king for access to the silver supply which he was exploiting to the full for his own mints? Better to let the issue pass and to please the king by supporting the royal minting efforts with all possible expertise and goodwill without calling unnecessary attention to themselves by pleading for a superfluous coinage.[110] If this was the occasion when the local coinage of Amphipolis came to an end, there is no need to assume that the decision was not made locally.

The cumulative evidence presented in this survey of the coinages of the north will make the point that suppression of local coinage cannot have been a policy of Philip's predecessors or of Philip himself. Another explanation for the end of local Greek coinage is at hand which fits the facts admirably. Philip's military and diplomatic successes put him and his immediate successors in a position to monopolize, if they chose, the supplies of

[108] *SVA* III, no. 403, b, line 5. On the history of relations between Thasos and Macedonia in this period, see Jean Pouilloux, *Recherches sur l'histoire et les cultes de Thasos*, vol. 1. *De la fondation de la cité à 196 avant J.-C.* (Paris, 1954, Etudes thasiennes 3), pp. 430–434.

[109] Cf. Pouilloux, *Recherches*, p. 431; Griffith, *HM*, pp. 358–361.

[110] Price, *Coins*, p. 21, suggests that Amphipolis may have continued to strike bronze coins after 357 but that the city no longer coined in silver because "such silver as was mined in her territory was transferred to the royal coffers."

gold and silver in the north. The very high rate of production of
their Macedonian royal coinage meant both that these supplies
were almost entirely used up by the mints of the king and that
royal coins were readily available over a wide area and probably
preferred for their quality and ease of recognition. Coins of Philip and Alexander, like the coins of Athens, had an international
appeal that most local Greek coinages could not match. No one
in Europe today would prefer a less-known currency to, let us
say, Swiss francs for investment value or ease of exchange or
buying power. The same would have been true for coins of
Aenus or Abdera or Neapolis compared with the prolific issues of
the Macedonian kings after the mid-350s. Like Liechtenstein
today, these small states needed no currencies of their own
because it was more advantageous to use the money of their
neighbors.

NINE. FINAL EVIDENCE

Up to this point, our attention has been of necessity focused primarily on the coinages of classical Greece and the historical evidence which bears on the chronologies of these coinages. In this final chapter, we will look at some further documentary and literary evidence which might be thought to support the idea that a close connection was recognized in the classical period between sovereignty and coinage. The unifying thread of the argument in this chapter, as throughout this study, is the demonstration that the evidence in question can be explained without reference to the usual assumption about sovereignty and coinage. Since the documentary evidence to be discussed is earlier in date, it will be treated first.

1
Documents of Classical Greek Cities
Concerning Coinage

The famous fifth-century "Athenian Coinage Decree" remains the single most important piece of evidence for the view that a close connection existed in classical Greece between the outright assertion of political sovereignty on an international scale and a monopoly of the right of coinage. The best and most decisive statement of this interpretation of the decree comes in Moses Finley's standard work on economics in classical antiquity:

Equally political was the fifth-century B.C. Athenian decree which laid down the rule that Athenian coins alone were to be current for all purposes within the Athenian empire. ... The political element is unmistakable: the unprecedented volume of Athenian military and administrative payments, at a time when foreign tribute was the largest source of public revenue, was much facilitated by a uniform coinage, and Athens was now able and willing to demonstrate who was master within the empire by denying the subject-states the traditional symbol of autonomy, their own coins. The Athenians may also have aimed at mint profits, but we shall not know until the missing bit of the text stating the mint charge for re-coining is found.

It is also held that there was a commercial motive, a desire to give Athenian merchants the advantage over others. The logic escapes me. Everyone had been equally the victim of a profusion of mints; had the Athenians been able to enforce their decree for a sufficient number of years, everyone within the empire would have benefited slightly but equally, the Athenians no more than the others, questions of pride and patriotism apart. Only the money-changers would have been the losers, and no one has yet suggested that such a powerful decree was passed just to hurt them.[1]

In a later work, Finley summarizes his view: whatever its precise date, the Coinage Decree was a "political act without any commercial or financial advantage to the Athenians."[2]

The situation is not as straightforward as this interpretation suggests. The decree involves more than just coins. When we can begin to follow its sense, the incomplete text which is preserved concerns provisions for the punishment of those officials throughout the empire who fail to act in accordance with what has been decreed. There follows a provision, whose full sense is unrecoverable because of the damaged state of the text, about the minting of silver which has been received. The fee to be charged for minting was specified, but the amount is not preserved. A charge of three percent is usually restored.[3] Next, there is a reference to a surplus of silver (assumed to be the silver which is being minted); in some (unrecoverable) circumstances,

---

[1] *The Ancient Economy* (London, 1973), pp. 168–169.

[2] "The Athenian Empire: A Balance Sheet," *Economy and Society in Ancient Greece*, p. 257, n. 46, with reference also to his comments in "Classical Greece," in *Deuxième Conférence internationale d'histoire économique Aix-en-Provence, 1962, I: Trade and Politics in the Ancient World* (Paris, 1965, repr. New York, 1979), pp. 22–24.

[3] ML, no. 45, pp. 111–117. Another fifth-century Athenian text concerned with coinage (*IG* I³ 90) is too poorly preserved to allow speculation on its possible relevance here. For a conservative translation of the decree, see C. W. Fornara, *Translated Documents of Greece and Rome 1. Archaic Times to the End of the Peloponnesian War* ² (Cambridge, 1983), no. 97.

it is to be given to the Athenian generals. There follows an obscure provision apparently dealing with a special fund, which is protected by the death penalty.[4] Death is specified as the punishment for proposing that foreign money (if this is the correct restoration) be used or be involved in loans. The election of heralds to announce the decree to the cities throughout the empire is then ordered, with provisions for setting up copies of the decree itself in the marketplaces of the cities and in front of the mint at Athens. Next, an addition is given to the oath to be sworn by members of the Athenian council which pledges them to punish anyone who coins money of silver in the cities of the empire and does not use Athenian coins or weights or measures but instead uses foreign coins and weights and measures.[5] The broken text is then restored to say that anyone may bring money to the mint in Athens to be reminted, and that a list is to be set up at the mint for anyone to see which will record the total of foreign coinage (both silver and electrum, according to a restoration for which there is no text surviving) turned in.

The problems of historical interpretation which this fragmentary document creates are many and mostly insurmountable. The only comfort is that for present purposes the vexed question of the precise date of the decree in the fifth century does not matter.[6] Enough of the text does survive, however, to show that Finley's interpretation is unsatisfactory. This text does not just concern coinage. The requirement that all the Athenian allies use Athenian weights and measures must also be explained. It hardly seems possible to identify local weights and measures as

[4] On this part of the decree, important because a reference to the nonuse of foreign coinage has been restored at this point, see D. M. Lewis, "Entrenchment-Clauses in Attic Decrees," in ΦΟΡΟΣ. *Tribute to Benjamin Dean Meritt*, ed. D. W. Bradeen and M. F. McGregor (Locust Valley, N.Y., 1974), pp. 83–85; H. Mattingly, "The Protected Fund in the Athenian Coinage Decree (*ATL* D 14, par. 7f.)," *AJP* 95 (1974), pp. 280–282; R. S. Stroud, "Three Attic Decrees," *CSCA* 7 (1974), pp. 281–282, 298.

[5] For the word order, see H. Mattingly, "The Second Athenian Coinage Decree," *Klio* 59 (1977), p. 83, n. 3, p. 87, n. 24.

[6] See the discussion in ML, no. 45, and E. Erxleben, "Das Münzgesetz des delisch-attischen Seebundes," *Archiv für Papyrusforschung* 19 (1969), pp. 91–139, 212; 20 (1970), pp. 66–132; 21 (1971), pp. 145–162.

"traditional symbols of autonomy," especially since this designation for coinage depends on the idea that the use of local types on local coins makes them symbols of autonomy because the Greek "passion for coins, and for beautiful coins at that" was "essentially a political phenomenon."[7] But the ban on minting coinage seems to apply only to silver coins, not to coins in other metals, electrum in particular. Yet electrum issues were the standard coinages of several mints in the Athenian Empire.[8] Electrum coinage, in fact, could be used by Athenian allies to make tribute payments.[9] If this decree is meant to be an assertion of sovereignty as a political act, the production of "symbols of autonomy" in other metals should have been banned as well as the production of such symbols in silver.

Various details in the decree strongly suggest a financial motivation for it. Above all, there is the fee to be charged for recoining non-Athenian currency. Even a nominal fee would bring in a gigantic sum to the state treasury if successfully levied on the entire amount of non-Athenian coinage in circulation in the Athenian Empire. Since the plural "drachmas" is preserved on

[7] Finley, *The Ancient Economy*, p. 166, quoting J. M. Keynes, *A Treatise on Money*, vol. 1. *The Pure Theory of Money* (London, 1930), p. 12. In fact, Keynes (who is referring to the kings of Lydia and not to the Greeks) is only arguing that the essential duty of the state is to establish the standard for coinage. Keynes explicitly says that it is not necessarily the duty of the state to produce this coinage. This is a very different point from the one Finley wishes to make.

As for weights and measures, the orator Gorgias in his late fifth-century *Defense of Palamedes* has Palamedes, who claims to have invented such things, call them "the convenient standards of commercial exchange" (section 30). The significance of the mention of weights and measures in the decree has tended to be slighted, as A. Giovannini remarks in *Rome et la circulation monétaire en Grèce au II e siècle avant Jésus-Christ* (Basel, 1968), pp. 75–76. His view is that "l'association, dans la loi, de l'unification de la monnaie avec celle des poids et des mesures montre que les Athéniens ont voulu d'abord faciliter les échanges et les transactions commerciales à l'intérieur de la ligue."

[8] Kraay, *ACGC*, pp. 243 (Chios), 262–267 (Lampsacus, Lesbos, Mytilene, Phocaea).

[9] On the importance of electrum coinage in the Athenian empire, see Friedrich Bodenstedt, *Phokäisches Elektron-Geld von 600–326 v. Chr. Studien zur Bedeutung und zu den Wandlungen einer antiken Goldwährung* (Mainz, 1976), pp. 71–73, 83–84.

the stone to indicate the fee charged for each *mina* (one hundred drachmas) recoined, the smallest possible fee is two drachmas, i.e., two percent. This is an important point. Two percent of the value of the non-Athenian coinage in the empire was a great sum of money. Moreover, it is likely that the fee was meant to be exacted after the recoining, not before.[10] In this way, the owners of the money bore any losses incurred in the melting down and restriking of their precious metal. Even if the Athenian mint bore these losses, the revenue to be expected from a successful program of this type was very large. But given the history of the Athenian Empire (one thinks of the mines of Thasos), it is unlikely that the Athenians intended to absorb a financial loss in the interest of an abstract idea of sovereignty.

As small a net gain as a fraction of a percent of the total of non-Athenian coinage in the empire was a delightful prospect for the Athenian public treasury. With the benefit of hindsight we may think that it was obvious for practical reasons that the Athenians were unlikely to be able to get their hands on all the foreign currency in the cities under their rule, but the decree clearly implies that they were eager to try.[11] This would not be the only example of inflated expectations about the amount of

[10] The minting charge is mentioned after the instructions for reminting (section 5). This order implies that the charge came after the reminting. With the text as commonly restored, however, the possibility remains that the charge was to be taken out before the reminting. It is perfectly conceivable that a formal ambiguity on this particular point may have been allowed to stand in the text, as often in Athenian decrees, because the Athenians knew what they meant to say.

[11] The enigmatic phrase in section 5 of the decree restored as "[to coin not] less than half" could make sense if it referred to the total of money somehow determined to be in the official possession of each city in the Empire rather than to the amount of currency presented to the mint by an individual. That is, the decree would have required each city to present not less than half its money for immediate recoining. This would have allowed each city to keep some funds on hand to pay expenses until the reminted coins came back from Athens and the remaining non-Athenian currency was sent to Athens for recoining. It would have been unrealistic even for the imperious Athenians to require allied cities to send all their funds to Athens at one time for recoining and thus to be completely without funds while their coins were shipped to Athens, recoined, and then shipped back again.

revenue the Athenians hoped to extract from their allies. [12] The mention of a surplus of some sort also implies that the Athenians intended to make a profit. The list of money turned in at Athens which was ordered to be erected at the mint makes sense as an indirect record of revenue analogous to the Tribute Quota Lists, to be kept in typical Athenian fashion as a guard against embezzlement on the part of those officials who would (the Athenians hoped) be handling tremendous sums of cash, and as a defense against any false accusations of peculation raised by suspicious fellow citizens. We really should not be surprised that the Athenians expected to be able to impose such a measure to their own profit. By comparison with the seigniorage charged in minting coins in the Middle Ages, for example, the Athenian fee may have been moderate. [13]

The explicit concern of the decree with silver coinage also suggests a direct connection with the assessment and the collection of the tribute owed to Athens from the cities of the empire (as Finley points out). This tribute was reckoned exclusively in terms of Athenian silver coinage, as the inscriptional records show, but it was (before the passage of this decree, anyway) not always paid in Athenian silver coinage. Some allied states appear to have paid with local silver coinage, with Persian silver coinage, or with electrum coinage. [14] At the very least this mixture of coinages was highly inconvenient because it required the

[12] Compare the reassessment decree of 425 (ML, no. 69), which set the extraordinary (and unfulfilled) goal of collecting approximately 1,500 talents as the annual tribute of the Empire.

[13] For example, a rate of 4.5 percent is attested in the early Carolingian period, and a rate of 8.5 percent is attested in A.D. 1174. See Thomas N. Bisson, *Conservation of Coinage* (Oxford, 1979), p. 5. For the rate of "agio" among the Greeks, see Raymond Bogaert, *Banques et banquiers dans les cités grecques* (Leiden, 1968), pp. 323–331. T. V. Buttrey, "The Athenian Currency Law of 375/4 B.C.," in *Greek Numismatics and Archaeology. Essays in Honor of Margaret Thompson*, ed. O. Mørkholm and N. M. Waggoner (Wetteren, Belgium, 1979), pp. 44–45, comments on the "considerable profit in seigniorage from the recoining of the issues which had been decried [i.e., of other states]" implied by the fifth-century Coinage Decree.

[14] Samuel K. Eddy, "Some Irregular Amounts of Athenian Tribute," *AJP* 94 (1973), pp. 47–70; Bodenstedt, *Elektron-Geld*, pp. 71–73, 83–84.

annually changing officials in charge of the tribute to check constantly on the fineness, the weight, and the authenticity of unfamiliar coinages and to calculate their value in Athenian coinage to see if each city was paying its assessed tribute in full. Moreover, other inscriptional evidence shows how complicated and cumbersome the Athenian procedure was for assessing tribute and verifying its proper level. Besides the relevant annual officials directly concerned, other citizens serving in official capacities were also supposed to check on the status of individual states and their payments.[15] This was no simple matter. The Athenian council and courts of the fifth century, moreover, were overloaded with other public business.[16] Hearing arguments about just how many foreign silver coins of a certain type equaled the amount of tribute owed in Athenian coinage and checking the reliability of these pieces was bound to become an unwelcome chore simply because the number of coins involved was so large.

The annual revenue from allied tribute payments was in the neighborhood of four hundred talents, an amount equal to 2,400,000 drachms or 600,000 tetradrachms.[17] Those totals meant that for purely practical reasons it would be much easier for the Athenians to get their revenue and to keep tabs on payment if at least most of the allies paid in Athenian coins in the first place.[18] An additional benefit would be that the state would no longer be burdened with odd amounts of foreign silver coinages which no one at Athens wanted to accept. As Xenophon says, non-Athenian silver coinages were often not welcome outside their local area.[19] The official financial records of Athens in this period show that funds in electrum tended not to be dispersed but kept in storage year after year, presumably because people demanded Athenian coins in payment from the city for services rendered or

---

[15] See ML, nos. 46, 68, 69, 77.

[16] Ps.-Xenophon, *Constitution of the Athenians* 3.1–9.

[17] See ML, pp. 87–88, for a discussion of this problematical figure.

[18] It would have been bothersome to count out a large sum even in Athenian tetradrachms, let alone in foreign coinages. See Demosthenes 27.58 for the counting out in public of an amount something over six talents.

[19] *Poroi* 3.2.

materials delivered.[20] Foreign silver accepted as payment of tribute would have to be melted down and then reminted as
Athenian coinage before it could be used by the city to pay its
bills. That process cost money and inevitably involved loss of
silver in the manufacturing of new coinage from old.[21] The
Athenians could most easily verify that they were getting the full
tribute if the silver they received was exclusively Athenian.
That would leave only the relatively limited payments in familiar
electrum coinages (which counted as gold) to be tallied in a
separate fashion. Of course, this goal could have been achieved
by a measure which merely stipulated that all tribute payments
(except those in electrum, i.e., in gold) would have to be made in
Athenian coinage and did not ban the production of foreign
silver coinage or the use of non-Athenian silver coinage, weights,
and measures. This is another reason to believe that the Athenians had in mind to charge the allies for recoining their money in
order to earn a large profit for the city (even from a small fee)
over and above the costs of the procedure.

This concern with revenue can also explain the inclusion of
weights and measures in the decree (apart from the direct link
between coins and weights as units of weight).[22] The Athenians
levied taxes on goods in order to raise revenue from im-
port/export traffic, and these taxes were set at a certain per-
centage of the value of the goods involved.[23] It was obviously
necessary to know the exact weight (for objects of precious
metal, for example) or volume (for bulk items such as grain) of
the goods in a shipment if the tax was to be levied and collected
accurately. Collecting these taxes was a complicated business so
long as it was necessary to contend with shipments of goods

---

[20] For example, ML, no. 59. See Bodenstedt, *Elektron-Geld*, pp. 83–84, who
perhaps goes too far in arguing that electrum served as a "Reservewährung" for
the Delian League.

[21] See E.J.P. Raven, *NC* 1950, pp. 1–22.

[22] For the link, see Kraay's discussion in *ACGC*, pp. 313–317, on the origins
of Greek coinage.

[23] Ps.-Xenophon, *Constitution of the Athenians* 1.17: a tax of 1 percent at the
Piraeus; Andocides 1.133–134: a tax of 2 percent in 399 B.C.; Xenophon, *Hellenica* 1.1.22: a tax of 10 percent on merchantmen from the Euxine. Cf. ML,
p. 161.

whose quantities were determined and recorded according to foreign weights and measures. As an example, let us suppose that a ship arrived in the Piraeus from the island of Thasos with a shipment of wine contained in amphoras made to conform to Thasian standards of measure rather than to Athenian. First, the number of amphoras in the shipment would have to be determined in order to levy the import tax. Next, the proper ratio between Thasian and Athenian liquid measures would have to be determined and the size of the shipment calculated on Athenian standards. Finally, to be absolutely certain of the accuracy of the calculations, an empirical test would have to be performed for each such shipment because the person doing all this could never be sure that the measures in question had not changed, or even been fraudulently altered, since the last time he had seen this particular standard. It would be far easier to check this sort of detail if one had to deal with only one kind of measure, the kind for which official Athenian standards were at hand as an easy and sure guide. [24] Many more shipments of foreign goods could be processed in the same amount of time and with far greater accuracy (i.e., full collection of the duty owed) if it was necessary to refer only to one universal set of weights and measures. Since the Athenians in the later fifth century enjoyed the benefits of a very large foreign trade in all sorts of goods in great quantities, these practical considerations were far from minor. [25] The amount of revenue involved was significant. We do not have the information to break down the revenues of Athens into precise categories, but at the start of the Peloponnesian War in 431 B.C. the Athenians took in about four hundred talents of their annual

[24] For the standards, see H. W. Pleket, *Epigraphica*, vol. 1 (Leiden, 1964), no. 14, sec. II (second century B.C.). Harold Mattingly, "Coins and Amphoras— Chios, Samos and Thasos in the Fifth Century B.C.," *JHS* 101 (1981), pp. 85–86, has argued that the Thasians changed the size of their amphoras in compliance with the decree.

[25] On the volume of trade, see Ps.-Xenophon, *Constitution of the Athenians* 2.7. The practical considerations were important even if these taxes were being collected by tax-farmers because the price for the tax contract to be paid to the state would be higher if it was expected that collection would be more efficient. On tax-farming, see, for example, Andocides 1.133–134; Demosthenes 24.122; Lycurgus, *Vs. Leocr.* 19, 58; Aristotle, *Ath. Pol.* 47.2–3; Plutarch, *Alcibiades* 5.

income of one thousand talents from "overseas revenue."[26] Although there is no way to determine how much of this total came precisely from taxes on trade, the figure gives some idea of the importance of the revenues which Athens derived from sources other than the tribute paid by the members of her empire. Measures to protect and to enhance that "overseas revenue" were important.

Analogous to the tax on goods was the requirement that Athenian allies as well as Athenian farmers send contributions in kind ("first fruits") to Eleusis each year in honor of the goddess Demeter.[27] These contributions were set at 1/600 of all barley and 1/1200 of all wheat. This was obviously a large amount when collected empirewide and was a form of imperial revenue. Uniform weights and measures would again have facilitated the assessment and collection of "first fruits" in the requisite quantities. The same was true in the case of Athenian regulation of the export of grain from the Black Sea region. From two inscriptions we learn that the Athenians set a limit to the number of measures of grain that certain cities could get from Black Sea sources. There were Athenian officials known as "guards of the Hellespont" whose job it was to see that these limits, defined by Athenian measures, were respected. [28] Again, their task was going to be much easier if they only had to deal with shipments in Athenian measures.

It is certainly not my intent to deny that the Athenian Coinage Decree was an expression of the power of an imperial state over subordinate states. Thucydides' account of Athenian action against the allied states of Naxos and Thasos in the 460s is more than enough to show the imperial attitude of Athens toward her

---

[26] Thucydides 2.13.3; Xenophon, *Anab.* 7.1.27. See Russell Meiggs, *The Athenian Empire* (Oxford, 1972), p. 258.

[27] ML, no. 73.

[28] ML, no. 65, lines 34–41 (Methone); B. D. Meritt, H. T. Wade-Gery, and M. F. McGregor, *The Athenian Tribute Lists* (Cambridge, Mass., 1939–1953), vol. 2, D 21 (Aphytis). On the *Hellespontophylakes*, see Finley, *Economy and Society*, pp. 54–55.

"free allies."[29] Ordering their allies to use Athenian coins, weights, and measures was entirely consistent with the attitude of the Athenians throughout this period of their history. But why was the order given? It seems reasonable to suggest that the Athenians wanted to improve the collection of revenue in the empire and to facilitate the regulation of the grain trade, so crucial to an Athens dependent on imported food. In other words, the Coinage Decree was not a "political act without any commercial or financial advantage to the Athenians." In contemporary American political jargon, it was a radical attempt to implement a "revenue enhancement act," which, as Finley says, also ensured Athenian imports of food.[30] When the Athenians in 425 greatly increased the amount of tribute owed by their allies, and in 413 abandoned the system of tribute in favor of a harbor tax, their principal motive was the same: an eminently practical concern to increase revenue.[31]

That the Coinage Decree was not long remembered as a special outrage against the sovereignty of other states is suggested by the failure of fourth-century sources to mention it in references to the repressive measures of the Athenian Empire in the fifth century.[32] For example, Isocrates fails to mention it both in

[29] 1.98, 1.100–101.

[30] *Economy and Society,* pp. 56–57. Cf. Will, "Les sources des métaux," *Numismatique antique,* p. 101, who argues that the Athenians by the mid-fifth century needed to melt down allied issues in order to produce more Athenian issues to pay their higher expenses. On his view, the Coinage Decree was intended to alleviate this shortage.

[31] See ML, no. 69; Finley, *Economy and Society,* p. 57. A similar concern with the practical advantages of eliminating diverse monetary and measuring systems can be seen in the Roman requirement that local systems in the provinces be compatible with the Roman system. On this requirement, see M. Crawford, "Finance, Coinage and Money from the Severans to Constantine," in *Aufstieg und Niedergang der römischen Welt,* vol. II, part 2, ed. H. Temporini (Berlin, 1975), p. 561.

[32] The one possible reference to the decree is, of course, in Aristophanes, *Birds,* lines 1040–1041 (414 B.C.), if one accepts Bergk's emendation. On later views of the Empire, see R. Meiggs, *The Athenian Empire* (Oxford, 1972), pp. 397–403; J. T. Chambers, "The IV Century Athenians' View of Their Fifth-Century Empire," *Parola del passato* 162 (1975), pp. 177–191. It was perhaps easier for the decree to fade from memory because it never seems to have been successfully implemented (so far as one can judge from the numismatic evidence).

his discussion of the harsh side of Athenian rule in *Panegyricus* 100–119 (380 B.C.) and in his report in *Panathenaicus* 53–73 (342 B.C.) of the criticisms leveled by others against the empire of the fifth century. Particularly significant is the lack of any explicit reference to the type of provisions included in the Coinage Decree in the inscribed list of practices which the Athenians swore not to inflict on their allies in their fourth-century league.[33] There is no mention in this inscription from 378/7 of coins or of weights or of measures in the list of "rights" which the Athenians guarantee to their new allies under the category of "freedom and autonomy." We can draw two conclusions from this evidence. First, neither the Athenians nor their allies in the fourth century had given any thought to the status of local coinage as an important component of "freedom and autonomy" which had to be guaranteed under the new arrangement. Second, the allies did not recall the Coinage Decree as derogating from their autonomy, as other practices named were remembered to have done.

The recently discovered Athenian law on silver coinage of 375/4 is equally unenlightening on any connection between sovereignty and coinage.[34] This law requires the acceptance of genuine Athenian silver coinage in financial transactions, specifies the duties of the public slaves whose job it is to verify the genuineness of silver coins, and lays down the penalties for failure to comply with its provisions. Whether the law also meant that foreign imitations of Athenian coinage in good silver had to be accepted is controversial.[35] But this point does not affect the present argument because, whatever its positive requirements, the law did not explicitly forbid the use of non-

[33] *IG* II² 43, for which now see Jack Cargill, *The Second Athenian League* (Berkeley, 1981), pp. 14–47.

[34] *Editio princeps* by R. S. Stroud, "An Athenian Law on Silver Coinage," *Hesperia* 43 (1974), pp. 157–188.

[35] Stroud believes that it did. For strong arguments against this view, see Buttrey, "Athenian Currency Law," *Greek Numismatics and Archaeology*, pp. 33–45; "More on the Athenian Coinage Law of 375/4 B.C.," *Quaderni ticinesi. Numismatica e antichità classiche* 10 (Lugano, 1981), pp. 71–94.

Athenian coinage in financial transactions. The motive of this law was to ensure a smoothly functioning currency system in Athens when circumstances about which we are uninformed had disrupted that system. [36] This inscription reveals a clear concern of the lawmakers with finance in the circumstances at hand, but considerations of sovereignty seem distant and irrelevant. The same can be said of the early-fourth-century agreement between Mytilene and Phocaea on the production of electrum coinage. [37] In the text as we have it, the main concern of the agreement is to protect the integrity of this "gold" coinage by setting up mechanisms to punish those who would try to debase it. The two states involved also apparently agreed to mint coins in alternate years, but there is no indication that this arrangement had any motive beyond the equitable sharing in a cooperative way of the practical responsibilities and rewards of minting this extremely valuable coinage. As has been well said, this was a commercial agreement. To read it, however, also as a statement with important implications for considerations of sovereignty seems unwarranted. [38]

The next document to be discussed is an incomplete inscription from the fourth century B.C. which refers to regulations

[36] For discussion with reference to other views, see H. Wankel, "Bemerkungen zu dem athenischen Münzgesetz von 375/4," *ZPE* 52 (1983), pp. 69–74, to which can be added T. R. Martin, "A Motive for the Athenian Law of 375/4 B.C. Concerning Silver Coinage," forthcoming in the *Acta* of the Eighth International Congress of Greek and Latin Epigraphy, Athens, 3–9 October 1982.

[37] *GHI*, no. 112 = *SVA* II, no. 228.

[38] See the comments of A. J. Graham, *Colony and Mother City in Ancient Greece* (Manchester, 1971), p. 123: "The issue of coins was a matter of political prestige, as may be seen from the agreement between Mytilene and Phocaea to issue coins in alternate years. . . . This is a commercial agreement, involving the use of the same coins by two cities, but it is necessary to establish strict equality in the issue of the coins: otherwise, it may be presumed, their status as independent cities was thought to be impugned." One might imagine that "strict equality" was important because significant amounts of money were involved in the production of electrum, and neither city wanted to suffer from the bargain. A. Giovannini, *Rome et la circulation monétaire en Grèce au II⁰ siècle avant Jésus-Christ* (Basel, 1978), pp. 75–76, agrees in emphasizing "le but économique ou financier" of this and other monetary measures known from Greece of the fifth to the second century B.C.

concerning coinage in the city of Olbia on the Black Sea. The text runs as follows:

There is to be access to Borysthenes [i.e., the territory of Olbia] on the following conditions. It was resolved by the council and the people; Kanobos son of Thrasydamas put forward the motion. There is to be import of all gold bearing a sign and silver bearing a sign [i.e., coinage] and export. The one wishing to sell or buy coined gold or silver, let him sell and buy at the stone in the assembly's meeting place. Whoever sells or buys elsewhere, the seller will be fined the amount of the silver sold, the buyer the amount of the price of what he bought. Everything is to be sold and bought with the coinage of the city, with the bronze and the silver of the Olbiopolitans. Whoever sells or buys with another [i.e., coinage], the seller shall be deprived of what he sells, the buyer of the amount of what he buys. Whoever buys the contract for collecting fines from transgressors shall exact the fines from those who transgress against this decree, having convicted them in court. In the selling and buying of gold, the Cyzicene stater is to be worth [? — the number is uncertain because the text is damaged] staters [of Olbian silver coinage], neither more nor less. All other gold and silver coinage is to be sold and bought as the parties involved may agree. There is to be no tax exacted on the sale or the purchase of gold or silver coinage . . . [the rest of the text is too damaged to be read].[39]

[39] *SIG* 3 218. The value of the Cyzicene stater is usually restored as 10 1/2, but 8 1/2 has been suggested by J. G. Vinogradov and P. O. Karyskowski, "The Canobus Decree on Money from Olbia and the Value of Precious Metals on the Black Sea in the Fourth Century," *VDI* 4 (138) 1976, pp. 20–42 (in Russian with English summary). The latter restoration would yield the normal rate of exchange between silver and electrum for the period of Alexander rather than an inflated value for the electrum staters. These authors date the inscription to the third quarter of the fourth century. The reference to bronze coinage shows that the decree is more recent than the introduction at Olbia of coinage in this metal, which obviously came earlier than the decree dated to the 320s which mentions it as apparently a relatively recent event. See J. G. Vinogradov, *Olbia. Geschichte einer altgriechischen Stadt am Schwarzen Meer* (Constance, 1981, Xenia. Konstanzer althistorische Vorträge und Forschungen 1), p. 29.

The use of πρὸς τὸ νόμισμα to mean to buy and to sell "with the coinage" is perhaps awkward. πρός seems to mean "with reference to" the coinage indicated in *SIG* 3 495, line 16. Cf. πρός in *IG* II 2 1013, line 14 and Aristotle, *Ath. Pol.* 51.3. To buy "with" coinage would perhaps be better expressed by the dative case (cf. Thucydides 3.40.1), or by διά with the genitive (cf. Plato, *Sophist* 223e3). In other words, the expression used in the text could conceivably imply that the city's coinage would be a kind of "money of account" to

It has recently been suggested that for reasons of civic pride
Olbia imposed the use of her own coins "for no other reason than
she imposes the use of her laws."[40] In other words, the aim of the
decree on this interpretation was to assert the sovereignty of the
city by means of a uniform monetary circulation. Again, as in
the case of the Athenian Coinage Decree, an explanation of this
kind fails to take into account the text as a whole. It hardly
seems possible to understand the situation at Olbia this decree
was addressing without considering the issues of the right of
access to the city and permission to import and export precious
metal in the form of coinage. The first lines of the text make it
clear that these are the issues of direct concern in this instance.

Another fourth-century inscription from Olbia shows the
importance of these same issues and of the policy on trade in precious metals which this decree specified. This second text is a
proxeny decree which grants special privileges to a man from the
city of Mesembria and to his descendants and family. Two of
the privileges listed are access to the city and permission to
import and export without tax all the money they like.[41] If these
are special privileges granted in this case to special friends of the
city, the implication is that at the time of this proxeny decree
other foreigners (and perhaps Olbian citizens) did not ordinarily
enjoy these rights. For example, there obviously was a regular
tax on the import and export of gold and silver coins. Otherwise, the special exemption granted in the proxeny decree would

---

serve as a yardstick for fast and precise comparisons by traders and merchants
of the prices being offered for precious metal coinage by different dealers operating in the Olbian market.

On the odd history of bronze coinage at Olbia, see M. J. Price, "Early
Greek Bronze Coinage," in *Essays in Greek Coinage Presented to Stanley Robinson*,
ed. C. M. Kraay and G. K. Jenkins (Oxford, 1968), pp. 101–103.

[40] M. M. Austin and P. Vidal-Naquet, *Economic and Social History of Ancient
Greece: An Introduction* (Berkeley, 1977), pp. 330–331. For further discussion
and earlier views, see Will, "Les sources des métaux," *Numismatique antique*, pp.
101–102; E. Belin de Ballu, *Olbia, cité antique du littoral nord de la Mer Noire*
(Leiden, 1972), pp. 67–68; H. Schmitz, *Ein Gesetz der Stadt Olbia zum Schutze
ihres Silbergeldes* (Freiburg in Baden, 1925).

[41] *SIG*[3] 219. For other comparable decrees, see *Inscriptiones Olbiae
1917–1965* (Leningrad, 1968), nos. 3, 6–9, 14–15, 20.

be pointless. The decree on coinage gives the right of access and free importation and exportation of coinage to everyone, not just to special friends of the city. This proxeny decree and others like it presumably reflect the situation before the passage of the coinage decree (or after its failure and repeal?), a measure which in effect turned Olbia into a duty-free port open to all for the sale and purchase of gold and silver coinage. This measure would have facilitated trade in precious metals in the form of coinage and boosted trade in general by making it easy for traders to import and export the coinage used in financial transactions of all kinds. [42]

On this interpretation, the various provisions of the decree make sense as an ensemble intended to promote an effective, popular, and lucrative market. Anyone can bring in or take out as much gold and silver coinage as he likes, and he can sell it as he pleases, so long as he does it at the specified location. This specification may mean that there was an official monopoly on money-changing, as, for example, there was at Byzantium for a time at least during the fourth century.[43] At the very least it suggests that there was some sort of official interest in the process of exchange. Since sales and purchases are to take place at a certain location, it was easy to enforce the sole price regulation of the decree (the value specified for Cyzicene staters) and to allow interested parties to get together to make mutually advantageous deals for their money. Just as in any concentrated, centralized market for one commodity which is peopled by various dealers trying to sell the same thing, the side-by-side competition was

---

[42] The word "everything" or "all" ($\pi\acute{\alpha}\nu\tau\alpha$) in line 14 of the Olbian coinage decree is usually taken to refer to all goods bought and sold in Olbia, but the decree otherwise mentions nothing except gold and silver coinage. It is not out of the question that the word means only "all gold and silver coinage."

[43] Ps.-Aristotle, *Oeconomica* II.ii.3a-d. See H. Seyrig, "Monnaies hellénistiques de Byzance et de Calcédoine," in *Essays in Greek Coinage Presented to Stanley Robinson*, ed. C. M. Kraay and G. K. Jenkins (Oxford, 1968), pp. 189–190. Cf. the arrangements attested in *OGIS*, nos. 484 (Pergamum) and 515 (Mylasa). Even when the rates charged for changing money were subject to competitive pressure, they were generally high. See Bogaert, *Banques*, pp. 323–331; M. Giacchero, "I motivi finanziari e commerciali dell'unione monetaria fra Mitilene e Focea," *RIN* 82 (1980), pp. 6–7.

going to keep prices in line and promote a volume business. (One can compare, for example, the central market of modern Athens, where the location of many small butchers' shops one next to another makes it convenient both for shoppers to look for the best meat at the best price and for the market police to enforce local regulations.) This arrangement of the market combined with the abolition of taxes on the importation of precious metals would have made Olbia an attractive port of call for foreign traders.

Ease in comparative shopping in the interests of an effective market could conceivably explain the requirement that Olbian coinage be used in transactions (if this is what the decree required). Sellers and buyers of different foreign gold and silver coinages (and of other goods, for that matter) would find it much simpler to compare prices and to find the best deal for their money if only one standard was in use against which all coinages had to be tariffed. But a better explanation of the requirement could be that the Olbians planned to profit from it. That is, a trader who wanted to exchange, for example, Athenian coinage for Macedonian coinage after striking a deal with another trader or with a money-changer would be required to change his Athenian coins into Olbian ones and then change the Olbian coins into Macedonian ones. He would then pay the exchange fee twice, once when buying Olbian coins and once when selling them. This practice will be familiar to travelers in Europe who wish to exchange one foreign currency for another in a third country and are forced to buy and then immediately sell the currency of the host country in order to complete the transaction, paying a bank charge twice. This "nuisance" fee would have been a good source of revenue for the Olbians as a whole if there was an official monopoly of money-changing, or for those individuals involved in this business if there was no state monopoly. (In the latter case, individuals may have paid a fee for the privilege of conducting this business.) The important consideration was to make Olbia an attractive place for traders to do their business despite any such expenses as exchange fees. The removal of the tax on the import and export of precious metals would have provided the necessary attraction. The Olbians were trying to become an international "free market" for currency, a phenomenon familiar from recent history at the time when the restrictions on European currencies made it profitable for distant places like Hong Kong and Singapore to turn themselves into such free markets for currency. If the variety of foreign coins found at Olbia is any indication, the Olbians had some success in attracting this kind of business.[44]

The one specified price in the decree illustrates how the standard was to work. By setting a price in Olbian money for Cyzicene staters (of electrum, which as usual passed as gold), the Olbians both made these staters serve in practice as the gold issue which the local coinage lacked and established a benchmark for the valuation of local coinage, the market standard. But the absence of taxes on the sale and purchase of gold and silver coinage in transactions which could be arranged without government interference confirmed the free nature of the market, a significant change from past practice when a tax had been imposed.

An interpretation which excludes commercial or financial motives for this decree in favor of political motives linked to the required use of local coinage misses the mark. Founded on a trade route with the interior, Olbia flourished in the sixth and fifth centuries. But by the fourth century, less happy times had perhaps begun, and the third century was a period of decline.[45] The decree concerned with coinage would fit well in a period when the Olbians were trying to prevent or ameliorate deterioration in the local economy by creating a convenient, price-competitive, and untaxed market for gold and silver coinage from which they could profit both directly and indirectly.[46] The Olbian monetary decree was a political decision in the sense that

[44] For the range of foreign coinage found in Olbia, see W. Ziebell, *Olbia. Eine griechische Stadt in Süd-Russland* (Hamburg, 1937), p. 75.

[45] On the history of Olbia, see M. Danoff, *RE* suppl. IX, *s. v.* "Pontos Euxeinos 17. Olbia," cols. 1092–1104; Belin de Ballu, *Olbia* (Leiden, 1972); A. Wąsowicz, *Olbia pontique et son territoire* (Paris, 1975).

[46] For the sort of indirect benefits to be expected from more commercial traffic, see the tax attested at Cyzicus in the sixth century (*SIG*³ 4) and the remarks of Ps.-Xenophon, *Constitution of the Athenians* 1.17.

it was made by the citizens of a *polis* in their own interest, but it was not a decision to do with the assertion of political sovereignty through the imposition of a uniform monetary system.

2
Views on Coinage in Classical Literature

The second category of evidence which must be treated here consists of the relevant references to coinage in the literature of the classical period. First, there are the opinions offered about the origin of coinage. The stories current in the fifth and fourth centuries on this subject should reveal traces of any contemporary notion that sovereignty and coinage were closely connected, especially since by this period Greek coinages were normally issued by states, not by private individuals.[47]

The sixth-century thinker Xenophanes is said to have attributed the invention of coinage to the Lydians.[48] No other details of his opinion are recorded, such as why it was invented or whether by a king (e.g., Croesus) or by private individuals. Herodotus in the fifth century held the same opinion, but he added another detail: "The first men we know to have coined money of gold and silver and used it were the Lydians; they were also the first retail merchants."[49] The second fact is not explicitly given as an explanation of the first, but there is an implied

[47] For recent discussion of the question whether early Greek coinage was produced by private individuals, see R. R. Holloway, "La ricerca attuale sull'origine della moneta," *RIN* 80 (1978), pp. 7–14; J. H. Kroll, "From Wappenmünzen to Gorgoneia to Owls," *ANSMN* 26 (1981), pp. 1–32; M. J. Price, "Thoughts on the Beginnings of Coinage," in *Studies in Numismatic Method Presented to Philip Grierson*, ed. C.N.L. Brooke, B.H.I.H. Stewart, J. G. Pollard, and T. R. Volk (Cambridge, 1983), p. 6. See Price, "Early Greek Bronze Coinage," *Essays . . . Robinson*, p. 100, and "The function of early Greek Coinage," in *Le Origini della monetazione di bronzo in Sicilia e in Magna Grecia. Atti del VI Convegno del Centro Internazionale di Studi Numismatici Napoli 17–22 Aprile 1977, AIIN* 25, suppl. (Rome, 1979), p. 356, for the idea that the bronze "kollyboi" from Athens in the later fourth century were issues of private individuals.

[48] H. Diels and W. Kranz, *Die Fragmente der Vorsokratiker* [6] (Berlin, 1951–1952), vol. 1, p. 130, F 4.

[49] 1.94.1.

connection. The Lydians, whether king or individuals, invented precious metal coinage in the interests of commerce. The same motive is spelled out more clearly by the fourth-century historian Ephorus, who reported that Pheidon, king and then tyrant of Argos, struck the first silver coins on the island of Aegina, "for the island became a place for foreign trade because the land was poor and the people engaged in trading by sea."[50] In this case the invention of coinage is attributed to a king, but there is no indication that his invention had anything to do with the assertion of his own royal or tyrannical sovereignty. Rather, Pheidon invented coinage to facilitate commerce, in this instance foreign trade.

Commercial motives for the invention of coinage are explicitly recorded as part of the tradition by Plato very briefly in *Republic* 2.371b8–9 and by Demosthenes in a speech of 353/2 B.C. which contains remarks he attributes to Solon.[51] According to Demosthenes, Solon argued that the counterfeiters of laws ought to be punished if, as was the case in all states, the counterfeiters of coinage were put to death; this argument was all the more compelling because the laws are the coinage of the state, so to speak, while silver coinage was invented by private individuals for private transactions and belonged to them. For our purposes, the important point is that Demosthenes in the mid-fourth century can attribute to Solon a view on the origin of coinage which is about as far as one can get from any tradition that coinage was invented by a sovereign as an assertion of sovereignty.

Aristotle echoes this idea that coinage was invented expressly to serve the needs of people in exchanges. In *Ethics* 5.1133a19–b28, he makes it clear that men invented coinage to facilitate the exchange of different kinds of goods. Money is therefore conventional rather than natural, as it functions among men "by agreement." Since this passage is concerned with the

---

[50] Strabo 8.6.16 (C376); cf. 8.3.33 (C358). On Pheidon, cf. Pollux 9.83–85. On the close correlation between the history of Aeginetan coinage and the development of the island's commerce, see R. Ross Holloway, "An Archaic Hoard from Crete and the Early Aeginetan Coinage," *ANSMN* 17 (1971), pp. 1–21.

[51] 24.212–214.

nature of exchange rather than with a historical description of
the role of money in society, one might argue that the context
explains Aristotle's failure here to assign any further significance
to money, such as a connection with the assertion of political
sovereignty. In *Politics* 1.1257a31-b7, however, Aristotle describes the historical development of money. At first, he says,
men relied on barter to exchange goods. The invention and use
of money came as natural developments from this more primitive
system of exchange. The development of money spurred profit
making in trade as a way of life.[52] Aristotle states again in this
second passage that coinage functioned as a medium of exchange
"by agreement." If he meant by this any kind of literal agreement, the context indicates that it was an agreement among individuals for their individual convenience.[53] If Aristotle perceived
an important connection between coinage and sovereignty, this
section of the *Politics* would have been a good place to make the
point because he explicitly comments on the change from precious metal used as money by size and weight to the use of actual
coins minted with a type ($\chi\alpha\rho\alpha\kappa\tau\dot{\eta}\rho$). All he says about this
$\chi\alpha\rho\alpha\kappa\tau\dot{\eta}\rho$ is that men put it on money to free themselves of the
necessity of measuring, i.e., of the need to determine the value of
money by weighing it in every transaction. The $\chi\alpha\rho\alpha\kappa\tau\dot{\eta}\rho$,
Aristotle states, was put on as a sign of the amount. There is
nothing here about the type as "the badge of the city" or coinage
as a symbol of autonomy.

From even this brief summary it should be evident that the
opinions current in the classical period on the origin of Greek
coinage reveal no interest in any notions about a connection
between sovereignty and coinage. Even when the invention of
coinage is attributed to a sovereign such as Pheidon, the motive
is to promote commerce, not to make a political statement.

A second body of evidence from literature to be scrutinized

[52] On these two complex passages, see Scott Meikle, "Aristotle and the Political Economy of the Polis," *JHS* 99 (1979), pp. 58-62. Cf. Ed. Will, "Fonctions
de la monnaie dans les cités grecques de l'époque classique," *Numismatique
antique*, pp. 233-246.

[53] For the view that it was a private international agreement, see J. Moreau,
"Aristote et la monnaie," *REG* 82 (1969), p. 351.

for traces of a classical tradition on sovereignty and coinage is political philosophy. It is especially to be regretted that the once considerable classical and early Hellenistic literature on monarchy is for all practical purposes lost.[54] For example, we cannot know whether Aristotle had anything to say about coinage in his treatise *On Kingship*, which he is traditionally believed to have written for Alexander's edification.[55] From what was originally perhaps a much larger body of material, only one item in fourth-century political philosophy has survived which discusses the place of coinage in a well-run state. In *Laws* 5.741e-742c, Plato sets out the ideal practical arrangements for a small city-state. One of the things he believes this state should forbid is excessive moneymaking and piling up wealth. To that end, there must be a law forbidding private individuals to possess any gold and silver. They are allowed to have only coinage that is valid within the confines of the home state for the use of craftsmen and the necessary payment of wages but is unacceptable as currency in the outside world. For the payment of the state's expenses in dealing with the outside world, it should acquire "regular Hellenic coinage" (κοινὸν Ἑλληνικὸν νόμισμα) which can be used, for example, on visits abroad by officials of the state. If a private person goes abroad with official permission and returns home with "foreign coinage" (ξενικὸν νόμισμα) left over, he is to deposit it with the state and take in return a corresponding amount of "local" (ἐπιχώριον) coinage. Failure to do so is a serious crime. This section of the *Laws* ends with a prohibition of dowry and of lending money at interest.

[54] On this genre of literature, see E. R. Goodenough, "The Political Philosophy of Hellenistic Kingship," *YCS* 1 (1928), pp. 55–102; L. Delatte, *Les traités de la royauté d'Ecphante, Diotogène et Sthénidas* (Bibliothèque de la Faculté de Philosophie et Lettres de l'Université de Liège 97, 1942), pp. 282–290; P. Hadot, "Fürstenspiegel," in *Reallexikon für Antike und Christentum*, vol. 8 (Stuttgart, 1972), cols. 555–632; Olaf Müller, *Antigonos Monophthalmos und "Das Jahr der Könige"* (Bonn, 1973), pp. 109–110. Kingship figures as a subject for discussion in the *Politicus* of Plato, but no substantive details are offered on mundane topics such as how to control the monetary system. When coinage is mentioned in 289b2–5, it is presented as of marginal importance for the subject at hand.

[55] See, for example, J. R. Hamilton, *Alexander the Great* (London, 1973), p. 33.

Such a system would naturally impose a uniform monetary circulation of only local coinage in the home state, but the goal is ethical, not political in the modern sense required if this uniform circulation was to be enforced in the interest of asserting the state's sovereignty. Plato is trying to devise a system that will promote the ethical well-being of the citizens in clear imitation of the arrangements for coinage at Sparta in the classical period.[56] His ethical goal requires the state to control the monetary system, and everything else for that matter, but this requirement is not imposed by the nature of coinage as, for example, a symbol of the state's sovereignty, but by the nature of men as imperfect beings.

In sum, then, one sees that neither the documentary nor the literary evidence from the classical period supports the idea that any close connection was perceived between sovereignty and coinage which would have made coins into the symbols of autonomy or badges of independence of every sovereign state. The conclusion already suggested by the numismatic and historical evidence is confirmed.

[56] See Glenn R. Morrow, *Plato's Cretan City: A Historical Interpretation of the Laws* (Princeton, 1960), pp. 139–140.

CONCLUSION

Thanks perhaps to its long and largely unquestioned history, the standard opinion on sovereignty and coinage in the classical Greek world continues to flourish even in unlikely places. D. B. Shelov, for example, offers "economic" explanations for the initiation and cessation of various civic coinages in his study of the coinages of the Bosporus region from the sixth to the second centuries B.C. Against the Marxist background sketched in Shelov's introduction, this sort of explanation is easily comprehensible. It is, then, surprising to find that Shelov also occasionally invokes the conventional notion of the relationship between sovereignty and coinage to explain the cessation of coinage as the result of suppression by a sovereign when an "economic" explanation would serve.[1] The idea is simply too pervasive to be ignored even though its application seems at variance with the basic presuppositions of the work.

It is my contention that the numismatic, historical, documentary, and literary evidence uniformly fails to support the idea that there was operative in the classical Greek world a strongly felt connection between an abstract notion of sovereignty and the right of coinage which implied the necessity to enforce a uniform monetary circulation. In particular, this idea has been misapplied in the history of the relations of Philip II, Alexander the Great, and the early successors with the Greeks. As we have seen, this idea has often been used to establish the dates at which coinages ended by argument from the supposed consequences of the imposition of royal "sovereignty." The cases of Ambracia, Thebes, Phocis, Corinth, and Abdera come to mind, for example,

[1] *Coinage of the Bosporus VI-II Centuries B.C.*, trans. H. Bartlett Wells (Oxford, 1978, British Archaeological Reports International Series, suppl. 46), pp. 59, 115–121.

as obvious examples of this misconceived method (to say nothing of Thessaly). There is no evidence to prove that any of these kings suppressed, or even tried to suppress, Greek autonomous coinage. Even the most obvious demonstration of a king's power over another state, the imposition of a garrison, demonstrably had nothing to do with the fate of the coinage of the garrisoned state.

Interpretation of this situation is difficult, to be sure. One might argue that the Macedonian kings did not suppress any Greek coinages, even in an area like Thessaly which was under their control, because they realized the strict connection the Greeks felt between the idea of their independence and the existence of their coinages. To demonstrate just how respectful of Greek freedom they were, the argument would go, the kings would have deliberately allowed the Greeks to continue to coin despite the problems this would have caused for the establishment of genuinely royal rule. If there is any truth in this interpretation, it need not be because great importance was attached to coins as "explicit badges" or "symbols." Any king who ordered a Greek state to stop minting its own coins would certainly have been interfering in the internal affairs of that state and would have been perceived as doing so. That sort of interference was not going to win goodwill or to encourage loyalty. It might have seemed preferable to avoid any meddling with coinage for such practical reasons, but these were the same reasons to avoid unnecessary meddling in general with the property and institutions of those one wanted to keep pacified in one's own self-interest. Coinage would not have been more sensitive in this context than other important concerns of the state.[2]

I would argue that a far more likely interpretation of the evidence is that the Macedonian kings gave hardly a thought to the existence or nonexistence of local Greek coinage. Their concern was, above all, to secure a steady and large supply of precious metal which could be turned into coinage for the efficient payment of their expenses, which were considerable now that their military and political activities were spread beyond the

---

[2] Such as a city's wall. See below.

boundaries of the homeland.[3] Their efforts to maximize their
supply of precious metal and their increased level of coin production had indirect adverse effects on local Greek coinage. It
became harder for most city-states (those without their own
mines) to acquire raw silver for conversion to coinage, and the
large Macedonian royal issues entered circulation in such
numbers that there was less and less need for locally produced
money. Whatever need there might have been from time to time
would have involved small denominations to serve as small
change in purely local use, the kind of service for which bronze
coinage was intended.

Greek states which regarded local coins as absolutely necessary as assertions of sovereignty, however, could have overcome
the problem of a diminished supply of raw silver by acquiring
Macedonian royal coins and melting them down for reissue as
local products. But this perhaps expensive solution seems not to
have been adopted, at least not in Thessaly, for example. Thessalian coinage just stopped. If the Macedonian king even
noticed this change, he would not have been inconvenienced by
it. It was, in fact, more convenient for him if the Thessalians
paid the customary revenues, due him in his capacity as their
leader, with Macedonian coins which he could spend immediately without added expense for exchange or reminting. Of
course, the Thessalians may not have been able to pay the Macedonian king with ease (or even at all) if their prosperity had been
destroyed by *ca.* 320 B.C. But if, as Demosthenes tells us, the
king's revenue as leader of the Thessalian confederacy came from
market and port taxes, it is likely that the Thessalians went on
paying him. Only now they paid him in whatever coinage they
themselves received in tax collection. More and more those
coins were Macedonian, and that suited everyone. The Thessalians were content to go on circulating their old local issues
despite their ever more worn appearance, in company with the
Attic-weight issues of Macedonia and Athens. It was expedient

[3] They could also conceivably have been concerned with the role of coinage
in standardizing and facilitating transactions, but I see no clear evidence that
they placed much importance on this function of coinage.

and convenient to do so, and those were the facts that mattered. Abstract notions of sovereignty need never have entered the picture.

One can insist on this last point because the abstract idea of sovereignty as commonly found in modern political philosophy is difficult to identify with precision in the thinking of the classical period. No word in classical Greek fully corresponds to this now familiar concept. The words which immediately come to mind in this context, such as ἐλευθερία and αὐτονομία, served more as terms of propaganda than as programmatic descriptions of a well-defined state of sovereign independence.[4] The word ἀρχή, on the other hand, tended to express a concrete notion of "rule."[5] The Greeks naturally recognized different varieties of

[4] See, for example, A. Heuss' recent discussion of ἐλευθερία in "Die Freiheitserklärung von Mylasa in den Inschriften von Labranda," in *Le monde grec. Pensée, littérature, histoire, documents. Hommages à Claire Préaux*, ed. J. Bingen, G. Cambier, and G. Nachtergael (Brussels, 1975), pp. 403–415. In his well-known monograph *Stadt und Herrscher des Hellenismus* (Leipzig, 1937, Klio Beiheft 26), Heuss made sovereignty as an abstract concept a central feature of the relationship of the Hellenistic kings to the Greek city-states. For an extensive collection of evidence, see Kurt Raaflaub, "Zum Freiheitsbegriff der Griechen. Materialien und Untersuchungen zur Bedeutungsentwicklung von ἐλεύθερος/ἐλευθερία in der archaischen und klassischen Zeit," in *Soziale Typenbegriffe im alten Griechenland und ihr Fortleben in den Sprachen der Welt. Band 4*, ed. E. C. Welskopf (Berlin, 1981), pp. 180–405. Martin Ostwald, *Autonomia: Its Genesis and Early History* (Chico, Calif., 1982, American Classical Studies 11), argues that the concept of αὐτονομία never received a proper definition in the fifth century and only began to be spelled out in the fourth century, most prominently (as we have the evidence) in the decree of Aristoteles for the Second Athenian League. For further discussion of the conceptual gap between these ancient Greek terms and the modern notion of sovereignty, see E. Badian, "Hegemony and Independence. Prolegomena to a Study of the Relations of Rome and the Hellenistic States in the Second Century B.C.," in the *Actes du VIIᵉ congrès de la F.I.E.C. Budapest, 1979*, vol. 1 (Budapest, 1983), pp. 399–400.

[5] The listing of "sovereignty" as one of the definitions in LSJ⁹, *s. v.* ἀρχή II.1, is overly interpretative. For a good example of how "rule" rather than "sovereignty" serves to translate ἀρχή into English with the proper connotation, see Aristotle, *Politics* 1.1254b16–20, and the translation by T. A. Sinclair, *Aristotle. The Politics* (Harmondsworth, 1962), p. 37. One might add in this context that the translation of πόλις as "state" in the usual modern sense of the word is, strictly speaking, also anachronistic. Cf., for example, Reinhard Koerner, "Die Bedeutung von πόλις und verwandten Begriffe nach Aussage der Inschriften," in *Soziale Typenbegriffe im alten Griechenland und ihr Fortleben in den*

ἀρχή, such as μοναρχία. Plato and Aristotle distinguished various forms of "the rule of one," including of course the rule of a king.[6] Neither of these theorists discussed coinage in relation to royal rule, nor do any fragments on this topic survive from the treatises written in the fourth and third centuries as advice to kings, when the appearance on the Greek scene of kings seems to have stimulated the production of this kind of literature.[7]

Only traces of this literature have survived to us, and one cannot say whether the subject of coinage was ever raised in these ancient *Fürstenspiegeln*. Even if, as seems likely, the philosophers were primarily concerned with the personal qualities of the king himself, as was Isocrates in his remarks on the topic of kingship, they could have made practical recommendations on coinage as the result of ethical concerns.[8] Zeno of Citium went Plato one better by denying the need for coinage even as a means of everyday exchange or trade, and such radical theorizing on the subject of money could conceivably have left its mark on the advice being proffered in the new handbooks for kings.[9] Exactly what, if anything, philosophers may have advised their royal pupils to do about coinage we cannot know. In any case, nothing substantial on the topic of the practical affairs of kingship survives from this period.

There is no obvious or universally applicable reason why a king should have wanted to suppress perfectly good Greek coinages even in areas he controlled. The suppression of traditional local coinage would probably have created a certain amount of monetary confusion in the affected region and perhaps even some financial hardship for the communities involved. Those conditions could only promote political discontent and instability. The case of Thessaly and the establishment and maintenance of

---

Sprachen der Welt. Band 3, ed. E. C. Welskopf (Berlin, 1981), pp. 360–367.

[6] *Politicus* 291e1–5; *Politics* 3.1284b35–1288a32.

[7] For references to discussions of this genre, see n. 54 in chapter 9.

[8] Isocrates, *Philip* 114, 116; *Nicocles* 5–6.

[9] Diogenes Laertius 7.33. Whether the kings actually took any advice that was offered is still another question. Victor Ehrenberg, *Man, State and Deity. Essays in Ancient History* (London, 1974), pp. 56–57, argues that the work of Greek philosophers had little if any influence on the Hellenistic kings.

the League of Corinth show that Macedonian policy under Philip and Alexander was to promote stability through the exploitation of traditional institutions, or of new institutions created in a traditional mold. Until the very end of the fourth century, the successors of Alexander found it expedient to pay lip service at least to the norms of rule which Philip and Alexander had observed. Success was sought in imitation of the great models of the recent past and in proclaiming allegiance to the cause of Greek "freedom."[10]

The question of what exactly a king was and how he was supposed to act took on new urgency, however, once the line of Alexander was extinguished beyond any doubt with the murder of his bastard son, Heracles, in 309/8 B.C.[11] Since no one could claim the succession to the Macedonian throne by blood (although Ptolemy may have tried), other criteria had to be brought into play to identify the next king.[12] Brute force was going to be the most important criterion, but pretenders to royal status could hope to win support by means of propaganda as well. Coins with their pictorial types and inscriptions offered one medium with which to spread a propagandistic message, and the inscription "of king so-and-so" (which began with the coinage of Alexander) became widespread at the end of the fourth century on issues of Cassander, Ptolemy, and Seleucus. These legends clearly advertised the status which the issuers claimed. They needed to advertise their claims because they had all claimed the title of "king" on their own initiatives and in competition with one another.[13] In a certain sense, their status as

[10] Only Cassander failed to join this hypocritical chorus. His policy was presumably to support the oligarchs in various Greek cities whom his father had put into power and who helped him to control their fellow Greeks. Forbidding his friends and supporters to mint coins was not in his interest, and he never did so in Athens despite the presence there of his garrison for ten years.

[11] Diodorus 20.28.1–3.

[12] There was a rumor that Ptolemy was a bastard of Philip II (Curtius 9.8.22; Pausanias 1.6.2).

[13] On the beginnings of the Hellenistic monarchies, see O. Müller, *Antigonos Monophthalmos und das "Jahr der Könige"* (Bonn, 1973); Will, *Histoire politique I* ², p. 76. For a caution, however, against the notion that coin types were always important in the formation of public opinion, see M. H. Crawford, "Roman Imperial Coin Types and the Formation of Public Opinion," *Studies . . . Grier-*

"kings" was independent of the territory they happened to control, at least in the way they laid claim to the status. Only Cassander was in Macedonia. The others were controlling detached sections of Alexander's empire. This new kind of kingship was, by necessity, largely personal and charismatic. As such, its content and its legitimacy were open to question. The legend "of king so-and-so" on a coin publicized, however indirectly, the claim to legitimate kingship, but it cannot tell us anything about the claims implied in that status. That is, the identification on his coins of, for example, Ptolemy as "King Ptolemy" does not mean that Ptolemy thereby was claiming an exclusive right of coinage as a royal prerogative.

What are we to make, then, of the evidence of the coin hoards from Egypt in the late fourth and early third centuries which show that a uniform monetary circulation was indeed created early in Ptolemy's rule? It is certainly not proof that Ptolemy enforced this pattern of circulation as a matter of policy to assert his new royal status. An economic explanation seems called for by the other evidence. As a result of his hostile relations with other successors and of the lack of precious metal resources in Egypt, Ptolemy encountered grave financial difficulties which led him to issue coinage of a lighter weight than that of the Attic standard of Macedonian royal coinage. His successive devaluations of his silver currency made it significantly less valuable than the other, non-Egyptian issues of coinage which it resembled in size and design. The only way Ptolemy could make such a coinage function was by enforcing its use to the exclusion of other coinages. In addition, he could profit from the demonetization of Attic-weight coinages, which would have to be turned in to the government in exchange for less valuable new issues. In other words, the overriding motive for the creation of the Ptolemaic system of uniform monetary circulation was clearly financial.[14] In any case, the system could not have had any

---

son, pp. 47–64.

[14] See O. H. Zervos, "A Ptolemaic Hoard of 'Athena' Tetradrachms at *ANS*," *ANSMN* 23 (1978), pp. 53–56, on Ptolemy's coinage. M. A. Levi, "Studi Tolemaici I. Moneta e politica dei primi Tolemei," *Parola del passato* 30 (1975), pp. 192–200, stresses the financial preoccupations of the first two Ptolemies.

relevance to considerations of sovereignty as related to the right of coinage because there were no local autonomous coinages in Egypt whose existence could have represented (on the traditional view of this subject) diminution of the king's status as sovereign. Ptolemy's monetary situation was special and had almost nothing in common with the circumstances in which the other successors found themselves. Like Ptolemy, they needed money, but they did not issue lightweight coinages, and they had to coexist with city-states with their own traditions of autonomous coinage.

It seems anachronistic to use an abstract concept of sovereignty as a definitive criterion in trying to explain why coinages started and stopped in the classical period. This is not to deny that there could be causal links between what we commonly mean by the expression "the sovereignty of a state" and the production of coinage. The predominant link, however, was practical, not theoretical. Independent states in the world of classical Greece had to be prepared to defend themselves militarily, and defense-related expenditures were probably by far the largest and most regularly occurring expenditures for most independent Greek states. These expenditures would be most urgent and greatest especially if a state succeeded in liberating itself from the domination of another power. In that case it was necessary for political survival to have money to pay for defense, not least against the real, or imagined, threat from the former oppressor. It would not, therefore, be surprising if occasionally coinage began for the first time when a previously oppressed state won its freedom. But these coins would have been produced to serve in the first instance as the currency required to finance a war effort in defense of freedom. Their intended function was a highly practical one: to pay soldiers, to buy military equipment, to pay for defense works, and so on. In other words, the state needed to produce coins as instruments of its policy on self-defense. It re-

Roger S. Bagnall, *The Administration of the Ptolemaic Possessions Outside Egypt* (Leiden, 1976), pp. 211–212, argues that considerations of profit and power determined royal decisions to create a zone of monetary isolation. See S. Kondis, "A propos des monnayages royaux lagides en Cyrénaïque sous Ptolémée I er et II," *RBN* 124 (1978), pp. 23–47, on the coexistence in Cyrene of autonomous and royal coinages.

mains to be demonstrated that it needed or wanted to produce coins to serve as symbols of an abstract notion of sovereignty. Perhaps an analogy can help to illuminate my point. Let us imagine a Greek city which had no city wall during a period of occupation or domination by another power, either because the city had never built a wall in the first place or it had lost the wall as a consequence of its defeat by the dominant power. As soon as the domination is ended, this city builds a wall. Why? To secure its own defense and to protect its newly won freedom, we must answer.[15] Should we also assume that the wall was built expressly as a symbol of that freedom? Surely not, or at least we should not assume that the citizens of the city built their wall explicitly and self-consciously for a symbolic purpose.[16]

One could extend this model to explain the augmentation of the production of coinage to cover other state expenses, too, as in the case of the great increase in the production of Macedonian coinage at the end of the reign of Philip II when the king had large expenses for diplomacy and war. Unfortunately, we are too poorly informed to make any reasonable statements about the relation of coin production in Greek city-states to, for example, public building projects or pay for public office. Many influences of different sorts may have contributed to the decision of a particular Greek state to start or to increase the production of coinage at a particular time, but practical considerations, so far as we can tell, ruled.[17] Another practical consideration, of

[15] The obvious example is Athens after the defeat of the Persians in 479 (Thucydides 1.89–93).

[16] This seems, however, to be the implication of M. Amit, *Great and Small Poleis* (Brussels, 1973), p. 118, in his discussion of the rebuilding of the walls of Plataea in the 330s: "Since the walls were the symbol of independence and the means of defense of the cities, the building or destruction of city-walls is sometimes described as the building or destruction of the city itself." (He refers to Xenophon, *Hell.* 2.2.20, 2.3.11, concerning Piraeus.)

[17] This was true not only in Greece, of course. See, for example, A. T. Cutroni, "Aspetti e problemi della monetazione arcaica di Selinunte (inizi-480 a.C.)," *Kokalos* 21 (1975), pp. 154–173 (whose discussion of the "political" role of coinage shows just how practical the politics of a *polis* were); R. F. Sutton, "The Populonia Coinage and the Second Punic War," *Contributi introduttivi allo studio della monetazione etrusca. Atti del V Convegno del Centro Internazionale di Studi Numismatici Napoli 1975*, in *AIIN* 22, Suppl. 1976 (publ. 1977), pp.

course, was to ensure the reliability of the coinage in circulation in the state so that the transactions for which coinage was necessary could go on smoothly. For this reason, it made sense for the production of coinage normally to be restricted to the state. Too many uncertainties would be created if coinage were to be produced by private individuals on a regular basis. [18] Yet another consideration was the possibility of making a profit from the operation of a well-run mint, although we are not in a position to say just how large this profit might have been, especially in the minting of coinages in precious metal rather than in bronze. [19] The most basic practical consideration of all, however, was that a state had to be financially solvent in order to produce coinage (in precious metals, at any rate). Without the resources of capital that only prosperity could bring in classical antiquity, when the present practices of deficit financing on the national level or the printing of more paper money were not in question, the state could not mint a gold or silver coinage even in the expectation of turning a profit at some point. It was necessary to have money, one might say, in order to produce currency. If a state became insolvent, it could no longer mint such coins.

For all these reasons, it seems to me that the demands of proper method in classical history and numismatics require us to try to understand changes in coin production as likely to have been dictated by practical necessity and practical possibility rather than by abstract theory. In many ways, it is misleading and anachronistic to speak of the "right of coinage" in this period. It might in the end be more profitable to think instead of the "fact of coinage." The case of Proconnesus can serve as an example of what I mean by this. When not long after 362 B.C.

199–211 (coinage produced to meet the expenses of war); R. C. Knapp, "The Date and Purpose of the Iberian Denarii," *NC* 1977, pp. 1–18 (native coinage began as a result of fiscal demands).

[18] For some discussion of the possible role of private persons in the production of Greek coinage, see the references in n. 47 of chapter 9. The facilitation of transactions, not the assertion of the sovereignty of the state, is the motive implied by Aristotle for putting a χαρακτήρ on coins. See *Politics* 1.1257a39–41.

[19] For this motive in the minting of bronze, see *OGIS*, no. 339, lines 45–46

Cyzicus absorbed Proconnesus by force, the coinage of Proconnesus naturally ended because Proconnesus no longer existed as a state. If there were to be no more citizens of the state of Proconnesus, and there were not, there could hardly continue to be a coinage marked with their ethnic. In one sense, perhaps, it would be possible to say that the closing of the mint of Proconnesus marked the loss of the state's independence, but this observation identifies only the inevitable historical connection between the abolition of the state of Proconnesus by the territorial expansion of the state of Cyzicus and the consequent abolition of the official functions and institutions of the state of Proconnesus, of which the production of coinage was one. That Proconnesus stopped minting coins is a historical fact of some significance, but it does not tell us anything about the possible function of coinage as a symbol of sovereignty in the eyes of the people of Proconnesus or of Cyzicus.[20]

I would agree with A. J. Graham that "no generally valid rules can be established for the political interpretation of

---

(discussed below).

[20] On the abolition of Proconnesus and its coinage, see Louis Robert, *Monnaies grecques. Types, légendes, magistrats monétaires et géographie* (Geneva, 1967), pp. 16–21. He summarizes in the following way the situation once the Proconnesians had been absorbed into the state of Cyzicus: "Dès lors il n'y eut plus d'Etat proconnésien, il n'y eut plus de monnayage, marque de l'indépendance d'une ville, qu'avait supprimée une guerre" (p. 18). The case of Delos in 168 B.C. is parallel to that of Proconnesus: the state was abolished, and therefore so was its coinage. On these events, see L. Robert, "Monnaies dans les inscriptions grecques," *RN* 1962, pp. 18–24 (who, it should be pointed out, maintains in the case of Delos, as in the case of Proconnesus, that local coinage was the symbol of the state, the mark of its existence and sovereignty); Raymond Bogaert, *Banques et banquiers dans les cités grecques* (Leiden, 1968), pp. 165–169; Will, *Histoire politique II²* (Nancy, 1982), pp. 282–284, 298–301. These cases call to mind the situation in 431 B.C. when the Athenians expelled the population of Aegina (Thuc. 2.27), an action which naturally brought about the closing of the local mint. The change of the Aeginetan coin type from turtle to tortoise is usually linked to Athenian action against the Aeginetans. See, for example, Russell Meiggs, *The Athenian Empire* (Oxford, 1972), p. 184. For a warning against relating this change to historical events, however, see R. Ross Holloway, "An Archaic Hoard from Crete and the Early Aeginetan Coinage," *ANSMN* 17 (1971), pp. 20–21.

coins." [21] That coinage was invented and produced for practical reasons which, if I am correct, had nothing originally to do in the classical period with a symbolic function in the affirmation of political sovereignty does not, of course, have to mean that coins never came to serve as symbols of this sort. Something can be invented for one purpose and in the course of time come to serve another, quite different purpose. According to circumstances, it might acquire a new function while continuing to serve its original function, or modifying that function, or even losing it partially or entirely. It has been suggested, for example, that the earliest electrum coinage was invented to facilitate the giving of "personalized gifts or payments" as part of the social structure of archaic society. Coins were not produced at this stage to make possible small payments of the kind involved in everyday transactions, but in the long run, it turned out that the existence of coins made their use for this latter purpose possible and led to the development of a system of currency for ordinary exchanges such as in shopping. [22] In the same way, it is conceivable that the minting of coinage eventually came to be regarded as a symbolic affirmation of sovereignty, even as coins continued to serve practical purposes. But it is far from necessary to assume that this secondary development, if it indeed occurred, happened almost simultaneously with the invention of coinage or even soon thereafter. On the other hand, one way in which such a development could indeed take place would be for one state to initiate action intended to suppress the coinage of another state. The citizens of the victimized state would certainly regard the suppression of their customary coinage as an infringement of their autonomy, just as if, let us say, they were forbidden to wear the traditional costume of their particular culture. The rallying cry of the resistance could be "They are taking away our coin-

---

[21] *Colony and Mother City*, p. 123 (in the context of a thoughtful discussion of the commercial and political character of coins in which he demonstrates how difficult it can be to draw strict connections between the production of coinage and political independence).

[22] For this scenario, see M. J. Price, "The Function of Early Greek Coinage," *Le Origini della monetazione di bronzo*, pp. 351–358, and "Thoughts on the Beginnings of Coinage," *Studies . . . Grierson*, pp. 1–10.

age; they are taking away our freedom." In this way, the minting of local coinage could come to be regarded as a symbol of
sovereign independence, as an institution of the state which had
to be maintained for its symbolic value. In other words, when
one group threatens to take away something which others usually
have, or actually succeeds in depriving them of it, the victimized
group can come to see this something as a symbol of its diminished or lost autonomy even though no symbolic value had been
attached to it originally. But, it must be emphasized, the victimized group does not necessarily have to react in this way.[23] It
may happen that the loss of other institutions or functions of the
state seems more important, or it may be that no such symboliza-
tion is necessary at all because the concept of freedom itself, as
expressed in words alone, is sufficient motivation to action, or at
least to discontent, for those whose status is in question. In any
case, if coinage really was an important affirmation of political
sovereignty in the classical period, rather than an essentially
practical response to concrete needs of the state, it would be
difficult to understand why Greek states often took so long after
the invention of coinage and the spread of its use to begin to produce their own coinage, and why they often went for long
periods without producing any coinage once minting had been
initiated. If Greek coins had served as the equivalent of modern
national flags, which are expressly meant to function as symbols
of political sovereignty and national pride, no self-respecting
Greek state would have gone without them if at all possible.[24]

[23] It is important to recall at this point that we have no evidence that the
Athenian Coinage Decree caused the minting of local coinage to be seen as an
important or symbolic component of sovereignty. See the discussion in chapter
9.

[24] On the symbolism of flags, see Raymond Firth, *Symbols. Public and Private*
(Ithaca, 1973), pp. 328–367. On p. 341, he quotes a brochure of the government of India: "The National Flag, the National Anthem and the National
Emblem are the three symbols through which an independent country proclaims
its identity and sovereignty. . . ." It is interesting that coinage is omitted.
Another instructive illustration (not found in Firth) of the contemporary recognition of the symbolic function of flags, arms, seals, and the like in the assertion
of the notion of sovereignty is supplied by the history of the long controversy in
the 1960s over the selection of a new Canadian flag. See the comments of J. R.
Matheson (who was, he says on p. 1, "an active participant in the battle") in

We must be careful not to confuse symbols with indications.
That is, something need not be a consciously produced symbol of
the abstract notion implied by a certain political condition in
order for its existence or nonexistence to be one possible indication of that condition. For example, the existence of local coinage could indicate that a state was independent, if it were
certifiably the case during the period concerned that, for whatever reason, only independent states issued such coinages.[25]
Similarly, the existence of a city wall, a local military force, or
various other official institutions one might think of could also
serve equally well to indicate the political condition of the state,
if the existence of that institution was only possible when the
state was in the specified political condition. Moreover, when a
distinction between symbols and indications is kept in mind, it
becomes clear that even in a situation in which only independent
cities could issue local coinage, it need not be true that the lack
of a local coinage would necessarily be a sign of a corresponding

---

Canada's Flag. A Search for a Country (Boston, 1980): "The search for a flag had
a single objective, namely Canadian symbolism in its purest form." This was
especially important because Canada's flag was "an assertion of her sovereignty"
(p. 3). Cf. the title of Conrad Swan's book on Canadian arms and seals,
Canada: Symbols of Sovereignty (Toronto, 1977). As he shows, the symbolic
value of banners in asserting sovereignty was explicitly recognized in the Middle
Ages (p. 3, with n. 2 on p. 11). It seems to me, however, that the equation of
ancient coins with modern flags and similar symbols is anachronistic. On civic
emblems in Greece, see L. Lacroix, "Les 'blasons' des villes grecques," in *Etudes
d'archéologie classique, I, 1955–1956* (Paris, 1958 Annales de L'Est, Mémoire 19),
pp. 89–115. Firth, *Symbols*, pp. 15–23, has an illuminating discussion of the
widespread contemporary use of the terms "symbol" and "symbolic" and the
ways in which they are often misapplied.

[25] For just such an analysis, see E. Bickerman on civic coinage in Syria under
the Seleucids, *Institutions des Séleucides* (Paris, 1938), p. 213. Cf. his remarks in
"La cité grecque dans les monarchies hellénistiques," *Revue de philologie* 13
(1939), p. 340, n. 1 (in an extended discussion of Heuss' *Stadt und Herrscher*).
For useful discussions of the distinction between symbols and other kinds of
signs, see Firth, *Symbols*, pp. 61–66 (in the context of a long treatment of the
meaning and scope of the term "symbol," pp. 54–91), and Terence Hawkes,
Structuralism and Semiotics (Berkeley, 1977), pp. 126–129. To use the terminology of the pioneering semiotician C. S. Peirce (on whom see the discussions just
cited), coinage could serve as an "index" of political circumstances without serving as a symbol of abstract political notions.

lack of independence. An independent city might simply choose, for a variety of reasons, not to produce its own coinage and to use the coinage of others. Independence could be, to use the terminology of philosophic argument, the necessary condition, at certain times and in certain places, for the production of local coinage. It would not be a sufficient condition.[26] In addition, that something is indicative of a certain condition is far from requiring that it also be symbolic of the abstract notions which contemporaries or later observers believe to lie behind that condition. A conceptual jump from indication to symbol is obviously possible, but it is not automatic.[27]

If we are to believe that an abstract notion of the sovereignty of the state became a central component of decisions on who in the Greek world should mint coins and who should not, I submit that there is no compelling evidence for such a development any earlier than the last decade of the fourth century, when a variety of self-appointed kings began to compete for status, recognition, and territory. In these new and uncertain circumstances, it is perhaps conceivable that these kings came to believe that their

[26] We should not, then, be surprised if the gaining of independence does not coincide with the initiation of the production of local coinage, as, for example, in the case of Commagene in the second century B.C. In his recent study, "Coinage of the Armenian Kingdoms of Sophene and Commagene," *ANSMN* 28 (1983), p. 80, Paul Z. Bedoukian finds it "a little surprising" that we have no coins of Ptolemaeus of Commagene once he had declared his independence because "one would expect that a ruler beginning a dynasty would have taken pains to issue coins in his name."

[27] Once something is identified as indicative of a certain historical situation, the temptation is natural also to assign it the function of a symbol. See, for example, Jean Ducat, "La confédération béotienne et l'expansion thébaine à l'époque archaïque," *BCH* 97 (1973), pp. 62, 71–72, on the earliest coinage of the Boeotian Confederacy: "Le monnayage béotien a vraisemblablement été créé pour répondre aux besoins propres, principalement militaires sans doute, da la Confédération. Il est en même temps l'affirmation que la nouvelle entité politique apparue en Grèce donne de son existence" (71–72). That the appearance of Boeotian federal coinage is an indication of the need of the organization to respond to important practical concerns no one can doubt; that it was issued to be a symbol of the political existence of the new body is no more than an assumption based on the tradition concerning coinage and sovereignty which is under examination here.

coins had some special significance for the assertion of their right to rule. Once the Hellenistic kings had broken with Macedonian tradition by placing their own portraits on their royal issues, such coins were in some sense special. (For examples of such portrait coins, see plate 2, nos. 3–4, of Ptolemy and Demetrius Poliorcetes respectively.) One might imagine, for example, that just as it would have been potentially offensive to the king for one of his subjects or allies to destroy a statue of the king, the presence of the king's portrait on a coin might have made his contemporaries think twice about doing anything to or with his coins that a sensitive monarch might construe as *lèse-majesté*. Like a statue of the current king, a coin bearing the portrait of the living monarch had the potential to serve as a symbol of the majesty and status which the ruler wished to claim as his own. One might recall in this context the report by Suetonius that it was a crime of treason under Tiberius to carry into a latrine or a brothel a ring or a coin which bore an image of the *princeps*.[28]

Even if royal coinage ever came to be regarded as in some sense symbolic after a portrait of the king began to appear on his coins, it does not automatically follow that the king had to impose a uniform monetary circulation on those under his control, Greeks included, or that the coinages of Greek city-states had to develop a similar symbolic function. Not for this reason alone would one like to know more about the subsequent history in the Hellenistic and Roman worlds of the relationship between

---

[28] *Tiberius* 58. Philostratus, *Apollonius of Tyana* 1.15, has the story that a man was convicted because he beat one of his slaves who happened at the time to be carrying a coin with Tiberius' image on it. As for statues of the monarch, Diodorus (20.93.6–7) records that even while Demetrius Poliorcetes was besieging Rhodes, the *demos* prudently rejected a proposal to destroy the statues of Antigonus and Demetrius. One can also cite the well-known incidents from the Roman Empire involving statues of the *princeps* or the *divi* and accusations of treason. See, for example, Tacitus, *Ann.* 1.73.2, 1.74.3, 3.70.1; Suetonius, *Tib.* 58; Dio 57.24.7; Philostratus, *Apollonius of Tyana* 1.15; *Digesta Iustiniani* 48.4.5, 6, 7.4; and the comments of F.R.D. Goodyear, *The Annals of Tacitus. Books 1–6. Vol. II* (Cambridge, 1981), pp. 161–162, on *Ann.* 1.74.3. For a general survey of the adoption of royal portraits as an obverse type, see N. M. Davis and C. M. Kraay, *The Hellenistic Kingdoms. Portrait Coins and History* (London, 1973).

sovereignty and coinage. All that seems certain is that the situation was complex.[29] This is not the place to try to explore that history, but it seems appropriate in conclusion to mention a few especially interesting pieces of evidence. We can begin with the case of Aradus and what has been called the *lex Seyrig.*[30]

In a series of important articles, Henri Seyrig used the coins of Aradus to illuminate the otherwise poorly known political history of that city in the Hellenistic period.[31] Following Bickerman, Seyrig looked to the coins of a city for an indication of its political status, which could be defined, on his analysis, as subjection to a king, or as an intermediate status between subjection and autonomy, or as autonomy.[32] This so-called law relates the kind of coinage produced by a city to the particular political status of that city: cities subject to Hellenistic kings could be forced to mint royal coins; cities in an intermediate status would not be required to mint royal coins; free cities could mint autonomous coinage, either as posthumous Alexanders or as issues with purely civic types. This analytical scheme forms the basis of Seyrig's treatment of the coins of Aradus as evidence for the political history of the city.[33] Until the Macedonian conquest, Aradus, in Seyrig's words, "forme un royaume vassal du roi de Perse, et frappe des monnaies d'argent en toute souveraineté." Under the Macedonians, however, the city ceases to issue its own coins and becomes a royal mint, which shows that it is "une ville sujette." That the city ceases to have a royal mint under

[29] To gain an impression of the complexity of the relations between Hellenistic kings and Greek cities, one can still profit from the summary of A.H.M. Jones, *The Greek City from Alexander to Justinian* (Oxford, 1940), pp. 95–112.

[30] For this term, see Attilio Mastrocinque, "Storia e monetazionne di Mileto all'epoca dei Diadochi," *AIIN* 27–28 (1980–1981), p. 62.

[31] "Aradus and Tyre in the War against Tryphon," in his volume *Notes on Syrian Coins* (New York, 1950), pp. 17–19; "Aradus et sa pérée sous les rois Séleucides," *Syria* 28 (1951), pp. 206–220 = *Antiquités Syriennes* (Paris, 1953), pp. 185–200; "Monnaies hellénistiques XII. Questions aradiennes," *RN* 1964, pp. 9–50.

[32] For Bickerman, see above, n. 25.

[33] For another excellent example of this same procedure, see his article "Parion au 3ᵉ siècle avant notre ère," in *Centennial Publication of the American Numismatic Society*, ed. Harald Ingholt (New York, 1958), pp. 603–625.

Seleucus perhaps indicates that it now enjoys a more favorable status which is nevertheless "une souveraineté incomplète." Aradus recommences the minting of autonomous coinage in late 259 B.C., when the dating era of the city begins.[34] This final observation depends on the assumption that Antiochus II in 259 gave the city its formal autonomy, which included the right of coinage, and that the city immediately began to exercise this right. This assumption cannot be confirmed from the numismatic evidence, however, because the earliest issues of autonomous tetradrachms from Aradus are posthumous Alexanders with no indications of their dates, unlike the later series which are inscribed with era dates. Moreover, it is interesting that from evidence Seyrig cites as part of his discussion of Aradus, we can see that cities did not necessarily start to issue autonomous coinages as soon as their eras had begun. That is, they did not immediately rush their local coinages into production the moment they had achieved the freedom which a local era is taken to imply.[35] Sidon and Seleuceia waited until the fifth year of their eras, Laodiceia until the fourth, and Tripolis until the third.[36] If autonomous coinage was in fact an important symbol to affirm the political sovereignty of these cities, why did they wait for years before producing the symbols of their new status? And why, like Aradus, should cities produce Alexanders that were very nearly anonymous instead of coins that were uniquely civic? Seyrig himself remarked that the early tetradrachms of Aradus "do not express the town's sovereignty: a mint-mark is the only sign of their origin."[37]

[34] *Syria* 28 (1951), pp. 206–208, 213–214; *RN* 1964, pp. 32–36, 42–43. For a survey of the history of Aradus which recapitulates Seyrig's conclusions, see J.-P. Rey-Coquais, *Arados et sa Pérée aux époques grecque, romaine et byzantine* (Paris, 1974), pp. 149–169.

[35] See Seyrig, *RN* 1964, p. 34, on this assumed connection.

[36] Seyrig, *Syria* 28 (1951), p. 213.

[37] *Notes on Syrian Coins* (New York, 1950), p. 18. Cf. his discussion of the identification of the previously unrecognized third-century tetradrachms of Parion, *Centennial Publication*, pp. 606–613. He explains in *Syria* 28 (1951), pp. 214–215, that the "commercial cities" favored the production of Alexanders for their coinages which were intended for a large circulation. This is obviously an economic rather than a political explanation. The same is true of Seyrig's explanation for the introduction of new series at Byzantium and Chalcedon *ca.*

Tyre is one city which did not delay in minting autonomous coinage. Its coins began in 126/5 B.C. as soon as its era had begun.[38] If it is true that Aradus also began to issue its coins as soon as its era had begun, a further coincidence is noteworthy. The beginning of autonomous coinage at Tyre in 126/5 coincides with the city's refusal to open its gates to Demetrius II and its direct involvement in the complex hostilities of the time in Syria.[39] The beginning of autonomous coinage at Aradus in 259 coincides with the start of the Second Syrian War, in which the city could not escape involvement.[40] Could it be that these two cities started to mint their own coins just at these particular times because they had pressing financial demands to meet, such as those imposed by the need to defend themselves or to contribute to the war efforts of the Seleucid kings whose causes the cities chose to favor, or were made to favor?[41] The point is that one could explain why the civic mints at Aradus and Tyre happened to begin producing coins at the beginnings of the eras of the cities without resorting to the idea that their coinages were

---

235 B.C. and for the abrupt initiation of inscriptions to identify the coinages of these cities *ca.* 205. In both cases, he plausibly posits a desire to increase civic revenues as the motive for the changes. See his article "Monnaies hellénistiques de Byzance et de Calcédoine," in *Essays in Greek Coinage Presented to Stanley Robinson*, ed. C. M. Kraay and G. K. Jenkins (Oxford, 1968), pp. 185–195.

[38] *Notes on Syrian Coins* (New York, 1950), pp. 28, 31; *Syria* 28 (1951), p. 213.

[39] Will, *Histoire politique II*², pp. 435–436.

[40] Seyrig, *Syria* 28 (1951), pp. 215–216; Will, *Histoire politique I*², pp. 234–243.

[41] Seyrig, *Notes on Syrian Coins* (New York, 1950), p. 19, and *Syria* 28 (1951), p. 220, suggested that the resumption of the minting of tetradrachms at Aradus in 138/7 after a hiatus of several decades represented a privilege given to the city by Antiochus VII as compensation for support from the navy of Aradus. This suggestion was presumably based on the idea that the minting of tetradrachms was of special political significance in the Seleucid kingdom. While maintaining this latter position in his subsequent work on Aradus in *RN* 1964 (p. 45: "On se rappelle que la frappe du tétradrachme, dans l'empire séleucide, est un privilège des villes libres."), Seyrig expressed doubts about his earlier idea that the minting of tetradrachms at Aradus had been suspended by Antiochus IV to punish the city. Since Aradus minted silver drachms throughout the period of hiatus in the production of the larger denomination, Seyrig asked "si cette suspension ne pourrait pas s'expliquer aussi bien par un simple épisode de politique monétaire" (p. 50).

meant to symbolize the new status of the cities. Practical reasons alone would suffice to explain the desire of these cities for coinage at these particular moments in their histories.

Seyrig acknowledges the importance of practical concerns in decisions about the coinages of the Hellenistic cities with his denial that they produced tetradrachms "par souci de prestige."[42] That these coins bore prominently the types and legends of Alexander, with only a monogram or municipal symbol to link them to the issuing city, shows, he argued, that the cities were interested in the profits their mints could bring in. Since the kings wanted to keep these profits for themselves, they did not allow the subject cities to mint tetradrachms. When a city gained its freedom, it too wanted to make a profit from coinage. In other words, in Seyrig's opinion, the kings were not restricting the freedom of the cities to coin for reasons having to do with an abstract notion of sovereignty. A desire for profit was their motive.

In making this argument, Seyrig refers to a well-known honorary inscription of the later second century B.C. from Sestus (*OGIS* 339) which praises the honorand Menas for many services to the city, one of which was to oversee the production of a local bronze coinage. In this context, an explanation is given for the decision of the *demos* to begin the minting of a local bronze coinage.

43 ... τοῦ τε δήμου προελομέ-
44 νου νομίσματι χαλκίνωι χρῆσθαι ἰδίωι, χάριν
     τοῦ νομειτεύεσθαι μὲν τὸν τῆς πό-
45 λεως χαρακτῆρα, τὸ δὲ λυσιτελὲς τὸ
     περιγεινόμενον ἐκ τῆς τοιαύτης προσόδου
46 λαμβάνειν τὸν δῆμον. ...

In the course of an illuminating analysis of the role of moneyers and the importance of "civic pride" in the Greek *polis*, Louis Robert refers to this text to make the important point that decisions on matters of public concern to a *polis* could be influenced by feelings of pride and sentiment as well as by cold calculation

[42] *Syria* 28 (1951), p. 214.

of material advantage. [43] This is true above all because decisions were made in the *polis* by people in public meetings of one kind or another, not by faceless entities operating in isolation from human psychology. It is certainly possible, as he says elsewhere, that a *demos* could have decided, for reasons of "fierté civique," on a course of action which was not financially necessary or advantageous. [44] But even if the *demos* of Sestus wanted to have its own coins for the "rendement aussi sentimental" which the existence of a local bronze coinage could conceivably have provided, [45] this inscription plainly shows the overriding importance to the *demos* in this particular case of making a profit from the introduction of bronze coinage. This is clear from the words τῆς τοιαύτης προσόδου in the δέ clause, which describe what has come before in the μέν clause. Since "the city's coin type being used as a current type" is explicitly described as a form of revenue, it will not do to see the μέν and the δέ clauses as describing two completely different and unrelated reasons for the introduction of bronze coinage, that is, self-advertisement (to use the term of J. R. Melville-Jones) on the one hand and revenue

[43] "Les monétaires et un décret hellénistique de Sestos," *RN* 1973, pp. 43–53.
[44] *Monnaies antiques en Troade* (Geneva, 1966), pp. 87–88.
[45] Robert, *RN* 1973, p. 50. J. R. Melville Jones, "Epigraphical Notes on Hellenistic Bronze Coinage," *NC* 1972, p. 40, suggests that the μέν clause expresses "the aim of self-advertisement, of giving currency to the city's emblem." He prefers this version to the alternative translation of the clause as (in his words) "to give currency to the city's coinage," despite the support lent this latter version by Polybius 18.34.7. The interpretative translation of χαρακτήρ as "emblem" recalls H. von Fritze's translation of it as "Stadtwappen," in his article "Sestos. Die Menas-Inschrift und das Münzwesen der Stadt," *Nomisma* 1 (1907), p. 4. M. M. Austin, *The Hellenistic World from Alexander to the Roman Conquest. A Selection of Ancient Sources in Translation* (Cambridge, 1981), no. 215, p. 349, translates the passage as "when the people decided to use its own bronze coinage, so that the city's coin type should be used as a current type and the people should receive the profit resulting from this source of revenue," with an annotation (p. 351, n. 16) to point out "the emphasis on civic pride in the issue of coinage" (citing Robert and Melville Jones). Further translations from this inscription will be taken from Austin's version, with line references to the Greek text in *OGIS*.

on the other.[46] Rather, it is made clear that under the circumstances at Sestus putting a local bronze coinage into use was a precondition to securing a new source of revenue. Funds were needed because the city had fallen into desperate financial straits.[47] The emphasis here is not on the bringing into existence of a local coinage to serve as a symbol of sovereignty, but on the institutionalizing of the use of local coinage as a current standard in order for the city to make a profit.[48] It can be mentioned at this point that, as argued in the previous chapter, the use of local coinage as a standard at Olbia may have served an analogous purpose in advancing the economic status of the city. Another revealing comparison with the situation at Sestus comes from the ruling of Hadrian that certain purchases of fish at Pergamum had to be paid for in bronze coinage, not in silver, "so as to preserve the revenue of the exchange for the city."[49] That the new coinage of Sestus was to be in bronze and not silver underlines the financial interest of the city in the production of its coinage. A principal impetus to the spread of the use of bronze coinage in

[46] The self-advertisement to be derived from the issuing of bronze coinage would have been limited in any case because bronze coins tended not to circulate beyond their local area. The advertising of the existence of the state implied by this idea would not have affected those outside the boundaries of the state, to whom one might suppose such advertising would be especially directed. With the production of a bronze coinage without a major silver coinage, the *demos* would have been advertising its existence only to itself.

[47] Lines 54–58, 102–104.

[48] νομειτεύεσθαι implies that the city's coinage was intended to become in some sense a customary standard. See the citations of this word in *OGIS* 339, n. 22, and *LSJ*⁹, s. v. νομιτεύομαι. Cf. the use of νομιστεύομαι in Polybius 18.34.7; Sextus Empiricus, *Adv. math.* 1.178; Suidas, s. v. νομιστευομένων, and of ἐνομίστευον in *Etym. mag.*, s. v. ὀβελίσκος. Robert, *RN* 1973, p. 50, is of course correct that no mention of profit is made in lines 48–49 when Menas is praised for implementing the decision of the *demos* to use its own coinage. Profit is not mentioned here, however, because this section only recapitulates what was said in lines 43–44 about the decision of the *demos* to use its own bronze coinage, a decision which was explained in the following μέν and δέ clauses in lines 44–46 to make it clear how Menas had been instrumental in securing for the people yet another of many "useful advantages" (line 8). Using local coinage, in this context, presupposed making a profit.

[49] *OGIS* 484, lines 16–23. See Raymond Bogaert, *Banques et banquiers dans les cités grecques* (Leiden, 1968), p. 233.

the Hellenistic period was the realization on the part of the cities
that they could make a greater profit from such "fiduciary" coinages.[50] Surely Seyrig was correct to regard this inscription as
excellent evidence for the profit motive in the production of
coinage. It seems less clear that it is appropriate to use the text
as evidence for the notion of coinage as a symbol of sovereignty.

Another inscription from Hellenistic Asia Minor, this one
from the time of Seleucus II, has also been regarded as evidence
for a well-recognized connection between an abstract notion of
sovereignty and coinage.[51] One of the documents recorded in
this long text is a treaty between Smyrna and Magnesia ad Sipylum. Under the terms of this treaty, the residents of Magnesia
are to become citizens of Smyrna. It is specified, among other
things, that these new citizens are to use the laws of Smyrna in
their dealings with the people of Smyrna and that they are to
accept the coinage of Smyrna in Magnesia.[52] It would be mistaken to regard these specifications as imposed by Smyrna in
order to assert its sovereignty as a *polis* over the sovereignty of
Magnesia as a *polis* because the inscription makes it clear that
the residents of Magnesia, a mixture of military settlers and
natives, had little, if any, civic organization. They can hardly be
seen as constituting a standard *polis*, and they had no coinage of
their own.[53] The natives were so lacking in the structures of a

[50] Melville Jones, *NC* 1972, p. 39.
[51] *OGIS* 229 = *SVA* III, no. 492. See Crawford, "Roman Imperial Coin
Types," *Studies . . . Grierson*, p. 51.
[52] Lines 54–55: δεχέσθωσαν δὲ καὶ ἐμ Μαγνησίαι τὸ νόμισμα τὸ τῆς πό-
λεως [ἔνν]ομον.
[53] On the nature of the community, see H. H. Schmitt, *SVA* III, p. 172;
Bezalel Bar-Kochva, *The Seleucid Army. Organization and Tactics in the Great
Campaigns* (Cambridge, 1976), pp. 21–23, 37–38 (esp. nn. 89–90 on p. 38);
Getzel M. Cohen, *The Seleucid Colonies* (Wiesbaden, 1978, Historia Einzelschriften 30), pp. 77–78. B. V. Head, *Historia Numorum* 2 (Oxford, 1911), p.
652, put the earliest coins of Magnesia after 190 B.C. Cf. his earlier survey,
Catalogue of the Greek Coins of Lydia (British Museum, London, 1901), pp. lxix-
lxxiii. E. T. Newell, *The Coinage of the Western Seleucid Mints from Seleucus I to
Antiochus III* (New York, 1941, reissued in 1977 with a summary of recent scholarship by O. Mørkholm), pp. 271–280, assigned a few issues to Magnesia
under Antiochus I toward the end of his reign during the period "246–242/1
B.C.(?)," as the products of a temporary mint operating for only a short time.
The coins he tentatively assigned to Seleucus II and Antiochus Hierax have

developed *polis*, in fact, that the military settlers had to provide the secretaries to draw up the necessary lists of the names of the natives who were "free and Greek" and therefore eligible for the citizenship of Smyrna. [54] Since Magnesia ad Sipylum at this point in its history apparently bore little resemblance to the organized type of city-state familiar from classical and Hellenistic history, the arrangements outlined for it in this inscription should be regarded as the creation of the minimum level of civic institutionalization required to make its residents into functional citizens of Smyrna. Before this treaty and the new organization which it brought, Magnesia ad Sipylum had very little political sovereignty, in the modern sense, to be imposed upon. The specification about coinage in this inscription amounted to a statement of the normal situation in a *polis*: the coinage of the *polis* would be what we might call "legal tender" for the citizens of that *polis*. The Athenian law of 375/4 B.C., already mentioned in the previous chapter, shows that it was sometimes necessary to make this sort of statement, and it should not be overlooked that the Athenians had such a statement inscribed and set up in public for the purpose of ensuring the smooth functioning of financial transactions. In the treaty between Smyrna and Magnesia ad Sipylum, it is stated that the coins of Smyrna would be the legal tender for the citizens of Smyrna, which is what the eligible residents of Magnesia were to become under the new arrangement described in the treaty.

A particularly tantalizing entry in this brief catalogue of evidence from the Hellenistic period is the letter from Antiochus VII to the Jewish leader Simon quoted in the Septuagint in the context of 139/8 B.C. Antiochus, looking for support in his struggle against a rival, is trying to win over Simon. Antiochus first confirms to Simon all the "exemptions" ($\dot{\alpha}\phi\acute{\epsilon}\mu\alpha\tau\alpha$) allowed him by earlier kings. The letter continues with "I grant you permission to strike your own coinage as currency for your country.

---

been reattributed to Parion by Henri Seyrig, *Centennial Publication*, pp. 609–610. No new attributions to Magnesia are listed by Mørkholm in his summary.

[54] Lines 46–47

Jerusalem and the temple are to be free."[55] The collocation of a king, coinage, and freedom here only increases one's frustration at the realization that everything about this episode works against our trying to understand what it means. Above all, there is the lack of any coins which can be attributed to Simon. This has led to speculation that the grant from Antiochus either was not historical or was withdrawn soon after it was extended, or that Simon abstained from coining for religious reasons.[56] It is also unclear whether the reference in the text to "freedom" is correct. It has ˙ been suggested that the text should read "Jerusalem shall be sacred and having the right of asylum."[57] Since numerous cities in Seleucid territory issued coinages in the mid-second century B.C., it is sadly ironic that this rare literary reference to coinage should pertain to a coinage which apparently never existed.[58]

The copious evidence from Roman history also raises important questions for this subject, but it would be far beyond the scope of this study to try to cite more than a tiny selection of scholarly opinion on points of interest. On the origin of Roman silver coinage, for example, Andrew Burnett has now suggested that the earliest issue of Roman silver coins "presumably reflects military spending of some sort (e.g. on supplies) . . ." rather than a decision by the Romans "to issue coins in their own name as a reflection of their growing awareness of their position in the Mediterranean World c. 300."[59] As for non-Roman coinages in

[55] I Maccabees 15.6–7: καὶ ἐπέτρεψά σοι ποιῆσαι κόμμα ἴδιον, νόμισμα τῇ χώρᾳ σου, Ιερουσαλημ δὲ καὶ τὰ ἅγια εἶναι ἐλεύθερα, translated by J. A. Goldstein, *I Maccabees* (Garden City, N.Y., 1976), p. 510.

[56] See Emil Schürer, *The History of the Jewish People in the Age of Jesus Christ (175 B.C.-A.D. 135)*, rev. Geza Vermes and Fergus Millar, vol. 1 (Edinburgh, 1973), pp. 190–191, 197; Goldstein, *I Maccabees*, p. 514. On the problem of the beginning of Hasmonean coinage, see Will, *Histoire politique II²*, p. 413.

[57] Goldstein, *I Maccabees*, p. 514.

[58] See Claire Préaux, *Le monde hellénistique*, vol. 1 (Paris, 1978), pp. 290–293, for a useful survey of the topic "monnayage des villes" in the context of Hellenistic history.

[59] "The First Roman Silver Coins," *Quaderni ticinesi. Numismatica e antichità classiche* 7 (1978), pp. 141–142, superseding his earlier remarks (i.e., the second quotation given here in the text) in "The Coinages of Rome and Magna Graecia in the Late Fourth and Third Centuries B.C.," *SNR* 56 (1977), p. 118.

the Republican period, A. R. Bellinger surmised that any effect
Rome may have had on local coinages under the Republic was
"neither systematic nor premeditated."[60] Augustus certainly
exercised a great influence on Roman coinage during his reign,
but the status of local coinages under his arrangement remains
far from clear. At the very least, it would seem unwarranted to
assume that he dealt with provincial coinage in any systematic
fashion.[61] Some local coinages continued to be minted until the
reforms of Diocletian.[62] "Unofficial" coinages still existed under
Constantine.[63] Nothing could better illustrate how ambiguous
(from the modern point of view) the relationship between sovereignty and coinage could sometimes be in Greco-Roman antiquity than the situation regarding the counterfeiting of bronze
coinage in the Roman Empire before the period of the Dominate.

[60] "Greek Mints under the Roman Empire," in *Essays in Roman Coinage
presented to Harold Mattingly*, ed. R.A.G. Carson and C.H.V. Sutherland
(Oxford, 1956), p. 138. For a recent discussion of provincial and civic as well
as state coinage, see A. M. Burnett, "The Authority to Coin in the Late Republic and Early Empire," *NC* 1977, pp. 37–63.

[61] See, for example, the discussions of Augustan coinage by Aase Bay, "The
Letters *SC* on Augustan *aes* Coinage," *JRS* 62 (1972), pp. 111–122; C.H.V.
Sutherland, *The Emperor and the Coinage. Julio-Claudian Studies* (London, 1976),
pp. 11–30, and "Some Observations on the Coinage of Augustus," *Quaderni
ticinesi. Numismatica e antichità classiche* 7 (1978), pp. 163–178; Dietmar Kienast,
Augustus: Prinzeps und Monarch (Darmstadt, 1982), pp. 315–336.

[62] See Bellinger, "Greek Mints," *Essays . . . Mattingly*, p. 148; Sutherland, *The
Emperor*, pp. 27–28, with reference to the arguments of Michael Grant, *From
Imperium to Auctoritas* (Cambridge, 1946); Michael Crawford, "Finance, Coinage
and Money from the Severans to Constantine," *Aufstieg und Niedergang*, vol. II.2,
p. 570. He argues (pp. 572–575) that the great increase both during and after
the Severan age in the number of Greek cities minting coins and in the volume
of production of such coinages reflects fiscal burdens imposed on the cities by
the central authority of the empire. There was, on his view, a "change from
city coinages being a symbol of autonomy and an aid to local economic activity
to their being a means of additional taxation and subservient to Imperial
finances" (p. 575). For a brief discussion of the situation in the early Empire,
see Harold Mattingly, *Roman Coins*[2] (London, 1967), pp. 177, 188–194; Sutherland, *The Emperor*, pp. 31–33. On the complex subject of Diocletian's
reforms, see, for example, Sutherland, *The Roman Imperial Coinage*, vol. 6 (London, 1973), pp. 93–100.

[63] Crawford, "Finance," *Aufstieg und Niedergang*, p. 561.

As Philip Grierson puts it, ". . . we are confronted by the surprising fact that under the principate no legislation against the counterfeiting of bronze is known to have existed. Indeed, the words of the jurists in describing the law with regard to the counterfeiting of gold and silver virtually imply that none did exist, as also do the terms of Constantine's constitution of 318."[64] In short, it seems that the postclassical history of sovereignty and coinage resists simple analysis. On present evidence, it is far from easy to locate in so complex a picture points at which we could properly speak of a relationship between sovereignty and coinage that

[64] "The Roman Law of Counterfeiting," *Essays . . . Mattingly*, pp. 244–245. He discusses the evidence from the Theodosian Code for the later situation with regard to the counterfeiting of coinage in all metals on pp. 250–253. For discussion of literary evidence taken to indicate a perceived connection between sovereignty and coinage under the Roman Empire, see Crawford, "Roman Imperial Coin Types," *Studies . . . Grierson*, p. 48 (*Scriptores Historiae Augustae, Firmus* 2.1), p. 51 (Dio 52.30.9, 64.6.1), and "Finance," *Aufstieg und Niedergang*, p. 561, n. 2 (Dio 52.30.9). It is obviously not the same thing for a pretender to the imperial throne to issue a coinage on which he is portrayed as Roman Emperor and for a city to issue a local coinage that has nothing to do with any challenge to Imperial authority. Moreover, in the passage just cited from the *SHA* the main evidence brought forth in the discussion there on whether Firmus was a *princeps* or a mere *latrunculus* is his assumption of the proper imperial titulature by calling himself *Augustus* on his coins and αὐτοκράτωρ in his edicts. Similarly, he is said to have been a *princeps* because he took over the imperial garb by wearing the purple. That imitation of the Emperor by employing his title on coins and by wearing similar clothes was surely a sign of open rebellion does not have to mean, however, that any and all coinages were universally regarded as symbols of sovereignty. Dio 52.30.9 comes from the famous speech in favor of monarchy put into the mouth of Maecenas. When Maecenas advises that the cities other than Rome should not be allowed their own coins or weights or measures, he has just been discussing the question of a proper financial policy for the monarch. The context is that of how to keep the cities well regulated and solvent. Dio 64.6.1 reports that Vitellius could act nobly despite his outrageously extravagant style of life, which had been previously described. The proof cited for this nobility is, first, that Vitellius retained the coinage struck under Nero, Galba, and Otho, the new emperor reportedly not being upset at the sight of their images (οὐκ ἀγανακτῶν ταῖς εἰκόσιν αὐτῶν), and, second, that Vitellius allowed everyone to keep whatever gifts had been previously bestowed. The point of the mention of coins is simply that Vitellius was too easygoing to try to obliterate the memory of his immediate predecessors on the throne by doing away with all portraits of them.

would have been strict enough to satisfy Jean Bodin on all counts.

In our current state of knowledge, it always seems better to start historical investigation of the relations between the Hellenistic kings and the Greek city-states from the premise that these relations were a matter of practical arrangements worked out in a context unaffected by considerations of the theoretical components of royal and civic sovereignty. On this principle, it would be valid to employ abstract notions of this sort for interpretative purposes only if it proved impossible to construct a satisfactory model to explain historical events without using such notions. All one can say at present is that if it is true, as one finds often asserted, that Greek states in the Hellenistic period customarily had their autonomous coinages suppressed by the kings who dominated them, the reason cannot have been that the Hellenistic kings were following classical precedent by insisting on an exclusive right of coinage and a uniform monetary circulation as a necessary and inevitable attribute of their royal sovereignty. That precedent never existed. When this fact is acknowledged, the subject of Hellenistic coinage can perhaps more easily be approached on its own terms. Various civic mints in European Greece suspended operations in the later fourth and early third centuries, but we are far from required to think that these mints were closed by royal decree. As we have seen, different city-states experienced hardships which made it impossible for their mints to remain financially viable when confronted with an influx of Macedonian coinage into Greece. It is a striking statistic that of the hoards listed in the *Inventory of Greek Coin Hoards* (1973) and *Coin Hoards I-VI* (1975–1981) as found in mainland Greece and dated between *ca.* 320 and 250 B.C., sixty-two percent contain Macedonian royal coins, in large enough numbers to show that these non-Greek coins were being commonly used and not just saved as valuable curiosities. By comparison, even during their heyday of popularity in Sicily *ca.* 350–280, the coins of Corinth turn up in only sixty-one percent of the hoards there. [65]

[65] Fifty-four of eighty-seven hoards from mainland Greece contain Macedonian royal issues (without counting coins of Ptolemy).

It is no exaggeration to say that Macedonian royal coins began to flood Greek monetary circulation at the end of the classical period and in the early Hellenistic age. These coins were instantly recognizable and familiar to (and perhaps preferred by) the many Greek veterans of military service under a Macedonian commander, and struck on the well-known Attic weight standard. This influx could have resulted in supplantation of Greek coinage in many places for purely practical reasons. But supplantation is not suppression, nor does it imply a uniform monetary circulation. [66] More than eighty-eight percent of the hoards from Greece dated to the period *ca.* 320–250 contain Greek coins. [67] One sees therefore that even during the years when local mints were closing, Greece never experienced the uniformity in monetary circulation which the hoards reveal as the norm in Ptolemaic Egypt in the early Hellenistic period. And as the case of Athens shows, it was possible for a Greek city to go on issuing its own coins long into the third century, even if it was occupied by a garrison and had lost its former political importance. [68] The proverbial quality of Athenian coins meant that demand for the mint's production sprang from a wider market than did the demand for other local coinages. Athenian coins were simply popular enough to survive the competition with the output of royal mints, and the Athenian state had the finances to support the expense. [69] In a remark about the relative virtues of elegant and rough modes of expression, the Hellenistic philosopher Zeno of Citium, a resident of Athens in the early Hellenistic period and a friend of King Antigonus Gonatas, used the lovely and rounded silver coins of Alexander type and the randomly and

[66] See the remarks of Tony Hackens, "A propos de la circulation monétaire dans le Péloponnèse au IIIᵉ s. av. J.-C.," in *Antidorum W. Peremans sexagenario ab alumnis oblatum* (Louvain, 1968, Studia Hellenistica 16), pp. 94–95.

[67] Seventy-seven of eighty-seven hoards.

[68] Ch. Habicht, *Studien zur Geschichte Athens in hellenistischer Zeit* (Göttingen, 1982, Hypomnemata 73), pp. 34–42, convincingly argues that Athens did not lose the right of coinage even in 261 B.C. after the Chremonidean War. Cf. Ralph W. Mathisen, "Antigonus Gonatas and the Silver Coinages of Macedonia circa 280–270 B.C.," *ANSMN* 26 (1981), p. 112, n. 51.

[69] Cf. Diodorus 18.18.6, who reports that Athens was prosperous in the early Hellenistic period.

awkwardly struck Athenian tetradrachms to make a comparison. Beautiful words, like the former type of coins, were no better for all their attractiveness; words of the other sort, like the tetradrachms of Athens, often counted for more in the scale. [70] Other Greek coinages, those of Thessaly for example, lacked the appeal and the financial backing which Athenian coinage enjoyed. When such coinages went out of existence, the Macedonian kings had no interest in financing their revival. They had other concerns to occupy them. As it turned out, the Greeks themselves had reasons to forgo further production of local coinage, but these reasons had nothing immediately to do with an abstract notion of sovereignty. They had everything to do with the facts of Greek economics, finances, and preference for the royal coins of Macedonia. [71] We can begin to understand the true significance of coinage in the Greek world only if we keep this axiom in mind.

[70] Diogenes Laertius 7.18.

[71] In a review of a recent book by Milton and Rose Friedman, William F. Rickenbacker poses what he calls a "fundamental question" which merits quotation here: "Does a country need its own currency anyway? Liechtenstein, for example, an important international financial haven, has no currency of its own. It operates in an environment of competitive currencies issued by other countries, and its citizens seek the soundest values in the world marketplace" (*National Review*, 27 July, 1984, p. 41). If one were to ask this question about Greco-Roman antiquity, the proper answer might be that, for practical reasons, sometimes they did, and sometimes they did not.

PLATES

PLATE 1

1. A silver drachm (6.13 gr.) of Larissa with a female head in profile on the obverse and a prancing horse on the reverse. Probably to be dated to the late fifth or early fourth century B.C. Dewing catalogue no. 1391.

2. A silver drachm (6.04 gr.) of Larissa with a female head facing three quarters left on the obverse and a horse with foal on the reverse. From the middle of the fourth century B.C. Dewing catalogue no. 1394.

3. A silver drachm (5.83 gr.) of Larissa with a female head facing three quarters left on the obverse and a horse with a branch under its belly grazing left on the reverse. From the middle of the fourth century B.C. Dewing catalogue no. 1407.

4. A silver drachm (6.12 gr.) of Larissa with a female head facing three quarters left on the obverse and a horse grazing right on the reverse. This was the last type produced at the mint of Larissa, in the latter half of the fourth century until *ca.* 320 B.C. Dewing catalogue no. 1406.

5. A silver drachm (4.23 gr.) of Alexander the Great with a head of Heracles wearing a lion's skin on the obverse and a seated Zeus on the reverse. Attributed to Miletus *ca.* 300–294 B.C. by Margaret Thompson, *Alexander's Drachm Mints 1. Sardes and Miletus* (New York, 1983), series XIII, no. 269. Dewing catalogue no. 1152.

Permission to illustrate these coins has kindly been granted by the Dewing Greek Numismatic Foundation, to which the coins belong. The coins are on loan to the Fogg Art Museum, Harvard University, Cambridge, Mass. The catalogue numbers refer to *The Arthur S. Dewing Collection of Greek Coins*, ed. Leo Mildenberg and Silvia Hurter (New York, 1985). The dates given represent my own opinion, unless otherwise specified.

PLATE 1

PLATE 2

1. A silver octadrachm (28.86 gr.) of Alexander I, king of Macedonia, with a man standing beside a horse on the obverse and an incuse square bordered by Alexander's name on the reverse, a type which mimicked that of his barbarian neighbors the Bisaltae. Probably to be dated to the first half of the 470s B.C. Dewing catalogue no. 1082.

2. A gold stater (8.57 gr.) of Philip II with a laureate head of Apollo on the obverse and a biga on the reverse. Attributed to Pella *ca.* 340–328 B.C. or *ca.* 336–328 B.C. by Georges Le Rider, *Le monnayage d'argent et d'or de Philippe II* (Paris, 1977), group II, 1, no. 101a. Dewing catalogue no. 1099.

3. A silver tetradrachm (14.13 gr.) of Ptolemy I with his portrait on the obverse and an eagle on a thunderbolt on the reverse. To be dated sometime after 305 B.C. Dewing catalogue no. 2743.

4. A silver tetradrachm (17.32 gr.) of Demetrius Poliorcetes with his portrait on the obverse and a standing Poseidon on the reverse. Of the type attributed to Amphipolis in 289–288 B.C. by E. T. Newell, *The Coinages of Demetrius Poliorcetes* (London, 1927), no. 124. Dewing catalogue no. 1201.

PLATE 2

APPENDIX ONE. Philip II and the Career
of Simus of Larissa: The Historical Evidence

The usual reconstruction of the career of Simus of Larissa as a collaborator with Philip II is based on various pieces of evidence from the historical sources. Difficulties of interpretation arise with each of these items. The first one occurs in the oration *On the Crown* (18.48, of 330 B.C.). As part of a list of Greek traitors, Demosthenes claims that a Eudicus and a Simus of Larissa were called friends of Philip until they had put Thessaly into Philip's hands. Neither the chronology nor the precise fate of those fallen from grace is made explicit, as so often in Demosthenes. He probably means to imply that Simus, along with the other Greek collaborators mentioned in the same passage, suffered exile as the penalty of Philip's lost friendship, but his language is not entirely clear on this point. [1]

Furthermore, it is an open question whether Demosthenes was correct, if this was his implication. Even if he knows the facts in

[1] Immediately after the list which includes Simus, Demosthenes says "Then the whole world has become full of traitors [reading προδοτῶν with all the manuscripts except S] exiled, treated violently, suffering every evil. What of Aristratus of Sicyon, and what of Perilaus of Megara? Are they not outcasts?" If the sentence beginning with "Then the whole world" refers in a generalizing way to the persons named in the list found in the preceding sentence (where the name of Simus occurs), it seems a bit odd that Demosthenes should then go on to cite additional specific examples of the generalizing statement. It is conceivable that the fate of the men in the first list was simply no longer to be regarded by Philip as special friends and therefore to have lost the benefits conferred by that status. The generalizing sentence would then introduce a new point in Demosthenes' description of the unhappy endings of those who collaborated with Philip, a point which is made specific by the mention of Aristratus and Perilaus. The usual interpretation is that this passage does presuppose the exile of all the men listed by Demosthenes. See Hermann Wankel, *Demosthenes. Rede für Ktesiphon. Ueber den Kranz* (Heidelberg, 1976), vol. 1, pp. 335, 339–41.

every case, Demosthenes can be quite cavalier in the assembling of a list of this sort. For example, Aristratus of Sicyon and Perilaus of Megara, whom Demosthenes explicitly names as exiles after the list in which Simus occurs, reappear later in the same oration in a list which purports to name traitors who gave away their cities' freedom first to Philip and *now* to Alexander.[2] Equally instructive is the case of Euthycrates of Olynthus, another traitor to Philip. Demosthenes claims that he too was treated as one of the king's intimates until he and an associate had betrayed their city. Then, says Demosthenes, "they came to the worst ruin of all."[3] The orator Hypereides, however, reports that the same Euthycrates was alive and apparently a man of some influence even after 338 B.C.[4] Demosthenes is simply not to be trusted in the matter of the fate of those who helped Philip because the orator was at pains to show how the crimes of traitors did not pay. Truth took second place to exaggeration and even invention in the interest of Demosthenes' partisan message against collaboration. We cannot safely conclude on the basis of Demosthenes' oratory that Simus' fall from Philip's favor meant expulsion from Larissa.

Next, we learn from Harpocration's notes to Demosthenes' oration *On the Crown* that Eudicus was "one of those established by Philip as lords of all Thessaly," but his comment on Simus mentions no special office or power. Simus was, according to Harpocration, "one of the Aleuads who was among those who seem to have cooperated with the Macedonian."[5] Since Diodorus tells us that the Aleuads called on Philip for help against the tyrants of Pherae in the 350s B.C., it makes sense to regard Simus as one of those who brought the Macedonian king to Thessaly and supported his election as leader of the Thessalian confederacy.[6] These are the only pieces of evidence which can confidently be considered as referring to Simus' career during the period of Philip's influence in Thessaly. So far, then, the evidence appears

[2] 18.295–296.
[3] 8.40.
[4] Frag. 76 (*OCT*) = frag. B 19.1 (LCL, *Minor Attic Orators*, vol. 2).
[5] *S. v.* Εὔδικος; Σῖμος.
[6] 16.14.1–2, 16.35, 16.38.1.

to indicate that Simus was already a prominent citizen of Larissa by the time Philip intervened in Thessaly, not that Simus owed his prominence to Philip. In fact, an earlier prominence would help to explain why Simus would have been an initially useful ally for Philip to select as one of his "friends" at Larissa.

Some extremely dubious evidence has been marshalled to reconstruct the later career of Simus. First comes an ambiguous passage in the *Politics* of Aristotle.[7] In a discussion of the causes of the overturning of oligarchies, Aristotle mentions the case of Larissa when it was under Aleuad rulership headed by Simus as an example of revolution in times of peace brought about by strife between factions in the oligarchy itself.[8] According to Aristotle, the factions chose a "mediating magistrate" backed by military force to resolve the difficulties. This magistrate did not operate as the factions had intended, however, but he instead used his position to acquire tyrannical power for himself, thereby overturning the oligarchy.

Aristotle unfortunately fails to make it clear who became mediating magistrate at Larissa in this episode, or when it took place. For example, Aristotle has been taken to mean that Simus

---

[7] 5.1306a26–31: ἐν δὲ τῇ εἰρήνῃ διὰ τὴν ἀπιστίαν τὴν πρὸς ἀλλήλους ἐγχειρίζουσι τὴν φυλακὴν στρατιώταις καὶ ἄρχοντι μεσιδίῳ, ὃς ἐνίοτε γίνεται κύριος ἀμφοτέρων, ὅπερ συνέβη ἐν Λαρίσῃ ἐπὶ τῆς τῶν Ἀλευαδῶν ἀρχῆς τῶν περὶ Σῖμον, καὶ ἐν Ἀβύδῳ ἐπὶ τῶν ἑταιριῶν ὧν ἦν μία ἡ Ἰφιάδου.

[8] The ambiguity arises from several sources. Since the expression οἱ περὶ Σῖμον could mean either "those associated with Simus" (cf. *Pol.* 5.1314b25) or simply "Simus" (cf. *Pol.* 5.1305b25–26), the exact translation is uncertain. It could be "at the time of the rule of the Aleuads associated with Simus," or "at the time of the rule of Simus the Aleuad." On these uses of περί in Aristotle, see Rudolf Eucken, *Ueber den Sprachgebrauch des Aristoteles. Beobachtungen über die Praepositionen* (Berlin, 1868), p. 66; Hermann Bonitz, *Index Aristotelicus* (Berlin, 1870), *s. v.* περί 3. Second, the name Σῖμον is an emendation (Schlosser) for σάμον found in all the manuscripts and the Latin translation.

The story of murder and revenge involving a Simus to which Callimachus alludes is sometimes connected with this episode, but it does not help with chronology. See Callimachus frag. 588 (Pfeiffer); Ch. Habicht, "Epigraphische Zeugnisse zur Geschichte Thessaliens unter der makedonischen Herrschaft," in *Ancient Macedonia*, vol. 1 (Thessaloniki, 1970), pp. 266–268.

himself became the magistrate and therefore tyrant. [9] Alternatively, the same words have been interpreted to mean that Philip
or one of his subordinates became magistrate to settle the factional strife that had arisen while Simus was in power. [10] Finally,
the same passage has been viewed as evidence that an
unspecified magistrate (neither Simus nor Philip) was chosen
when strife arose at Larissa over the association of Simus and the
Aleuads with Philip and Simus' "controversial position." [11] The
difficulty is only compounded when one remembers that there is
no guarantee that the episode described so briefly by Aristotle
belongs to this period. [12] Aristotle's Simus could be the Simus of
Demosthenes at an earlier date before Philip's appearance in
Thessaly, or even a completely different person. [13]

The evidence used to establish the view that Simus was
expelled by Philip in 344 B.C. inspires even less confidence. As
we have seen, Demosthenes' testimony on this point is not

[9] See J. R. Ellis, *Philip II and Macedonian Imperialism* (London, 1976), pp.
137 – 138.

[10] See Sordi, *LT*, p. 286, and *AIIN* 3 (1956), pp. 18 – 19.

[11] See Griffith, *HM*, pp. 525 – 526.

[12] The only independent argument offered in order to date the episode from
the *Politics* is that Aristotle would have further identified Simus if he had not
been describing a recent and familiar event involving the Simus who had collaborated with Philip. See H. D. Westlake, *Thessaly in the Fourth Century B.C.*
(London, 1935), p. 191, n. 1, and Sordi, *LT*, p. 365. But we cannot judge how
familiar even the Simus of Philip's time would have been to Aristotle's audience,
and a glance at this section of the *Politics* shows how wide ranging Aristotle was
in his references. For example, he begins his discussion of revolutionary change
in oligarchies with a reference to Lygdamis in the sixth century B.C. (5.1305a41),
and the episode of Simus is linked with an otherwise unattested incident at
Abydus involving the obscure Iphiades (5.1306a31).

[13] Ulrich Kahrstedt, "Grundherrschaft, Freistadt und Staat in Thessalien," in
*Nachrichten von der Gesellschaft der Wissenschaften zu Göttingen aus dem Jahre
1924. Philologisch-historische Klasse* (Berlin, 1925), pp. 136 – 137, suggests that
this episode took place between 394 and 364 B.C. For other possible candidates
for this Simus besides the one involved with Philip, see Sordi, *LT*, p. 365. One
can add that if the Simus who collaborated with Philip was a relatively young
man at the time, his grandfather could have been active at Larissa early in the
fourth century. By a well-known pattern of Greek nomenclature, they could
have both been named Simus. This pattern was observed among the Aleuads,
as the Daochus inscription shows (*SIG* 3 274).

necessarily reliable. The remaining evidence is certainly unreliable. In his narrative, Diodorus succinctly reports that in 344/3 B.C. Philip won the goodwill of the Thessalians "by expelling the tyrants from the cities."[14] Diodorus goes on to say that Philip's aim was to win over the Greeks once he had the Thessalians as allies. His plan succeeded: joining themselves with the decision of the Thessalians, the neighboring Greeks allied themselves with Philip. This passage is odd and disturbing because the clear implication is that Philip acquired the Thessalians as allies as a result of his actions in 344/3 B.C., which is absurd because Philip had done that long before in his interventions of the 350s B.C. In the light of the generally muddle-headed nature of the details of this passage, in which Diodorus seems to be at the very least amalgamating events of the 350s and the 340s, we cannot be certain of the accuracy of Diodorus' statement that Philip expelled tyrants from more than one city in 344/3 B.C. The only city where this certainly took place was Pherae, Philip's perennial trouble spot in Thessaly. If a second city is required, an obvious possibility would be nearby Pagasae, where the tyrants of Pherae had been established at the time of Philip's earlier expulsion of them. If tyrants had returned to Pherae by 344 B.C., they could also have returned to Pagasae. But it may simply be the case that Diodorus is generalizing here from a single case of the expulsion of tyrants.

Nevertheless, Larissa has been nominated as another city from which Philip expelled tyrants in 344 B.C. because the scholia to Demosthenes refer to the Aleuads as tyrants whom Philip expelled. It is a simple matter, however, to show that this testimony is worthless. Schol. Dem. 2.14 (Dindorf vol. 8, p. 92, on 22,7) incorrectly explains Demosthenes' reference to the "tyrannical house" which Philip recently helped the Thessalians combat as a reference to the Aleuads of Larissa. As Diodorus' account shows, at the time of this oration of Demosthenes the expression "tyrannical house" can only be a reference to the tyrants of Pherae whom Philip fought on behalf of the Aleuads. The scholiast has reversed the identification of the Aleuads and the

[14] 16.69.8.

tyrants of Pherae. The same mistake occurs in a more egregious fashion in schol. Dem. 1.22 (Dindorf vol. 8, p. 64, on 15,18). There, the scholiast essentially relates the story of Philip's intervention in Thessaly against the tyrants of Pherae in the 350s while managing to interchange the roles of Pherae and Larissa, the leader of the Thessalian confederacy against Pherae. Thanks to this outrageous blunder, the scholiast has Philip drive out the Aleuads, rather than the tyrants of Pherae, in the period before the events described in the oration to which the note is appended, i.e., in the period before the war with Olynthus in 349 B.C. This scenario is ridiculous, and it would be unjustified to say that the scholiast knows of a later expulsion of the Aleuads by Philip which he has retrojected into the 350s B.C. Nothing of historical value can be gleaned from these two scholia. We cannot use them as the basis for assuming that Philip expelled Simus and the other Aleuads in 344 B.C.[15]

[15] One cannot use Polyaenus, *Strat.* 4.2.11, to argue that Philip expelled the Aleuads. Since Polyaenus says that Philip tried to take action against "some Aleuads," it appears that he was intervening in an Aleuad factional fight and no more. As it turned out, Philip failed to catch even the Aleuads he was after.

APPENDIX TWO. Two External Models
for Philip II

One might conceivably argue that Philip's views on sovereignty
and coinage could have been shaped by familiarity with the practices of other sovereigns. The question is whether Philip's
knowledge of such external models could have induced him to
think about sovereignty and coinage along the lines commonly
assumed for ancient kings by modern scholars. Dietmar Kienast,
for example, has argued that Philip's rule as a Macedonian king
was influenced by the practices of Persian kingship in both
foreign and domestic policy. Kienast points to Philip's treatment
of Thrace as a prime example of this phenomenon: the region
had been under Persian control before it was joined to Macedonia.[1] E. A. Fredricksmeyer has recently argued that Philip
aimed at absolute monarchy in the style of the Persian king.[2] In
reality it is very difficult to say what influences worked on Philip
as he met the changing challenges of ruling his kingdom, and
how important any external models were. Common sense, ambition, and the limits imposed by the traditions of the Macedonian
nobility were the principal influences on Philip as king. If he
did pay any attention to Persian arrangements for coinage, he
could not have reached the conclusion from this model that as a
king he should suppress local coinage. Coinage in Persia owed
its start to a king, the innovative Darius, but as we saw in the
discussion of Ellis' theory on suppression as a policy of Alexander in chapter 5, the Great King did not enforce a monopoly

[1] *Philipp II von Makedonien und das Reich der Achaimeniden* (Munich, 1973,
Abhandlungen der Marburger Gelehrten Gesellschaft 6), p. 249.

[2] "On the Final Aims of Philip II," in *Philip II, Alexander the Great and the
Macedonian Heritage*, ed. W. L. Adams and E. N. Borza (Lanham, Md., 1982),
pp. 85–98.

on the right of coinage in his domain. There was no precedent to be found in the Persian model for Philip to insist on a royal monopoly of the right of coinage or a uniform monetary circulation.

A second external model to be considered is that of Boeotia. Since Philip was held hostage for a time at Thebes as a young man and was later involved in Boeotian affairs, it is obvious that he had the opportunity to learn about the policy on coinage which Thebes enforced as the *hegemon* of the Boeotian League. Could he have found in Theban practice an inspiration for a policy of the suppression of local coinage by a powerful *hegemon*?

The earliest coin with a Boeotian type (the famous shield) on the obverse is marked with the letter chi, has a type of Chalcis on the reverse, and is on the Euboic standard. A reasonable guess is that this odd coin was part of an issue produced at Chalcis in the later sixth century to finance some joint enterprise undertaken by the Chalcidians and the Boeotians.[3] The first coins from Boeotia proper were issued in the last years of the sixth century by three mints and have the same types. Initials identify Tanagra and Haliartus as two of the mints. The coins without any inscription are assumed to have been produced at Thebes. By *ca.* 500 B.C, seven different cities are issuing coins with the same types, all seven issues identified by the initial of the particular mint on the reverse. Orchomenus at the same time issued a fractional coinage with different types. These coinages appear to dwindle away after the Persian Wars, perhaps because they had been produced as a response to the financial demands of the war years. In the second quarter of the fifth century, Tanagra may have tried to issue a coinage purporting to be a federal issue, but the chronology of these coins is very uncertain.[4] The point to notice here is that coinage in Boeotia from the earliest times was usually a cooperative effort among various cities. There was no strong tradition of individual civic coinages issued in complete independence of the other cities in Boeotia.

[3] Kraay, *ACGC*, pp. 108–111.

[4] See B. H. Fowler, "Thucydides I.107–108 and the Tanagran Federal Issues," *Phoenix* 11 (1957), pp. 164–170; R. J. Buck, *A History of Boeotia* (Edmonton, Alberta, 1979), pp. 141–142.

Since the Boeotian League was in existence already in the sixth century, it is obvious that the cities of the region had decided early, no doubt under the dominant influence of Thebes, that their situation called for cooperation.[5] The *Hellenica Oxyrhynchia* confirms the tradition of the Boeotian confederacy that "in all matters, financial, legal and others, the members shared in proportion to their provision of federal officers and military contingents."[6]

This tradition probably explains the "revival of civic issues" at Acraephia, Coronea, Haliartus, Tanagra, and Thebes which is postulated for the period *ca.* 456 – 447 B.C. when the Athenians controlled most of Boeotia after a defeat of League forces under the leadership of Thebes. These issues have the usual shield on the obverse and individual reverse types with identifying initials. Since Tanagra and Thebes certainly, and Coronea probably, were Athenian opponents in this period, these issues were likely produced in cooperation to finance military resistance either before the defeat in 456 or before the victory in 447. The Boeotian victory at Coronea in 447 forced the Athenians to evacuate Boeotia and allowed the cities to regain their autonomy.[7] The state of Boeotian coinage after 446 is an unresolved mystery. Kraay in his handbook assumes that the series with shield on the obverse and Theban types and inscription on the reverse begins by the third quarter of the century. J.A.O. Larsen, on the other hand, points out that Orchomenus, not Thebes, dominated the Boeotian League until 426 and puts the start of the series after that date.[8] The hoards do not help us to decide which opinion, if

[5] Cf. Buck, *History of Boeotia*, p. 112. For a discussion of Boeotian coinage in this period as a political phenomenon, see Jean Ducat, "La confédération béotienne et l'expansion thébaine à l'époque archaïque," *BCH* 97 (1973), pp. 61–62, 71–72.

[6] In the London papyrus, section XVI (XI), 4 (Bartoletti): τῶν κοινῶν ἀπέλαυνον. For the quotation, see I.A.F. Bruce, *An Historical Commentary on the 'Hellenica Oxyrhynchia'* (Cambridge, 1967), p. 163.

[7] Thucydides (1.113.4) and Diodorus (12.6.2) are explicit on this point: the Boeotians were "autonomous" again.

[8] *ACGC*, p. 111; *GFS*, p. 37.

either, is correct.[9] But the striking thing is that there are no "civic issues" known which can fit into the period of autonomy after 446 when Orchomenus and its friends led Boeotia. If coins were truly badges of autonomy, the Orchomenians should have produced some while free of Theban control.

The issues just mentioned with particularly Theban types on the reverse, which are assumed to end with the King's Peace in 386, do not represent a radical break with earlier Boeotian tradition on coinage. That is, coins are produced for a confederacy with the Boeotian shield on the obverse and local identification on the reverse, presumably financed by the contributions of various Boeotian cities and intended to pay joint expenses. One city or the other may dominate the confederacy, Thebes more often than not, but the principle remains the same.[10]

It makes sense to suppose that the cities in Boeotia found it convenient for various practical reasons to forego individual civic coinages in favor of a confederate production. Most cities in Boeotia were small, and the establishment of a mint would have meant an initial capital outlay that was unnecessary. Much more important, a confederate coinage, produced either at one central mint or at several locations, simplified the regularization of contributions toward paying for a confederate military force and ruled out disputes among the troops over whose pay was issued in more valuable or less valuable currency. Finally, a confederate coinage did give a powerful *hegemon* the opportunity to exploit the financial resources of subordinates. If Thebes or any other city in Boeotia could require other cities to send in funds to be made into a coinage to serve, as the leader would say, "the needs of all," so much the better for the dominant city. It could control the funds to its own financial advantage. That was a gain

[9] The chronological conclusions drawn by Kraay (*ACGC*, p. 111) on the basis of *IGCH* 42 are not reliable because O. Picard, *Chalcis et la confédération eubéenne: étude de numismatique et d'histoire (IVᵉ – Iᵉʳ siècle)* (Athens, 1979), p. 167, has lowered its date from *ca.* 400 B.C. to *ca.* 350 on the strength of information supplied by Herbert Cahn.

[10] The two fourth-century issues from Boeotia marked with personal names and the legend "of the Boeotians" respectively, Kraay's series I(c) and II, are discussed in section 1 of chapter 8.

to expect from the fact of exercising domination; it was not a demonstration of a theoretical connection between sovereignty and coinage. The model provided by the situation in Boeotia was not going to influence Philip to suppress Greek coinages in the interest of such a notion.

APPENDIX THREE. The Aristotelian
Oeconomica and Coinage

Oikonomia as the administration of a household is discussed in the first book of the short, peculiar treatise conventionally referred to as the Aristotelian *Oeconomica*, but the second book has a wider scope. *Oec.* II.i gives a very brief description of four different kinds of *oikonomia*: royal, satrapal, polis, and private. In this case, *oikonomia* means not household administration but "financial administration," or "management of public revenues." [1] *Oec.* II.ii, on the other hand, is a list of anecdotes describing how various states and individuals raised money in extraordinary circumstances with stratagems ranging from the sale of state monopolies to outright trickery. None of these incidents is later in date than the reign of Alexander the Great (336–323). Furthermore, as B. A. van Groningen observes in his commentary, the details of administration mentioned in *Oec.* II.i suggest that the kingdom in question is not a theoretical one but precisely the Achaemenid kingdom, either in its purely Persian form or as ruled by Alexander the Great and the early successors before its dissolution at the end of the century. The entire disposition of *Oec.* II.i, as well as the specific mention of satrapal administration, points to a historical context in which the Persian Empire could be thought of as an existing unit.

The most plausible context into which Book Two can be fitted, van Groningen argues, is the latter years of Alexander's reign and the following decade or so during which his empire

[1] For the former definition, see B. A. van Groningen, *Aristote. Le second livre de l'Economique* (Leiden, 1933), commentary, p. 25; for the latter, see M. I. Finley, *The Ancient Economy* (London, 1973), p. 20, who says of *Oec.* II.i that "what is noteworthy about these half a dozen paragraphs is not only their crashing banality but also their isolation in the whole of surviving ancient writing."

was maintained as at least a conceptual unit. This view contrasts with, for example, Niebuhr's idea that Book Two was written in the second half of the third century B.C. in Syria, then under the rule of a Seleucid king, who ruled through satrapies in the general area of the old Persian Empire in the East. Niebuhr's argument is undermined, however, by the observations that none of the anecdotes is later than the 320s and that by the latter third century satrapal administration would have been more familiar to any interested Greek than is implied by the discussion in *Oec.* II.i. Since Book Two appears to be directed at those who may be governing in a satrapal system but have little or no knowledge of such a system, van Groningen places the composition of Book Two *ca.* 325–300, perhaps by a student of the Peripatetic school originally inspired to the task by Aristotle.[2]

If *Oec.* II.i does belong in the last quarter of the fourth century, it has a potential bearing on the relation between royal sovereignty and the right of coinage at the start of the Hellenistic period. In the survey of four types of "financial administration" in *Oec.* II.i, coinage is mentioned only in connection with royal *oikonomia*. The text at this point is not without its own problems.

Let us look first at royal *oikonomia*. It has power with respect to everything; it has four aspects: concerning coinage, concerning exportations, concerning importations, concerning expenditures.

With respect to each of these, I say that concerning coinage it is

[2] See van Groningen, *Aristote*, introduction, pp. 37–48, with references to earlier opinions from Niebuhr onwards. Renato Laurenti, *Studi sull' Economico attribuito ad Aristotele* (Milan, 1968), reviews the evidence for the nature and the date of the work, concluding that Book Two is indeed a unit composed at the end of the fourth century (pp. 54, 57). Giacomo Manganaro, "La caduta dei Dinomenidi e il *politikon nomisma* in Sicilia nella prima metà del V sec. a.C.," *AIIN* 21–22 (1974–1975), p. 30, suggests the author was Clearchus of Soli. M. I. Finley, *CR* 20 (1970), p. 317, rejects the idea of Peripatetic authorship. Heinz Kreissig, *Wirtschaft und Gesellschaft im Seleukidenreich* (Berlin, 1978), pp. 77–78, identifies discrepancies between *Oec.* II.i and Seleucid practice. For a brief survey of the situation of the Greek cities in Asia Minor in relation to the *diadochoi*, see Wolfgang Orth, *Königlicher Machtanspruch und städtische Freiheit* (Munich, 1977), pp. 12–15, with detailed treatment of the status of the cities under the early Seleucids in the main body of his text.

what sort should be made and when valuable or cheap. . . . (Ps.-Arist., *Oec.* II.i.2–3)

The controversy involves the last phrase of the excerpt translated above. The text of the manuscripts is περὶ μὲν τὸ νόμισμα λέγω ποῖον καὶ πότε τίμιον ἢ εὔωνον ποιητέον. Although van Groningen says that "it is not impossible that the explanation had already been added in the original," he regards τίμιον ἢ εὔωνον ("valuable or cheap") as a gloss to explain ποῖον ("of what sort") and excludes these words from the text.[3] The translation given with his approval in the Budé edition of the *Oeconomica* is "Pour les monnaies, il s'agira de savoir de quel type il faut en faire, et quand."[4]

The ambiguity of the text at this point causes difficulties in the interpretation of this remark on coinage. According to van Groningen (following Andreades), the remark as a whole means that the Persian King reserved to himself the minting of coinage, a monopoly which is to be explained by three motives: to affirm and maintain the unity of the kingdom, to facilitate commerce, and to standardize tribute payments and pay and prevent others from profiting from a coinage of poor alloy. With the exclusion of the words "valuable or cheap," he interprets the last phrase of the remark to mean that the King has to decide whether to coin silver or gold from his vast store of bullion at any particular moment, in order either to restore the desired rate of exchange between silver and gold when an imbalance has developed or to profit from the temporary imbalance in the rate. Since the King's decision to coin in one metal or the other would in fact affect the relative values of the two precious metal coinages in circulation, he would in effect be deciding whether these coinages should be valuable or cheap.[5]

There are grave difficulties with van Groningen's interpreta-

[3] See van Groningen, *Aristote*, commentary, pp. 31–32. His suggestion is rejected by P. Thillet, "Les économiques d'Aristote," *REG* 82 (1969), p. 578.

[4] B. A. van Groningen and André Wartelle, *Aristote. Economique* (Paris, 1968), pp. XXVII, 9.

[5] See D. Schlumberger, *L'Argent grec dans l'empire achéménide* (Paris, 1953), p. 16, n. 2, against the modern idea that the Persian king established a legal exchange rate between gold and silver.

tion. He reasonably assumed that *Oec.* II.i reflects the historical reality of the time when it was composed. [6] But if that is the case, and the historical context is the last quarter of the fourth century, the remark on coinage either does not mean that the King maintained a royal monopoly of the right of coinage, or the author of the treatise is very much mistaken. As we have seen, neither the Achaemenid Kings nor Alexander the Great maintained such a monopoly. The historical facts do not match the theory if one is to understand these words as the claim for the King of a monopoly of the right of coinage. [7] It is a contradiction to assume, as van Groningen does, that the treatise both reflects the "reality of things" and indicates that the King monopolized the right of coinage.

Further difficulties ensue with the idea that the last phrase of the quoted passage refers to the impact of royal mint production on the exchange rate between gold and silver. It may be right (we have no way to tell) to assume that the Great King did oversee the relative values of gold and silver in his territory, but it is more likely that if he did so, he did it by edict rather than by regulating the production of royal coinage. The Persian king preferred to mint as little coinage as possible, and this amount only as special financial needs required it. He cannot have used the "money supply" (as it is called in the United States today) as a tool for indirect financial management of the exchange rate. After all, that was not his style. As for Alexander, although he minted a great deal of gold and silver coinage, it would be hard to believe that he would have tried to use different levels of mint activity for this sort of sophisticated and certainly anachronistic monetary policy. [8]

The Persepolis Treasury Tablets, discussed in chapter 5, allow us to explain the last phrase of the passage under consideration and to construe the text as it stands. The phrase would mean

[6] See van Groningen, *Aristote*, introduction, p. 42: "Constatons tout d'abord que l'exposé n'a de sens pour son auteur et ses lecteurs, que s'il décrit la réalité des choses."

[7] As Bellinger saw, *Essays*, p. 41.

[8] See Bellinger, *Essays*, p. 31, for what is known about the gold-silver exchange rate in this period.

that the King has to decide what sort of coinage is to be struck. This could involve deciding whether to mint gold or silver depending on his financial needs and precious metal reserves at the moment, as well as whether large or small denominations were needed for the kind of payments which were to be made. The King also has to decide when his money will be valuable and when it will be cheap, i.e., what its value will be in terms of the commodities which represented the most common standard of payment in the Persian Empire, as we have already seen. We cannot take *Oec.* II.i.2–3 as implying that a royal monopoly of the right of coinage existed at the time when the work was written or as advocating such a monopoly as a necessary aspect of royal *oikonomia*. Rather, the author was describing the king's unique responsibility for issuing two precious metal coinages and for establishing their value in relation to the most common standard of value in the predominantly nonmonetary Persian economy, that is, in relation to commodities. On this view, the author of the treatise essentially ignored the minting of coinage as an aspect of *oikonomia* at the various levels he treats. This was surely shortsighted on the author's part, but one can hardly argue that *Oeconomica* II.i, a very short text, even begins to cover all the topics one could reasonably expect to learn about in the financial administration of a kingdom or a satrapy or a polis. We can assume, in line with the other evidence, that it was taken for granted that kings and their satraps and the cities in their territories would issue coins when they found it expedient to do so for practical reasons.

APPENDIX 4. Historical Probability
and the Chronology of the Silver and Gold
Coinage of Philip II

"History textbooks of the future will have to take note of all this, however daunting such a specialized numismatic work may seem." This is the comment of M. Jessop Price in the introductory paragraph of his important review article on Georges Le Rider's monumental study of the coinage of Philip II, *Le monnayage d'argent et d'or de Philippe II, frappé en Macédoine de 359 à 294* (Paris, 1977).[1] Price is certainly correct in his evaluation of the importance of Le Rider's work for ancient historians. Comprehensive discussion of the reign of Philip can no longer be conducted without reference to the historical implications of Le Rider's conclusions about the chronology of Philip's coinage. Especially important are Le Rider's conclusions that almost all of Philip's gold coinage was posthumous and that the posthumous production of both gold and silver in Philip's name continued until *ca.* 329/8 B.C. J. R. Ellis, for one, has already used Le Rider's chronology to draw up a provisional scheme for the coinage of Philip and of Alexander which has far-reaching implications for the political and economic history of the period. Ellis' most striking suggestion is that Alexander *ca.* 329/8 B.C. instructed Antipater to terminate all coinages under Macedonian control that were not the king's own, including the posthumous coinage of Philip and the autonomous coinages of Philippi and of Larissa in Thessaly. This order to terminate all coinages except Alexander's own, Ellis then suggests, "would likely be interpreted (as, perhaps he [Alexander] intended it) as a further step in the progressive devaluation of things Macedonian and towards

---

[1] "The Coinage of Philip II," *NC* 1979, pp. 230–241.

the transfer eastwards of the imperial centre of gravity."[2] One could add that such an order would also have had enormous implications for Alexander's relations with ostensibly independent Greek states such as Larissa. Since historians will certainly rely on Le Rider's great achievement in organizing Philip's coinage as they interpret the history of this period, it is essential to examine the two major conclusions of Le Rider just mentioned in the light of the historical context of Philip's reign.

Le Rider divides the silver issues bearing the name and types of Philip into three groups minted at Pella and four minted at Amphipolis. At Pella, group I runs from 359 B.C. to *ca.* 349/8, followed by group II from *ca.* 348/7 to *ca.* 329/8. Group III is entirely posthumous, running from *ca.* 323/2 to *ca.* 315. The four groups at Amphipolis have as their chronological limits *ca.* 357/6–349/8 (I), *ca.* 348/7 – *ca.* 329/8 (II), *ca.* 323/2 – *ca.* 316/5 (III), and *ca.* 315/4 – *ca.* 295/4 (IV). [3] Regrettably, the hoards offer no help at all with the absolute chronology of the issues in either silver or gold which Le Rider assigns to Philip's lifetime. Le Rider, therefore, offers only tentative dates for these issues. [4] General considerations of finance and of sovereignty in combination with his study of the relative chronology of the different groups lead Le Rider to conclude that Philip began to coin in silver at Pella in the very beginning of his reign in 359 B.C. [5] Silver coinage started to be produced at Amphipolis within several years, and both mints produced their group I coins until *ca.* 348/7 B.C., when the changeover to the issues of group II took place. Group II is subdivided for both mints. At Amphipolis, IIA is dated *ca.* 348/7–343/2, with IIB placed *ca.* 342/1–329/8. At Pella, IIA1 is dated *ca.* 348/7–343/2, IIA2 *ca.*

[2] *Philip II and Macedonian Imperialism* (London, 1976), pp. 235–239 (he had access to Le Rider's conclusions before the publication of the latter's work).

[3] *Monnayage*, pp. 386–400.

[4] *Monnayage*, pp. 387–388: "la chronologie que je propose dépend-elle, jusqu'à la mort de Philippe II, de considérations relatives au nombre des émissions et à l'importance respective des groupes: les dates absolues que j'avancerai doivent donc être regardées comme fort approximatives et sujettes à révision."

[5] *Monnayage*, pp. 386–387.

342/1 – 337/6, and IIB *ca.* 336/5 – 329/8.[6] A crucial point for the present discussion is the *terminus* of *ca.* 329/8 for group II at both mints. Le Rider chooses this *terminus* for the silver because that is the date he establishes as the end of group II of Philip's gold coinage.[7] The various groups of the gold coinage are dated as follows: group I (Pella and Amphipolis) *ca.* 345 to *ca.* 340, or *ca.* 342 – 340 to *ca.* 336; group II (Pella and Amphipolis) *ca.* 340 to 329/8, or *ca.* 336 to *ca.* 329/8; group III A-B-C (Amphipolis) *ca.* 323/2 to *ca.* 315(?).[8] The placement *ca.* 329/8 B.C. of the *terminus* of group II of both the silver and the gold issues is the catalyst for the formation of Ellis' historical interpretation of Alexander's policy on the termination of coinages at this time. Le Rider accepts Ellis' view.[9] What, then, are the reasons for thinking that this date is correct?

The issues of silver tetradrachms of Amphipolis' second group (IIB) were, as Le Rider shows, produced under a new arrangement at the mint. Different issues with different moneyers' marks were produced simultaneously rather than only one at a time, and the volume of production was large. As E. T. Newell pointed out, some of these coins carry the same moneyers' marks as do some tetradrachms of Alexander III. Newell believed that this sharing of marks meant that there had been a brief period after Philip's death during which the minting of coins of Philip continued under Alexander's reign until the new king's own coins could be put into production by the same mint officials who had overseen the production of the posthumous issues of Philip. Once the switch to Alexander's coins had been made, the production of posthumous issues of Philip ceased. Newell accordingly thought that late 336 was the most likely date for the

[6] *Monnayage,* pp. 389 – 395.

[7] *Monnayage,* p. 390.

[8] *Monnayage,* pp. 428 – 434. The arrangement of Le Rider's groups in gold and silver is analyzed and conveniently schematized in tables by Price in his review article (*NC* 1979, pp. 230 – 241). Price outlines an arrangement which is very different from that of Le Rider, and he suggests that Aegae was a third mint.

[9] *Monnayage,* pp. 437 – 438.

end of Philip's posthumous issues.[10] (Since Philip actually died
late in the year 336, it would be more accurate to refer to this
date as 336/5, thereby allowing for the possibility that the posthumous production envisioned by Newell spilled over into
335.)[11] Although Le Rider has shown Newell's argument in favor
of a similar situation at the mint in Pella to be wrong, he continues to date the commencement of the minting of Alexander's
own coins at Amphipolis to the start of his reign.[12] Others would
delay the introduction of coinage in Alexander's name until 333
or 332.[13]

Le Rider, however, prolongs the period during which posthumous silver issues of Philip were produced on analogy with his
chronology of the posthumous gold coinage of Philip. This
longer period of production allows Le Rider to postulate a more

[10] *Reattribution of Certain Tetradrachms of Alexander the Great* (New York,
1912), p. 21. See now M. J. Price, "Alexander's Reform of the Macedonian
Regal Coinage," *NC* 1982, pp.180–190, with a discussion of the die links and
shared symbols on the final issues of Philip and the first issues of Alexander
(pp. 186–187).

[11] On the date of Philip's death, see M. B. Hatzopoulos, "The Oleveni
Inscription and the Dates of Philip II's Reign," in *Philip II, Alexander the Great
and the Macedonian Heritage*, ed. W. L. Adams and E. N. Borza (Lanham, Md.,
1982), pp. 37–41.

[12] *Monnayage*, pp. 390–394. Price, *NC* 1982, pp. 180–190, argues that
Alexander's coinage began in Macedonia near the start of his reign. Philip's
silver would have ceased at this point, but, Price suggests, the production of
Philip's gold may have continued (pp. 187–188). Nancy J. Moore, "The Lifetime and Early Posthumous Coinage of Alexander the Great from Pella" (Diss.,
Princeton University, 1984), appendix II, suggests that the first issues at Amphipolis should be the so-called eagle tetradrachms, produced for a very short time
and followed by the regular series of Alexanders. (I am indebted to the author
for a copy of her work.) On the question of the earliest issues of Alexander and
the "eagle tetradrachms," see, in addition to *Monnayage*, pp. 394–395, and the
references in the following note, E. Pegan, "Die frühesten Tetradrachmen Alexanders des Grossen mit dem Adler, ihre Herkunft und Entstehungszeit," *JNG*
18 (1968), pp. 99–111; Price, *Coins of the Macedonians* (London, 1974), p. 23.

[13] See N.G.L. Hammond, *Alexander the Great: King, Commander and Statesman*
(Park Ridge, New Jersey, 1980), pp. 156–157; O. H. Zervos, "The Earliest
Coins of Alexander the Great: Notes on a Book by Gerhard Kleiner," *NC* 1982,
pp. 166–179; F. de Callataÿ, "La date des premiers tétradrachmes de poids
attique émis par Alexandre le Grand," *RBN* 128 (1982), pp. 1–25.

nearly constant level of production of the issues of group IIB in silver, even with some augmentation in production posited for the years *ca.* 342/1 – 337/6 (IIB at Amphipolis, IIA2 at Pella) to correspond with Philip's preparations for his Asian campaign. If, like Newell, one puts the end of group II near the beginning of Alexander's reign, the level of production in the last years of Philip's reign would be greatly augmented by comparison with his earlier years as king.[14]

Since the *terminus* of *ca.* 329/8 for the silver issues of group II at both Pella and Amphipolis is taken from the chronology of group II of the gold issues, it is essential to examine the evidence for the *terminus* of this latter group. Le Rider's date for the end of group II in gold depends on the analysis of one hoard found at Corinth in 1930 during archaeological excavation.[15] The coins in this hoard consisted entirely of Macedonian gold: forty-one staters of Philip II (according to Le Rider's classification, there are thirteen from the mint at Pella, twenty-eight from Amphipolis) and ten of Alexander III (Amphipolis four, Tarsus three, Salamis one, Sidon one, uncertain one). A date for the hoard of *ca.* 329/8 was established by Margaret Thompson on the basis of Newell's dates for the coins of Alexander of the same type as those found in the hoard. Since none of these staters of Alexander appears to have been minted later than 329/8 B.C. and the later specimens show no signs of wear, the burial of the hoard is assumed to have taken place "within a very few years" of 329/8. [16] The archaeological context in which the hoard was found and the style of the piece of pottery which was used to

[14] The numbers of dies identified from the various subgroups of tetradrachms show clearly that IIB at Amphipolis had a greater relative level of production than did IIA. At Pella, the same is true of IIA2 as compared to IIA1 and IIB. See the table in *Monnayage*, p. 385. Le Rider's chronology depends on the assumption that the mints usually produced coins at a "normal" rate year after year, that is, at a more or less constant and regular level of production. See, for example, *Monnayage*, p. 431. On this assumption, issues of coins are to be dated by distributing them as evenly as possible across the span of time believed to have been available for their production.

[15] *Monnayage*, pp. 429 – 430. The hoard is *IGCH* 77.

[16] G. Roger Edwards and Margaret Thompson, "A Hoard of Gold Coins of Philip and Alexander from Corinth," *AJA* 74 (1970), p. 349.

cover the cache are compatible with this date but cannot help to establish a precise date.[17]

Le Rider accepts Thompson's date for the hoard and makes three observations on the staters of Philip found in it.[18] First, on the whole they are in a good state of preservation, although five of the early specimens show the traces "d'une certaine usure." The other thirty-six are in good condition, some even in superb condition (*fleur de coin*). Second, the twenty-eight coins of Philip from the mint of Amphipolis exhibit a total of four different moneyers' marks, with twenty-one of them in two groups which are later than the other two. In the first of these later groups, which has thirteen coins, three sets of two coins each were struck from the same dies, and in the second group of eight coins, one set of two coins and one set of three coins were struck from the same dies. The appearance together of coins struck from the same dies, Le Rider says, indicates that these coins had not circulated much before they were hoarded, an observation confirmed by their good state of preservation. It is probable, he adds, that they were minted shortly before the burial of the hoard. Third, the last dies of group II of the mint of Amphipolis are represented in the hoard. Since Le Rider thinks that group II would have been terminated at the same time in Amphipolis as in Pella, it is possible that the production of this group did not extend beyond the date of burial of the Corinth hoard.

These observations lead Le Rider to the conclusion that the latest staters of Philip in the hoard could have been minted "jusqu'en 329/8" and that this could therefore be the date of the end of group II. If the production of Philip's coins had stopped in 336/5 B.C., it would be hard, Le Rider believes, to see how the Philips could have been so well preserved and how there could have been so many coins struck from the same dies in the same hoard. Once 329/8 is postulated as the *terminus* of group II in gold, Le Rider establishes the chronology of earlier issues in gold by working backward because the date at which Philip's gold first began to be minted cannot be fixed independently. On Le

[17] Edwards, *AJA* 74 (1970), p. 346.
[18] *Monnayage*, p. 430.

Rider's assumption that the nine separate issues of group II at Amphipolis extend over seven or eight years, the start of group II would be placed *ca.* 336/5, which would make the group entirely posthumous. Nevertheless, Le Rider concludes that "par prudence" it is perhaps better to propose a slightly expanded chronology of *ca.* 340 to *ca.* 328. The same is true for Pella. Again working backward in time, Le Rider proposes to place the start of group I in gold *ca.* 345 or even as late as *ca.* 342–340 based on the number and sizes of the issues in this group. This chronology would require us to believe that Philip did not begin to mint gold until almost fifteen years (at the earliest) after the start of his reign. Le Rider insists that this remarkable chronology for Philip's gold is not explicitly contradicted by any literary or documentary evidence. [19]

Obviously the crux of the numismatic argument for the *terminus* of group II is the chronological information derived from the Corinth hoard. In his article on Le Rider's book, Price points out that the establishment of *ca.* 329/8 as the date of the Corinth hoard depended on the now discredited attribution of certain Alexanders to a mint in Sicyon. He argues that the date of 329/8 has been "undermined." [20] Other hoard evidence, he suggests, hints at a later burial date. The argument is not conclusive, however. [21] Moreover, the Alexanders once attributed to Sicyon

[19] *Monnayage*, pp. 431–432.

[20] *NC* 1979, p. 234.

[21] He refers to three other hoards: from Samovodéné, Bulgaria, 1957 = *IGCH* 395 = Le Rider no. 3, pp. 259–261; from Saïda, Lebanon, 1829, 1852, 1863 = *IGCH* 1508 = Le Rider no. 4, p. 262; in commerce, 1967 (perhaps from the Balkans; not in *IGCH*) = Le Rider no. 5, pp. 262–264. Price states that Le Rider nos. 3 and 5 "confirm that period II of the gold must, in the main, be contemporary with the lifetime coinage of Alexander the Great" (*NC* 1979, p. 234). It must be pointed out, however, that these two hoards (as reported, anyway) consisted entirely of gold coinage. Le Rider does not describe the states of wear of the coins he saw; one might suspect that most of the coins are well preserved because caches of gold tend to be savings deposits. If the hoards are savings hoards, it is risky to draw precise conclusions about chronology from their contents. (See the text below.)

As for the Saïda hoard, Price reports that it has a "firm date of deposit" of 324/3 but contains "only issues of period I of 'Pella' and issues of period II at 'Amphipolis' earlier than those of the Corinth hoard" (*NC* 1979, p. 234). No reliable chronological conclusions can be drawn from the contents of this hoard,

have now been attributed to Pella, beginning *ca.* 328/7 B.C.[22] If this new dating is correct, the absence of these coins from the Corinth hoard would still be an indication of a burial date no earlier than *ca.* 328. The question of the burial date of the Corinth hoard and its significance for the chronology of Philip's coinage cannot be evaluated separately, however, from the questions of the nature of the hoard and the implications of its nature for the dates of the coins in it. There are two striking features of this particular hoard which mean it should not be regarded as an ordinary circulation hoard, consisting of an essentially random selection of coins from current circulation which was assembled on the spot and hidden as soon as possible, such as would be characteristic, for example, of the cash drawer of a merchant who suddenly found it expedient to hide his money.[23] First, all the coins in it were gold staters. Such very valuable coins were not components of ordinary monetary circulation, especially in central and southern Greece, where gold coins were not even minted. Pieces of such high value were the best choice for hoarding one's treasure, however, because they made it easy to

---

however, as a result of the complicated circumstances of its recovery. Thousands of coins from the deposit were abstracted and never recorded (see the reports listed under *IGCH* 1508). The coins actually recovered were part of an enormous deposit of coinage which had been stored in large jars, some of which at least contained separate groups of coins of the same type. (See, for example, W.-H. Waddington, "I. Trouvaille de Saïda," *RN* 1865, pp. 3–25. In the third discovery of coins from this deposit, two of the three jars contained only "staters of Alexander." The third had some different coinages mixed in.) It seems possible that later issues of Philip, for example, could have originally been part of the deposit but were stored separately in jars whose contents were never recorded. Alternatively, they could be missing because the jars had originally been part of some sort of treasury or repository for official funds which periodically received large shipments of cash for eventual dispersement as needed. The "missing coins" could have been stored in jars from which funds had been dispersed before the rest were hidden away. U. Westermark, "Notes on the Saïda Hoard (*IGCH* 1508)," *Nordisk Numismatisk Årsskrift* 1979–80, pp. 22–35, reviews the contents of the hoard and concludes that the three deposits were parts of a single cache.

[22] Moore, *Coinage of Alexander*, chapter 2. Price, *NC* 1979, pp. 238–239, puts some of these issues at Aegae.

[23] On the classification of hoards, see n. 23 in chapter 2.

stash away a large amount with only a small bulk. The generally good condition of the coins is also characteristic of a savings hoard, although this observation is not as significant in the case of gold coins as it is in the case of silver because gold coins with their high value in general circulated less than did their less valuable silver colleagues. Second, the original excavator discovered a striking gold necklace buried just beside the coins. [24] There seems to be no doubt that the piece of jewelry was part of the same cache as the coins. They were all buried under an earthen floor near a pillar in the basement floor of a stoa-like building adjacent to the temple of Apollo at Corinth. Since this "stoa" appears to have been a public building which may have been used to store military arms, its lower level would have been a good place for an official or magistrate to hide treasure, but it was not the obvious place for the burial of an ordinary circulation hoard. [25]

If this hoard was indeed some sort of savings hoard, then one must be very careful in drawing chronological conclusions from its contents. The coins in a savings hoard are usually not, as a group, specimens which have been extracted from circulation just before the hoard was hidden away. (Obviously, some of the coins in a savings hoard could have been put into the group soon before the hiding of the cache, but not even this need have happened.) Rather, it is likely that coins of large value in good condition would be put away from time to time as the saver added to his hoard. Even if one prefers to think of this as an "emergency" hoard suddenly assembled on one occasion for hiding away, its contents show that it was not assembled from everyday circulation. For whatever reasons, this was a special hoard.

[24] F. J. DeWaele, "The Greek Stoa North of the Temple at Corinth," *AJA* 35 (1931), p. 405. Cf. Edwards *AJA* 74 (1970), p. 343. Gladys R. Davidson, *Corinth Vol. XII. The Minor Objects* (Princeton, 1952), pp. 256–257, no. 2055, points out that the necklace resembles jewelry from the Balkan area. A northern provenance would make it easy to believe that the necklace belonged to a Macedonian who brought it to Corinth as a personal possession.

[25] On the nature of the stoa, see Robert L. Scranton, *Corinth Vol. I, Part II. Monuments in the Lower Agora and North of the Archaic Temple* (Princeton, 1951), pp. 175–179.

It is easy to reconstruct a history of the assembly and hiding away of this hoard which would be consistent with its nature but does not require us to think that the gold coins of Philip in good condition which it contained had to have been minted only a short time before the burial of the hoard. The owner of the hoard, for example, could have obtained and put away his gold coins of Philip years before he acquired the coins of Alexander which represented the final additions to his savings cache. He could have then added, from time to time, staters of Alexander to the gold Philips he had acquired earlier. He would have kept these valuable coins in a safe place as his private savings, thus ensuring that the gold Philips stayed out of circulation and incurred only little, if any, wear from handling. At some point, he put together his accumulation of gold coins with a valuable necklace in a hoard which he buried in the stoa but never recovered. That there are quite a few shared dies among the gold staters of Philip (three of the ten staters of Alexander also share dies) certainly means, as Le Rider says, that these coins had not circulated much, if at all, before they were hoarded. Otherwise, one would expect to find no, or only a few, shared dies because coins from the same dies are inevitably dispersed in different directions in the course of extended circulation after their production together at the mint. But this situation does not have to mean, as Le Rider assumes, that the coins in question had been minted not long before the date at which the hoard as we have it was put together and buried. Since Corinth was the civic headquarters for the Hellenic League which Philip founded after the battle of Chaeronea in 338 B.C., it was a very likely destination for periodic large shipments of money sent from the kings or their representatives. Philip kept troops in Corinth, for one thing, as did Alexander throughout his reign. [26]

Since the Macedonian kings necessarily had considerable expenses to pay in what amounted to the "head office" of their Hellenic League, they needed to send money to Corinth on occasion. Under Alexander, some of the funds could have come from the East, accounting for the presence in Corinth of Alexanders

[26] On Corinth's garrison, see Polybius 38.3.3; Plutarch, *Aratus* 23.4.

minted outside Macedonia. That Alexander sent money back to Greece is attested.[27] Various people could have had direct access to official shipments of recently coined money, such as a Macedonian in the employ of the king or an official of the League. Someone of this sort could have put together the coins in the Corinth hoard by acquiring gold Philips and Alexanders, either legitimately as compensation or illegitimately by theft or fraud, directly from Macedonian shipments of money sent to support Macedonian royal interests in this vital garrison post.[28] The hoarder would have gotten his coins as soon as there was access to the cash, before the king's gold was dispersed into general circulation. Thus he was likely to get coins with shared dies and in good condition. Over the course of time, the hoarder would have built up a cache of gold coins obtained in this way. It is also possible to think that there was some sort of official storehouse or treasury at Corinth in connection with the Macedonian presence and the League, to which sums were added from time to time from official shipments of money from Macedonia and the East. The hoarder could have assembled his coins, gradually or all on a single occasion, from the money which had accumulated in such a depository. He could have acquired the money either in the course of his regular duties or perhaps during the confusion created by an emergency such as the revolt of Agis. Indeed, when Antipater came to the Peloponnese with an army to defeat Agis in 331/0, he undoubtedly brought money with him from reserves in Macedonia and the funds which Alexander had sent to him from the East.[29] Some of this money could have found its way into a hoard in Corinth. It is not difficult, then, to account for the formation of the Corinth hoard without assuming that its

[27] In 334, Alexander sent Cleander to the Peloponnese with funds to recruit mercenaries. See Arrian 1.24.2, 2.20.5; Curtius 3.1.1 (*cum pecunia*).

[28] Cf. Thompson, *AJA* 74 (1970), pp. 349–350; Griffith, *HM*, p. 639, n. 2.

[29] For the money, see Arrian 3.16.10. On the chronology of the revolt, see E. Badian, "Agis III," *Hermes* 95 (1967), pp. 170–192; G. L. Cawkwell, "The Crowning of Demosthenes," *CQ* 19 (1969), pp. 170–173; E. N. Borza, "The End of Agis' Revolt," *CP* 66 (1971), pp. 230–235; G.E.M. de Ste. Croix, *The Origins of the Peloponnesian War* (Ithaca, 1972), pp. 376–378; P. A. Brunt, *Arrian*, vol. 1, pp. 480–485.

coins in good condition had to have been minted just before the burial of the hoard.

Although he never addresses the issue explicitly, Le Rider apparently regards the Corinth hoard as an ordinary circulation hoard. But this cannot be. As a result, his chronology cannot be said to rest on a firm footing because the dates he proposes for the early posthumous issues of Philip in gold and in silver depend on the assumption that the hoard is not a savings hoard. It is still quite possible to believe that the early posthumous issues of Philip (as distinct from the later posthumous issues which begin *ca.* 323/2) should be regarded as ending not long after Philip's death at the point when Alexander's own coinage was in full production. [30] Le Rider's principal objection to placing the *terminus* of his group II in silver and in gold as early as *ca.* 336/5 is the much greater rate of production for the later issues of this group which such a date would imply. [31] Although, as already mentioned, Le Rider assumes an increased rate of production at the end of Philip's reign, he prefers to extend these copious issues well into Alexander's reign in order to spread them over a greater number of years, thereby postulating a less noticeable augmentation in mint output during the minting of these coins.

A very noticeable augmentation of production, however, is exactly what one would expect in the last years of Philip's reign because he had truly enormous expenses in that period. First, there was the large-scale campaign which culminated in the battle of Chaeronea. After this victory, Philip had to finance the foundation of his League of Corinth and the great preparations for the invasion of Asia. [32] Already in 336 Philip had sent to Asia

[30] Cf. Price, *NC* 1982, pp. 186–190.

[31] See, for example, *Monnayage*, p. 390: "Si nous adoptions le point de vue de Newell, nous aurions à placer le groupe IIB des tétradrachmes amphipolitains de Philippe II entre *c.* 342/1 et 337/6. Il y aurait eu à cette époque une très sensible augmentation de la production de l'atelier, le groupe IIB étant trois fois plus important que le groupe IIA et ayant couvert un laps de temps à peu près égal."

[32] Diodórus 16.89.3, 16.91.2.

a vanguard of ten thousand men. [33] There was also his own wedding to Cleopatra to pay for, followed by the grandiose celebration on an international scale for the wedding of his daughter. [34] All of this required a great deal of cash. As Theopompus disparagingly pointed out, Philip could expend prodigious sums of money with the speed of a whirlwind because, for one thing, he was a military man with no time for accounting. [35] Never was that more true than on the eve of the departure of Philip's main army for the land of the Great King, who was backed by enormous financial resources. Once he had finalized his plans for the attack on Persia and the great celebration of his newly won Panhellenic leadership in conjunction with his daughter's wedding, Philip could count on huge expenses to come. Clearly he needed coinage and lots of it. Group IIB in silver would fit well as that coinage. Some of it could certainly be posthumous, of course, especially if it was in production to finance the invasion of Asia, because Alexander, who had many other things to attend to at the beginning of his reign, could simply have directed the mints to continue to produce money for the expedition with the dies in hand until he had the time and the inclination to see to the introduction of his own coins. Newell thought the transition took place within a matter of a few weeks after Philip's death, but there is really no satisfactory way to determine how long it took Alexander to arrange for the production of the new issues. [36]

No strictly comparable proliferation of issues exists for the gold of group II, but the two final issues of this group, which were produced simultaneously, are represented by a relatively large number of dies. [37] Again, this evidence for a greater rate of production of gold coinage at the end of group II would make

[33] Diodorus 16.91.2, 17.7.10; Polyaenus, *Strat.* 5.44.4; Justin 9.5.8–9. Cf. E. Badian, "The Death of Philip II," *Phoenix* 17 (1963), pp. 244–250.

[34] On Philip's wedding, see Griffith, *HM*, pp. 676–678; for the lavish expenditure on his daughter's wedding, see Diodorus 16.91.4–92.

[35] *FGrH* 115 F 224. Cf. Griffith, *HM*, pp. 442–443.

[36] Newell, *Reattribution*, p. 21. Price, *NC* 1982, p. 190, believes that "the radical reform of the coinage was one of Alexander's first actions."

[37] They have 31 of the 83 obverse dies of the group and 40 of the 122 reverse dies (*Monnayage*, p. 425).

sense in the context of Philip's activities in what turned out to be the last years of his reign. As we have seen, Le Rider's *terminus* of *ca.* 329/8 for group II leads to the hypothesis that Philip minted no gold coinage at all before *ca.* 345 at the earliest. Le Rider emphasizes that no ancient source provides incontrovertible evidence to prove that this chronology is impossible. Nevertheless, it must be said that the historical arguments for a much earlier start for Philip's gold coinage are compelling. Above all, it is simply inconceivable that Philip had large amounts of gold at his disposal from his own gold mines as early as the mid-350s but did not coin any of it in order to pay his expenses as king and as commander. Paying in bullion would have been cumbersome, difficult, and unnecessary. Why in the world would he have refrained from minting his gold? As we could guess even if the sources were totally silent about Philip's gold, there were many ways in which the king could exploit his holdings in this most valuable of natural resources by minting gold coins well before the last years of his reign. But the sources are not silent.

In his description of Philip's dealings in 357/6 B.C. with the town of Crenides on the Thracian coast (renamed Philippi by the king), Diodorus remarks that Philip exploited the gold mines of the region to produce his famous gold coins, the so-called Philips. [38] With these coins, says Diodorus, Philip greatly increased the strength of Macedonia because he used them to pay large numbers of mercenary soldiers and to bribe many Greeks to become traitors. The tone of the passage is rhetorical to be sure, and as Le Rider points out, Diodorus does not explicitly say that Philip began to mint his gold coins soon after his takeover of the gold mines of Crenides (although that is certainly the implication). [39] Le Rider, of course, thinks that Philip waited for a decade or more after the acquisition of these mines before he minted any gold coins. There are reasons to be found in the history of the earlier years of Philip's reign to think otherwise.

[38] 16.8.6–7. Cf. E. Borza, "The Natural Resources of Early Macedonia," *Philip II*, p. 10.

[39] *Monnayage*, p. 432.

First, Philip had mercenaries in his army well before 345 B.C.
Polyaenus mentions that Philip had them in Thessaly in (probably) the second half of the 350s B.C.[40] Demosthenes in 349 B.C.
(*Olynthiac* I.22) says that Philip had them to use against
Olynthus. Many of these mercenaries were probably recruited
from the tribes to the north of Macedonia, some of whom, and
probably all, had a special fondness for gold.[41] Gold staters
would have been very handy to win the loyalty of such men. But
there is an even more noteworthy reason to suppose that Philip
began to mint these coins earlier than 345 B.C.

Philip's first move outside the natural sphere of influence of
Macedonia in the north came when he intervened in Thessaly
early in the 350s against the tyrants of Pherae and their very
powerful Phocian allies.[42] This intervention ultimately involved
Philip in the Third Sacred War on the side of those who claimed
to represent the interests of Apollo and his sanctuary at Delphi.
Philip's decision to come to the aid of (in Diodorus' terminology)
"the Thessalians" was a momentous one which involved great
risks. His opponents were formidable, his allies were vacillating
and prone to split up in fits of pique at each other, and his own
troops might well be less than eager to fight away from home for
goals that had more to do with considerations of grand strategy
than with any immediate threat to their homeland. Philip was
going to need to resort to every possible weapon to win this gamble. He had to encounter his enemies' thrusts, or he was apt to
lose everything he had worked for in Macedonia and all he had
hoped for in Greece. He would have been keenly aware of the
tactics of the Pheraeans and especially of the very dangerous
Phocians. They could fight, as Philip was going to find out, and
they could corrupt, as Philip already knew. The Phocian flair for
corrupting their opponents by playing on their greed is the

[40] *Strat.* 4.2.18.

[41] See Griffith, *HM*, pp. 438–444, on Philip's mercenaries. The Gallic mercenaries of Antigonus Gonatus were paid in gold, their favorite wage:
Polyaenus, *Strat.* 4.6.17. Cf. Polybius 4.46.3; Memnon of Heraclea, *FGrH* 434 F
11 (19). The rebellious pharaoh Tachus minted gold coins to pay his mercenaries in 361 B.C. See Kraay, *ACGC*, p. 76.

[42] See the references in n. 4 of chapter 4.

particular point to notice here, while keeping it in mind that
Philip had the good fortune to acquire the gold mines of
Crenides after he had become embroiled in Thessalian affairs
and just about the time that the Third Sacred War erupted.[43]
From the beginning, the Phocian effort in the Sacred War
depended on lavish spending. The first Phocian general, Philomelus, attracted mercenaries by offering fifty percent more
than the customary rate of pay, relying at first on his own resources and a contribution by the Spartan commander Archidamus.[44] When other Greek states began to unite against the Phocian occupation of Delphi, Philomelus gathered still more mercenaries. Eventually he plundered the treasures of the sanctuary
of Apollo in order to finance his operations. [45]Philomelus' successor as Phocian commander, Onomarchus, also plundered the
sanctuary, minting coins from Apollo's silver and gold. He used
these coins to secure the loyalty of his allies and to bribe as many
of his enemies as possible to desert to his side or to remain neu-
tral. Most notably, Onomarchus corrupted even the Thessalians,
a principal adversary, to retire from the field, abandoning their
allies, the Boeotians. [46] The retirement of the Thessalians was a
tremendous coup for Onomarchus; so long as they stayed out of
the fight, Apollo's sacred cause was lost. It is easy to suspect
that the Phocian issues of gold were particularly effective in per-
suading the Thessalians to change their course. Such a weapon
could influence policy in a less obtrusive and swifter fashion than
even hordes of mercenaries. Onomarchus was equally successful
in using his money to pay Chares to keep Philip occupied in

---

[43] For the chronology, see Griffith, *HM*, pp. 246–250; E. Badian, "Philip II
and Thrace," *Pulpudeva* 4 (1983), pp. 55–57.

[44] Diodorus 16.24–25.1.

[45] Diodorus 16.28–30.2. Diodorus later (16.56.5) says that Philomelus did
not plunder the god's dedications, but his earlier narrative contradicts this report (16.30.1, 16.32.1). The statement at 16.56.5 probably recalls only the report of Philomelus' restraint at the beginning of the war. Compare the similar
wording of 16.28.2 (τῶν μὲν ἱερῶν ἀναθημάτων ἀπείχετο) and 16.56.5 (ἀπέ-
σχετο τῶν ἀναθημάτων).

[46] Diodorus 16.33.2–3.

Thrace.[47] Phyallus, the next Phocian commander, continued to turn Apollo's treasures into silver and gold coinage. [48] In short, the Phocians minted gold as well as silver coinage throughout the Sacred War to pay mercenaries, to buy the loyalty of allies, and to win over collaborators among their enemies who could control the actions of their cities. The amount of precious metal which the Phocian commanders turned into coinage was large, and the impact of so much gold on Greeks who had previously seen rather little of it was powerful. [49] Had it not been for the intervention of Philip against them, the Phocians could have marched victoriously down their road of gold to domination of central Greece.

But Philip stopped them. Not immediately perhaps, but stop them he did. (The war was finally ended only in 346 B.C.) [50] I would suggest that Philip's gold coinage served as a weapon in the struggle with an opponent who wielded the same weapon

[47] Theopompus, *FGrH* 115 F 249. Cf. Griffith, *HM*, p. 281.

[48] Diodorus 16.36.1.

[49] Diodorus 16.56.5–7; Athenaeus 6.231b-d. M. Crawford, "The Treasures of Delphi," *AIIN* 27–28 (1980–1981), pp. 299–300, has argued that the Phocians did not melt down the treasures and mint coins from them, but rather that the treasures were sold in order to procure Greek coinage. The argument essentially depends on the suggestion that κατακόπτειν εἰς νόμισμα (e.g., in Diodorus 16.56.6) could mean "to convert into cash (by sale)." But the words εἰς νόμισμα must mean that coins were made from the material which was "cut up." Cf. Diogenes Laertius' description (5.77) of the fate of the statues of Demetrius of Phalerum at Athens: κατασπάσαντες αὐτοῦ τὰς εἰκόνας καὶ τὰς μὲν ἀποδόμενοι, τὰς δὲ βυθίσαντες, τὰς δὲ κατακόψαντες εἰς ἀμίδας. The climax of the story is that the Athenians made chamber pots from some of the statues, not that they sold the statues in order to procure chamber pots.

That none of the gold or large silver coins from the Phocian coinage of the Sacred War has survived is understandable because the coinage was sacrilegious. Anyone who held on to such coins risked the human and divine punishment meted out after the war against everyone who could be connected with the plundering of Apollo's sanctuary (Diodorus 16.56.8–57, 16.60–64). The only way to avoid the pollution of sacrilege while preventing financial loss was for owners of this Phocian coinage to melt it down into bullion, or have it recoined into another, blameless coinage.

[50] See Griffith, *HM*, pp. 329–347 on this tangled affair, and the recent discussion by E. M. Harris, "The Political Career of Aeschines" (Diss. Harvard University, 1983), chapter 5 (summary in *HSCP* 88 [1984], pp. 262–264).

with great skill and effect. The power of gold to pay soldiers and to cement alliances would have been handy from the start of the Sacred War, but after Philip's crushing defeat by the Phocians it would have been invaluable. The Macedonian army had almost come apart in the aftermath of this crushing failure, and Onomarchus had subsequently beaten the Boeotians in a separate engagement. There can have been few occasions when Philip's prospects as a successful leader of Greeks as well as of Macedonians looked darker. What to do? First, whip the cowed Macedonian army into shape. Second, in the words of Diodorus, "persuade the Thessalians to fight the war in common."[51] It was going to be a delicate matter to persuade defeated men like the Thessalians who, recent history showed, were more than ready to listen to reason from the other side when there was money to be made in being reasonable. That Philip did persuade them to marshal a total of twenty thousand infantry and three thousand cavalry speaks well for his powers of persuasion. Were they merely oratorical? It seems reasonable to think that Philip saw fit to fight the Phocians with their own weapon: gold coinage.

When Philip returned to Thessaly after his defeat at the hands of the Phocians, a return he did not have to make, he was clearly putting his army, his reputation, and his future on the line. It would have been a good idea to buy some loyalty. And there were propaganda points to be made as well. The Phocian coinage was an unspeakable outrage against Apollo's divine dignity, struck from the god's precious possessions which the Phocian mint masters had melted down. Philip was very conscious of the benefits to be hoped for in a visible commitment to Apollo. He had his soldiers wear laurel crowns into battle to prove that they were the avengers of sacrilege committed against Apollo at Delphi and not just the defenders of Thessalian pride.[52] Le Rider points out that the laureate head of Apollo on Philip's gold coins very likely has something to do with the king's public and osten-

[51] 16.35.1–4.
[52] Justin 8.2.3.

tatious devotion to the god's banner in the Sacred War. [53] But his chronology for these issues requires him to believe that the Apollo type commemorates Philip's success in the Sacred War when the coins were issued at some point after the war's end in 346, perhaps even well after the end. It makes better sense to think that Philip's gold coinage with its garlanded head of Apollo (Plate 2, no. 2) represents a useful rival to the Phocian gold coinage stolen from Apollo of Delphi. Useful for bribery and appropriate for a propaganda campaign, the first issues of Philip's gold coins would fit very comfortably in the chronological context of the early years of the Sacred War in the middle and later 350s, soon after Philip had fortuitously acquired his own source of gold. Philip needed his gold coins to fight the Phocians as effectively as possible. Silver coinage alone could of course pay mercenaries and bribe Greeks, but without a gold coinage the odds against Philip in his desperate struggle with the Phocians and their potent weapon, gold coinage, were going to be worse. Philip was inclined to gamble only on sure bets. He needed a great deal of money at once, and he had gold mines. The obvious course was to coin in gold. The savings in production costs alone made it worthwhile.

It is very difficult to accept Le Rider's contention that none of the historical references which we have to Philip's use of gold need imply that Philip had his own gold coinage as early as the 350s or even the first half of the 340s. Demosthenes states that Philip bribed his way to prominence, starting with the Thessalians in the 350s. [54] When Demosthenes describes Philip's attempt to bribe Athenian ambassadors in 346 B.C., he is explicit about the king's chosen currency for the tactic: a great deal of χρυσίον, which should mean "gold coinage" in this context. [55] Le Rider suggests that Philip in fact offered Persian gold coinage, or electrum from Cyzicus, not his own gold issues. [56] What he does not explain is why Philip should have paid to acquire

[53] *Monnayage*, pp. 412–413.

[54] 19.259–267. Cf. Hypereides, *Vs. Demosthenes* 15.

[55] 19.167. The immediately preceding reference to χρήματα shows that χρυσίον here indicates coinage.

[56] *Monnayage*, p. 432.

foreign gold coinage when he had available a supply of gold from his own mines with which to mint his own gold coins. The evidence of Demosthenes is against Le Rider's chronology for Philip's gold coinage.

The same is true of the evidence of Diodorus. He reports that Philip proceeded to bribe many important men in various cities after having successfully bribed officials of Olynthus to betray that city to him. [57] Diodorus concludes this story with the observation that Philip used to declare that he had "enlarged his kingdom" more with the help of gold (διὰ χρυσίου) than with the help of arms. It is interesting to note that Diodorus used the same phrasing earlier to refer proleptically to Philip's successes in Thessaly against Pherae and the Phocians. [58] A little later in his narrative, Diodorus tells the undated story of Philip's remark when told that he was attacking a city with impregnable walls: Are the walls so high that even gold cannot scale them? asked the king. [59] It seems clear that Diodorus received from his sources the distinct impression that Philip had his own gold coins well before the late 340s B.C.

Simplicity in historical hypotheses is not always a virtue, but a simple hypothesis which fits the historical context as otherwise known is preferable to a more complex hypothesis which fails to make sense of the context. Based on the size of the various issues of Philip's gold (and apparently assuming an uninterrupted production of coins), Le Rider assigns five to six years to the gold coins of group I and seven to eleven years to those of group II. It is, however, always a risky business to date issues of coinage based on the assumption of a roughly uniform rate of production in "normal" times. I would suggest that the various issues of Philip's gold coinage in groups I and II could reasonably be distributed over the period from the middle or later years of the 350s to sometime in the mid-330s after his death in 336/5. The hypothesis would be that Philip began to mint his own gold coins because he needed a lot of money quickly, especially to

---

[57] 16.53.2–3.

[58] 16.38.2: "having enlarged his kingdom."

[59] 16.54.3–4. Here the reference is generic (χρυσός).

meet the Phocian threat, that a great increase in production took
place near the end of his reign, and that these particular issues
came to an end sometime early in the reign of Alexander (with,
of course, the resumption of the minting of posthumous Philips
in 323).[60] If this chronology for Philip's gold is right, there is
then no reason (on Le Rider's own evidence) to think that posthumous issues in silver continued for as long as seven years after
the death of Philip.[61]

In his discussion of Zervos' revival of the idea that Alexander
began to mint his own silver coins only several years after his
accession to the Macedonian throne, Price makes it clear that the
numismatic evidence is inadequate to decide the question. As
he puts it, the argument "must fall back on to historical
probability."[62] The same applies to the argument that makes
nearly all of Philip's gold coins posthumous issues. Further
study of the coinage may help to clarify the situation, but it
would be a mistake to treat the numismatic evidence as divorced

[60] For a different estimation of the date at which Philip began to mint his
famous gold Philips, see the views of N.G.L. Hammond, "The Lettering and the
Iconography of 'Macedonian' Coinage," in *Ancient Greek Art and Iconography*, ed.
Warren G. Moon (Madison, 1983), pp. 245–258.

[61] Since so much remains uncertain about the chronology and even the location of the mints of Philip's coinage, it is difficult to draw firm conclusions about
the relation between the silver and the gold. There are, for example, many
moneyers' marks which are not shared between the gold and the silver from the
same mint (according to Le Rider's attributions). For the gold staters of Amphipolis, there are twelve different markings (counting no mark as one category)
in groups I and II. Nine of these do not appear in the silver of groups I and II
of Amphipolis. The three which are shared occur in group II of the gold but in
group I of the silver. At Pella, on the other hand, all the marks from groups I
and II of the staters which are shared appear in group II of the silver, except
for one in IC. Most of the marks from group II of the gold at Amphipolis which
do not appear in the silver from Amphipolis do, however, turn up in the
silver of group II from Pella. This brief observation is naturally not meant to
do justice to a complicated subject, but only to point out that the situation is
complex and confusing. For one thing, in the absence of die links, what
guarantee is there that similar marks on different issues of coins mean that these
coins belong together chronologically? The same marks could be used over
again at the same mint after a period of time, or by different officials at different
mints.

[62] *NC* 1982, p. 188.

from historical probability. Le Rider's chronology for Philip's gold seems incredible on historical grounds. Certainly no historical reconstruction which is built on this foundation, such as that of J. R. Ellis concerning Alexander's policy on non-Alexander coinages, can be accepted.[63]

[63] In *NC* 1982, p. 188, n. 20, Price expresses a reservation about the chronology which makes the vast majority of Philip's gold coinage posthumous: "The possibility that all the gold issues of period II are lifetime Philips cannot be completely discarded." This is especially so because it is impossible to accept Price's hypothesis (pp. 187–188) that Alexander may have been compelled by a motion of the League of Corinth to continue to mint gold coinage of Philip as the official medium of payment for the expenses of the League's campaign against the Persians. Macedonian royal mint production was not regulated by any motion of the king's Greek allies. Moreover, Alexander had been officially recognized as the *hegemon* of the League, and he had the same standing as had Philip. His coinage was just as good as his father's for the payment of League expenses, as the Corinth hoard itself clearly implies. Why would the Greeks have cared whether the gold they received carried the types of Philip or of Alexander? They were not ignorant northern barbarians who would insist on having the same type of coinage even after the accession of a new king in Macedonia. Finally, the Greek allies were probably expected to pay for their own troops. See A. J. Heisserer, *Alexander the Great and the Greeks. The Epigraphic Evidence* (Norman, Okla., 1980), pp. 22–23. The Greeks of the League of Corinth, like the king's Macedonian troops, would have been happy to receive Alexander's own gold whenever he saw fit to distribute some to them.

APPENDIX FIVE. *Pegasi* of Ambracia
in Hoards

In *IGCH* and *CH* vols. 1–6, *pegasi* of Ambracia occur in eight hoards which have been dated to the reigns of Philip and Alexander: from Aetolia, *IGCH* 72 (350–325): 1 Ambracian coin in a total of 12; from Sicily, *IGCH* 2127 (*ca.* 350): 4 in 29+; *IGCH* 2130 (*ca.* 350–340): 4 (5) in 91; *IGCH* 2131 (*ca.* 340): 10 in 88; *IGCH* 2132 (*ca.* 340–330): 1 in 26; *IGCH* 2133 (*ca.* 340–330): 16 in 327; *IGCH* 2135 (350–325): 2 in 47; *CH* 3.20 (340): 2 in 42?

There are *pegasi* of Ambracia in eighteen hoards dated *ca.* 325–275 B.C.: from western Greece? *IGCH* 88 (*ca.* 325–300): 3 in 28+; from Cephallenia, *IGCH* 140 (*ca.* 300–275): ? in *ca.* 350–400; from southern Italy, *IGCH* 1948 (*ca.* 300?): 2 in a large hoard; from Sicily, *IGCH* 2144 (333–332, or 320–310): 5 in *ca.* 245; *IGCH* 2145 (320–310): 16 in *ca.* 300?; *IGCH* 2147 (*ca.* 310): 1 in 277+; *IGCH* 2148 (*ca.* 310): 2 in 58+; *IGCH* 2149 (*ca.* 310?): 3 in 65; *IGCH* 2151 (*ca.* 300): 9 in 642; *IGCH* 2152 (*ca.* 300 or *ca.* 220): 1 in 16; *IGCH* 2153 (*ca.* 300): 2 in 77; *IGCH* 2180 (early 3rd): 6 in *ca.* 530; *IGCH* 2181 (early 3rd): ? in 460; *IGCH* 2185 (*ca.* 289): 1 in 269; *IGCH* 2187 (early 3rd): 19 in 169; *IGCH* 2189 (early 3rd): 1 in 23; from southern Italy, *CH* 1.39 (late 4th): 1 in 13; from Sicily, *CH* 2.63 (280): 1 in 13+. I have not included *IGCH* 201 from Epirus, which has an unknown number of Ambracian drachms and is dated only to the "3rd cent. B.C. "

The available information on the state of wear of the coins in these hoards is, as usual, not extensive. Of the coins illustrated from *IGCH* 2131, one of the Ambracian coins is corroded, but the other is approximately as worn as the E series *pegasus* of Cor-

---

[1] See *NotSc* 1954, p. 72, figs. 2.5 (Corinth) and 2.12 (Ambracia).

inth also shown.[1] The E series appears to belong to the 340s.[2] The condition of the one Ambracian coin in *IGCH* 72 is "très bien" as opposed to the "bien" of the most recent Corinthian coin in the hoard, a stater of Ravel's group IV, which is probably to be dated to the first half of the fourth century.[3] This information need not mean that Ambracian coinage continued past *ca.* 338–336, but in *IGCH* 2144 there are two Ambracian coins illustrated (*NC* 1928, pl. 6, nos. 11–12) whose condition is slightly worse than that of the two Corinthian *pegasi* of the AΛ series (pl. 6, nos. 5–6) but better than that of a Δ series *pegasus* (pl. 6, no. 9). Both the AΛ and Δ series are more recent than the E series. In *IGCH* 2149, the condition of the only Ambracian coin described is "buona," while the Corinthian staters range from "buona" to "ottima conservazione."[4] Unfortunately the other two Ambracian coins of *IGCH* 2149 cannot be identified from the publication, but one of them is, according to Ravel's scheme in his arrangement of Ambracian coinage, more recent than the coin listed as "buona." In *IGCH* 88, two of the Ambracian coins are apparently more worn than the Corinthian staters of the letter series, all of which are described as in good (καλή) condition.[5] These two Ambracian coins, however, are not of Ravel's most recent types. The third Ambracian coin, of a type (quiver and bow symbol) not found in Ravel's catalogue, is as well preserved as the Corinthian coins (καλή).

In *IGCH* 2151, there are tetradrachms of Alexander III together with Ambracian and Corinthian coins.[6] The condition of five of the eight tetradrachms is given as "media," of the remaining three, "buona." Only eight of the nine Ambracian staters have their condition listed, five "media" and three "cattiva." As a group, therefore, the Ambracian coins are more worn than the Alexander tetradrachms, but as a smaller denomination

[2] See G. K. Jenkins, "A Note on Corinthian Coins in the West," in *Centennial Publication of the American Numismatic Society*, ed. Harald Ingholt (New York, 1958), pp. 373–374.
[3] See *BCH* 86 (1962), p. 421.
[4] See *AIIN* 5–6 (1958–1959), pp. 167–177.
[5] See *JIAN* 11 (1908), pp. 258–260.
[6] See *AIIN* 5–6 (1958–1959), pp. 125–165.

the staters would have shown more evidence of wear than would the tetradrachms in a similar period of circulation. Therefore, the staters in this hoard do not have to be older than the tetradrachms of Alexander.

The condition of the Corinthian staters from the letter series in this hoard ranges from "cattiva" to "buona." One gains the impression that the Ambracian staters could be contemporary with the earlier Corinthian staters from the letter series but that the letter series continued to be produced for a longer period than did the issues of Ambracia. This impression is reinforced by the state of wear of the coins in *IGCH* 2187.[7] The condition of the Ambracian staters ranges from "media" to "ottima." As a group they are at least as well preserved as the letter-series staters of Corinth in the hoard ("pessima" to "buona"). The conditions of the two *pegasi* of the period of Agathocles at Syracuse found in the hoard are given as "quasi-buona" and "buona." Of the Ambracian coins, the condition of two is "quasi-buona," of three "buona," and of one "ottima." Since the Agathocles coins probably belong to the period *ca.* 306 – 289 B.C., while the letter-series staters of Corinth are to be dated to the last four decades of the fourth century, the date of at least some of the Ambracian coins should be later than the 330s, perhaps a good deal later.

[7] See *AIIN* 5 – 6 (1958 – 1959), pp. 91 – 124.

APPENDIX SIX. Sicyonian Silver Coins in Hoards

The following hoards from the period *ca.* 330–200 B.C. , all from mainland Greece, are on record in *IGCH* and *CH* vols. 1–6 as containing silver coins of Sicyon. *IGCH* 67 (350–325): 10 Sicyonian coins in a total of *ca.* 150; *IGCH* 68 (*ca.* 350–325): 2 in 38; *IGCH* 70 (350–325): 12 in 42; *IGCH* 73 (*ca.* 350–325?): 60 in 62; *IGCH* 75 (*ca.* 330–320): 78? in *ca.* 100; *IGCH* 76 (*ca.* 327): 6 in 35; *IGCH* 78 (*ca.* 323): 15 in 133; *IGCH* 81 (*ca.* 319): 3 in 37+; *IGCH* 83 (*ca.* 315–310): 2 in 150+; *IGCH* 93 (*ca.* 310–300): 1 in 112; *IGCH* 111 (late 4th): 3 in *ca.* 69; *IGCH* 115 (end of 4th): 22 in 22; *IGCH* 117 (*ca.* 300): 2 in 38; *IGCH* 122 (*ca.* 300): 5 in 28; *IGCH* 129 (310–290): 13 in 478+; *IGCH* 130 (early 3rd): 3 in 37+; *IGCH* 132 and *CH* 3.31 (280): 7 in 55+; *IGCH* 133 (early 3rd): 2 in 11+; *IGCH* 159 (*ca.* 264 or 260–240): 3 in 61; *IGCH* 162 (*ca.* 250): 1 in 30; *IGCH* 170 (250–240): 31 in 33; *IGCH* 173 (*ca.* 250–225): 26 in 50; *IGCH* 176 (*ca.* 235–225): 2 in 82; *IGCH* 182 (after 265 or *ca.* 220): 31 in 55; *IGCH* 195 (*ca.* 225–200?): 27 in 63; *IGCH* 199 (3rd): 7 in 11; *IGCH* 207 (late 3rd): 1 in 15; *CH* 2.42 (350–325): 4 in 25+; *CH* 2.51 (323–320): 1 in 9+; *CH* 2.74 (3rd?): 52 in 75+; *CH* 2.75 (3rd?): an abundance in a large hoard; *CH* 3.43 (229–228): 2 in 38; *CH* 6.24 (270): 9 in 575.

Information on the condition of these coins is available only in a limited number of cases. The Sicyonian obols in *IGCH* 78 are in FDC condition, which is better than the condition of all but one of the accompanying Olympian coins.[1] Furthermore, the Sicyonian coins in *IGCH* 78 are contemporary with those in *IGCH* 76, which Newell dated to the early 320s by comparison

---

[1] These latter specimens are from the most recent period of production of the mint at Olympia, 363–323 B.C., according to C. T. Seltman, *The Temple Coins of Olympia* (Cambridge, 1921), pp. 111–113.

with the condition of the Macedonian coins in the latter hoard.[2] The condition of the Sicyonian staters in *IGCH* 83 matches that of the lifetime and early posthumous Alexander tetradrachms in the hoard.[3] In *IGCH* 122, four of the five Sicyonian coins are better preserved than the coins of Thebes, which of course should be no later than 335 B.C.[4]

In *ICGH* 159 the staters of Sicyon are worn, but not as badly as are the smaller denomination Alexander III drachms. On the other hand, the condition of the two Theban staters in the hoard is perhaps comparable to that of the more worn Sicyonian staters but much worse than that of the best preserved specimen of the latter group.[5] The Theban and Sicyonian coins are the same denomination, but we should notice that the Theban types have almost no raised detail which would show signs of wear as quickly as would the fine detail of the more elaborate Sicyonian types. After a similar period of circulation, coins of Sicyon should perhaps appear more worn than Theban coins of the same denomination. Therefore, the Sicyonian staters in *IGCH* 159 should be more recent than the Theban staters in the hoard. But it must be admitted that reliable analysis is difficult when the coins from a hoard have experienced extremely extended periods of circulation. Of the specimens illustrated from *IGCH* 173, the triobol and stater of Sicyon are in better condition than the tetradrachm and drachm of Alexander III and in approximately the same condition as the drachm of Lysimachus (Lampsacus, 299 B.C.).[6] Similar comparisons can be made from *IGCH* 176. The two Sicyonian staters are at least as well preserved as four of the five Alexander drachms in the hoard, and their condition is

---

[2] See Seltman, *Temple Coins*, p. 112.

[3] See E. T. Newell, *Alexander Hoards III: Andritsaena* (New York, 1923). Compare, for example, no. 107 (Sicyon) in pl. 5 with no. 53 (posthumous Alexander) in pl. 3.

[4] See *ArchDelt* 18 (1963), *Chronica* p. 6; 24 (1969), *Chronica* p. 9.

[5] See *AA* 1958, pp. 38–62. Nos. 47–49 are Sicyonian, nos. 38–39 Theban.

[6] See *BCH* 80 (1956), p. 227, pl. 6, nos. 5–6 (Alexander), 7 (Lysimachus), and 12–13 (Sicyon).

significantly better than that of the Theban stater in the hoard.[7] In *IGCH* 182, the Sicyonian triobols seem to be slightly better preserved as a group than either the drachms of Chalcis or the drachm and triobol of Corinth.[8]

In *CH* 3.31, the three Sicyonian drachms illustrated seem to be at least as well preserved as the three drachms of Alexander III and one of Philip III. In *CH* 3.43, the two Sicyonian staters are generally comparable in their condition to the other later fourth-century coins in the hoard. Obviously none of these comparisons can be regarded as precise, especially when they are made from photographs. On the basis of the available evidence, one might guess that the mint of Sicyon may have closed at least for a while in the last quarter of the fourth century, like the mints in Thessaly.

[7] See E. T. Newell, *Alexander Hoards IV: Olympia* (New York, 1929), nos. 32–33 (Sicyon), 50 (Thebes), and 58–61 (Alexander).

[8] See *ArchDelt* 14 (1931–1932), pp. 71–77.

BIBLIOGRAPHY

In the case of authors with more than one item, books are listed first, followed by articles and reviews in that order. Items are arranged alphabetically within these categories.

Albini, U. *[Erode Attico] περὶ πολιτείας* (Florence, 1968).

Amit, M. *Great and Small Poleis: A Study in the Relations between the Great Powers and the Small Cities in Ancient Greece* (Brussels, 1973).

Anderson, J. K. *Ancient Greek Horsemanship* (Berkeley, 1961).

———. *Military Theory and Practice in the Age of Xenophon* (Berkeley, 1970).

Aucher, J. B. *Eusebii Pamphili Chronicon Bipartitum, Pars I* (Venice, 1818).

Audoin, R., and P. Bernard. "Trésor de monnaies indiennes et indo-grecques d'Aï Khanoum (Afghanistan)," *RN* 1973, pp. 238–289; *RN* 1974, pp. 7–41.

Austin, M. M. *The Hellenistic World from Alexander to the Roman Conquest: A Selection of Ancient Sources in Translation* (Cambridge, 1981).

Austin, M. M., and P. Vidal-Naquet. *Economic and Social History of Ancient Greece: An Introduction* (Berkeley, 1977).

Babelon, E. *Traité des monnaies grecques et romaines,* vol. 4 (Paris, 1926–1932).

Badian, E. "The Administration of the Empire," *Greece and Rome* 12 (1965), pp. 166–182.

———. "Agis III," *Hermes* 95 (1967), pp. 170–192.

———. "Alexander the Great and the Greeks of Asia," in *Ancient Societies and Institutions. Studies Presented to Victor Ehrenberg on His 75th Birthday* (Blackwell, Oxford, 1966), pp. 37–69.

———. "A Comma in the History of Samos," *ZPE* 23 (1976), pp. 289–294.

———. "The Death of Philip II," *Phoenix* 17 (1963), pp. 244–250.

———. "Harpalus," *JHS* 81 (1961), pp. 16–43.

———. "Hegemony and Independence. Prolegomena to a Study of the Relations of Rome and the Hellenistic States in the Second Century B.C.," *Actes du VIIᵉ congrès de la F.I.E.C. Budapest, 1979,* vol. 1

(Budapest, 1983), pp. 397–414.

———. "Philip II and Thrace," *Pulpudeva* 4 (1983), pp. 51–71.

Bagnall, R. S. *The Administration of the Ptolemaic Possessions Outside Egypt* (Leiden, 1976).

Bakhuizen, S. C. *Mnemosyne* 35 (1982), pp. 435–437, review of R. Etienne and D. Knoepfler, *Hyettos de Béotie et la chronologie des archontes fédéraux entre 250 et 171 avant J.-C.* (Paris, 1976, *BCH*, suppl. 3).

Bar-Kochva, B. *The Seleucid Army: Organization and Tactics in the Great Campaigns* (Cambridge, 1976).

Bay, A. "The Letters *SC* on Augustan *aes* Coinage," *JRS* 62 (1972), pp. 111–122.

Bedoukian, P. Z. "Coinage of the Armenian Kingdoms of Sophene and Commagene," *ANSMN* 28 (1983), pp. 71–88.

Belin de Ballu, E. *Olbia, cité antique du littoral nord de la Mer Noire* (Leiden, 1972).

Bellinger, A. R. *Essays on the Coinage of Alexander the Great* (New York, 1963).

———. "Greek Coins from the Yale Numismatic Collection, II," *YCS* 12 (1951), pp. 251–265.

———. "Greek Mints under the Roman Empire," in *Essays in Roman Coinage Presented to Harold Mattingly*, ed. R.A.G. Carson and C.H.V. Sutherland (Oxford, 1956), pp. 137–148.

———. "Notes on Coins from Olynthus," in *Studies Presented to David Moore Robinson*, ed. G. E. Mylonas and D. Raymond, vol. 2 (St. Louis, 1953), pp. 180–186.

———. "The Thessaly Hoard of 1938," in *Congresso internazionale di numismatica Roma 1961: II. Atti* (Rome, 1965), pp. 57–60.

Bengtson, H. *Die Strategie in der hellenistischen Zeit: Ein Beitrag zum antiken Staatsrecht* vol. 1 (Munich, 1937, Münchener Beiträge zur Papyrusforschung und antiken Rechtsgeschichte 26).

Benveniste, E. *Le vocabulaire des institutions indo-européennes*, vol. 2 (Paris, 1969).

Béquignon, Y. "Etudes thessaliennes," *BCH* 59 (1935), pp. 36–77.

Berthold, R. M. *Rhodes in the Hellenistic Age* (Ithaca, 1984).

———. "Fourth Century Rhodes," *Historia* 29 (1980), pp. 32–49.

Berve, H. *Das Alexanderreich auf prosopographischer Grundlage* (Munich, 1926).

Bickerman, E. *Institutions des Séleucides* (Paris, 1938, Bibliothèque archéologique et historique 26).

———. "La cité grecque dans les monarchies hellénistiques," *Revue de philologie* 13 (1939), pp. 335–349.

Bickerman, E., and J. Sykutris. *Speusipps Brief an König Philipp* (Leipzig,

1928, Berichte über die Verhandlungen der Sächsischen Akademie der Wissenschaften zu Leipzig, Philologisch-historische Klasse 80, 3).

Biel, G. *Treatise on the Power and Utility of Moneys,* trans. R. B. Burke (Philadelphia, 1930).

Bisson, T. N. *Conservation of Coinage: Monetary Exploitation and its Restraint in France, Catalonia, and Aragon (c. A.D. 1000–c. 1225)* (Oxford, 1979).

Blanchet, A., and A. Dieudonné. *Manuel de numismatique française* (Paris, 1912–1936).

Blondel, G. "Etude sur les droits régaliens et la constitution de Roncaglia," in *Mélanges Paul Fabre. Etudes d'histoire du Moyen Age* (Paris, 1902, repr. Geneva, 1972), pp. 236–257.

Bluck, R. S. *Plato's Meno* (Cambridge, 1961).

Bodenstedt, Fr. *Phokäisches Elektron-Geld von 600–326 v. Chr. Studien zur Bedeutung und zu den Wandlungen einer antiken Goldwährung* (Mainz, 1976).

Bodin, J. *Six livres de la république* (1576). See McRae below.

Bogaert, R. *Banques et banquiers dans les cités grecques* (Leiden, 1968).

Bonitz, H. *Index Aristotelicus* (Berlin, 1870).

Borza, E. N. "The End of Agis' Revolt," *CP* 66 (1971), pp. 230–235.

————. "The Natural Resources of Macedonia," in *Philip II, Alexander the Great and the Macedonian Heritage,* ed. W. L. Adams and E. N. Borza (Lanham, Md., 1982), pp. 1–20.

Bosworth, A. B. *A Historical Commentary on Arrian's History of Alexander,* vol. 1 (Oxford, 1980).

Bousquet, J. "Le compte de l'automne 325 à Delphes," in *Mélanges hellénistiques offerts à Georges Daux* (Paris, 1974), pp. 21–32.

Bridrey, E. *Nicole Oresme. Etude d'histoire des doctrines et des faits économiques: la théorie de la monnaie au XIVe siècle* (Paris, 1906).

Briscoe, J. "The Antigonids and the Greek States 276–196 B.C.," in *Imperialism in the Ancient World,* ed. P.D.A. Garnsey and C. R. Whittaker (Cambridge, 1978), pp. 145–157.

Bruce, I.A.F. *An Historical Commentary on the 'Hellenica Oxyrhynchia'* (Cambridge, 1967).

Brunt, P. A. *Arrian,* vol. 1 (Cambridge, Mass., 1976, Loeb Classical Library).

Buck, C. D. *The Greek Dialects* (Chicago, 1955).

Buck, R. J. *A History of Boeotia* (Edmonton, Alberta, 1979).

Buckler, J. *The Theban Hegemony 371–362 B.C.* (Cambridge, Mass., 1980).

Budelius, R. *De monetis et re nummaria libri duo* (Cologne, 1591).

Burnett, A. M. "The Authority to Coin in the Late Republic and Early

Empire," *NC* 1977, pp. 37–63.

———. "The Coinages of Rome and Magna Graecia in the Late Fourth and Third Centuries B.C.," *SNR* 56 (1977), pp. 92–121.

———. "The First Roman Silver Coins," *Quaderni ticinesi. Numismatica e antichità classiche* 7 (1978), pp. 121–142.

Buttrey, T. V. "The Athenian Currency Law of 375/4 B.C.," in *Greek Numismatics and Archaeology. Essays in Honor of Margaret Thompson*, ed. O. Mørkholm and N. M. Waggoner (Wetteren, 1979), pp. 33–45.

———. "More on the Athenian Coinage Law of 375/4 B.C.," *Quaderni ticinesi. Numismatica e antichità classiche* 10 (1981), pp. 71–94.

Cahn, H. *SNR* 1977, pp. 279–287, review of M. J. Price and N. M. Waggoner, *Archaic Greek Coins. The Asyut Hoard* (London, 1975).

Callataÿ, F. de. "La date des premiers tétradrachmes de poids attique émis par Alexandre le Grand," *RBN* 128 (1982), pp. 1–25.

Cameron, G. G. *Persepolis Treasury Tablets* (Chicago, 1948).

Camp, J. McK. II. "A Drought in the Late Eighth Century B.C.," *Hesperia* 48 (1979), pp. 397–411.

Cargill, J. *The Second Athenian League: Empire or Free Alliance?* (Berkeley, 1981).

Carney, T. F. *The Economies of Antiquity: Controls, Gifts and Trade* (Lawrence, Kans., 1973).

Carreau, D. *Souveraineté et coopération monétaire internationale* (Paris, 1970).

Cary, M. "The Sources of Silver for the Greek World," in *Mélanges Gustave Glotz*, vol. 1 (Paris, 1932), pp. 133–142.

Castritius, H. "Die Okkupation Thrakiens durch die Perser und der Sturz des athenischen Tyrannen Hippias," *Chiron* 2 (1972), pp. 1–15.

Cawkwell, G. L. *Philip of Macedon* (London, 1978).

———. "The Crowning of Demosthenes," *CQ* 19 (1969), pp. 163–180.

Chadwick, J. "Ταγά and ἀταγία," in *Studi linguistici in onore di Vittore Pisani* (Brescia, 1969), vol. 1, pp. 231–234.

Chambers, J. T. "The IV Century Athenians' View of Their Fifth-Century Empire," *Parola del passato* 162 (1975), pp. 177–191.

Cohen, G. M. *The Seleucid Colonies. Studies in Founding, Administration and Organization* (Wiesbaden, 1978, Historia Einzelschriften 30).

Coin Hoards vols. 1–6 (Royal Numismatic Society, London, 1975–1981).

Cook, J. M. *The Persian Empire* (New York, 1983).

Copernicus, N. *Monetae Cudendae Ratio* (1526).

Crawford, M. H., ed. *Sources for Ancient History* (Cambridge, 1983).

———. "Finance, Coinage and Money from the Severans to

Constantine," in *Aufstieg und Niedergang der römischen Welt* II.2, ed. H. Temporini (Berlin, 1975), pp. 560–593.

———. "Money and Exchange in the Roman World," *JRS* 60 (1970), pp. 40–48.

———. "Roman Imperial Coin Types and the Formation of Public Opinion," in *Studies in Numismatic Method Presented to Philip Grierson*, ed. C.N.L. Brooke, B.H.I.H. Stewart, J. G. Pollard and T. R. Volk (Cambridge, 1983), pp. 47–64.

———. "The Treasures of Delphi," *AIIN* 27–28 (1980–1981), pp. 299–300.

Cutroni, A. T. "Aspetti e problemi della monetazione arcaica di Selinunte (inizi-480 a. C.)," *Kokalos* 21 (1975), pp. 154–173.

Dale, A. M. *Euripides. Alcestis* (Oxford, 1954).

Dandamayev, M. A. "Politische und wirtschaftliche Geschichte," *Beiträge zur Achämenidengeschichte*, ed. G. Walser (Wiesbaden, 1972, Historia Einzelschriften 18), pp. 15–58.

Danoff, M. *RE* suppl. 9, *s. v.* "Pontos Euxeinos 17. Olbia."

Daux, G. "Dédicace thessalienne d'un cheval à Delphes," *BCH* 82 (1958), pp. 329–334.

Davanzati, B. *Lezione delle monete* (presented orally 1588, publ. 1638) in *Ecrits notables sur la monnaie. XVIᵉ siècle. De Copernic à Davanzati*, ed. J.-V. Le Branchu (Paris, 1934), vol. 2, pp. 223–241 (in French translation).

Davidson, G. R. *Corinth Vol. XII. The Minor Objects* (Princeton, 1952).

Davis, N. M. and C. M. Kraay. *The Hellenistic Kingdoms. Portrait Coins and History* (London, 1973).

Delatte, L. *Les traités de la royauté d'Ecphante, Diotogène et Sthénidas* (Bibliothèque de la Faculté de Philosophie et Lettres de l'Université de Liège 97, 1942).

Denina, C. *Istoria politica e letteraria della Grecia libera* (Venice, 1784).

Derathé, R. "La place de Jean Bodin dans l'histoire des théories de la souveraineté," in *Jean Bodin. Verhandlungen der internationalen Bodin-Tagung in München* (Munich, 1973), pp. 245–260.

DeWaele, F. J. "The Greek Stoa North of the Temple at Corinth," *AJA* 35 (1931), pp. 394–423.

Diels, H., and W. Kranz. *Die Fragmente der Vorsokratiker*⁶ (Berlin, 1951–1952).

Dieudonné, A. "La théorie de la monnaie à l'époque féodale et royale d'après deux livres nouveaux," *RN* 1909, pp. 90–109.

Dittmar, H. *Aischines von Sphettos* (Berlin, 1912).

Dohrn, T. "Die Marmor-Standbilder des Daochos-Weihgeschenks in Delphi," *Antike Plastik* 8 (1968), pp. 33–53.

Drews, R. *Basileus. The Evidence for Kingship in Geometric Greece* (New Haven, 1983, Yale Classical Monographs 4).

Droysen, J. G. *Geschichte des Hellenismus I: Geschichte der Nachfolger Alexanders* (Hamburg, 1836).

Ducat, J. "La confédération béotienne et l'expansion thébaine à l'époque archaïque," *BCH* 97 (1973), pp. 59–73.

Düring, I. *Aristoteles: Darstellung und Interpretation seines Denkens* (Heidelberg, 1966).

Eckhel, J. *Doctrina Numorum Veterum* (Vienna, 1792–1798).

Eddy, S. K. "Some Irregular Amounts of Athenian Tribute," *AJP* 94 (1973), pp. 47–70.

Edson, C. F. "The Antigonids, Heracles and Beroea," *HSCP* 45 (1934), pp. 213–246.

———. "Perseus and Demetrius," *HSCP* 46 (1935), pp. 191–202.

Edwards, G. R., and M. Thompson. "A Hoard of Gold Coins of Philip and Alexander from Corinth," *AJA* 74 (1970), pp. 343–350.

Ehrenberg, V. *The Greek State* 2 (London, 1969).

———. *Man, State and Diety. Essays in Ancient History* (London, 1974).

Ehrhardt, C. "The Coins of Cassander," *Journal of Numismatic Fine Arts* 2 (1973), pp. 25–32.

Ellis, J. R. *Philip II and Macedonian Imperialism* (London, 1976).

Engel, A., and R. Serrure. *Traité de numismatique moderne et contemporaine* (Paris, 1897–1899).

Engels, D. W. *Alexander the Great and the Logistics of the Macedonian Army* (Berkeley, 1978).

Erhart, K. P. *The Development of the Facing Head Motif on Greek Coins and Its Relation to Classical Art* (New York, 1979).

Errington, R. M. *Philopoemen* (Oxford, 1969).

———. "Alexander the Philhellene and Persia," in *Ancient Macedonian Studies in Honor of Charles F. Edson* (Thessaloniki, 1981), pp. 139–143.

———. "From Babylon to Triparadeisos: 323–320 B.C.," *JHS* 90 (1970), pp. 49–77.

———. "Macedonian 'Royal Style' and Its Historical Significance," *JHS* 94 (1974), pp. 20–37.

———. "The Nature of the Macedonian State Under the Monarchy," *Chiron* 8 (1978), pp. 77–133.

Erxleben, E. "Das Münzgesetz des delisch-attischen Seebundes," *Archiv für Papyrusforschung* 19 (1969), pp. 91–139, 212; 20 (1970), pp. 66–132; 21 (1971), pp. 145–162.

Estrup, H. "Oresme and Monetary Theory," *Scandinavian Economic History Review* 14 (1966), pp. 97–116.

Euken, R. *Ueber den Sprachgebrauch des Aristoteles. Beobachtungen über die Praepositionen* (Berlin, 1868).

Felsch, R.C.S., H. J. Kienast, H. Schuler, G. Hübner, K. V. Woyski, and H. Becker. "Apollon und Artemis oder Artemis und Apollon? Bericht von der Grabungen im neu entdeckten Heiligtum bei Kalapodi 1973–1977," *AA* 1980, pp. 38–123.

Ferguson, W. S. *AJA* 39 (1935), pp. 154–155, review of M. Gude, *A History of Olynthus* (Baltimore, 1933).

Fine, J.V.A. "The Problem of Macedonian Holdings in Epirus and Thessaly in 221 B.C.," *TAPA* 63 (1932), pp. 126–155.

Finley, M. I. *The Ancient Economy* (London, 1973).

———. *Ancient Slavery and Modern Ideology* (London, 1980).

———. *Economy and Society in Ancient Greece,* ed. B. D. Shaw and R. P. Saller (London, 1981), for revised versions of "Was Greek Civilisation Based on Slave Labour?" *Historia* 8 (1959), pp. 145–164, and "The Athenian Empire: A Balance Sheet," in *Imperialism in the Ancient World,* ed. P.D.A. Garnsey and C. R. Whittaker (Cambridge, 1978), pp. 103–126.

———. *Politics in the Ancient World* (Cambridge, 1983).

———. "Classical Greece," in *Deuxième Conférence internationale d'histoire économique Aix-en-Provence, 1962, I: Trade and Politics in the Ancient World* (Paris, 1965, repr. New York, 1979), pp. 11–35.

———. *CR* 20 (1970), pp. 315–319, review of B. A. van Groningen and A. Wartelle, *Aristote. Economique* (Paris, 1968).

Firth, R. *Symbols. Public and Private* (Ithaca, 1973).

Forbes, R. J. *Studies in Ancient Technology,* vol. 8 (Leiden, 1964).

Fornara, C. W. *Translated Documents of Greece and Rome, 1. Archaic Times to the End of the Peloponnesian War* 2 (Cambridge, 1983).

Fowler, B. H. "Thucydides I.107–108 and the Tanagran Federal Issues," *Phoenix* 11 (1957), pp. 164–170.

Franke, P. R. "Geschichte, Politik und Münzprägung im frühen Makedonien," *JNG* 3–4 (1952–1953), pp. 99–111.

———. "Phethaloi–Phetaloi–Petthaloi–Thessaloi. Zur Geschichte Thessaliens im 5. Jahrhundert v. Chr.," *AA* 85 (1970), pp. 85–93.

Franklin, J. H. *Jean Bodin and the Rise of Absolutist Theory* (Cambridge, 1973).

Friedricksmeyer, E. A. "On the Final Aims of Philip II," in *Philip II, Alexander the Great and the Macedonian Heritage,* ed. W. L. Adams and E. N. Borza (Lanham, Md., 1982), pp. 85–98.

Frisk, H. *Griechisches etymologisches Wörterbuch,* vol. 2 (Heidelberg, 1970).

Fritze, H. von. "Sestos. Die Menas-Inschrift und das Münzwesen der Stadt," *Nomisma* 1 (1907), pp. 1–13.

Frye, R. N. *The History of Ancient Iran* (Munich, 1984).

Gallis, C. J. "A Short Chronicle of Greek Archaeological Investigations in Thessaly from 1881 until the Present Day," in *La Thessalie, Actes de la Table-Ronde 21–24 Juillet 1975 Lyon*, ed. B. Helly (Lyon, 1979), pp. 1–30.

Gardner, P. *British Museum Catalogue of Greek Coins. Thessaly to Aetolia* (London, 1883).

———. *A History of Ancient Coinage 700–300 B.C.* (Oxford, 1918).

Garlan, Y. *Les Esclaves en Grèce ancienne* (Paris, 1982).

Garnsey, P., T. Gallant, and D. Rathbone, "Thessaly and the Grain Supply of Rome During the Second Century B.C.," *JRS* 74 (1984), pp. 30–44.

Giacchero, M. "I motivi finanziari e commerciali dell'unione monetaria fra Mitilene e Focea," *RIN* 82 (1980), pp. 1–10.

Gillies, J. *The History of Ancient Greece, its Colonies and Conquests; from the Earliest Accounts till the Division of the Macedonian Empire in the East* (London, 1786).

———. *A View of the Reign of Frederick II of Prussia; with a parallel between that Prince and Philip II of Macedon* (Dublin, 1789).

Giovannini, A. *Rome et la circulation monétaire en Grèce au IIe siècle avant Jésus-Christ* (Basel, 1978, Schweizerische Beiträge zur Altertumswissenschaft 15).

Goldsmith, O. *The Grecian History from the Earliest State to the Death of Alexander the Great*² (London, 1800).

Goldstein, J. A. *I Maccabees* (Garden City, N.Y., 1976).

Goodenough, E. R. "The Political Philosophy of Hellenistic Kingship," *YCS* 1 (1928), pp. 55–102.

Goodyear, F. R. D. *The Annals of Tacitus Books 1–6. Vol. II* (Cambridge, 1981).

Graham, A. J. *Colony and Mother City in Ancient Greece* (Manchester, 1971).

Grant, M. *From Imperium to Auctoritas* (Cambridge, 1946).

Grierson, P. *Bibliographie numismatique* (Brussels, 1966).

———. "The Roman Law of Counterfeiting," in *Essays in Roman Coinage presented to Harold Mattingly*, ed. R.A.G. Carson and C.H.V. Sutherland (Oxford, 1956), pp. 240–261.

———. *Numismatics* (Oxford, 1975).

Griffin, A. *Sikyon* (Oxford, 1982).

Groningen, B. A. van. *Aristote. Le second livre de l'Economique* (Leiden, 1933).

Groningen, B. A. van, and A. Wartelle. *Aristote. Economique* (Paris, 1968).

Gruen, E. S. "Philip V and the Greek Demos," in *Ancient Macedonian Studies in Honor of Charles F. Edson* (Thessaloniki, 1981), pp. 169–182.

Gschnitzer, F. *Abhängige Orte im griechischen Altertum* (Munich, 1958, Zetemata 17).

———. "Namen und Wesen der thessalischen Tetraden," *Hermes* 82 (1954), pp. 451–464.

Gullath, B. *Untersuchungen zur Geschichte Boiotiens in der Zeit Alexanders und der Diadochen* (Frankfurt, 1982, Europäische Hochschulschriften. Reihe III. Geschichte und ihre Hilfswissenschaften 169).

Habicht, Ch. *Studien zur Geschichte Athens in hellenistischer Zeit* (Göttingen, 1982, Hypomnemata 73).

———. *Untersuchungen zur politischen Geschichte Athens im 3. Jahrhundert v. Chr.* (Munich, 1979, Vestigia 30).

———. "Eine neue Urkunde zur Geschichte Thessaliens unter der makedonischen Herrschaft," in *Ancient Macedonian Studies in Honor of Charles F. Edson* (Thessaloniki, 1981), pp. 193–198.

———. "Epigraphische Zeugnisse zur Geschichte Thessaliens unter der makedonischen Herrschaft," *Ancient Macedonia*, vol. 1 (Thessaloniki, 1970), pp. 265–279.

———. "Literarische und epigraphische Ueberlieferung zur Geschichte Alexanders und seiner ersten Nachfolger," in *Akten des VI. internationalen Kongresses für griechische und lateinische Epigraphik München 1972* (Munich, 1973), pp. 367–377.

Hackens, T. "A propos de la circulation monétaire dans le Péloponnèse au IIIe s. av. J.-C.," in *Antidorum W. Peremans sexagenario ab alumnis oblatum* (Louvain, 1968, Studia Hellenistica 16), pp. 69–95.

Hadot, P. "Fürstenspiegel," *Reallexikon für Antike und Christentum*, vol. 8 (Stuttgart, 1972), cols. 555–632.

Hallock, R. T. "A New Look at the Persepolis Treasury Tablets," *JNES* 19 (1960), pp. 90–100.

Hamilton, J. R. *Alexander the Great* (London, 1973).

Hammond, N.G.L. *Alexander the Great: King, Commander and Statesman* (Park Ridge, New Jersey, 1980).

———. *A History of Greece to 322 B.C.* ^{2} (Oxford, 1967).

———. "The Lettering and the Iconography of 'Macedonian' Coinage," in *Ancient Greek Art and Iconography*, ed. W. G. Moon (Madison, 1983), pp. 245–258.

———. "The Narrative of Herodotus VII and the Decree of Themistocles at Troezen," *JHS* 102 (1982), pp. 75–93.

Hammond, N.G.L. and G. T. Griffith. *A History of Macedonia. Volume II. 550–336 B.C.* (Oxford, 1979).

Hannick, J.-M. "Remarques sur les lettres de Philippe V de Macédoine à la cité de Larissa (*IG* IX, 2, 517)," in *Antidorum W. Peremans sexagenario ab alumnis oblatum* (Louvain, 1968, Studia Hellenistica 16), pp. 97–104.

Harris, E. M. "The Political Career of Aeschines" (Diss., Harvard University, 1983).

Hartung, F. *Deutsche Verfassungsgeschichte vom 15. Jahrhundert bis zur Gegenwart* [7] (Stuttgart, 1950).

Hatzopoulos, M. B. "The Oleveni Inscription and the Dates of Philip II's Reign," in *Philip II, Alexander the Great and the Macedonian Heritage*, ed. W. L. Adams and E. N. Borza (Lanham, Md., 1982), pp. 21–42.

Hauben, H. "Rhodes, Alexander and the Diadochi from 333/332 to 304 B.C.," *Historia* 26 (1977), pp. 307–339.

Hawkes, T. *Structuralism and Semiotics* (Berkeley, 1977).

Hayek, F. A. *Denationalisation of Money: The Argument Refined. An Analysis of the Theory and Practice of Concurrent Currencies* [2] (London, 1978).

Head, B. V. *Catalogue of the Greek Coins of Lydia* (British Museum, London, 1901).

———. *Historia Numorum* (Oxford, 1887).

———. *Historia Numorum* [2] (Oxford, 1911).

———. *On the Chronological Sequence of the Coins of Boeotia* (London, 1881).

Heisserer, A. J. *Alexander the Great and the Greeks. The Epigraphic Evidence* (Norman, Okla., 1980).

Helly, B. "Une liste des cités de Perrhébie dans la première moitié du IVe siècle avant J.-C.," in *La Thessalie, Actes de la Table-Ronde 21–24 Juillet 1975 Lyon*, ed. B. Helly (Lyon, 1979), pp. 165–200.

Helly, B., G. J. Te Riele, and J. A. Van Rossum. "La liste des gymnasiarches de Phères pour les années 330–189 av. J.-C.," in *La Thessalie, Actes de la Table-Ronde 21–24 Juillet 1975 Lyon*, ed. B. Helly (Lyon, 1979), pp. 220–255.

Herrmann, F. "Die Silbermünzen von Larissa in Thessalien," *ZfN* 35 (1924–1925), pp. 1–69.

———. "Die thessalische Münzunion im 5. Jahrhundert," *ZfN* 33 (1922), pp. 33–43.

Heuss, A. *Stadt und Herrscher des Hellenismus* (Leipzig, 1937, Klio Beiheft 26).

———. "Die Freiheitserklärung von Mylasa in den Inschriften von Labranda," in *Le Monde grec. Pensée, littérature, histoire, documents. Hommages à Claire Préaux*, ed. J. Bingen, G. Cambier, and

G. Nachtergael (Brussels, 1975), pp. 403–415.

Heyman, C. "Achille-Alexandre sur les monnaies de Larissa Cremaste en Thessalie," in *Antidorum W. Peremans sexagenario ab alumnis oblatum* (Louvain, 1968, Studia Hellenistica 16), pp. 115–125.

Higgins, W. E. "Aspects of Alexander's Imperial Administration: Some Modern Methods and Views Reviewed," *Athenaeum* 58 (1980), pp. 129–152.

Holloway, R. R. "An Archaic Hoard from Crete and the Early Aeginetan Coinage," *ANSMN* 17 (1971), pp. 1–21.

———. "Il problema dei 'pegasi' in Sicilia," *Quaderni ticinesi. Numismatica e antichità classiche* 11 (1982), pp. 129–136.

———. "La ricerca attuale sull'origine della moneta," *RIN* 80 (1978), pp. 7–14.

Hooker, J. T. "Thessalian ΤΑΓΑ," *ZPE* 40 (1980), p. 272.

Hornblower, S. *Mausolus* (Oxford, 1982).

An Inventory of Greek Coin Hoards, ed. M. Thompson, O. Mørkholm, and C. M. Kraay (New York, 1973).

Isager, S. and M. H. Hansen. *Aspects of Athenian Society in the Fourth Century B.C.* (Odense, 1975, Odense Univ. Class. St. 5).

Jaschinski, S. *Alexander und Griechenland unter dem Eindruck der Flucht des Harpalos* (Bonn, 1981, Habelts Dissertationsdrucke, Reihe alte Geschichte 14).

Jeffery, L. H. *Archaic Greece: The City-States c. 700–500 B.C.* (London, 1976).

Jenkins, G. K. "A Note on Corinthian Coins in the West," in *Centennial Publication of the American Numismatic Society*, ed. Harald Ingholt (New York, 1958), pp. 367–379.

Jones, A. H. M. *The Greek City from Alexander to Justinian* (Oxford, 1940).

Jouvenal, B. de. *Sovereignty. An Inquiry into the Political Good*, trans. J. F. Huntington (Chicago, 1957).

Kahrstedt, U. "Grundherrschaft, Freistadt und Staat in Thessalien," in *Nachrichten von der Gesellschaft der Wissenschaften zu Göttingen aus dem Jahre 1924. Philologisch-Historische Klasse* (Berlin, 1925), pp. 128–155.

Kaiser, W. B. "Alexander and Mytilene," in *Münzen und Medaillensammler Berichte aus allen Gebieten der Geld-, Münzen- und Medaillenkunde* (Freiburg, 1970), pp. 795–800.

Kann, R. A. *A History of the Hapsburg Empire 1526–1918* (Berkeley, 1974).

Karst, J. *Die Chronik des Eusebius* (Leipzig, 1911).

Keynes, J. M. *A Treatise on Money*, vol. 1. *The Pure Theory of Money* (London, 1930).

Kienast, D. *Augustus: Prinzeps und Monarch* (Darmstadt, 1982).

————. *Philipp II von Makedonien und das Reich der Achaimeniden* (Munich, 1973, Abhandlungen der Marburger Gelehrten Gesellschaft 6).

————. *RE* 47, *s. v.* "Pyrrhos" (13).

Kinns, P. "The Amphictyonic Coinage Reconsidered," *NC* 1983, pp. 1–22.

Kirsten, E. *RE* suppl. 7, *s. v.* "Pherai."

Kleiner, G. "Zur Chronologie der Münzen von Abdera," *JNG* 2 (1950–1951), pp. 14–20.

Knapp, R. C. "The Date and Purpose of the Iberian Denarii," *NC* 1977, pp. 1–18.

Koeppler, J. "Frederick Barbarossa and the Schools of Bologna: Some Remarks on the 'Authentica Habita,'" *English Historical Review* 54 (1939), pp. 577–607.

Koerner, R. "Die Bedeutung von πόλις und verwandten Begriffe nach Aussage der Inschriften," in *Soziale Typenbegriffe im alten Griechenland und ihr Fortleben in den Sprachen der Welt. Band 3. Untersuchungen ausgewählter altgriechischer sozialer Typenbegriffe*, ed. E. C. Welskopf (Berlin, 1981), pp. 360–367.

Kondis, S. "A propos des monnayages royaux lagides en Cyrénaïque sous Ptolémée Iᵉʳ et II," *RBN* 124 (1978), pp. 23–47.

Koumanoudes, S. N. "Prosopographika Thebaikon nomismaton," *Neon Athenaion* 5 (1964–1966), pp. 62–69.

Kraay, C. *Archaic and Classical Greek Coins* (Berkeley, 1976).

————. *Greek Coins and History* (London, 1969).

————. "The Coinage of Ambracia and the Preliminaries of the Peloponnesian War," *Quaderni ticinesi. Numismatica e antichità classiche* 8 (1979), pp. 37–66.

————. "The Earliest Issue of Ambracia," *Quaderni ticinesi. Numismatica e antichità classiche* 6 (1977), pp. 35–52.

————. "Timoleon and Corinthian Coinage in Sicily," in *Actes du 8ème Congrès internationale de numismatique New York-Washington 1973* (Paris, 1976), pp. 99–105.

————. *NC* 1977, pp. 189–198, review of M. J. Price and N. M. Waggoner, *Archaic Greek Coins. The Asyut Hoard* (London, 1975).

Kramolisch, H. *Demetrias II. Die Strategen des thessalischen Bundes vom Jahr 196 v. Chr. bis zum Ausgang der römischen Republik* (Bonn, 1978, Beiträge zur ur- und frühgeschichtlichen Archäologie des Mittelmeer-Kulturraumes 18).

Kreissig, H. *Wirtschaft und Gesellschaft im Seleukidenreich* (Berlin, 1978,

Schriften zur Geschichte und Kultur der Antike 16).

Kroll, J. H. "A Chronology of Early Athenian Bronze Coinage, *ca.* 350–250 B.C.," in *Greek Numismatics and Archaeology. Essays in Honor of Margaret Thompson*, ed. O. Mørkholm and N. M. Waggoner (Wetteren, 1979), pp. 139–154.

———. "From Wappenmünzen to Gorgoneia to Owls," *ANSMN* 26 (1981), pp. 1–32.

Lacroix, L. "Les 'blasons' des villes grecques," in *Études d'archéologie classique, I, 1955–1956* (Paris, 1958, Annales de l'Est, Mémoire 19), pp. 89–115.

Landry, A. *Le Moyen Age* 22 (1909), pp. 145–178, review of E. Bridrey, *Nicole Oresme* (Paris, 1906).

Larsen, J.A.O. *Greek Federal States* (Oxford, 1967).

———. "The Thessalian Tetrades in Plutarch's *Moralia* 822 E," *CP* 58 (1963), p. 240.

Lattimore, S. "The Chlamys of Daochus I," *AJA* 79 (1975), pp. 87–88.

Laurenti, R. *Studi sull'Economico attribuito ad Aristotele* (Milan, 1968).

Lehmann, G. A. "Der 'Erste Heilige Krieg'—eine Fiktion?" *Historia* 29 (1980), pp. 242–246.

———. "Thessaliens Hegemonie über Mittelgriechenland im 6. Jh. v. Chr.," *Boreas* 6 (1983), pp. 35–43.

Leland, T. *The History of the Life and Reign of Philip King of Macedon* 2 (London, 1775).

Le Rider, G. *Le Monnayage d'argent et d'or de Philippe II frappé en Macédoine de 359 à 294* (Paris, 1977).

———. "Les monnaies," in *Fouilles d'Aï Khanoum I. Campagnes de 1965, 1966, 1967, 1968*, ed. P. Bernard (Paris, 1973, Mémoires de la délégation archéologique française en Afghanistan 21), pp. 203–205.

———. "Numismatique grecque," in *Annuaire 1968–1969. Ecole pratique des Hautes Etudes. IVe section. Sciences historiques et philologiques* (Paris, 1969), pp. 173–187; and *Annuaire 1969–1970* (Paris, 1970), pp. 255–269; *Annuaire 1970–1971* (Paris, 1971), pp. 241–262.

Lévêque, P. *Pyrrhos* (Paris, 1957).

Levi, M. A. "Studi Tolemaici I. Moneta e politica dei primi Tolemei," *Parola del passato* 30 (1975), pp. 192–200.

Lewis, D. M. "Entrenchment-Clauses in Attic Decrees," in ΦΟΡΟΣ. *Tribute to Benjamin Dean Meritt*, ed. D. W. Bradeen and M. F. McGregor (Locust Valley, N.Y., 1974), pp. 81–89.

Lintott, A. *Violence, Civil Strife and Revolution in the Classical City 750–330 B.C.* (Baltimore, 1982).

Lock, R. "The Macedonian Army Assembly in the Time of Alexander the Great," *CP* 72 (1977), pp. 91–107.

314   BIBLIOGRAPHY

Lotze, D. Μεταξὺ ἐλευθέρων καὶ δούλων. *Studien zur Rechtsstellung unfreier Landbevölkerungen in Griechenland bis zum 4. Jahrhundert v. Chr.* (Berlin, 1959, Deutsche Akademie der Wissenschaften zu Berlin. Schriften der Sektion für Altertumswissenschaft 17).

Mably, Abbé G. B. *Observations sur les Grecs* (Geneva, 1749).

McRae, K. D. *Jean Bodin. The Six Bookes of a Commonweale* (Cambridge, Mass., 1962).

Mandel, J. "Jason: The Tyrant of Pherae, Tagus of Thessaly, as reflected in Ancient Sources and Modern Literature: The Image of the 'New Tyrant,'" *Rivista storica dell'antichità* 10 (1980), pp. 47–77.

Manganaro, G. "La caduta dei Dinomenidi e il *politikon nomisma* in Sicilia nella prima metà del V sec. a. C.," *AIIN* 21–22 (1974–1975), pp. 9–40.

Martin, T. R. "The Chronology of the Fourth-Century B.C. Facing-Head Silver Coinage of Larissa," *ANSMN* 28 (1983), pp. 1–34.

———. "Diodorus on Philip II and Thessaly in the 350s B.C.," *CP* 76 (1981), pp. 188–201.

———. "A Phantom Fragment of Theopompus and Philip II's First Campaign in Thessaly," *HSCP* 86 (1982), pp. 55–78.

———. "A Third-Century B.C. Hoard from Thessaly at the ANS (IGCH 168)," *ANSMN* 26 (1981), pp. 51–77.

Mastrocinque, A. "Storia e monetazione di Mileto all'epoca dei Diadochi," *AIIN* 27–28 (1980–1981), pp. 61–78.

Matheson, J. R. *Canada's Flag. A Search for a Country* (Boston, 1980).

Mathieu, G. *Isocrate. Tome IV*, ed. with E. Brémond (Paris, 1962).

Mathisen, R. W. "Antigonus Gonatas and the Silver Coinages of Macedonia circa 280–270 B.C.," *ANSMN* 26 (1981), pp. 79–124.

Mattingly, H. *Roman Coins* 2 (London, 1967).

———. "Coins and Amphoras—Chios, Samos and Thasos in the Fifth Century B.C.," *JHS* 101 (1981), pp. 78–86.

———. "The Protected Fund in the Athenian Coinage Decree (ATL D 14, par. 7f.)," *AJP* 95 (1974), pp. 280–285.

———. "The Second Athenian Coinage Decree," *Klio* 59 (1977), pp. 83–100.

May, J.M.F. *Ainos. Its History and Coinage 474–341 B.C.* (Oxford, 1950).

———. *The Coinage of Abdera 540–345 B.C.* (Oxford, 1966).

———. *The Coinage of Damastion and the Lesser Coinages of the Illyro-Paeonian Region* (Oxford, 1939).

———. *NC* 1953, pp. 165–170, review of D. Raymond, *Macedonian Regal Coinage to 413 B.C.* (New York, 1953).

Meiggs, R. *The Athenian Empire* (Oxford, 1972).

Meiggs, R., and D. Lewis. *A Selection of Greek Historical Inscriptions to the End of the Fifth Century* (Oxford, 1969).

Meikle, S. "Aristotle and the Political Economy of the Polis," *JHS* 99 (1979), pp. 57–73.

Melville-Jones, J. R. "Epigraphical Notes on Hellenistic Bronze Coinage," *NC* 1972, pp. 39–43.

———. "The Value of Gold at Athens in 329/8 B.C.," *AJAH* 3 (1978), pp. 184–187.

Mendels, D. "Polybius, Philip V and the Socio-Economic Question in Greece," *Ancient Society* 8 (1977), pp. 155–174.

Menut, A. D. *Maistre Nicole Oresme. Le livre de Politiques d'Aristote* (Philadelphia, 1970).

Meritt, B.D., H. T. Wade-Gery and M. F. McGregor. *The Athenian Tribute List* (Cambridge, Mass., 1939–1953).

Merker, I. L. "Lysimachos—Thessalian or Macedonian?" *Chiron* 9 (1979), pp. 31–36.

Millar, F. "The Phoenician Cities: A Case-Study of Hellenisation," *Proceedings of the Cambridge Philological Society* 209 (1983), pp. 55–71.

Milojčič, V., and D. Theocharis, eds. *Demetrias I* (Bonn, 1976, Beiträge zur ur- und frühgeschichtlichen Archäologie des Mittelmeer-Kulturraumes 12).

Minguijón, S. *Historia del derecho espagñol* 4 (Barcelona, 1953).

Momigliano, A. "George Grote and the Study of Greek History," in *Studies in Historiography* (London, 1966), pp. 56–74.

———. "Tagia e tetrarchia in Tessaglia," *Athenaeum* 10 (1932), pp. 47–53.

Montanari, G. *Della Moneta* (1687), in *Scrittori classici italiani di economia politica. Parte antica*, vol. 3 (Milan, 1804).

Moore, N. J. "The Lifetime and Early Posthumous Coinage of Alexander the Great from Pella" (Diss., Princeton University, 1984).

Moreau, J. "Aristote et la monnaie," *REG* 82 (1969), pp. 349–364.

Moretti, L. *Iscrizioni storiche ellenistiche*, vol. 1 (Florence, 1967), vol. 2 (Florence, 1975).

Mørkholm, O. "Cyrene and Ptolemy I: Some Numismatic Comments," *Chiron* 10 (1980), pp. 145–159.

———. "The Hellenistic Period. Greece to India," in *A Survey of Numismatic Research 1972–1977*, ed. R. Carson, P. Berghaus and N. Lowick (Berne, 1979), pp. 60–97.

Morrison, J. S. "Meno of Pharsalus, Polycrates and Ismenias," *CQ* 36 (1942), pp. 57–78.

Morrow, G. R. *Plato's Cretan City: A Historical Interpretation of the Laws* (Princeton, 1960).

Mosshammer, A. A. *The Chronicle of Eusebius and Greek Chronographic Tradition* (Lewisburg, Pa., 1979).

Müller, L. *Numismatique d'Alexandre le Grand suivie d'un appendice contenant les monnaies de Philippe II et III* (Copenhagen, 1855).

Müller, O. *Antigonos Monophthalmos und "das Jahr der Könige"* (Bonn, 1973, Saarbrücker Beiträge zur Altertumskunde 11).

Monroe, A. E. *Monetary Theory before Adam Smith* (Cambridge, Mass., 1923), pp. 91-92.

Munz, P. *Frederick Barbarossa: A Study in Medieval Politics* (London, 1969).

Newell, E. T. *Alexander Hoards III. Andritsaena* (New York, 1923, Numismatic Notes and Monographs 21).

———. *Alexander Hoards IV. Olympia* (New York, 1929, Numismatic Notes and Monographs 39).

———. *The Coinages of Demetrius Poliorcetes* (London, 1927).

———. *The Coinage of the Western Seleucid Mints from Seleucus I to Antiochus III* (New York, 1941, reissued 1977 with a summary of recent scholarship by O. Mørkholm).

———. *Reattribution of Certain Tetradrachms of Alexander the Great* (New York, 1912) = *American Journal of Numismatics* 45 (1911), pp. 1-10, 37-45, 113-125, 194-200, and *American Journal of Numismatics* 46 (1912), pp. 22-24, 37-49, 109-116.

Oakley, J. H. "The Autonomous Wreathed Tetradrachms of Kyme, Aeolis," *ANSMN* 27 (1982), pp. 1-37.

Oeconomides, M. Caramessini. "Contribution à l'étude du monnayage d'Alexandre le Grand. A propos d'un trésor inédit du Musée Numismatique d'Athènes," *Studia Paulo Naster Oblata I. Numismatica Antiqua*, ed. S. Scheers (Leuven, 1982, Orientalia Lovaniensia Analecta 12), pp. 89-96.

———. "Deux trésors de statères éginètes au Cabinet des Médailles d'Athènes," *SM* 30 (1980), pp. 81-90.

———. "The 1970 Myrina Hoard of Aeginetan Staters," in *Greek Numismatics and Archaeology. Essays in Honor of Margaret Thompson*, ed. O. Mørkholm and N. M. Waggoner (Wetteren, 1979), pp. 231-239.

Oman, C. "Some Problems of the Later Coinage of Corinth," *NC* 1926, pp. 20-35.

Orth, W. *Königlicher Machtanspruch und städtische Freiheit* (Munich, 1977, Münchener Beiträge zur Papyrusforschung und antiken Rechtsgeschichte 71).

Ostwald, M. *Autonomia: Its Genesis and Early History* (Chico, Ca., 1982, American Classical Studies 11).

Ott, I. "Der Regalienbegriff im 12. Jahrhundert," *Zeitschrift der Savigny-Stiftung für Rechtsgeschichte, Kanonistische Abteilung* 35 (1948), pp. 234–304.

Papahadjis, N. D. "Magnesia polis, 'at the foot of Mount Pelium,'" *Thessalika* 2 (1959), pp. 22–28.

Patin, C. *Introduction à l'histoire par la connaissance des médailles* (Paris, 1665).

Peek, W. "Griechische Inschriften," *AthMitt* 59 (1934), pp. 35–80.

Pegan, E. "Die frühesten Tetradrachmen Alexanders des Grossen mit dem Adler, ihre Herkunft und Entstehungszeit," *JNG* 18 (1968), pp. 99–111.

Petitot-Biehler, C. Y., and P. Bernard. "Trésor de monnaies grecques et gréco-bactriennes trouvé à Aï Khanoum (Afghanistan)," *RN* 1975, pp. 23–69.

Picard, O. *Chalcis et la confédération eubéenne: étude de numismatique et d'histoire (IV ^{e}-I ^{er} siècle)* (Athens, 1979, Bibliothèque des Ecoles françaises d'Athènes et de Rome 234).

Pleket, H. W. *Epigraphica*, vol. 1 (Leiden, 1964).

Pouilloux, J. *Recherches sur l'histoire et les cultes de Thasos*, vol. 1. *De la fondation de la cité à 196 avant J.-C.* (Paris, 1954, Ecole française d'Athènes. Etudes thasiennes 3).

Préaux, C. *Le monde hellénistique. La Grèce et l'Orient (323–146 av. J.-C.)*, vol. 1 (Paris, 1978).

Prestianni Giallombardo, A. M. "'Diritto' matrimoniale ereditario e dinastico nella Macedonia di Filippo II," *RSA* 6–7 (1976–1977), pp. 81–110.

Price, M. J. *Coins of the Macedonians* (London, 1974).

———. "Alexander's Reform of the Macedonian Regal Coinage," *NC* 1982, pp. 180–190.

———. "The Coinage of Philip II," *NC* 1979, pp. 230–241.

———. "Early Greek Bronze Coinage," in *Essays in Greek Coinage Presented to Stanley Robinson*, ed. C. M. Kraay and G. K. Jenkins (Oxford, 1968), pp. 90–104.

———. "The Function of Early Greek Coinage," *Le Origini della monetazione di bronzo in Sicilia e in Magna Grecia. Atti del VI Convegno del Centro Internazionale di Studi Numismatici Napoli 1977, AIIN* 25 suppl. (1979), pp. 351–358.

———. "On Attributing Alexanders—Some Cautionary Tales," in *Greek Numismatics and Archaeology. Essays in Honor of Margaret Thompson*, ed. O. Mørkholm and N. M. Waggoner (Wetteren, 1979), pp.

241–250.

―――. "Thoughts on the Beginnings of Coinage," in *Studies in Numismatic Method Presented to Philip Grierson*, ed. C.N.L. Brooke, B.H.I.H. Stewart, J. G. Pollard, and T. R. Volk (Cambridge, 1983), pp. 1–10.

Price, M. J., and N. M. Waggoner. *Archaic Greek Coinage. The Asyut Hoard* (London, 1975).

Pufendorf, S. "De rebus gestis Philippi Amyntae F.," in *Dissertationes Academicae Selectiores* (Lund, 1675), pp. 109–195.

Raaflaub, K. "Zum Freiheitsbegriff der Griechen. Materialien und Untersuchungen zur Bedeutungsentwicklung von ἐλεύθερος/ἐλευθερία in der archaischen und klassischen Zeit," in *Soziale Typenbegriffe im alten Griechenland und ihr Fortleben in den Sprachen der Welt. Band 4. Untersuchungen ausgewählter altgriechischer sozialer Typenbegriffe und ihr Fortleben in Antike und Mittelalter*, ed. E. C. Welskopf (Berlin, 1981), pp. 180–405.

Ravel, O. *The "Colts" of Ambracia* (New York, 1928, Numismatic Notes and Monographs 37).

―――. *Corinthian Hoards (Corinth and Arta)* (New York, 1932, Numismatic Notes and Monographs 52).

―――. *Les "poulains" de Corinthe*, vol. 2 (London, 1948).

―――. "Corinthian Hoard from Chiliomodi," in *Transactions of the International Numismatic Congress*, ed. J. Allan, H. Mattingly, and E.S.G. Robinson (London, 1938), pp. 98–108.

Raven, E.J.P. "The Amphictyonic Coinage of Delphi 336–334 B.C.," *NC* 1950, pp. 1–22.

Raymond, D. *Macedonian Regal Coinage to 413 B.C.* (New York, 1953, Numismatic Notes and Monographs 126).

Regling, K. "Phygela, Klazomenai, Amphipolis," *ZfN* 33 (1922), pp. 46–67.

Rey-Coquais, J.-P. *Arados et sa Pérée aux époques grecque, romaine et byzantine* (Paris, 1974, Institut français d'archéologie de Beyrouth. Bibliothèque archéologique et historique 97).

Rhodes, P. J. *A Commentary on the Aristotelian Athenaion Politeia* (Oxford, 1981).

Riesenberg, P. N. *Inalienability of Sovereignty in Medieval Political Thought* (New York, 1956).

Robert, L. *Monnaies antiques en Troade* (Geneva, 1966, Hautes Etudes numismatiques I.1).

―――. *Monnaies grecques. Types, légendes, magistrats monétaires et géographie* (Geneva, 1967, Hautes Etudes numismatiques I.2).

―――. "Les monétaires et un décret hellénistique de Sestos," *RN* 1973, pp. 43–53.

―――. "Monnaies dans les inscriptions grecques," *RN* 1962, pp. 7–24.

Robertson, N. "The Myth of the First Sacred War," *CQ* 28 (1978), pp. 38–73.

―――. "The Thessalian Expedition of 480 B.C.," *JHS* 96 (1976), pp. 100–120.

Robinson, D. M., and P. A. Clement. *Excavations at Olynthus Part IX. The Chalcidic Mint and the Excavation Coins Found in 1928–1934* (Baltimore, 1938).

Roesch, P. *Etudes béotiennes* (Paris, 1982, Institut Fernand-Courby. Centre de recherches archéologiques URA 15).

Rogers, E. *The Copper Coinage of Thessaly* (London, 1932).

Rollin, C. *Histoire ancienne*, vol. 3 (Paris, 1740).

Roscher, W. H. *Ausführliches Lexikon der griechischen und römischen Mythologie*, vol. 5 (Leipzig, 1916–1924).

Rosen, K. "Der 'göttliche' Alexander, Athen und Samos," *Historia* 27 (1978), pp. 20–39.

Rostovtzeff, M. *The Social and Economic History of the Hellenistic World* (Oxford, 1953).

Roux, G. *L'Amphictionie, Delphes et le temple d'Apollon au IVᵉ siècle* (Lyon, 1979, Collection de la Maison de L'Orient méditerranéen 8, série archéologique 6).

Sabine, G. H. (revised by T. L. Thorson). *A History of Political Theory* 4 (Hinsdale, Ill., 1973).

Ste. Croix, G.E.M. de. *The Class Struggle in the Ancient Greek World* (London, 1981).

―――. *The Origins of the Peloponnesian War* (Ithaca, 1972).

Salmon, P. *Etude sur la Confédération béotienne (447/6–386)* (Brussels, 1978, Académie royale de Belgique, Mémoires de la classe des lettres 63,3).

Schlumberger, D. *L'argent grec dans l'empire archéménide* (Paris, 1953) = R. Curiel and D. Schlumberger, *Trésors monétaires d'Afghanistan* (Paris, 1953, Mémoires de la délégation archéologique française en Afghanistan 14), pp. 1–64.

Schlumberger D., and P. Bernard. "Aï Khanoum," *BCH* 89 (1965), pp. 590–657.

Schmitt, H. H. *Die Staatsverträge des Altertums III. Die Verträge der griechisch-römischen Welt von 338 bis 200 v. Chr.* (Munich, 1969).

Schmitz, H. *Ein Gesetz der Stadt Olbia zum Schutze ihres Silbergeldes* (Freiburg in Baden, 1925).

Schoene, A. *Eusebii Chronicorum Liber Prior* (Berlin, 1931).

Schönert-Geiss, E. "Das Geld im Hellenismus," *Klio* 60 (1978), pp. 131–136.

Schürer, E. *The History of the Jewish People in the Age of Jesus Christ (175 B.C.–A.D. 135)*, rev. G. Vermes and F. Millar, vol. 1 (Edinburgh, 1973).

Scranton, R. L. *Corinth Vol. I, Part II. Monuments in the Lower Agora and North of the Archaic Temple* (Princeton, 1951).

Sealey, R. "Dionysius of Halicarnassus and Some Demosthenic Dates," *REG* 68 (1955), pp. 77–120.

Segre, M. "Grano di Tessaglia a Coo," *Rivista di filologia* 12 (1934), pp. 169–193.

Seibert, J. *Alexander der Grosse* (Darmstadt, 1972, Erträge der Forschung 10).

———. *Die politischen Flüchtlinge und Verbannten in der griechischen Geschichte* (Darmstadt, 1979, Impulse der Forschung 30), vol. 1.

———. *Das Zeitalter der Diadochen* (Darmstadt, 1983, Erträge der Forschung 185).

Seltman, C. T. *Greek Coins* 2 (London, 1955).

———. *The Temple Coins of Olympia* (Cambridge, 1921).

Seyrig, H. *Notes on Syrian Coins* (New York, 1950, Numismatic Notes and Monographs 119).

———. "Ardus et sa pérée sous les rois Séleucides," *Syria* 28 (1951), pp. 206–220 = *Antiquités Syriennes* (Paris, 1953), pp. 185–200.

———. "Monnaies hellénistiques XII. Questions aradiennes," *RN* 1964, pp. 9–50.

———. "Monnaies hellénistiques de Byzance et de Calcédoine," in *Essays in Greek Coinage Presented to Stanley Robinson*, ed. C. M. Kraay and G. K. Jenkins (Oxford, 1968), pp. 183–200.

———. "Parion au 3e siècle avant notre ère," in *Centennial Publication of the American Numismatic Society*, ed. Harald Ingholt (New York, 1958), pp. 603–625.

Shelov, D. B. *Coinage of the Bosporus VI-II Centuries B.C.*, trans. H. B. Wells (Oxford, 1978, British Archaeological Reports International Series, suppl. 46).

Sinclair, T. A. *Aristotle. The Politics* (Harmondsworth, 1962).

Shishova, I. A. "The status of the *penestai*," *VDI* 3 (133) 1975, pp. 39–57 (in Russian with English summary).

Sivignon, M. *La Thessalie. Analyse géographique d'une province grecque* (Lyon, 1975, Institut des études rhodaniennes. Mémoires et documents 17).

Snodgrass, A. *Archaic Greece* (Berkeley, 1980).

Sordi, M. *La lega tessala fino ad Alessandro Magno* (Rome, 1958).

————. "Aspetti della propaganda tessala a Delfi," in *La Thessalie, Actes de la Table-Ronde 21–24 Juillet 1975 Lyon,* ed. B. Helly (Lyon, 1979), pp. 157–164.

————. "La dracma di Aleuas e l'origine di un tipo monetario di Alessandro Magno," *AIIN* 3 (1956), pp. 9–22.

Stählin, Fr. *Das hellenische Thessalien* (Stuttgart, 1924).

Stählin, Fr., E. Meyer, and A. Heidner. *Pagasai und Demetrias. Beschreibung der Reste und Stadtgeschichte* (Berlin, 1934).

Stanyan, T. *The Grecian History* (London, 1751).

Stroud, R. S. "An Athenian Law on Silver Coinage," *Hesperia* 43 (1974), pp. 157–188.

————. "Three Attic Decrees," *CSCA* 7 (1974), pp. 281–298.

Sutherland, C.H.V. *The Emperor and the Coinage. Julio-Claudian Studies* (London, 1976).

————. *The Roman Imperial Coinage,* vol. 6. *From Diocletian's Reform (A.D. 294) to the Death of Maximinus (A.D. 313)* (London, 1973).

————. "Some Observations on the Coinage of Augustus," *Quaderni ticinesi. Numismatica e antichità classiche* 7 (1978), pp. 163–178.

Sutton, R. F. "The Populonia Coinage and the Second Punic War," in *Contributi introduttivi allo studio della monetazione etrusca. Atti del V Convegno del Centro Internazionale di Studi Numismatici Napoli 1975, AIIN* 22 suppl. (1976, publ. 1977), pp. 199–211.

Swan, C. *Canada: Symbols of Sovereignty* (Toronto, 1977).

Taillardat, J., and P. Roesch. "L'inventaire sacré de Thespies. L'alphabet attique en Béotie," *Revue de philologie* 40 (1966), pp. 70–87.

Talbert, R.J.A. *Timoleon and the Revival of Greek Sicily 344–317 B.C.* (Cambridge, 1974).

Tarn, W. W. *Antigonus Gonatas* (Oxford, 1913).

————. Chap. 14, "Greece: 335 to 321 B.C.," and chap. 15, "The Heritage of Alexander," in *Cambridge Ancient History. Vol. VI. Macedon 401–301 B.C.* (Cambridge, 1927).

Thillet, P. "Les économiques d'Aristote," *REG* 82 (1969), pp. 563–589.

Thiron, M. *Les Trésors monétaires gaulois et romains trouvés en Belgique* (Brussels, 1967).

Thompson, M. "The Cavalla Hoard (IGCH 450)," *ANSMN* 26 (1981), pp. 33–49.

————. "Posthumous Philip II Staters of Asia Minor," in *Studia Paulo Naster Oblata I. Numismatica Antiqua,* ed. S. Scheers (Leuven, 1982, Orientalia Lovaniensia Analecta 12), pp. 57–61.

Tod, M. N. *A Selection of Greek Historical Inscriptions Vol. II. From 403 to 323 B.C.* (Oxford, 1948).

Tourreil, J. de. *Démosthène. Oeuvres* (Paris, 1721).

Trifone, R. "La variazione del valore della moneta nel pensiero di Bartolo," in *Bartolo di Sassoferrato. Studi e documenti per il VI centenario* (Milan, 1962), vol. 2, pp. 691–704.

Troxell, H. "The Peloponnesian Alexanders," *ANSMN* 17 (1971), pp. 41–94.

Vinogradov, J. G. *Olbia. Geschichte einer altgriechischen Stadt am Schwarzen Meer* (Constance, 1981, Xenia. Konstanzer althistorische Vorträge und Forschungen 1).

Vinogradov, J. G., and P. O. Karyskowski. "The Canobus Decree on Money from Olbia and the Value of Precious Metals on the Black Sea in the Fourth Century," *VDI* 4 (138) 1976, pp. 20–42 (in Russian with English summary).

Wachsmuth, W. *Hellenische Altertumskunde aus dem Gesichtspunkte des Staats* (Halle, 1828, 2nd ed. 1846).

Waddington, W.-H. "I. Trovaille de Saïda," *RN* 1865, pp. 3–25.

Wade-Gery, H. T. "Jason of Pherae and Aleuas the Red," *JHS* 44 (1924), pp. 55–64.

Wankel, H. *Demosthenes. Rede für Ktesiphon. Ueber den Kranz* (Heidelberg, 1976).

————. "Bemerkungen zu dem athenischen Münzgesetz von 375/4," *ZPE* 52 (1983), pp. 69–74.

Wąsowicz, A. *Olbia pontique et son territoire* (Paris, 1975, Univ. Besançon annales littéraires 168, Centre du recherches d'histoire ancienne 13).

Welles, C. B. *Royal Correspondence in the Hellenistic Period: A Study in Greek Epigraphy* (London, 1934).

Westermann, W. L. "New Historical Documents in Greek and Roman History," *American Historical Review* 35 (1929–1930), pp. 14–32.

Westermark, U. "Notes on the Saïda Hoard (*IGCH* 1508)," *Nordisk Numismatik Årsskrift* 1979–1980, pp. 22–35.

Westlake, H. D. *Thessaly in the Fourth Century B.C.* (London, 1935).

————. "The Aftermath of the Lamian War," *CR* 63 (1949), pp. 87–90.

Wilhelm, A. "Zu Ehren des Pelopidas," *Oesterr. Jahreshefte* 33 (1941), pp. 35–45.

Will, Ed. *Histoire politique du monde hellénistique Tome I* 2 (Nancy, 1979), *Tome II* 2 (Nancy, 1982).

————. "Les sources des métaux monnayés dans le monde grec," and "Fonctions de la monnaie dans les cités grecques de l'époque classique," in *Numismatique antique. Problèmes et méthodes*, ed. J.-M. Dentzer, Ph. Gautier, and T. Hackens (Nancy, 1975, Etudes d'archéologie classique 4), pp. 97–102 and 233–246.

Will, Ed., C. Mossé, and P. Goukowsky. *Le monde grec et l'orient. Tome II. Le IVᵉ siècle et l'époque hellénistique* (Paris, 1975).

Williams, R. T. *The Silver Coinage of the Phokians* (London, 1972).

Zervos, O. H. "The Earliest Coins of Alexander the Great: Notes on a Book by Gerhard Kleiner," *NC* 1982, pp. 166–179.

———. "A Ptolemaic Hoard of 'Athena' Tetradrachms at ANS," *ANSMN* 23 (1978), pp. 43–58.

Ziebell, W. *Olbia. Eine griechische Stadt im Süd-Russland* (Hamburg, 1937).

INDEX

Abdera, 190–92, 195, 219
Acanthus, 188
Achaemenid kingdom, 266, 269. *See also* Persia
Acnonius, 106
Acraephia, 263
Aegina, 41, 46, 175, 215
Aenianes, 44
Aenus, 190–91, 195
Aetolia, 164
Aetolians, 135–36, 160
Agis, 281
agricultural production in Thessaly, 154–55, 158–59, 162
Aleuads, 35, 62, 74, 79, 86, 89–91, 103, 115, 256, 258–60
Aleuas, 107
Alexander I, 186–87
Alexander II, 86, 89–90, 188
Alexander III, 25, 29, 32, 48, 52, 56, 59, 96, 109, 114, 122–23, 126, 133, 157, 219, 224, 269, 273, 280–83, 291
Alexander IV, 133, 136–37, 141
Alexander of Pherae, 83, 87, 89
Alexander, son of Cassander, 142–43, 174, 179
Alexarchus, brother of Cassander, 142n27
Ambracia, 32, 54, 173–75, 180, 219, 293–95
Amit, M., 227n16
Amphictyony, 69, 93, 100, 110–11, 141, 171. *See also* Delphi
Amphipolis, 95, 190, 192–94; mint of Philip II, 272–77
Amyntas III, 89

ancestral constitution, 66, 81, 93
Andreades, A. M., 268
Antigonus Doson, 149
Antigonus Gonatas, 5, 148, 178–79, 183, 247
Antigonus Monophthalmus, 141, 178
Antiochus II, 236
Antiochus IV, 237n41
Antiochus VII, 237n41, 242
Antipater, 27, 32, 58, 117–18, 133–38, 140, 158, 160, 271, 281
Apollo, of Corinth, 279; of Delphi, 90, 107, 171, 285–89
Aradus, 235–37
Arcadian League, 38n11
Archelaus, 89
Archidamus of Sparta, 286
Arethusa, 39
Argos, 46, 156, 175n39, 215
aristocrats in Thessaly, 61, 72, 79, 84, 86, 89, 91
Aristotle, 215–17, 223, 267
Aristratus, 256
Arrian, 117
Aryandes, 119–120
Arybbas, 96
Asia Minor, 35, 126–29, 241, 282
Athena Itonia, 148
Athenian Coinage Decree, 196–207, 210, 231n23
Athenian Confederacy (fourth century), 191, 207
Athenian law on silver coinage, 207–208, 242
Athenians, 82, 85, 90, 111, 132–33, 137, 263
Athens, 46, 48, 59, 61, 67, 70, 86, 115,

Library of Congress Cataloging in Publication Data

Martin, Thomas R., 1947 –
  Sovereignty and coinage in classical Greece.

  Bibliography: p.
  Includes index.
  1. Coins, Greek. 2. Coinage—Greece. I. Title.
CJ351.M37   1985   737.4938   84-26292
ISBN 0-691-03580-6 (alk. paper)